Physiological Anthropology

Physiological Anthropology

Edited by ALBERT DAMON

New York   OXFORD UNIVERSITY PRESS   London Toronto 1975

Second printing, 1977

Copyright © 1975 by Oxford University Press, Inc.
Library of Congress Catalogue Card Number: 75-4349
Printed in the United States of America

PUBLISHER'S PREFACE

The Chapters of the book were first prepared for a seminar at Harvard University conducted by Professor Albert Damon. Professor Damon completed the editing of the papers before he died, but many of the details that accompany the editing of a book of this kind were left to Damon's colleague, Dr. Jonathan S. Friedlaender, without whose help this book would not have been possible. Further editorial advice was generously provided by Dr. Paul Baker, of Pennsylvania State University.

March 1975

FOREWORD

This book is both rewarding and revealing as a statement of present-day human biology. In its early days, anthropology looked at external appearance and its variety, focusing on the differences between populations or races. This focus emphasized the significance of human variation as a scientific resource, but if there was any interest in the causes of the differences, such as Darwinian adaptation, it did not lead to rigorous investigation, for which there were then few tools in any case. The failure of conclusive classifications of race to emerge, and thus of any automatic racial history, caused these studies to lag. This was in part abetted by the coincidental rise of human genetics—not very long ago—as the availability of blood polymorphisms of simple genetic determination opened the way for fresh investigation of populations. In spite of some expectations, this served to classify mankind no better than the calipers, but it did act to bring genetical population theory into anthropology, by forcing the view of the individual and the population as genetic complements of one another and by showing the search for fundamental cleavages between races to be illusory. It is in this sense, of working and thinking through populations and individuals, that anthropology continued a natural forward progress.

Still, while working with these two static aspects of an individual, genetics and adult morphology, anthropology had yet to tread the field lying between them: physiology, all the functional responses by which individuals adapt and survive and by which the gene pool of a population is modified. For whatever reasons, there were before World War II no physiological anthropologists (and no anthropological physiologists). The discussions in this book show how great the void has been; sensing it early, Albert Damon himself took degrees in both anthropology and medicine before settling down to professional work. Baker, an experienced and thoughtful worker in the field, in reviewing what has happened seems to doubt that there should in fact be "physiological anthropologists" and finds a feeling of discomfort with physiology on the part of the anthropological writers in this book. Time will tell. As a nonphysiological anthropologist, however, I am impressed by two things about these writers. They are staunchly anthropological in viewpoint, seeing things in terms of populations and evolutionary processes and demanding clear definitions of such concepts as "adaptation." And they manifest an awareness of the volume and complexity of the physiological variables involved and of how much there is to be done, a marked departure from the kind of simplistic assumptions earlier anthropologists were forced to make.

The physiologists among the writers recognize the anthropological adherence to population premises in variation, but they themselves deal with responses or adaptation in particular organs or systems, or what Mazess calls infra-individual problems. Their contribution is to broaden understanding of physiological research useful to anthropology. Finally, Damon sounds another note, one of urgency. The other anthropologists, seeing so much on the platter, are rather conservative, writing more in the realm of "pure" science, but Damon, expressing a theme of lifelong interest to him, stresses the need for "applied" research and our lateness in training human biologists for the job. Whether or not this should be the last book entitled *Physiological Anthropology*, a query of Baker's, it does seem late in the day to be the first, and one hopes that its impact will make up for lost time.

Peabody Museum
Harvard University   WILLIAM WHITE HOWELLS
Cambridge, Massachusetts
March 1975

CONTENTS

11. Behavioral Response and Adaptation to Environmental Stimulation   295

Joachim F. Wohlwill

12. Effects of Noise on Human Performance   335

David C. Glass and Jerome E. Singer

13. Biological Anthropology as an Applied Science   360

Albert Damon

Physiological Anthropology

1. The Place of Physiological Studies in Anthropology

PAUL T. BAKER*

In their efforts to fulfill the often used subtitle to anthropology, "The Study of Man," anthropologists have produced a series of sub-disciplines with such titles as philosophical anthropology, economic anthropology, political anthropology, psychological anthropology, ecological anthropology, and, now, physiological anthropology. Although it may be premature to speak of physiological anthropology as a real sub-discipline, this title for a book has a certain terminological validity; it can be used to encompass a body of information that has become important in anthropology and other man-oriented academic disciplines.

Despite the breadth of topics studied by anthropologists, at least two aspects of the subject prevent the discipline from really encompassing all human-oriented science. First, it is aggregating in approach, i.e., studies are focused on cultures or societies or populations rather than on individuals or genes. Second, although it has both a social and a biological scientific component, the two components meet only in the study of the distant evolutionary past, and there are very few areas where they have been conjoined in a study of living populations.

Although I am quite content that anthropology is concerned with the group rather than the individual, it does seem to me that if anthropologists are to provide any meaningful insights into why the behavior of one group of human organisms varies from that of another, they will have to understand the interaction of the biological and social systems for each group.

* Department of Anthropology, Pennsylvania State University, University Park, Pennsylvania.

Perhaps one of the problems in anthropology has been the failure to study the links between the behavior of a population and its genetic and morphological structure. Disciplines concerned with individuals have not missed these links. Thus, medicine contains bridging disciplines, such as endocrinology or physiology, which link the genetic and anatomical aspects of man to his health. Psychology includes not only social psychology and behavioral genetics but psychophysiology and psychopharmacology. I certainly do not mean to imply that the contents of this book or even all the information available on the physiology of human populations can fill this gap between genetics and behavior in anthropology, but I do suggest that this direction in research will provide us not only with new descriptive information on how human populations differ but will eventually help us to understand why they differ.

HISTORY

The idea that groups of men vary in their physiological responses and capabilities is certainly not a new idea. As a product of our biologically and culturally based ethnocentricity, most peoples attribute to other groups not only some inferior functions but also some superior functions. The behavior of early European explorers and scientists was no exception, and they frequently alleged that particular populations had such unique capabilities as better cold tolerance or the ability to survive altitudes and diseases, which they as Europeans did not have. Because the tools for testing these hypotheses were lacking, there was much disagreement among scientists in this area. The views of anthropologists, in particular, tended to polarize between those who felt all human responses to environmental stress were the same and those who believed there must be enormous differences. During the first half of this century, some anthropologists (Hrdlicka, 1908) and physiologists (Hicks *et al.*, 1931; Monge, 1948) attempted to determine whether populations varied in their physiological responses, but their techniques were crude and their attempts methodologically unsophisticated. World War II, however, facilitated the development of new methods. Governments deploying armies into varying climates not only supported research on ways to improve field performance but also provided funds to find out more about the opposition. New quantitative scientific concerns grew out of this. In biological anthropology, the intellectual challenge was clearly stated by Coon and others in their claims that the biological differences between human groups could best be understood by reference to the effects of morphological differences on the physiological responses of populations to their traditional physical environments (Coon *et al.*, 1950; Coon, 1955).

As the literature reviewed in this volume indicates, the study of population differences in terms of physiological functions was well under way by the late 'fifties, even though anthropologists were only peripherally involved. The research efforts that concentrated on man's response to the physical climate stresses was undertaken primarily by environmental physiologists and was concentrated in government laboratories in the United States and England.[1] Those Japanese scientists in a medical school setting also made significant contributions.

Nutritional research had its place in government laboratories, but perhaps the major impetus for research arose as a consequence of the international aid programs in attempts to improve world nutrition. Through surveys and studies of world-wide nutrition, it became apparent that populations were not necessarily identical in their nutritional needs and that the nutritional status of a population had considerable impact on behavioral style and potential.

Theoretical developments in still other academic disciplines led these scientists to a concern with population physiology. Thus, population geneticists, looking for the causes of man's extensive genetic polymorphisms, wondered if the polymorphisms developed because of their effect on physiological function and disease. Psychologists once again wondered whether the responses they were measuring on modern industrial man were indeed species-wide universals, and so they took a cautious interest in population differences.

All of these developments produced a significant amount of population-oriented research in the early 'sixties, but it also generated significant doubts as to the results. Almost all of the studies were small, single popu-

---

1 Many of these studies are available only through the U.S. defense documentation series but some were published as laboratory series. These include the following:

Environmental Protection Research Division Technical Report Series. Headquarters Quartermaster Research and Engineering Command, U.S. Army, Quartermaster Research and Engineering Center, Nattick, Mass.

Proceedings: Symposia on Arctic Medicine and Biology Series. Arctic Aeromedical Laboratory, Fort Wainwright, Alaska.

WADC *Technical Report* Series. Wright Air Development Center, Air Research and Development Command, United States Air Force, Wright-Patterson Air Force Base, Ohio.

lation comparisons, and, although they generally showed population differences, the investigator could seldom state the reason for the difference. To overcome this deficiency, more unified research plans, such as the Human Adaptability Project of the International Biological Program, were developed.

Having given this brief historical résumé, we will now shift the focus of this introduction.

THEORIES, DEFINITIONS, AND METHODOLOGICAL PROBLEMS

With so many disciplines involved, it is not surprising to find that the theoretical bases for individual studies are quite diverse nor is it surprising that similar findings have been variously interpreted by different investigators. With exceptions, of course, we may say that physiologists, nutritionists, and psychologists begin with a different set of assumptions than do biological anthropologists and population geneticists. The former group tends to assume that all men will react in the same way to an environmental stress and that, therefore, differences found between groups can probably be accounted for by differences in such short-term processes as acclimatization or by other environmental factors, such as disease, which have affected the responses. Biological anthropologists or population geneticists, on the other hand, tend to believe that processes of evolution should have produced population differences in physiological responses much as they have produced population differences in genetic structure and general morphology. Indeed, much of the early work of anthropologists concerned testing the hypothesis that the evolutionarily derived morphological differences between populations were the results of selection operating on the physiological correlates of the morphological variation.

Although these differences in theoretical position probably do not affect the results of these studies, they do influence both methodology and interpretation. A careful reading of this volume will reveal the still somewhat polarized viewpoints and the differences between them. Physiologists will tend to study small samples, which are selected as healthy and representative. They will probably study this sample in more detail, and individual or group differences in response, which are not of a major order, will often be dismissed. Anthropologists are more likely to study larger samples less rigorously and call any difference of statistical significance important.

Another major problem that has plagued interpretation is that of terminology. This problem is so serious that the majority of the authors in this volume find it necessary to discuss the subject and clarify their own terminological set. Although terminological struggles have often been rather sterile scientific endeavors in the past, they are probably necessary in physiological anthropology, since such terms as adaptation, acclimatization, and habituation carry major theoretical implications. I have in the past wandered in this scientific jungle (Baker, 1965, 1974) and might be tempted to again in this introduction, if the subject were not adequately covered by such authors as Thomas and Mazess. As it is, I will only note that I agree with their major point on the definition of adaptation. It is a complex concept and obviously means quite different things when applied to such subjects as the welfare of a social group, the survival of a population, the functional capacity of an individual, or the fate of a particular human gene.

As if theoretical and terminological problems were not enough, it must be stated that significant methodological and technical problems remain. Most studies have been based on classic experimental comparisons. Whether the comparison was performed under laboratory or field conditions, almost all used investigators as controls. Nutritional studies are an exception, but this is more apparent than real, since conclusions from data collected on various human populations were derived from comparisons with American or European standards. If all of the studies had been made under the same experimental conditions, one could still directly compare the physiological responses of the various groups. This was not the case, and, thus, population differences must always be deduced from comparison with the rather amorphous population known as European-derived investigators. In addition to the problems of the control (European) sample, it is also clear that the samples of non-Europeans studied are seldom representative of the chosen native population. For a variety of reasons, the sample is usually composed of healthy young adult males. Only recently have studies been extended to include other sex and age groups. Thus, the authors in this book are generally forced to look for generalities about populations based on results from perhaps unrepresentative young males in one population compared to European-derived scientists from various countries who may or may not resemble each other in their physiology.

There are, of course, additional problems, since we must work with man in natural experimental situations rather than with man under carefully controlled laboratory conditions. Thus, one must always be cogni-

zant of the fact that a group difference in physiological response to altitude or climate, for example, may be the product of a broad variety of
environmental or biological forces, which were not controlled for in the
particular comparison (Weiner, 1966).

Finally, there is the ever-present problem of differences in research techniques and tools, which often make cross-population comparisons impossible. The standardizations suggested by the International Biological Program have produced somewhat more uniform methods and techniques in
recent years (Weiner and Lourie, 1969), but the problems of interpretation are formidable. With so many problems, it is reassuring that the
authors of this book have been able to reach at least some generalizations
of import to anthropology.

STATE OF KNOWLEDGE

Although this volume does not contain all of the physiological data and
theory pertinent to anthropology, it does include most of the basic issues
and approaches. In general, the authors have devoted their chapters to
man's physiological responses to particular environmental stimuli or stressors. The implied objectives of the data reviews vary considerably, however. I detect four principal themes in these reviews. These are:

1. A description of man's physiological response to a particular environmental stimulus. This is the case, to some extent, in most chapters, but
for those stimuli where little is known of the response, description may be
the major chapter content. Responses to light and psychological stresses
are examples.

2. An exploration of population differences in physiological response
and a search for the causes of the difference. This is best exemplified by
the chapters on response to heat, cold, work requirements, and, to a lesser
extent, altitude. In these instances, some comparative data are available,
the basic nature of the human physiological response is known, and an
exploration for causes has at least begun.

3. An examination of the relationships of morphological and genetic
variation in man to physiological responses. As noted earlier in this chapter, the problems raised by evolutionary theory and the heterogeneity of
our species have made this topic popular.

4. An examination of the way physiological responses of men in stressful environments affect or are effected by culturally defined behavior
patterns. The rather simplistic previous view held that physiological re-

sponses to the physical environment were the cause of group differences in behavior or that culture determined the behavior regardless of physical environment. Physiological and ecological analysis suggests a much more subtle interaction of these factors.

Viewed in terms of these four objectives, the contents of this volume make it clear that physiological anthropology has developed a substantial body of information and even that some conclusions have been drawn since the basic problems were first formulated. Although other readers will undoubtedly select different salient conclusions, it may be useful to raise some tentative generalizations for discussion.

In temperature regulation, where the data are most complete, some generalizations derived from population comparisons are justified. As R. Newman notes, adult populations do not seem to differ in their basic responses to heat. Most differences in physiological responses to heat appear to be related to population variations in short-term acclimatization and/or body morphology. Infant and child variation in response to heat should be explored further, particularly for children living in hot desert areas.

Population responses to cold are more complex. Acclimatizational responses remain debatable and poorly defined. Adult population differences in response to total body cooling certainly occur, but the causes and significance are not clear. The population differences in peripheral response to cold is more dramatic, but new techniques and research designs seem called for, since, for most groups, it is not possible to segregate acclimatizational, developmental, and heritability factors in examining the response. Neither is it possible to differentiate the relative roles of such anatomical features as counter-current exchange from such neurophysiological factors as vasoconstriction and vasodilation control.

The relationships between body morphology and temperature regulatory responses have now been well explored in adults. These studies have confirmed earlier suggestions that morphological variation affects physiological responses to heat and cold. But comparisons of different populations have failed to support the simple evolutionary relationships between body morphology, physiological strain, and selection that were previously postulated by such authors as myself (Baker, 1960). As several chapter authors, M. Newman, in particular, point out, nutritional and disease variations between populations may have a more significant effect on morphological variation than has climatic stress.

The amount of information on nutritional variation among human populations is becoming truly prodigious, and M. Newman has made a bold effort to place it in anthropological perspective. One must agree with his statement that nutritional variation and man's responses to this variation is of major importance to anthropology. Some new discoveries, such as the lactase deficiency syndrome (McCracken, 1971), sex differences in the response to undernutrition (Stini, 1971), and the damaging effects on health of overnutrition (Dubos, 1965), have shown how the physiology of nutrition is critical to an understanding of the sources of biological variation in man. At the same time, I find it impossible to accept the often implicit assumption made in many nutritional studies that all morphological and much behavioral variability can be attributed to the nutritional adequacy of varying diets (Kallen, 1973).

The authors discussing work capacity, altitude, and infectious disease in this volume have chosen not to summarize the knowledge in these areas and to concentrate, instead, on some of the theoretical and methodological approaches, which they feel gives better insight into the causes and significance of population differences. Research in all these areas has increased tremendously since 1960, and I suspect that any attempt to summarize even the major findings within the confines of a chapter would be doomed to failure. In each instance, it has been established that there are substantial intra- and inter-population variations in physiological response, and, at present, the critical problems range from the need for detailed analytic studies to identify the causes of variation to broad synthetic studies to define the consequences of these variations.

As can be seen from Damon's chapter, his inclusion of the psychologist's views of stress and adaptation was no accident. He believed that biological anthropologists should be concerned not only with our past and the underdeveloped parts of the world but also with the complex new stresses faced by men in industrial societies. I sympathize with his concern and agree that many of the psychophysiologists' findings are pertinent. At the same time, I am not quite sure how anthropologists can contribute in this area. We can, of course, suggest that there is probably intra- and inter-populational variation in the responses under examination. But our basic theory of evolution has little predictive value for any hypothesis about how populations will respond to stresses that have never existed before. This does not mean that the psychologists' findings are not of any use. Indeed there are perception, cognition, and performance data that the population anthropologist must integrate if he wishes to understand human behavioral variation.

PROSPECTUS

In one sense I would not object if this book were to be not only the first one titled *Physiological Anthropology* but also the last. I say this because the title suggests that human physiology as such should be pursued by anthropologists. This has happened, and some biological anthropologists, myself included, have published their results in physiology journals. This helps physiology because it creates informational bridges, but I doubt that this is the primary objective of most anthropologists working with physiological techniques. Indeed, most of the contributors to this volume manifest an obvious discomfort with the subject of physiology as such. And, instead, they discuss the implications of the topic for various aspects of human ecology. I suggest that, like myself, the contributors to this volume believe that the underlying purpose of anthropological research utilizing human physiology is the construction of a transdisciplinary subject, which addresses itself to why human variability exists and how it contributes to our behavior as a species.

Finally, the hope of all science is the dual goals of explanation and prediction. Anthropology has pursued this hope by synthesis from the analytic parts. Physiology, here, is a new tool in the analytic structure and should achieve its function as such.

REFERENCES

Baker, P. T. 1960. Climate, culture and evolution. *Human Biol.* 32:1-61.

Baker, P. T. 1965. Multidisciplinary studies of human adaptability: Theoretical justification and method. In *International Biological Programme: A Guide to the Human Adaptability Proposals*, ed. J. S. Weiner. Handbook IBP No. 1. ICSU Special Committee for the International Biological Programme. (2nd ed. 1969.)

Baker, P. T. 1974. An evolutionary perspective on environmental physiology. In *Environmental Physiology*, ed. N. B. Slonim. St. Louis: Mosby.

Coon, C. S. 1955. Some problems of human variability and natural selection in climate and culture. *The Amer. Naturalist* 89:257-80.

Coon, C. S., S. M. Garn, and J. B. Birdsell. 1950. *Races: A Study of the Problems of Race Information in Man*. Springfield, Ill.: Charles C. Thomas, 153 pp.

Dubos, R. 1965. *Man Adapting*. New Haven: Yale University Press, 527 pp.

Hicks, C. S., R. F. Matters, and M. L. Mitchell. 1931. The standard metabolism of the Australian aboriginals. *Aust. J. Exptl. Biol. Med. Sci.* 8:69-82.

Hrdlicka, A. 1908. *Physiological and Medical Observations among the Indians of Southwestern United States and Northern Mexico. Bull. Bur. Am. Ethnol.* 460 pp.

Kallen, D. J. (ed.) 1973. *Nutrition, Development and Social Behavior.* Proceedings of the Conference on the Assessment of Tests of Behavior from Studies of Nutrition in the Western Hemisphere. U.S. Department of Health, Education, & Welfare, Washington, D.C., 386 pp.

McCracken, R. D. 1971. Lactase deficiency: An example of dietary evolution. *Current Anthropol.* 12 (4-5):479-500.

Monge, C. 1948. *Acclimatization in the Andes.* Baltimore: The Johns Hopkins Press. (Republished by Blaine Ethridge-Books, Detroit, 1973), 130 pp.

Stini, W. A. 1971. Evolutionary implications of changing nutrition patterns in human populations. *Am. Anthropol.* 73:1019-30.

Weiner, J. S. 1966. Major problems in human population biology. In *The Biology of Human Adaptability*, eds. P. T. Baker and J. S. Weiner. Oxford: Clarendon Press.

Weiner, J. S. and J. A. Lourie. 1969. *Human Biology: A Guide to Field Methods.* IBP Handbook No. 9. Philadelphia: F. A. Davis Co., 621 pp.

2. The Effects of Light on Man

DANIEL P. CARDINALI *

RICHARD J. WURTMAN **

LIGHT AS A COMPONENT OF THE ENVIRONMENT

Solar radiation has always constituted a ubiquitous and essential component of man's environment. Until the invention of artificial light sources, reflected rays from the visible portion of the solar spectrum were the major stimuli enabling man to see. Besides serving as the ultimate source of his food and energy, solar radiation acts directly on man, altering his chemical composition, controlling the rate of his maturation, and driving his biological rhythms. This chapter describes the known direct effects of sunlight on man. In it, we also consider the possible consequences to man's health of living in environments illuminated by artificial light sources, with spectra that differ significantly from those provided by the Sun.

Characteristics of natural lighting

Man evolved in an environment characterized by a particular kind of photic energy, the light of the Sun, filtered through the atmosphere and its surrounding layer of ozone. On the average, solar light is present for 12 hours out of every 24 at every point on Earth. The actual number of

* The Carrera del Investigador, Comisión Nacional de Estudios Geo-Heliofisicos, Argentina.
** Professor of Endocrinology and Metabolism, Massachusetts Institute of Technology, Cambridge, Massachusetts.

daylight hours at any point on any particular day varies with an annual rhythm of an amplitude that depends on the angular distance between that point and the Equator. In the Northern Hemisphere, the daylight period is longest on the first day of summer and shortest 6 months later.

Spectral composition of sunlight and light emitted by artificial light sources

The spectrum of the solar energies reaching the Earth is shown in Fig. 2-1. Essentially no wavelengths shorter than 290 nm (that is, essentially no short-ultraviolet and relatively few mid-ultraviolet photons) penetrate the atmospheric shield. The radiant flux at the longer wavelengths increases sharply in the near-ultraviolet (320-380 nm) and visible (380-770 nm) portions of the spectrum, reaching a peak in the blue-green range (between about 450 and 500 nm) and decreasing gradually well into the infrared portion of the spectrum. The intensity of the ultraviolet light that penetrates the atmosphere varies markedly with season. In the northern United States, the total erythemal radiation (solar radiation capable of producing sunburn, between 290 and 320 nm) reaching the Earth's surface in December may be as little as one-fifteenth that present in June; also, ultraviolet light may be essentially absent from the environment before 9 A.M. or after 3 P.M. The spectral quality and quantity of radiation from the visible portion of the solar spectrum usually vary less with the season. For instance, the illumination from direct sunlight (normal incidence) at noon in Boston is about 6400-8800 foot candles (34-47 mW/cm²) for wavelengths between 290 and 770 nm, regardless of the time of year.

The spectral composition of light from the Sun's disk roughly approximates that of the white light emitted by a theoretical black body heated to about 5600° K, minus the ultraviolet radiation below 290 nm, which is unable to penetrate the ozone layer and atmospheric shield surrounding the Earth. Hence, the solar spectrum is continuous, and the relative intensities of any of its component visible wavelengths do not differ by more than twofold; the average radiant fluxes of the blue, yellow, and red portions contained in the white light of the midday Sun are all approximately equal.

Incandescent light sources also emit spectra that approximate those of heated black bodies. Their color temperatures (the temperatures to which theoretical black bodies would have to be heated to emit compara-

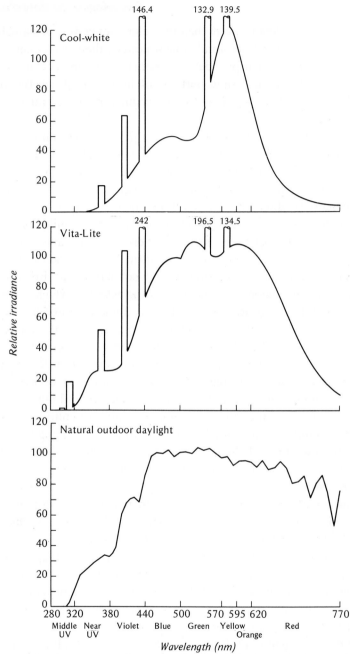

Fig. 2-1. Emission spectra of common fluorescent bulbs (cool-white) and of an artificial sunlight illuminant (Vita-Lite) compared with the relative spectral distribution of the natural light environment (CIE D-5500° K phase of natural outdoor daylight). Curves normalized to 100 ($\lambda = 560$ nm). (Reprinted from Wurtman and Weisel, 1969.)

ble spectra) are considerably lower than the color temperature of sunlight; hence, a larger fraction of their total radiant power (about 90%) consists of infrared radiation, which provides heat rather than light (Thorington *et al.*, 1971). Within the visible portions of incandescent spectra, the relative fluxes at different wavelengths are maximal in the red range and minimal in the blue.

Fluorescent bulbs generate visible light by a physical mechanism different from that of the Sun or of incandescent bulbs. Their light output comes not as a consequence of heating but as a consequence of the activation of chemical phosphors by ultraviolet light generated in a low-pressure mercury arc discharge. The spectra emitted by fluorescent sources can thus be modified at will; the design of such spectra is limited only by the ability of the chemist to devise novel phosphors. The inherent flexibility of fluorescent light sources has allowed the lighting engineer to design bulbs that are as bright as possible for a given total output. Brightness is a subjective phenomenon, depending upon the extent to which the retinal foveal photoreceptors are stimulated. Since these photoreceptors are most sensitive to visible light in the yellow-green range (555 nm for photopic vision) (Wald, 1964), fluorescent light sources have been designed to emit a considerably larger fraction of light in this region of the visible spectrum than is present in sunlight. Fluorescent sources are also usually designed to minimize emission in the ultraviolet and infrared ranges. It is thus apparent that, because of the wide use of fluorescent bulbs in offices, schools, and factories, a large number of Americans are spending most of their waking hours under light spectra that differ considerably from the range of spectra characteristic of natural sunlight (see Fig. 2-1). The premise governing the design of such spectra by industry was that the only significant effect of light on man was to provide the substrate for vision—that is, light acting on the retina, enabling man to perceive objects by their relative brightness. There is considerable evidence now that, in addition to subserving vision, environmental lighting has a major effect on man. Biologically active, visible light is not limited to the yellow-green portion of the spectrum. Further reflecting and perpetuating the notion that light's only effect on man is to enable him to see is the propensity of biologists to express the intensity of light emission in foot candles. Foot candles are units of illumination defined subjectively as lumens, i.e., units of brightness per square foot. Thus, when the intensity of any light source is described in foot candles, only the yellow-green emissions have actually been quantified. For a given total irradiance, the higher the proportion of emissions contained in the yellow-green range, the greater the foot-candle rating. It should be apparent that, if one is interested in studying a metabolic effect of light that results from emissions outside the yellow-green range (for example, the photoactivation of vitamin D precursors by ultraviolet light), foot-candle measurements give misleading information about the capacity of a particular lighting environment to produce that effect. It seems reasonable that the intensities of light emissions should be measured in absolute irradiance units, such as microwatts per square centimeter for each spectral band, rather than in subjective foot-candle units. Inasmuch as a major portion of the literature on biological effects of light provides data in terms of foot candles, both foot-candle and absolute energy units will be utilized in the following discussion.

Intensity of natural and artificial lighting

The illumination provided at eye level in most artificially lighted rooms is on the order of 50-100 foot candles (160-320 mW/cm^2 for cool-white fluorescent light). This level is less than 10% that present outdoors in the shade. The decision that this particular lighting intensity was appropriate for indoor use seems to have been based on economic and technological considerations rather than on any knowledge of man's biological needs. As long as rooms were being lit with incandescent bulbs, the amount of heat that would have been generated by providing more than 50 foot candles of light would have been inconvenient, if not intolerable. And, although fluorescent sources could provide higher light intensities without excessive heat production, the cost of the electric power used in the process would have been greater than that deemed appropriate for providing light to see by. As a consequence, if a citizen of Boston lives in a conventionally lighted indoor environment for 16 hours each day, he is exposed to considerably less visible light than would impinge on him were he to spend a single hour each day outdoors.

Summary

In summary, the characteristics of man's exposure to visible light can be defined in terms of three factors: the spectrum of the light, the irradiance level, and the number of hours per day the individual is exposed. All three factors have been changed drastically as man has moved indoors and taken advantage of artificial light sources.

RESPONSES OF HUMANS AND OTHER MAMMALS TO LIGHT

Direct and indirect effects of light on mammalian tissues

The effects of light on mammalian tissues can be classified as direct and indirect, depending on the mechanisms involved (Wurtman, 1970). In this section, we describe both kinds of effects and the experimental evidence that can be used to classify them.

Direct effects

The direct effects of light can be defined as chemical changes in tissue constituents resulting from the absorption of light energy in tissue. The molecule that absorbs the photon may or may not be photochemically transformed in the process; more commonly it is not, and the photic energy is dissipated as heat. Moreover, light can cause chemical changes through the process of photosensitization in molecules other than those actually absorbing photic energy. Certain photoabsorbent dyes and naturally occurring body constituents (such as riboflavin) are reversibly converted to photosensitizers (Enns and Burgess, 1965; Smith and Hanawalt, 1969) by absorbing photons of specific wavelengths. These high-energy intermediates can then catalyze the oxidation of a wide variety of circulating compounds and tissue constituents, which would not themselves absorb light.

In general, compounds containing conjugated double bonds strongly absorb ultraviolet light. As the size of the conjugated structure increases, the amount of light absorbed and the wavelength of the photons absorbed tend to increase also. In addition to its range, the absorption spectrum of any particular compound is also influenced by the polarity, temperature, and pH of its solvent, its concentration, and the presence of such charged side chains as amines and hydroxyl groups. The absorption of light by proteins occurs largely within such constituent aromatic amino acids as tyrosine and tryptophan and is usually maximal at wavelengths of about 280 nm. The purines and pyrimidines in nucleic acids absorb maximally at wavelengths near 260 nm (Smith and Hanawalt, 1969).

In order to prove that a particular chemical change in a tissue occurs as a direct response to light, it must first be shown that light energy of the required wavelength does, in fact, penetrate the body to reach that tissue. The visible portion of the solar spectrum can apparently penetrate all of the metaphoric nooks and crannies of the body, even the brain of a live sheep (Ganong *et al.*, 1963). Ultraviolet light, which is far more active photochemically, penetrates tissues considerably less effectively; even erythemal irradiation (290-320 nm), however, can pass through the epidermis into the dermis, where it has access to the blood circulating in dermal capillaries. Next, the postulated photochemical or photosensitization reaction must be fully characterized *in vivo* as well as *in vitro* (in simple solutions or tissue homogenates). This characterization entails defining the action spectra (the relative abilities of particular wavelengths to produce a given chemical or biological response) and isolating and identifying all of the reactants, intermediates, and products of the reaction both *in vivo* and *in vitro*.

The identification of *in vivo* action spectra is difficult and time-consuming; few, if any, such spectra have been defined for tissue responses occurring beneath the epidermis. In practice, the possibility that light might produce a chemical change in the intact organism is first explored using simple model systems. The reactions to controlled artificial light of dilute solutions of potentially photoabsorbent compounds and photosensitizers are examined in the hope of identifying substances that might be chemically altered by light *in vivo*. Experiments are then performed to determine whether light exposure does, in fact, modify the fate or the turnover of a particular substance in the whole organism. Even when it is possible to show such a modification (for instance, the fall in plasma bilirubin that occurs when jaundiced, premature infants are exposed to sunlight; see pp. 27 and 28 and Fig. 2.2) (Lucey *et al.*, 1968), one still cannot conclude that the mechanism of the *in vivo* effect is the same as the one that operates in the model system until the specific reactants, intermediates, and products of the reaction have been characterized. Unfortunately, in almost all cases, the acquisition of these sorts of data remains a goal for the future.

It should be noted in passing that any demonstration that light exposure modifies the fate of any body constituent *in vivo* challenges the prevailing view that all chemical reactions occurring in mammals are catalyzed and controlled by enzymes. Indeed, one might wonder why Evolution would "allow" the continued occurrence of non-enzymatic,

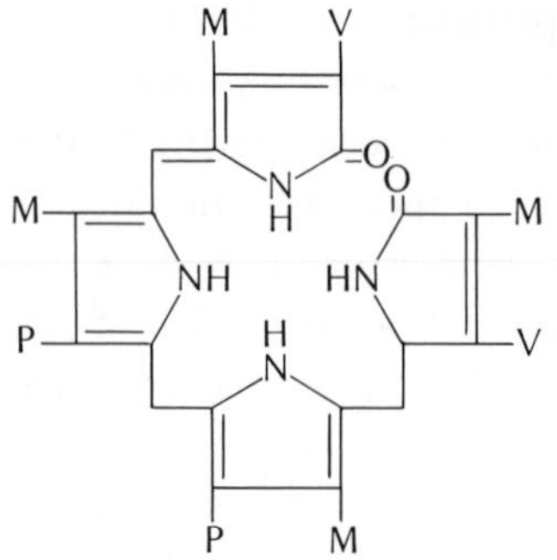

Bilirubin

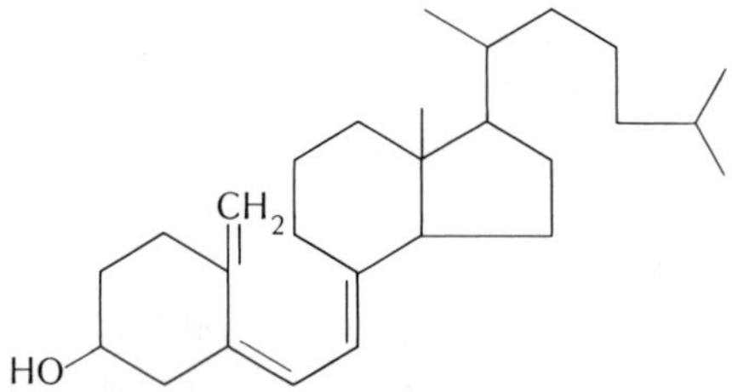

Vitamin D

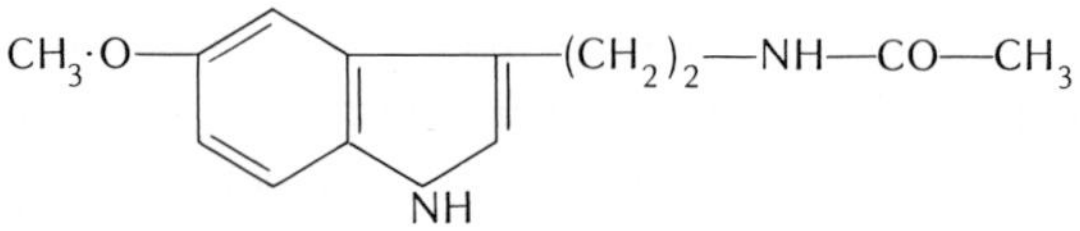

Melatonin

Fig. 2-2. Structures of bilirubin, vitamin D, and melatonin.

open-ended reactions when it could have provided man with a body surface less permeable to light.

Indirect effects

The indirect effects of light can be defined as those ultimately mediated by endogenous chemical signals with amplitudes that depend on the responses of specialized photoreceptor cells to light. Light activates a photoreceptor cell; this, in turn, activates a train of cells specialized for communications (neurons, neuroendocrine transducers, and/or endocrine glandular cells), causing the release of a neurotransmitter or the secretion of a hormone. The neurotransmitter, or the hormone, actually produces the light effect. As a case in point: When young rats were kept continuously under light, photoreceptive cells in their retinas responded by liberating neurotransmitter substances that activated other brain neurons; these neurons, in turn, transmitted signals (over complex neuroendocrine pathways) that reached the anterior pituitary. Here they stimulated the secretion of gonadotropic hormones, which accelerated the maturation of the ovary. When the eyes or pituitary glands were removed from other rats before they were placed under continuous lighting, the light exerted no measurable influence on their ovarian growth or function (Wurtman, 1967). Thus, in order for ovarian maturation to be stimulated by light, both the retina and the anterior pituitary gland of the rat must be intact; only the retina is the photoreceptor, however. The retina allows light to pass in, which initiates a train of internal signals, whereas the pituitary simply carries out one of the steps in transmitting these signals to the ovary.

Photoreceptors

Three types of evidence are required before a particular mammalian cell can be categorized as a photoreceptor. These are (a) anatomical evidence. The cell must contain organelles ("outer segments") thought to be the loci of the photochemical transduction process (Sjostrand, 1961). (These can be observed by electron microscopy.) It must also be demonstrated that axons originating from the cell make synapses with true neurons. (b) Chemical evidence. Rhodopsin or another of the vitamin A photopigments must be identified in the cell. (c) Physiological evidence. The particular cell must be shown to be essential for the occurrence of a physiological response to light. Its destruction must block the response.

Applying these criteria, we find that in adult mammals only the retina has clearly been shown to contain photoreceptor cells. These cells—the rods and the cones—are present in differing proportions in each species and tend to be concentrated in specific zones of the retina. Indirect evidence has been presented that some neuroendocrine effects of light persist in immature mammals following removal of the eyes (Zweig *et al.*, 1966), but this evidence cannot as yet be regarded as compelling. In lower vertebrates, it appears that the retina is not the sole photoreceptive organ. In the blinded duck, the hypothalamus responds directly to light transmitted via quartz rods placed in the eye socket, liberating factors that cause the pituitary to secrete gonadotropins (Benoit and Assenmacher, 1959). The duck pineal body also appears to be involved in this phenomenon. It has been shown that light can act directly on duck pineal bodies maintained in organ culture, thereby affecting several biochemical processes (Rosner *et al.*, 1971). In the frog, the pineal body and several adjacent epithalamic structures respond to specific wavelengths of visible light by varying the rates at which they emit nerve impulses (Dodt and Heerd, 1962).

Effects of light on the skin and subcutaneous tissues

Natural sunlight acts directly on the cells of the skin and subcutaneous tissues, producing both pathological and protective responses. Examples of the former include sunburn and, in highly susceptible individuals, a particular variety of skin cancer, squamous cell carcinoma. Examples of protective responses include an increase in the synthesis of melanin pigments by epidermal melanocytes and an acceleration of cell division, leading to a thickening of the ultraviolet-absorbing layers of the epidermis. Light also initiates photochemical and photosensitization reactions that affect compounds present in the extracellular fluid, including the circulating blood, or stored in cells. These reactions may be beneficial to the organism, as in the case of photoactivation of vitamin D precursors (Fig. 2-2), or they may produce substances that are toxic to tissues, as in photosensitive porphyria.

Cellular injury

Mid-ultraviolet erythemal radiation (290-320 nm) causes sunburn to appear within several hours of exposure. It is generally believed that this inflammatory reaction, which may persist for several days, results from the release of vasoactive substances from damaged epidermal cells. These substances presumably diffuse into the dermis where they damage the capillaries, causing erythema or reddening, heat, swelling, and pain. A variety of substances have been proposed as the offender (the biogenic amines, serotonin and histamine, and the polypeptide, bradykinin, for example); their identities have not yet been confirmed, however.

Sunburn can be considered an affliction of civilization. If, weather permitting, people were to expose themselves to sunlight for 1 or 2 hours each day throughout the year, their skin's reaction to the gradual increase in erythemal solar energies occurring during the winter and spring months would provide them with a protective layer of pigmentation to withstand summertime levels of sunlight. Instead, most people spend all the daylight hours during the winter and spring months indoors and are thus susceptible to the classic occurrence of sunburn: An office worker may spend his first day in 6 months out of doors maximally exposed in a bathing suit. The severe sunburn he experiences can be compared with the pancreatitis that develops in a starving man fed a large steak.

Chronic exposure to the Sun for many hours each day over many decades can cause permanent changes in skin structure. In the epidermis, these changes include skin atrophy, the formation of keratin plaques, and the appearance of squamous cell carcinomas in susceptible individuals (Kligman, 1969; Urbach, 1969). Dermal changes include the disintegration of collagen and elastic fibers. Genetic factors and the extent of skin pigmentation appear to be of major significance in determining the likelihood that an individual chronically exposed to sunlight will develop skin cancer (Urbach, 1969). For example, skin cancer is more common among people of Irish descent than would be anticipated if its distribution were random, yet it is reputed to be rare among Indians living high in the Andes who are exposed to considerably higher intensities of ultraviolet light.

Squamous cell carcinomas tend to appear on areas of the skin normally exposed to the greatest amounts of sunlight (for instance, the nose). Fortunately, most are readily removed surgically; but, all the same, they constitute a preventable, potentially lethal disease, and their manifest correlation with exposure to ultraviolet light has led some dermatologists to suggest that it would be best for man to avoid ultraviolet irradiation entirely. We find no experimental evidence to support this conclusion (see Blum, 1964). The threshold level of ultraviolet exposure, beyond which man's general incidence of skin cancer would increase, has not been determined. On intuitive grounds, however, it seems likely that this level is appreciably higher than that amount normally obtained from sunlight; otherwise, our species would have become extinct eons ago. It has recently been suggested that man may hasten his ultimate extinction by flying supersonic aircraft that modify the mass of the ultraviolet-absorbing ozone layer surrounding the Earth's atmosphere. Any major decrease in the shielding effects of this layer could increase the incidence of skin cancer among susceptible populations.

Protective responses

Immediately after people are exposed to sunlight, the amount of pigment in their skin increases, and they remain hyperpigmented for a few hours.

This effect is probably the result of the photooxidation of a colorless melanin precursor; it is apparently caused by all of the ultraviolet and visible radiations present in sunlight (Szabó, 1969). After a day or two, when the initial response to sunlight has subsided, melanocytes in the epidermis begin to divide and to synthesize and extrude melanin granules at an increased rate. This secondary hyperpigmentation can persist for several weeks following exposure to an erythemal dose of mid-ultraviolet light and provides considerable protection against further tissue damage by sunlight. The melanin granules extruded from the melanocytes can be taken up in squamous epithelial cells. They are lost from the body as these cells slough off, which explains the disappearance of tan a week or two after a vacation in the Sun. Exposure to ultraviolet light also increases the thickness of the superficial stratum corneum (or horny layer) of the epidermis. This helps retard the passage of ultraviolet light into the deeper layers of the skin.

Photochemical and photosensitization reactions

It is increasingly apparent that a large number of substances in the blood and tissues can be chemically altered by solar radiations, either as a direct result of photochemical reactions or by photosensitizer-catalyzed oxidations (Smith and Hanawalt, 1969). Considered below are three such substances, which are present in the skin and subcutaneous tissues, whose responses to sunlight clearly contribute to the maintenance of health or the genesis of disease. In the next decade, it is probable that researchers will find more and more body constituents with concentrations that are affected by exposure to sunlight.

VITAMIN D

Vitamin D_3, or cholecalciferol, is formed in the skin and subcutaneous tissue when ultraviolet light is absorbed by its provitamin, 7-dehydrotachysterol; it can also be obtained by eating fish. The precise action spectrum for the activation of the provitamin *in vivo* is not known; it may include both mid-ultraviolet (290-320 nm) and long-wave ultraviolet (320-400 nm) irradiations. A related, biologically active compound, vitamin D_2, can be obtained by consuming milk and other foods fortified with irradiated ergosterol (ergocalciferol); it remains to be demonstrated, however, that this exogenous source is as biologically effective as the vitamin D formed in the skin. In a population of Caucasian adults from St. Louis, Missouri, 71-91% of the total vitamin D activity in the blood was observed to be associated with vitamin D$_3$ and its derivatives (Haddad and Hahn, 1973); hence sunlight remains vastly more important than food as a source of vitamin D.

Recent studies by De Luca and others have shown that vitamin D compounds are further transformed by the liver and kidneys to the more active metabolites that are hydroxylated at the 1- and 25-positions; these metabolites act on the intestinal mucosa to facilitate calcium absorption and on bone to facilitate calcium exchange (De Luca, 1971). Loomis has suggested that the term "vitamin D" is a misnomer; the active compound is normally synthesized endogenously and, thus, is much more a hormone than a vitamin (Loomis, 1970). Like the hormone thyroxin, which cannot be synthesized in the absence of the dietary constituent iodine, the hormone vitamin D cannot be formed in the absence of the environmental input light. Just as one could substitute the consumption of irradiated milk for exposing oneself to sunlight, a person could fulfill his need for dietary iodine by consuming bovine thyroids. This does not mean that thyroxin should be considered a vitamin.

It has been recognized for some years that children chronically exposed to inadequate amounts of sunlight may develop rickets, a deforming disease characterized by undermineralization of the bones. This disease can be cured by irradiating the skin with ultraviolet light or by feeding afflicted children 200-400 IU of vitamin D daily (Loomis, 1970). Recent studies in Boston showed that apparently normal, elderly males deprived of ultraviolet light for 3 months (by remaining indoors during the winter in environments illuminated by standard incandescent or fluorescent sources) and consuming about 200 IU of dietary vitamin D per day developed an impairment in the ability of their intestinal mucosa to absorb calcium. Concurrent exposure of similar males for 8 hours/day to a lighting environment designed to simulate the solar spectrum in the visible and near-ultraviolet ranges blocked the 40% fall in calcium absorption observed in the control subjects (Neer et al., 1971) (Fig. 2-3). The amount of ultraviolet light impinging on these subjects was equivalent to the quantity that they might be expected to receive during a 15-minute lunchtime walk in the summer. It seems possible that the appropriate design of artificial lighting environments may provide a powerful public health measure for the prophylaxis of bony undermineralization.

BILIRUBIN

Bilirubin (Fig. 2-2) is a yellow degradation product of the hemoglobin released when red blood cells die (Poland and Odell, 1971). Apparently, it

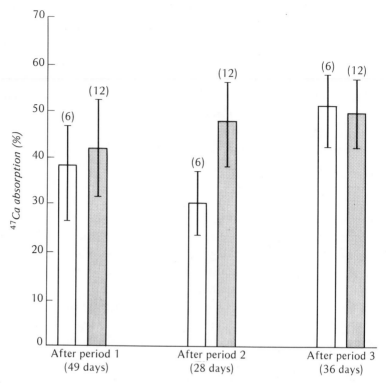

Fig. 2-3. Stimulation by artificial lighting of calcium absorption in elderly human subjects. From December 20, 1968 to April 25, 1969, eighteen healthy males between 57 and 80 years of age were asked to stay indoors and away from open windows during daylight. The subjects were divided into two groups, twelve of whom were to be considered the experimental group and six of whom were considered the controls. During period 1, all subjects were exposed to regular fluorescent lighting; at the end of this period, the ability of each subject to absorb calcium was estimated by measuring the percentage of ^{47}Ca passed in feces within six days of ingestion. During period 2, the twelve experimental subjects were exposed to an artificial sunlight illuminant (Vita-Lite, stippled columns), whereas the six controls remained under regular fluorescent luminaires that lacked significant ultraviolet emissions (white columns). At the end of this period, ^{47}Ca absorption was again measured. In period 3, all subjects were again exposed to the conditions of artificial light used during period 1. Differences between experimental and control groups after period 2 were significant ($p < 0.01$). (Reprinted from Neer et al., 1971.)

is gravely toxic for humans only during the first few days of life. An increase in the concentration of bilirubin in the blood causes the skin to exhibit the characteristic yellow of jaundice; such hyperbilirubinemia may occur because too much bilirubin is being formed, the rate of destruction of red blood cells being too great, or because the removal of bilirubin from the body, a process initiated by the liver, is abnormally slow. A dangerous form of hyperbilirubinemia occurs not infrequently in the newborn, premature infant whose liver is biochemically immature and whose red blood cells are being destroyed at a pathological rate because their blood type (usually Rh positive) is incompatible with that of their mother (usually Rh negative). The lipid-soluble bilirubin becomes concentrated in certain parts of the brain, where it can destroy neurons and produce a clinical syndrome known as kernicterus ("yellow brain"). The resulting cerebral damage is irreversible and can cause various degrees of motor and mental retardation, leading to cerebral palsy and even to death (Gartner *et al.*, 1970).

At present, all therapies for hyperbilirubinemia of the neonate are designed to keep the concentration of bilirubin in the plasma from reaching levels that might cause brain damage (about 10 to 15 mg %). Therapy is continued until the maturing liver is able to clear the bilirubin from the blood (about the end of the first postnatal week). One widely used therapy involves exchange transfusion, in which the jaundiced blood from the baby is completely replaced by bilirubin-free blood from a blood type-compatible donor (McKay, 1964).

Like rhodopsin in the retinal photoreceptors, bilirubin in solution can be bleached by light. Unlike rhodopsin, however, bilirubin photodecomposition is not reversed by darkness. These observations, made several years ago, prompted intensive clinical research on the possible use of light ("phototherapy") to lower plasma bilirubin levels in cases of neonatal hyperbilirubinemia. There was anecdotal evidence that newborn infants whose cribs had been placed near open windows became significantly jaundiced less often than infants whose cribs were at a distance from the windows; perhaps sunlight was accelerating the destruction of circulating bilirubin, and perhaps artificial light could produce the same effect. This hypothesis was confirmed, and, in the last few years, literally thousands of jaundiced infants have been exposed to light for 3 or 4 days as the sole therapy for their hyperbilirubinemia.

Many questions concerning the mechanism of, and even the long-term safety of the use of phototherapy for, hyperbilirubinemia remain. The final products of the photodecomposition of bilirubin *in vivo* have not yet been identified. It is thought that these substances are not toxic and, unlike bilirubin, water soluble and therefore easily excreted from the body (Ostrow, 1967). The effect of light on pure solutions of bilirubin has been studied extensively. In these studies, blue light has been found to be most effective in decomposing bilirubin. In the normal infant, all full-spectrum light sources thus far tested lower plasma bilirubin levels, regardless of the proportion of radiant energy in the blue range. Hence, the mechanism by which light destroys bilirubin *in vivo* may not be the same as the simple photochemical reaction occurring in pure solutions. The *in vivo* mechanism could involve a photosensitization reaction or even some effect of light on plasma albumin, the protein to which most of the circulating bilirubin binds. Since "natural" white light appears to be highly effective in treating jaundiced infants, and since exposure to blue light constitutes a novel and possibly unsafe experience in man's evolutionary history, there seems to be little justification at the present time for the treatment of infants with the more radical, blue-light phototherapy.

The observation that environmental light from the Sun or from artificial sources modifies the plasma levels of one endogenous substance opens a Pandora's Box for the student of human biology. It raises the possibility that the plasma levels of many additional substances are similarly dependent on light.

PHOTOSENSITIZING FOODS AND DRUGS

A number of widely used drugs (for example, the tetracyclines) and constituents of foods are potential photosensitizers—that is, they can be activated in the body in response to light, producing intermediates that can cause tissue damage in sensitive persons. A characteristic sign of such a reaction in sensitive persons is the appearance of a rash on the portions of the body most exposed to sunlight, the hands and face, for example. The rash invariably disappears when treatment with the drug or ingestion of the dietary sensitizer is curtailed.

In individuals with the congenital disease, erythropoietic protoporphyria, unusually large quantities of photosensitizing substances are released into the bloodstream as a result of a biochemical abnormality of the cells. These porphyrin compounds absorb long-wave ultraviolet radiation to generate toxic intermediates. Victims complain of a burning sensation in those portions of the skin that are exposed to light, which is followed by reddening and swelling. Since these symptoms can be induced at will and without major hazard by exposing patients suffering from relatively mild forms of the disease to light, erythropoietic protoporphyria constitutes one of the few clinical situations in which the action spectrum for a direct effect of light can be investigated in detail. It appears that skin damage is produced by a relatively narrow band of light in the region of 400 nm; this band coincides with one of the *in vitro* absorption peaks of the abnormal porphyrins. The symptoms of this disease can be ameliorated by the use of such photoprotective agents as carotenoids (Mathews-Roth *et al.*, 1970). These may quench the free radicals and the singlet-excited oxygen produced as intermediates of the photosensitization reaction.

Indirect effects of light

Light and biological rhythms

The amount of time all living things are exposed to light varies with two cycles, a 24-hour, light-dark cycle of day and night and an annual cycle of changing day length, absent only at the Equator. These light cycles correspond to many rhythmic changes in mammalian biological functions. Motor activity, sleep, food and water consumption, body temperature, and the rates at which many glands secrete their hormones all vary with rhythms with periods that approximate 24 hours (see Table 2-1). Thus,

Table 2-1   Some Rhythmic Functions in Man

Rhythmic function	*Usual time of peak level of activity*
Sleep	1–4 A.M.
Eosinophils in blood	1–3 A.M.
ACTH in plasma	2–5 A.M.
Cortisol in plasma	6–9 A.M.
Magnesium and calcium in urine	9–11 A.M.
17-Hydroxycorticosteroids in urine	10–12 A.M.
Sodium and potassium in urine	1–3 P.M.
Wakefulness	1–4 P.M.
Urine volume	3–6 P.M.
Catecholamine metabolites in urine	4–7 P.M.
Body temperature	4–6 P.M.
Skin reaction to subcutaneously injected histamine	7–11 P.M.
Phosphates in urine	10–12 P.M.

the concentration of cortisol in the blood of human subjects varies with a characteristic 24-hour rhythm; it is maximal in the morning hours and minimal in the evening. When people elect to reverse their activity cycles (for example, by working during the hours of darkness and sleeping during daylight), their plasma cortisol rhythms require about 5 to 10 days to adapt to the new environmental conditions (Eisenstein, 1969).

Annual rhythms in sexual activity, hibernation, and migratory behavior are widespread among animal species. The physiological significance of these rhythms probably derives from their ability to synchronize the activities of individuals within a species with regard to one another and with regard to their changing environmental conditions. For example, sheep ovulate and are fertilized in the Fall, thus anticipating, by many months, Spring, when larger quantities of food will be available to the mother for nursing the newborn. For humans, the pressure of the environment to adapt is of less significance. Psychosocial factors quite possibly are of greater importance than light cycles in generating or synchronizing biological rhythms. The biological utility of the sleep-wakefulness rhythm and of other consequent rhythms remains to be identified.

Cycles in environmental lighting may interact with biological rhythms in several ways. The light cycle may induce the rhythm. In this event, placing a mammal in an environment of continuous light or darkness should rapidly abolish the rhythm. Such was found to be the case for the content of norepinephrine in the rat pineal body, which varies each day with a characteristic rhythm that disappears in the absence of day-night light cycles (Wurtman et al., 1967). (The neuroanatomical and physiological mechanisms by which environmental lighting affect pineal body metabolism are described on pp. 31 to 34.) Another cyclic environmental input—dietary protein—has been shown to generate a daily rhythm. Amino acids, consumed as protein, travel to the liver via the portal circulation after each meal and induce aggregation of the protein-synthesizing units (polysomes). The amino acids thereby accelerate the synthesis and increase the tissue levels of tyrosine transaminase enzyme protein (Wurtman et al., 1968a; Fishman et al., 1969).

Rather than inducing the rhythm, the light cycle might simply entrain it, causing all animals in the same species to exhibit maxima and minima at the same time of the day or night. The factor that generates the rhythmicity per se could be a different cyclic environmental input (such as dietary protein) or an intrinsic oscillator (perhaps that metaphysical monstrosity, the "biological clock"). In either case, placing the mammal in an environment of continuous light or darkness should not extinguish the rhythm. If the rhythmic function can be sampled repeatedly in the same animal, it is possible to show that, in the absence of a cyclic lighting input, the rhythms in different animals become dissociated from each other. Presumably, this dissociation occurs because the rhythm "free-runs" or becomes "circadian" (Aschoff, 1965; Halberg, 1963; Pittendrigh and Skopik, 1970); that is, its precise period changes from exactly 24 hours to something that is more or less characteristic for each animal. If the rhythm does "free-run," this is good evidence that it is not generated by a cyclic environmental input exhibiting a 24-hour periodicity (such as light, ambient temperature, humidity). It could be generated, as we said above, by other cyclic environmental inputs, such as food and water, which also "free-run" in the absence of light, or it could result from intrinsic oscillators. In any case, only a few rhythms are amenable to this sort of experimental analysis in mammals, since only rhythms in behavior, body temperature, and plasma and urinary concentrations can be studied conveniently by repeated sampling from a single subject.

Relatively little information is available concerning the action spectra or intensities required for light to generate or entrain daily rhythms in mammals; it is known that light is the dominant environmental input affecting rhythms and that light exerts its effects indirectly, via retinal photoreceptors. The action spectrum for the entrainment of the body temperature rhythm in rats (McGuire and Wurtman, 1973) is similar to that required for the inhibition of the rat pineal body (Cardinali *et al.*, 1972) and to the absorption spectrum of rhodopsin (Wald, 1964) (see Fig. 2-4).

Light and the mammalian pineal body

Of all the indirect effects of light on mammalian processes, the photic control of hormone synthesis in the pineal body is probably the best characterized, next to vision. Experiments performed largely during the past decade have provided abundant evidence that nervous impulses reaching the pineal body via its sympathetic nerves control the rate at which this body synthesizes its hormone, melatonin (Wurtman *et al.*, 1968b) (Fig. 2-2). These impulses vary inversely with the amount of visible light impinging on the retina (Taylor and Wilson, 1970). They are carried through the brain, spinal cord, and sympathetic nervous system by a circuitous route, which differs from the pathway responsible for vision and which apparently is unique to mammals. This route is shown in Fig. 2-5.

Experiments have shown that, if rats are maintained for several days under conditions of continuous illumination, the activity of the pineal en-

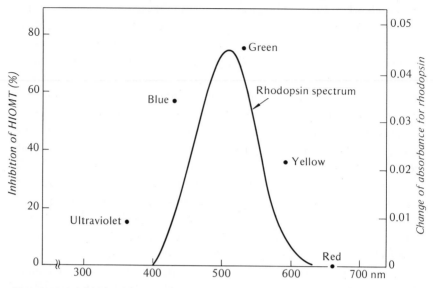

Fig. 2-4. Inhibition of the pineal enzyme hydroxyindole-O-methyl transferase (HIOMT) by various colors of light. Groups of rats were exposed to five narrow-spectrum light sources (ultraviolet, blue, green, yellow, and red) for 96 hours each. These sources were all at the same level of radiant energy (65 μW/cm^2). The percentage of inhibition of the melatonin-synthesizing enzyme is co-plotted with the absorption spectrum of rhodopsin, the visual pigment present in the rat retina. (Reprinted from Cardinali *et al.,* 1972.)

zymes involved in melatonin biosynthesis decrease many-fold (Wurtman *et al.,* 1964). This effect is absent in animals whose eyes have been removed and animals in which the nerves to the pineal body have been cut. The decrease in pineal enzyme activity appears to be an exaggeration of the "normal" response of the pineal body to natural light cycles; melatonin synthesis is also slowest at the end of the daily light period among animals kept in a cyclically lighted environment (Axelrod *et al.,* 1965). Although the precise role of melatonin (the major pineal body hormone thus far characterized) in the physiology of the intact mammal has not yet been ascertained, it is well established that the administration of melatonin affects the brain and secretion by various endocrine organs probably by acting on neuroendocrine control centers in the brain (Wurtman *et al.,* 1968b). In the brain, it induces sleep, modifies the electroencephalogram, and raises the levels of the neurotransmitter, serotonin; it affects secretion by the pituitary, the gonads, and the adrenals. Melatonin administration blocks the cyclic release of luteinizing hormone, the hormone

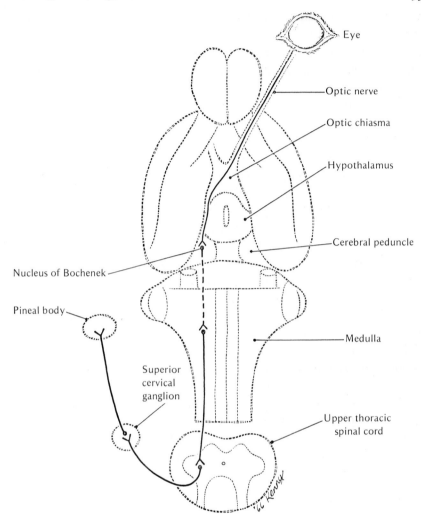

Fig. 2-5. Neural pathways by which light indirectly controls the synthesis of the pineal hormone, melatonin. Light stimuli reach the pineal body by a circuitous route ultimately involving the sympathetic nervous system. Photoreceptors in the eye respond to environmental lighting by generating nerve impulses, which are transmitted along the optic nerve. Most of these impulses travel to brain centers associated with vision. A small fraction diverge from the main visual pathway and, instead, travel along a nerve bundle (the inferior accessory optic tract), which leads to the central hypothalamic neurons involved in the regulation of the sympathetic nervous system. From this point, the pathway descends via the spinal cord to the preganglionic neurons supplying the superior cervical ganglia; the postganglionic neurons then ascend to the pineal body where they act by liberating the neurotransmitter, norepinephrine. Norepinephrine enhances the activity of several pineal enzymes involved in the synthesis of melatonin. (Reprinted from Wurtman *et al.*, 1968b.)

responsible for ovulation, from the anterior pituitary gland. Immature rats kept under continuous illumination became sexually mature at an earlier age than animals kept under a 24-hour, light-dark cycle (Wurtman, 1967); this effect may have been mediated by the photic inhibition of melatonin secretion.

In summary, although the pineal body is not directly responsive to light, its secretory activity is controlled by light. The secretion of melatonin by the pineal body may serve to synchronize the lighting environment with intrinsic biological processes not primarily dependent on light. In certain lower vertebrates, the pineal body is directly responsive to environmental lighting (Rosner *et al.*, 1971; Dodt and Heerd, 1962), serving as a photoreceptive "third eye," which sends messages about the state of environmental lighting to the brain. In the mammalian pineal body, all such traces of direct photoreceptive function are lost. The retinal photoreceptor that mediates the control of the mammalian pineal body by light has not yet been identified. Recent studies suggest, however, that this photoreceptor utilizes rhodopsin and may thus be a rod cell (Cardinali *et al.*, 1972). Figure 2-4 illustrates the similarity between the action spectrum for the photic inhibition of pineal hydroxyindole-O-methyl transferase (HIOMT), an enzyme required for melatonin biosynthesis, and the absorption spectrum for rhodopsin.

Very recently, a method has been developed for measuring melatonin in human urine, and it has been shown that melatonin excretion in man exhibits a 24-hour rhythmicity. The amounts of melatonin present in urine samples collected between 11 P.M. and 7 A.M. were 10- to 20-fold greater than the amounts present in 7 A.M. to 4 P.M. or 3 P.M. to 11 P.M. samples (Lynch and Wurtman, 1975).

Light and mammalian gonadal function

Environmental lighting has been shown to influence the maturation and the subsequent cyclic activity of the gonads in all mammalian and avian species thus far examined (Wurtman, 1967). The particular responses of each species to light seem to depend on whether the species is monoestrous or polyestrous (that is, whether it normally ovulates once a year, in the Spring or Fall, or at regular intervals throughout the year). Examples of the latter are laboratory rats (every 4 to 5 days); guinea pigs (every 12 to 14 days); and humans (every 29 days). The gonadal responses of each species to light also seem to depend on whether its members are physically active during the daylight hours or at night. Thus, if weanling rats (a nocturnal, polyestrous species) are kept, from birth, under continuous illumination, they mature at a younger age than control animals kept under cyclic illumination, but they then fail to ovulate cyclically, exhibiting instead a state of "persistent estrus" (Wurtman, 1967). Blindness in humans (a diurnally active, polyestrous species) is also associated with early gonadal maturation (Zacharias and Wurtman, 1969) (see Table 2-2). The gonads of most birds and of most diurnally active, monoestrous

Table 2-2   Effect of Blindness on Age of Menarche in Humans

Group[a]	Number	Mean age (months)	S.D.	S.E.
IA (premature,[b] blind)	85	143.0	14.5	1.6[c]
IB (premature, blind)	107	144.0	14.3	1.4[c]
II (premature, non-blind)	98	150.8	16.1	1.6
III (term,[d] blind)	68[e]	146.0	14.6	1.9[f]
IV (term, non-blind)	235	150.5	10.2	0.7

(Reprinted from Zacharias and Wurtman, 1969)
[a] Females in Group IA had no light perception; those in Group IB some.
[b] Prematurely born females.
[c] Differs from Group II, $p < 0.01$.
[d] Females born at full term.
[e] The nine subjects in this group without light perception were not included in the study.
[f] Differs from Group IV, $p < 0.01$.

mammals mature in Spring, in response to the gradual increase in day length. Ovulation can be accelerated in these animals by exposing them to artificially "long days." The annual period of gonadal activity in domestic sheep (also a diurnally active, monoestrous species) occurs in the Fall, in response to decreasing day length. The mechanisms that cause some species to be monoestrous and others polyestrous or that cause some animals to sleep by day and others by night are entirely unknown, as are those explaining why the gonadal responses of various species to light vary as widely as they do.

In birds, photoreceptors capable of mediating gonadal responses apparently exist in the brain as well as the eye. Hence, light reaching the brain of the duck via quartz rods placed in the eye socket can be used to accelerate gonadal enlargement (Benoit and Assenmacher, 1959). In adult mammals, however, only the retina appear to contain the photoreceptor cells necessary for stimulating gonadal responses (or any other neuroendocrine effects, for that matter). In support of this conclusion, removal of the eyes completely blocks the ability of experimental illumination to accelerate maturation or to interfere with the mechanisms responsible for causing ovulation (Wurtman, 1967). The neural and neuroendocrine pathways connecting the retina and the gonads are poorly defined; one such pathway probably involves the pineal body and melatonin (Wurtman *et al.*, 1968b); another may utilize cells in the hypothalamus, which, by secreting "releasing factors," control the secretion of gonadotropic hormones from the anterior pituitary. The action spectra for the effects of light on mammalian gonads have not yet been identified.

CONCLUSIONS

Visible and ultraviolet light in the environment affect a variety of structures and physiological mechanisms in mammals. Light interacts directly with the cells of the skin and with substances near the surface of the body. It stimulates photoreceptor cells, present in adult mammals only in the retina, to generate vision and to control biological rhythms, gonadal growth, ovulation, secretion from the pineal body, and, probably, additional processes as yet uncharacterized. The recent discovery that visible light can be used to lower the plasma concentration of one substance (bilirubin) indicates that there is a good possibility that the fate of many other biologically active circulating substances depends on environmental lighting. The lighting environments in which most humans spend most of their time differ considerably in spectrum and intensity from the environment in which man evolved. The biological consequences of living in such novel lighting environments have yet to be discovered.

REFERENCES

Aschoff, J. (ed.) 1965. *Circadian Clocks.* Amsterdam: North Holland Publishing Co.
Axelrod, J., R. J. Wurtman, and S. H. Snyder. 1965. Control of hydroxyindole-O-methyl transferase activity in the rat pineal gland by environmental lighting. *J. Biol. Chem.* 240:949-54.
Benoit, J. and I. Assenmacher. 1959. The control by visible radiations of the gonadotropic activity of the duck hypophysis. *Recent Prog. Hormone Res.* 15:143-64.
Blum, H. F. 1964. Does sunlight cause skin cancer? *Univ. Mag.* 21:10-13.

Cardinali, D. P., F. Larin, and R. J. Wurtman. 1972. Control of the rat pineal by environmental lighting: Dependency of the light spectrum. *Proc. Natl. Acad. Sci. (U.S.A.)* 69:2003-2005.

De Luca, H. F. 1971. Role of the Kidney tissue in metabolism of vitamin D. *New Engl. J. Med.* 284:554.

Dodt, E. and E. Heerd. 1962. Mode of action of pineal nerve fibers in frogs. *J. Neurophysiol.* 25:405-29.

Eisenstein, A. B. (ed.). 1969. *The Adrenal Cortex*. Boston: Little, Brown.

Enns, K. and W. H. Burgess. 1965. The photochemical oxidation of ethylene-diaminetetraacetic acid and methionine by riboflavin. *J. Am. Chem. Assoc.* 87:5766-70.

Fishman, B., R. J. Wurtman, and H. N. Munro. 1969. Daily rhythms in hepatic polysome profiles and tyrosine transaminase activity: role of dietary protein. *Proc. Natl. Acad. Sci. (U.S.A.)* 64:677-82.

Ganong, W. F., M. D. Shepherd, J. R. Wall, E. E. von Brunt, and M. T. Clegg. 1963. Penetration of light into the brain of mammals. *Endocrinology* 72:962-63.

Gartner, L. M., R. N. Snyder, R. S. Chabon, and J. Bernstein. 1970. Kernicterus: High incidence in premature infants with low serum bilirubin concentrations. *Pediatrics* 45:906-17.

Haddad, J. G., Jr., and T. J. Hahn. 1973. Natural and synthetic sources of circulating 25-hydroxyvitamin D in man. *Nature* 244:515-16.

Halberg, F. 1963. Circadian (about twenty-four hour) rhythms in experimental medicine. *Proc. Royal Soc. Med.* 56:253-60.

Kligman, A. M. 1969. Early destructive effect of sunlight on human skin. *J.A.M.A.* 210:2377-80.

Loomis, W. F. 1970. Rickets. *Sci. Am.* 223:77-91.

Lucey, J. F., M. Ferreiro, and J. Hewitz. 1968. Prevention of hyperbilirubinemia of prematurity by phototherapy. *Pediatrics* 41:1047-56.

Lynch, H. J. and R. J. Wurtman. 1975. Human urinary melatonin: A 24-hour rhythm. In *Fertility Regulation through Basic Research*, eds. W. A. Sadler and S. Segal. New York: Plenum Press.

McGuire, R. A., W. M. Rand, and R. J. Wurtman. 1973. Entrainment of the body temperature rhythm in rats: Effect of color and intensity of environmental light. *Science* 181:956-57.

McKay, J. 1964. Current status of use of exchange transfusion in newborn infants. *Pediatrics* 33:763-73.

Mathews-Roth, M. M., M. B. Pathak, T. B. Fitzpatrick, L. C. Harber, and E. H. Kass. 1970. Beta-carotene as a photoprotective agent in erythropoietic protoporphyria. *New Engl. J. Med.* 282:1231-34.

Neer, R. M., T. R. A. Davis, A. Walcott, S. Koski, P. Schepis, I. Taylor, L. Thorington, and R. J. Wurtman. 1971. Stimulation by artificial lighting of calcium absorption in elderly human subjects. *Nature* 229:255-57.

Ostrow, J. D. 1967. Photo-oxidative derivatives of [14C]-bilirubin and their excretion by the Gunn rat. *International Symposium on Bilirubin*. London: Blackwell, pp. 117-43.

Pittendrigh, C. S. and S. D. Skopik. 1970. Circadian systems. V. The driving oscillation and the temporal sequence of development. *Proc. Natl. Acad. Sci. (U.S.A.)* 65:500-507.

Poland, R. L. and G. B. Odell. 1971. Physiological jaundice: The enterohepatic circulation of bilirubin. *New Engl. J. Med.* 284:1-6.

Rosner, J. M., G. D. Perez Bedéz, and D. P. Cardinali. 1971. Direct effect of light on duck pineal explants. *Life Sci.* 10:1065-68.

Sjostrand, F. S. 1961. Electron microscopy of the retina. In *The Structure of the Eye*, ed. G. K. Smelser. New York: Academic Press, pp. 1-28.

Smith, K. C. and P. C. Hanawalt. 1969. *Molecular Photobiology*. New York: Academic Press.

Szabó, G. 1969. *The Biology of the Pigment Cell*. New York: Academic Press.

Taylor, A. N. and R. W. Wilson. 1970. Electrophysiological evidence for the action of light on the pineal gland in the rat. *Experientia* 26:267-70.

Thorington, L., L. Parascandola, and L. Cunningham. 1971. Visual and biological aspects of an artificial sunlight illuminant. *J. Illum. Eng. Soc.* 1:33-41.

Urbach, F. 1969. Geographic pathology of skin cancer. In *The Biological Effects of Ultraviolet Irradiation*, ed. F. Urbach. Oxford: Pergamon, pp. 635-50.

Wald, G. 1964. The receptors of human color vision. *Science* 145:1007-16.

Wurtman, R. J. 1967. Effects of light and visual stimuli on endocrine function. In *Neuroendocrinology*, vol. 2, eds. L. Martini and W. F. Ganong. New York: Academic Press, pp. 19-59.

Wurtman, R. J. 1970. Effects of light on metabolic processes. *Birth Defects: Original Article Series* 6:60-62.

Wurtman, R. J. and J. Weisel. 1969. Environmental lighting and neuroendocrine function: Relationship between spectrum of light source and gonadal growth. *Endocrinology* 85:1218-20.

Wurtman, R. J., J. Axelrod, and J. E. Fischer. 1964. Melatonin synthesis in the pineal gland: Effect of light mediated by the sympathetic nervous system. *Science* 143:1328-30.

Wurtman, R. J., W. Shoemaker, and F. Larin. 1968a. Mechanism of the daily rhythm in hepatic tyrosine transaminase activity: Role of dietary tryptophan. *Proc. Natl. Acad. Sci.* (*U.S.A.*) 59:800-807.

Wurtman, R. J., J. Axelrod, and D. E. Kelly. 1968b. *The Pineal*. New York: Academic Press.

Wurtman, R. J., J. Axelrod, G. Sedvall, and R. Y. Moore. 1967. Photic and neural control of the 24-hour epinephrine rhythm in the rat pineal gland. *J. Pharmacol. Exptl. Therap.* 157:487-92.

Zacharias, L. and R. J. Wurtman. 1969. Blindness and menarche. *Obstet. Gynecol.* 33:603-608.

Zweig, M., S. H. Snyder, and J. Axelrod. 1966. Evidence for a nonretinal pathway of light to the pineal gland of newborn rats. *Proc. Natl. Acad. Sci.* (*U.S.A.*) 56:515-20.

3. The Human Skin as an Adaptive Organ

GEORGE SZABÓ *

GENERAL CONSIDERATIONS

Environment and the cell

Our skin is the first line of encounter with the external environment. The integument is, indeed, continuously exposed to fluctuations in temperature, solar radiation, friction, and various biological and chemical agents. Furthermore, our skin also presents a barrier toward the internal milieu so that fluid balance is maintained.

In this chapter, we shall attempt to correlate the structure of skin with its role of "defense and containment" of the individual.

First, we have to prove to ourselves that our tools for investigating biological structures (light and electron microscopy) are not *too* refined to detect the adaptive changes in *cell* structure caused by environmental agents acting on the *individual* as a whole. Careful observations and well-planned experiments narrow "the resolution gap" between the various levels of investigation (Fig. 3-1) so that one can obtain meaningful data by looking at certain cells of an individual.

Many years ago, George Cuvier was able to draw valid conclusions as to the gross appearance and habitat of fossil animals by looking at their bones; in the 20th century, we are also able to gain some ideas about the environmental influences exerted on these animals by looking at their cells.

* Department of Periodontology, Harvard School of Dental Medicine and Departments of Anatomy and Dermatology, Harvard Medical School, Boston, Massachusetts.

Physiological Anthropology

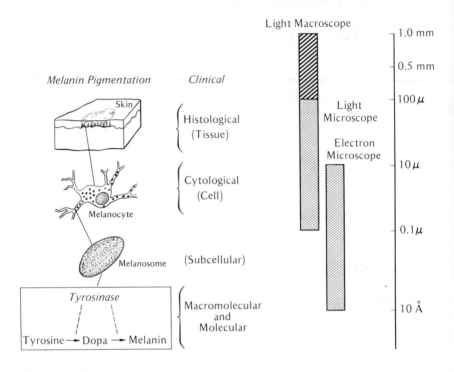

Fig. 3-1. Levels of organization of the melanin pigmentary system. (From Fitzpatrick *et al.,* 1971. By permission McGraw-Hill Book Co.)

For example, it is known that exposure of hamsters to phenobarbital drastically increases the area in the liver occupied by the smooth endoplasmic reticulum (Jones and Fawcett, 1966). It is also known that the lungs of city dwellers are heavily laden with smoke particles (Happleston, 1969). As a third example, it is now possible to visualize the color complexion of the whole individual by examining the pigment granules of his epidermal cells in the electron microscope (Szabó *et al.,* 1972).

Structure of skin

The skin consists of two types of tissues. Several layers of epithelial cells comprise the epidermis, which is supported and maintained by an underlying connective tissue, the dermis (Fig. 3-2). Although the specialized products of the epidermis, keratin and melanin, play an important role in the protection of the organism, it is the dermis that is primarily respon-

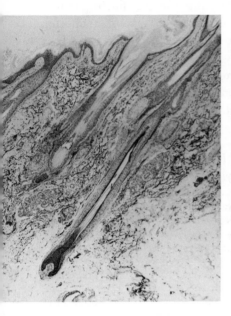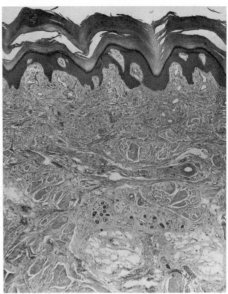

Fig. 3-2. Regional adaptation of skin structure to stresses. (A) *Section of human scalp.* Acid-Orcein-Giemsa stain ×50. Note the growing hair follicle deep in the dermis; to the left is a resting follicle. There is very little keratin at the top of the dermis. (B) *Section of human toe.* H&E stain. ×50. Note the very thick keratin, top of epidermis, which is thicker than that in (A). There are sweat glands in the dermis and a coil of a sweat duct in the keratin.

sible for the differentiation and maintenance of the epidermis (Billingham and Silvers, 1968).

The epidermal differentiation is the fascinating story of variability of the basal epidermal or Malpighian cell. The main function of this Malpighian cell is to form a fibrous protein, keratin. All of the cell's organelles, including the nucleus, disappear, and the cell itself becomes a "dead" carrier of this keratin. During this process, the cell leaves the basal layer of the epidermis (the junction of the epidermis with the dermis) and slowly approaches the surface of the skin. In man, this process takes about 28 days. Finally, the cell matures and is exfoliated, shed, or sloughed off the surface of the skin.

The Malpighian cell in other circumstances may take a different line of development, depending upon the inductive influence of the dermis. When Malpighian cells are associated with a group of dermal cells forming the hair or feather papillae, keratinization does not progress horizontally to form a flat surface, but, rather, the cells pile up to produce the hair or the feather shaft. Hairs and feathers are very important appendages of the skin, playing a vital role in the thermoregulation and protection of the individual. Man has lost his furry coat from most of his body surface, although there are about 60 hairs/cm^2 on even the most "hairless" part of the human body, with the exception of the palms and soles (Szabó, 1967). These hairs are very small and non-pigmented and, therefore, practically invisible (Table 3-1).

Table 3-1   The Number of Hair Follicles, Sweat Ducts,
and Melanocytes in the Human Skin

	Hair follicles (av. No./cm^2 ± S.E.)	Sweat glands (av. No./cm^2 ± S.E.)	Melanocytes (av. No./mm^2 ± S.E.)
Face	700 ± 40	270 ± 25	2120 ± 90
Trunk	70 ± 10	175 ± 20	890 ± 70
Arm	65 ± 5	175 ± 15	1160 ± 40
Leg	55 ± 5	130 ± 10	1130 ± 60
Average	330 ± 20	215 ± 15	1560 ± 110

(From Szabó, 1967)

There are some other modifications of these epidermal basal cells: like any other epithelial cell, they are able to form glands. One of these glands is the sebaceous gland, which produces the lipid, sebum. These sebum-producing glands are usually associated with hair follicles and put out their content into the hair canal, the pilosebaceous canal. In these glands, the Malpighian cells basically follow the same course of differentiation as a keratinizing cell; while they continue to produce sebum, they also approach the surface of the pilosebaceous canal, lose all cell organelles, and finally are keratinized.

Other types of glands derive from the basal epidermal cells. These include the *sweat glands*, which play a very important role in the regulation of the fluid balance and in the thermoregulation of the individual. They have a duct system, which penetrates the epidermis and opens on the surface of the skin ("pore"). Secretion of sweat takes place in the gland, and some reabsorption of the electrolytes has been observed at the beginning of the duct. Anatomically, there are two types of sweat glands. The phylogenetically more ancient type is associated with hair follicles (apocrine glands) and is very common in fur-bearing animals. These glands are present in man usually in the axillae and some other regions and are functional only after the onset of puberty. (The milk-producing mammary gland is also derived from apocrine glands.) Most of the sweat glands in man, however, are not associated with hair follicles but are free (eccrine glands). Such free sweat glands also occur on the plantar and solar surfaces of other mammals. Some of these free sweat glands are primarily under nervous control, like those on the plantar and solar surfaces, where sweating occurs under nervous stimulation. Other sweat glands play an important role in the thermoregulatory mechanism of the body; these include those on the forehead and on the trunk, which produce sweat under thermal stress.

The Malpighian cells also produce nails and claws, which are specialized keratinized appendages protecting the last digits of fingers and toes.

These appendages are not distributed on the body surface at random, but form an integumentary system where their number, size, and shape are strictly region-specific. Furthermore, the interface of the epidermis and dermis is not a smooth horizontal line, but an interdigitation forming an intricate pattern of hills and valleys. This pattern is also region-specific. Table 3-1 and Figs. 3-3 through 3-6 show some examples of this regional specificity in the adaptation of the skin to regional stresses.

Skin pigments

Skin is not only characterized by such products as keratin, sebum, or sweat, but it also contains coloring substances—pigments that, in the case of man, are melanin or "black" pigment, red blood cell pigment (reduced or oxidized hemoglobin), and carotenes or yellow pigments (Edwards, 1953). Melanin is the most characteristic pigment of the skin and is located mainly in the epidermis. Although the Malpighian cell shows a remarkably wide variety of functional variations, it cannot produce this melanin pigment, which is manufactured in another epidermal cell, the melanocyte. Melanocytes originate in the neural crest near the embryonic central nervous system and invade the fetal epidermis. They retain their "neural" morphology as shown by their dendritic processes, which are firmly inserted between the Malpighian cells.

Melanocytes synthesize an enzyme, tyrosinase, which catalyzes the oxidation of tyrosine (hydroxyphenylalanine, formed from the essential amino acid, phenylalanine, in the liver) into dihydroxyphenylalanine or DOPA. Following this oxidative process, DOPA is polymerized into melanin. There are differing views as to the exact nature of this final polymerizate:

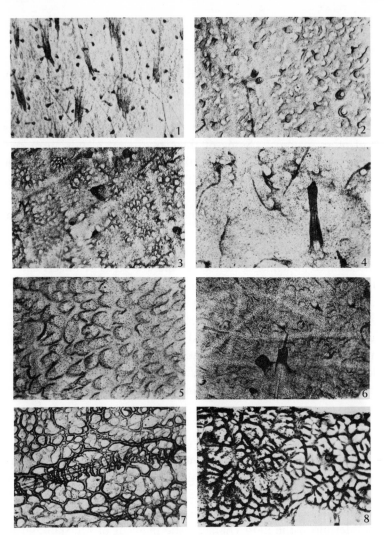

Fig. 3-3. Comparative anatomy of the dermo-epidermal interface: Dopa-treated pure epidermal sheets, viewed from the dermal side. ×30. I. Extremities.

(1) *Thigh,* full-term fetus. Paracarmine counterstain. Hair follicles solitary or grouped, two or three in a group; sweat ducts between the hair follicles in large numbers some indication of ridges; no melanocytes. (2) *Thigh,* 18-month-old baby. Paracarmine counterstain. Hair follicles and sweat ducts reduced in number per unit area; well-developed system of ridges; melanocytes dopa-positive; note impression of flexure lines. (3) *Thigh,* adult. Number of skin appendages per unit area further reduced; melanocyte population less dense than in (2); impressions of flexure lines more marked than in (2). (4) *Leg* (frontal aspect over shinbone). Basal layer mostly flat; ridges restricted around sweat ducts and hair follicles. (5) *Heel.* Absence of appendages or very low number of sweat ducts; dermal papillae penetrate the epidermis at an acute angle; melanocytes strongly dopa-positive. The structure of the calf and the knee is similar to that of the heel. (6) *Forearm* (frontal aspect), 8-year-old child. Two hair follicles, grouped, lower half of section; high density of melanocytes; shallow ridges or flat areas between well-developed flexure lines. (7) *Elbow.* Well-developed pattern of deep ridges. The flexure lines (straight lines across the field) are "bridged over" by ridges. (8) *Wrist.* Deep ridges with sweat glands; vitiliginous epidermis, with only the left half of the field showing dopa-positive melanocytes. (By permission of the Royal Society.)

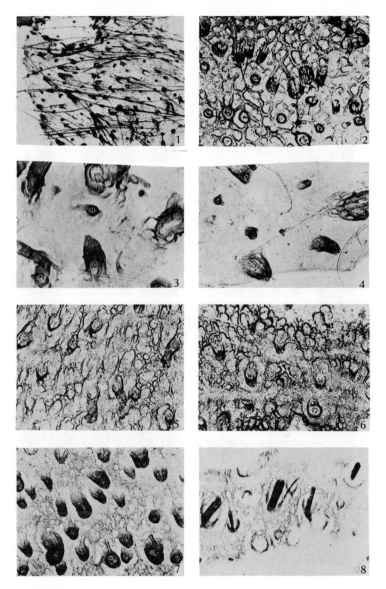

Fig. 3-4. Comparative anatomy of the dermo-epidermal interface: Dopa-treated pure epidermal sheets, viewed from the dermal side, ×30. II. The head.

(1) *Forehead,* 7-month-old fetus. Large number of hair follicles and sweat ducts; small number of dopa-positive melanocytes; system of ridges not yet developed. (2) *Forehead,* adult. Well-developed pattern connecting hair follicles; large number of melanocytes. (3) *Scalp* (with macroscopically visible hair), adult. Very large hair follicles with "anchoring ridges," and relatively smooth epidermis between; weakly dopa-positive melanocytes. (4) *Scalp* (bald site), same patient as in (3). The number and the distribution hair follicles are the same. (5) *Skin from behind the right* ear and (6) *from behind the left* ear, 9-year-old boy. Great similarity in ridge patterns, although the left side has a greater population of melanocytes. No sweat ducts. (7) *Helix.* Large hair follicles, pattern similar to forehead pattern, but melanocyte population less dense. (8) *Eyebrow.* Deeply pigmented, coarse hair with the usual circular pattern of the basal layer. (By permission of the Royal Society.)

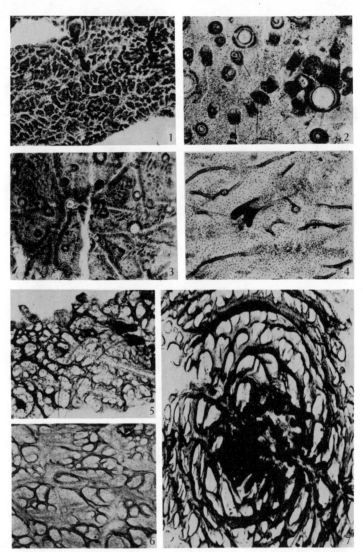

Fig. 3-5. Comparative anatomy of the dermo-epidermal interface: Dopa-treated pure epidermal sheets, viewed from the dermal side. ×30. III. The head and the trunk.

(1) *Eyelid.* Very characteristic pattern of angular epidermal ridges. (2) *Cheek.* No epidermal ridges; great variation in the size and the shape of melanocytes and hair follicles. (3) *Chin* (thin Thiersch graft). Flexure lines connect hair follicles; small circular or oval epidermal ridges. (4) *Neck* (frontal aspect). Indian. Abruptly ending parallel ridges; circularly arranged melanocytes around sweat duct, mid-section. The melanocytes are much less dense here than in the cheek, although this skin is more deeply pigmented. (5) *Chest.* Basic circular pattern of ridges with well-developed flexure lines; sweat duct, left lower corner, in "bay." (6) *Nipple areola,* Adult. Well-developed pattern of epidermal ridges; no skin appendages; melanocytes much less dense, although nipple is usually well pigmented. (7) *Nipple areola,* female, near-term fetus. Circular ridges; lactiferous ducts, mid-section.

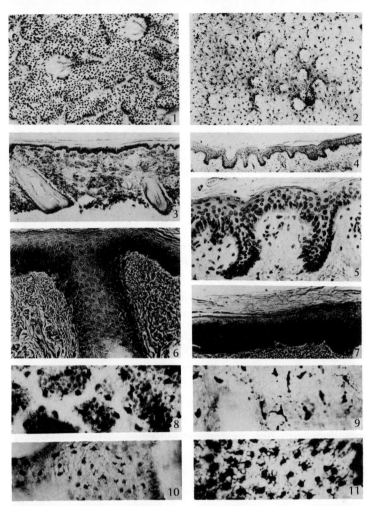

Fig. 3-6. Regional differences in the frequency distribution of melanocytes. Magnification as noted. The head and the thigh.

(1) *Pure epidermis from behind the ear.* Even distribution of melanocytes; two hair follicles. Dopa. ×60. (2) *Pure epidermis from the thigh.* Fewer melanocytes per unit area than preceding specimen; one or two melanocytes in circular imprints of dermal papillae; one sweat duct. Dopa. ×60. (3) *Skin from behind the ear* (transverse section). Almost continuous "melanocyte layer" with some melanocytes parallel to the basal layer. Nonspecific reaction in dermis and stratum corneum. Dopa. ×60. (4) *Thigh* (transverse section). Melanocytes mainly at tips of ridges; sparse between ridges. Dopa and Paracarmine. ×60. (5) *Thigh* (higher magnification of preceding section). Dopa-positive melanocytes mostly in basal layer of epidermal ridges. Dopa and Paracarmine. ×250. (6) *Skin from behind the ear* (higher magnification of (3). Basal layer melanocytes closely placed; clear halo around some melanocytes; "clear cells." In the outer root sheath, decreasing intensity of dopa reaction toward hair bulb. Dopa and Paracarmine. ×250. (7) *Skin from behind the ear* (same specimen as preceding section). Very strong dopa reaction in basal layer; melanocytes mostly at an acute angle to the basal layer; at left, a spindle-shaped melanocyte below the basal layer. Dopa. ×250.

Examples of melanocyte distribution from various regions

(8) *Nasal cavity.* Melanocytes chiefly on ridges (in focus). Dopa and Paracarmine. ×300. (9) *Forehead, 7-month-old fetus.* Low density of melanocytes with long dendrites. (Compare section 11.) Dopa ×300. (10) *Sole of foot.* Melanocytes on epidermal ridge. Dopa. ×300. (11) Forehead, adult. High density of melanocytes, round and with short dendrites. ×300.

some workers, like Mason (1967) think that it is a single polymerizate; others (Nicolaus and Hempel, 1967; Blois, 1967) consider it to be a mixture of compounds with varying degrees of polymerization.

This enzymatic reaction can be demonstrated by histochemical methods using DOPA as a substrate (cf. Szabó, 1969), when all functioning melanocytes rapidly metabolize DOPA and form DOPA melanin; or tyrosine, when the functional activity of the melanocytes (depending on exposure to sunlight) can be tested (Szabó, 1957). Malignant changes can also be detected by this tyrosine reaction (Fitzpatrick *et al.*, 1950) as can melanocytes in actively growing follicles (Foster, 1952).

Tyrosinase catalyzes the reaction that takes place inside the melanocyte in a specific cell organelle, the melanosome. The melanosome shows a species-specific size, shape, and internal structure, being oval in man (Fig. 3-7). Its long axis is longer in certain racial types, such as Negroids or Australian Aborigines ($\sim$ 0.8-1.0 μm), and shorter in Mongoloids ($\sim$ 0.5 μm); Caucasoids have melanosomes that vary in length. The diameter of the organelle is about 0.25-0.5 μm. Except for this difference in size of the melanosomes, *Homo sapiens* have a remarkably uniform melanosome structure in contrast to mice, for example (Rittenhouse, 1968).

The melanosome is produced by the melanocytes and "enters" the Malpighian cells by a unique phenomenon of cell-to-cell propagation. It has been observed in time-lapse cinematography that these melanin granules are incorporated by the epidermal cells directly from the processes of melanocytes (Cruickshank *et al.*, 1964; Cohen and Szabó, 1968; Klaus, 1969; Prunieras, 1969). Thus, the melanocytes function as unicellular "glands." Pierre Masson (1948) coined the word, *cytocrinia*, for the phenomenon of deposition or injection of melanin granules into the Malpighian cells.

The mechanism of incorporation of these melanosomes into keratinocytes is not yet fully understood. It is clear that there is a "size-sorting mechanism" operating in the keratinocytes: they incorporate granules (including artificial latex particles) above a certain size (about 1 μm) in separate units. If the granules are smaller (about 0.1 μm), the keratinocytes aggregate them into complexes. This is true for melanosomes (Szabó *et al.*, 1969) and also for latex particles (Wolff and Konrad, 1971, 1972) applied to migrating keratinocytes under wound-healing conditions. It is very interesting that the hue of the individual is controlled by mechanisms occurring in both the melanocytes and the keratinocytes. The number, size, and shape of melanosomes and their melanization process is ob-

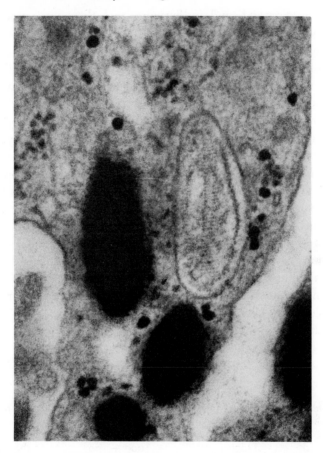

Fig. 3-7. *Negroid skin.* Electron micrograph of human melanosomes in a melanocyte. One completely melanized melanosome (Stage 4) can be seen beside an unmelanized melanosome (Stage 2). The internal structure of this Stage 2 melanosome consists of small particles and filaments in a rosette-like arrangement. Original ×30,000.

viously controlled by the genome of the melanocytes—the transfer process must be controlled by both partners in this process, the melanocytes and the keratinocytes. The keratinocytes, however, control the dispersion of the melanosomes after their transfer: they are either kept in complexes (when the melanosomes are small) or are dispersed individually (when they are large). Finally, there is a hypothetical, not yet proved process of digestion of melanosomes (not that of melanin but the carrier proteinous matrix, which may occur in the keratinocytes. One would wish that all these processes would be taken into consideration when melanogenesis in mammals is discussed—and furthermore, that these vital processes be studied further.

The "anatomical" differences between various human racial groups in regard to the distribution of melanosomes, however, are very minute. In the hair of all races investigated, the melanosomes are long and singly distributed. Furthermore, there is some, but not yet conclusive evidence that, after chronic solar radiation, the number of long melanosomes increases, and they become singly distributed in the keratinocytes. The melanosomes in the retinal pigment epithelium of the eye (which are derived not from the neural crest but from the neural cup), are always very long and, needless to say, are never transferred from these cells into any other type of cell, although they are able to migrate within the processes of the retinal pigment cells.

Melanocytes show regional variations in their size, shape, and frequency distribution in the integument (Table 3-1; Figs. 3-3 through 3-6). All human racial groups (and all other mammals so far investigated) have the *same* number of melanocytes in corresponding areas of the body regardless of the color of the skin (Table 3-2).

*Table 3-2   Comparison of Melanocyte Numbers
among Color Variants of Mammals*

Species	Area (no.of indiv.)	Melanocytes ($mm^2 \pm$ S.E.)	References
Man			
Caucasoid	Thigh (35)	1000 + 70	Szabó, 1969;
Mongoloid	Thigh (3)	1290 ± 45	Szabó, Gerald
Negroid	Thigh (7)	1415 ± 255	et al., 1971
Guinea Pig			
Black	Ear (8)	920 ± 145	Billingham and
Red	Ear (8)	865 ± 100	Medawar,
			1953
Mouse			
C57 Black	Tail (4)	590 ± 65	Gerson and
DBL Dilute	Tail (4)	590 ± 165	Szabó, 1969

The color of the human skin depends not only on the melanin content, but on other coloring substances. Hemoglobins (oxidized and reduced) and the carotenes also contribute to produce the final hue of the integument (Edwards, 1953). The location of the melanin is important in producing the color. For example, if the melanin is found in the dermis, as in the so-called Mongolian spot, then the skin is deep blue in color. In man, melanin is located mainly in the epidermis and gives rise to various shades of brown.

In hair follicles, melanocytes donate melanosomes to the cells of the keratinizing hair matrix, and there is a periodic activity of melanin production and regression synchronous with the periodic growing and resting activity of the hair follicle itself. The graying of hair is due to a gradual loss of functioning melanocytes in the follicle (Fitzpatrick *et al.*, 1964). Functioning melanocytes also decline in number in the epidermis (about 10%/1 decade of life) (Snell and Bischitz, 1963), but this decline is not drastic enough to cause loss of pigment in the epidermis.

THE SKIN AS AN ADAPTIVE ORGAN

The skin as a fluid barrier

We now turn our attention to modifications or adaptations of the skin in changing environments. We are not going to deal in great detail with the adaptation of skin to chemical agents; we will only state that the skin is a very efficient barrier for most chemicals (Scheuplein and Blank, 1971). The effectiveness of this barrier depends upon the adhesion of the keratinized epidermal cells, which are firmly attached to each other up to the last few layers of cells nearest to the surface. The low permeability of the *stratum corneum*, it now seems, is relatively constant throughout its thickness, with the possible exception of the upper two or three layers, which are not continuous and are in the process of being shed. This barrier also works very effectively in maintaining the fluid balance of the individual by not allowing excessive water loss. The sweat glands, however, function to quickly adjust to changes in the ambient temperature, providing a channel for water loss if necessary.

Temperature regulation

Man also must be able to lose heat to the environment to maintain a constant body temperature. In most cases, the temperature of the environment is lower than that of the body. Again, sweating plays an important role in this maintenance, but the vasculature of the dermis can also adapt to a quickly changing environment by such means as the "shunt" system between the arterial and venous circulation, which can quickly open or close according to the demands put on the integument by a changing external temperature. Furthermore, the blood vessels, by dilating or constricting, can adapt themselves to warm or cold environments.

Color changes

It is also well known that the color of human skin changes upon exposure to solar radiation. There is considerable controversy in the literature as to the usefulness of this suntanning mechanism. We shall discuss in more detail this mechanism and its possible adaptive value for man.

"Racial" differences in skin structure

There are no obvious racial differences in the structure of the skin on the light microscopic level when one considers the thickness of the stratum corneum and the numerical distribution of melanocytes, hairs, and sweat glands in the epidermis. Furthermore, light microscopic sections from a dark Mediterranean skin can be very similar to those from a Negroid skin.

It is true that it is exceedingly difficult to measure the thickness of the keratin layer exactly, and accurate quantitative studies are few, but it is also true that chronically exposed skin shows a thicker keratin layer than skin that is not exposed or exposed infrequently.

There are a number of studies claiming that there is a higher number of sweat glands in some races, e.g., the Japanese (Kawahata et al., 1961). These studies, however, usually refer to the number of *functioning* glands and not to the absolute number of glands present. The data of Thomson (1954), based on the number of glands present regardless of function, show that there is no difference between various human racial groups. There is a great need for future studies in this field.

Under the influence of continuous exposure to the Sun, the skin of less pigmented Caucasoids and other groups may show age changes in the dermis not shown by pigmented Negroids or Australoids. Therefore, the *senile* human skin may show "racial" differences due to environmental factors, i.e., more elastic degeneration is present in fair-skinned individuals than in "colored" individuals (Mitchell, 1967, 1968).

The protective role of melanin pigment

In the literature, discussion of this question usually falls into two categories. There are proponents of the idea that only keratin is of importance as a defensive agent against solar radiation (Blum, 1948, 1961, 1968) or that melanin pigment is the only agent of importance. It is obvious, however, that neither substance should be regarded as a panacea for all ills produced by the environment. Furthermore, discussions of this sort usually choose an environment exceedingly hostile to man, such as the Arctic Circle or a hot desert, where man's adaptive abilities are tested *in extremis* and where man (such as the Bushman and other displaced tribes) live by necessity, not choice. Very few sane individuals would choose to spend many hours in zenith sunshine (which doesn't last for many hours, anyway) or to go to Antarctica to live permanently.

When discussing the value of melanin pigmentation, one should first remind oneself that this pigment does indeed play a vital role for the survival of the individual, in the retinal pigment epithelium of the eye. Melanin or other pigments are always associated with photoreceptors in the animal kingdom (cf. Fox, 1960), and the genetically determined absence of such pigment, as in albinos, thus seriously hinders the normal visual functioning of such an individual, resulting in nystagmus and eventual blindness. We are, therefore, justified when we say that, in discussing the importance of melanin, we should start with the statement that melanin plays a vital role in vision.

What is our position, however, as far as the melanin content of the skin goes? We can say that, in cold-blooded vertebrates, the pigmentary effector system, which is under hormonal and neural control, is very important for the survival of the individual. This pigmentary effector system, which adapts quickly and efficiently to environmental color changes, is based on the dispersion or aggregation of melanosomes in dermal melanophores and epidermal melanocytes (cf. Bagnara and Hadley, 1973). This system is non-existent in homeotherm vertebrates, in which pigmentation of the plumage or the furry coat plays an important role in protecting the body from radiation. In the case of arctic animals, seasonal color changes, which are under hormonal control, do occur and are mediated via the eye and the hypothalamic-hypophyseal complex.

Man, as noted previously, has lost most of his furry coat, but he has retained a functioning epidermal melanocyte system known to respond to solar radiation. It is also known that blond individuals, when exposed for too long a time to sunlight without previous exposure, suffer serious damage to the skin, sunburn, which may eventually lead to cancerous changes in the epidermis of the skin (cf. Szabó, 1969; Fitzpatrick *et al.*, 1971).

The absence of high intensity ultraviolet radiation of long duration, the relatively cold climate, and the low humidity provided a suitable environment for the development of the blond Nordic racial variation of man. Blond or near albinotic individuals (e.g., the San Blas Indians; see Keeler, 1953, 1969) appear in other regions of the globe as well (Fitzpatrick *et al.*, 1971), but, in the tropics, such individuals are at a serious disadvantage because they usually develop cancer of the skin and may die before attaining sexual maturity. Nobody would deny that a rate of melanogenesis adequate for the Nordic race for survival in its original habitat is deleterious when these Nordics are exposed to a higher intensity of solar radiation. Individuals with a higher content of melanin present in the skin or with a higher rate of melanogenic activity are not subject to sunburn or cancerous changes of the skin under the conditions Nordic individuals are (McGovern and Russell, 1973, see pp. 222-260).

It is obvious that it is an advantage for an individual to have melanin pigment present in the skin and to have a high level of melanogenic activity if he is to survive in regions of the globe where the ultraviolet radiation is high and of long duration. To a naturalist, it is also obvious that there is an intricate interplay of many factors and characteristics of the body to ensure survival, and certain factors may be advantageous under one set of conditions and less advantageous or even harmful under some others. As far as the human skin goes, the presence of keratin is also of great importance and plays an important role in scattering light, protecting the underlying tissue, and, when melanin is absent or very much reduced in its quantity, it may come in as a second line of defense and, to a degree, may protect the individual. Fitzpatrick, however, has reported that vitiliginous Negro individuals are sunburned in vitiliginous areas of their integument, whereas they are not sunburned in areas where there is still some melanin present, although the thickness of keratin is the same in both areas. Furthermore, if all the keratin is removed by stripping the skin by the scotch tape method, the area with melanin is still protected, whereas the area without melanin is sunburned (personal communication).

How can we answer the question about the origin of the less pigmented races? Loomis (1967, 1968) has very ably summarized the role melanin may play in enhancing or suppressing the ultraviolet-induced synthesis of vitamin D in the skin. It has been found that, under identical conditions and social environment, colored children, when their diet is not supplemented with vitamin D, are more likely to develop vitamin D deficiency in temperate climates than their playmates who are fair in complexion. He proposes that it is not only "not disadvantageous" to be less pigmented in the Northern Hemisphere, but explicitly advantageous! Therefore, the naturally occurring mutations of blonds prevailed over darker individuals in lower latitudes. As Daniels *et al.* (1972) put it: "The degree of melanization is regarded as a compromise between vitamin D requirements and requirements to protect the DNA of the basal cell from mutational change."

Skin color not only plays a protective role against ultraviolet radiation, but, as we have already pointed out, the pigmentary effector system is an effective environmental camouflage. Thus, it not only protects the individual from radiation but also from predators. It has been suggested that the melanin content of the naked human skin has survival value by blending the individual in to the surroundings more efficiently. Therefore, it is advantageous to be black in a jungle or brown in a desert. We should also remember, however, that man invaded the present temperate climates during the glacial periods when clothing was necessary for survival, so pigmentation of the skin had less survival value there than in the hot regions of the Earth.

Finally, we should discuss the apparent disadvantage of high melanin content of the skin in a warm environment where highly pigmented skin absorbs much more heat than less pigmented skin. It is safe to assume that the protective role of melanin against carcinogenic ultraviolet radiation is of much greater value than its somewhat uncomfortable heat absorbing ability, and it is preferable to be free of cancer than to be uncomfortably hot. It is also true that the absorption of heat may be counterbalanced by a more efficient heat-dissipating mechanism by some highly pigmented races (Thomson, 1954).

Our common sense tells us that it is advantageous to have some melanin in reserve in order to form new melanin if we are exposed to ultraviolet radiation. Observing man on the beach, one would soon notice that young children who are blond instinctively seek the shade, whereas the children who are more pigmented do not care about exposure. Although melanin is not a panacea against all assaults of the environment, it is a good protective agent. The reader is referred to the excellent article of Daniels *et al.* (1972) concerning the theories of the role of melanin in human evolution.

CONCLUSIONS

Melanin is a life-saving, protective substance *par excellence*. It is associated with structural components of the skin (e.g., keratin) or other products of the integument (sweat) in providing a defense mechanism for the individual. By itself it can also be of great survival value, both in man and such other species as the mollusk, whose "ink" provides a smoke screen for the escape of the attacked animal (cf. Szabó, 1969). The production of melanin has a great adaptive value for man—whereas it is advantageous to be highly pigmented in regions of the Earth where there is much sunshine in order to avoid cancer, melanin is less advantageous in temperate regions, where too much melanin may filter out the ultraviolet radiation that is vitally important for the synthesis of vitamin D, which is required for normal development of the skeletal system. The parameters of the melanogenesis (rate of formation of melanosomes; the melanization of these particles; their transfer to the keratinocytes; and their fate within these cells), offer a scientific approach to the study of the effect of the environment on the genetic process of transcription and translation, since the tyrosine-tyrosinase system is very susceptible to environmental radiation. Nature and nurture really mimic each other in this field.

Finally, the natural scientist cannot help but register, with regret, the fact that such an important mechanism as environmentally adaptable melanogenesis and its end result, the magnificent variation in coloration of man, induces misery and motivates discrimination in society—an insanity that can only be compared to the sadism of such peoples who would kill, not a mocking bird, but a cardinal because of its flamboyant colors or would withhold food from egrets because they are white! How fortunate we should feel that *Homo sapiens* was not created by a Procrustes who would have made all of us of the same size, height, and color. . . .

REFERENCES

Bagnara, J. T. and M. E. Hadley. 1973. *Chromatophores and Color Change: Comparative Physiology of Animal Pigmentation.* New York: Prentice-Hall.

Billingham, R. E. and W. K. Silvers. 1968. Dermoepidermal interactions and epithelial specificity. In *Epithelial-Mesenchymal Interactions,* eds. R. Fleischmajer and R. E. Billingham. Baltimore: Williams & Wilkins, pp. 252-66.

Blois, M. S. 1967. A note on the problem of melanin structure. In *Advances in Biology of Skin,* Vol. VIII, *The Pigmentary System,* eds. W. Montagna and F. Hu. New York: Pergamon Press, pp. 319-21.

Blum, H. F. 1948. Light and the melanin pigment of human skin. In *The Biology of Melanomas,* ed. R. W. Miner. New York: Special Publication of the New York Academy of Sciences, Vol. IV, pp. 388-98.

Blum, H. F. 1961. Does the melanin pigment of human skin have adaptive value? *Quart. Rev. Biol.* 36:50-63.

Blum, H. F. 1968. Vitamin D, sunlight, and natural selection. *Science* 159: 652.

Cohen, J. and G. Szabó. 1968. Study of pigment donation *in vitro. Exp. Cell Res.* 50:418-34.

Cruickshank, C. N. D. and S. A. Harcourt. 1964. Pigment donation *in vitro. J. Invest. Derm.* 42:183-84.

Daniels, F., Jr., P. W. Post, and B. E. Johnson. 1972. Theories of the role of pigment in the evolution of human races. In *Pigmentation, its Genesis and Biologic Control*, ed. V. Riley. New York: Appleton-Century Crofts, pp. 13-22.

Edwards, E. A. 1953. Analysis of skin color in living human subjects by spectrophotometric means. In *Pigment Cell Growth*, ed. M. Gordon. New York and London: Academic Press, pp. 149-58.

Fitzpatrick, T. B., S. W. Becker, Jr., A. B. Lerner, and H. Montgomery. 1950. Tyrosinase in human skin: Demonstration of its presence and of its role in human melanin formation. *Science* 112:223-25.

Fitzpatrick, T. B., G. Szabó, and R. E. Mitchell. 1964. Age changes in the human melanocyte system. In *Advances in Biology of Skin*, Vol. VI, *Aging*. New York: Pergamon Press, pp. 35-50.

Fitzpatrick, T. B., K. A. Arndt, W. H. Clark, Jr., A. Z. Eisen, E. J. Van Scott, and J. H. Vaughn. 1971. *Dermatology in General Medicine*. New York: McGraw-Hill.

Foster, M. 1952. Manometric and histochemical demonstration of tyrosinase in foetal guinea-pig skin. *Proc. Soc. Exp. Biol. and Med.* 79:713-15.

Fox, H. M. and G. Vevers. 1960. *The Nature of Animal Colours*. Seattle: University of Washington Press.

Heppleston, A. G. 1969. Pigmentation and disorder of the lung. In *Pigments in Pathology*, ed. M. Wolman. New York and London: Academic Press, pp. 33-73.

Jones, A. L. and D. W. Fawcett. 1966. Hypertrophy of the agranular endoplasmic reticulum in hamster liver induced by phenobarbital (with a review of the functions of this organelle in liver). *J. Histochem. & Cytochem.* 14:215-32.

Kawahata, A. and T. Adams. 1961. Racial variations in sweat gland distribution. *Proc. Soc. Exp. Biol. Med.* 106:862-65.

Keeler, C. E. 1953. The Caribe Cuna moon-child and its heredity. *J. Heredity* 44:162-71.

Keeler, C. E. 1969. Description of the Cuna albino syndrome. *CSH Bul. Cur. Res.* 8:23.

Klaus, S. 1969. Pigment transfer in mammalian epidermis. *Arch. Derm.* 100: 756-62.

Loomis, W. F. 1967. Skin-pigment regulation of vitamin-D biosynthesis in man. *Science* 157:501-6.

Loomis, W. F. 1968. Vitamin D, sunlight and natural selection. *Science* 159: 653.

Mason, H. S. 1967. The structure of melanin. In *Advances in Biology of Skin*, Vol. VIII, *The Pigmentary System*, eds. W. Montagna and F. Hu. New York: Pergamon Press, pp. 293-312.

Masson, P. 1948. Pigment cells in man. In *The Biology of Melanomas*, ed.

R. W. Miner. New York: Special Publication of the New York Academy of Sciences, Vol. IV, pp. 15-51.

McGovern, V. J. and P. Russell (eds.). 1973. *Mechanisms in Pigmentation.* Basel: S. Karger.

Mitchell, R. E. 1967. Chronic solar dermatosis: a light and electron microscopic study of the dermis. *J. Invest. Derm.* 48:203-20.

Mitchell, R. E. 1968. The skin of the Australian Aborigine: A light and electron microscopical study. *Aust. J. Dermat.* 9:314-28.

Nicolaus, R. A., K. Hempel, and H. S. Mason. 1967. Comments on Howard S. Mason's paper "The structure of melanin." In *Advances in Biology of the Skin,* Vol. VIII, *The Pigmentary System,* eds. W. Montagna and F. Hu. New York: Pergamon Press, pp. 313-17.

Prunieras, M. 1969. Interaction between keratinocytes and dendritic cells. *J. Invest. Derm.* 52:1-17.

Rittenhouse, E. 1968. Genetic effects on fine structure and development of pigment granules in mouse hair bulb melanocytes. I. and II. *Dev. Biol.* 17:351-81.

Scheuplein, R. J. and I. H. Blank. 1971. Permeability of the skin. *Physiol. Rev.* 51:702-47.

Snell, R. S. and P. G. Bischitz. 1963. The melanocytes and melanin in human abdominal wall skin: A survey made at different ages in both sexes and during pregnancy. *J. Anat. Lond.* 97:361-76.

Szabó, G. 1957. Tyrosinase in the epidermal melanocytes of white human skin. *A.M.A. Arch. Dermatol.* 76:324-29.

Szabó, G. 1967. The regional anatomy of the human integument with special reference to the distribution of hair follicles, sweat glands and melanocytes. *Philos. Trans. Roy. Soc. B.* 252:447-85.

Szabó, G. 1969. The biology of the pigment cell. In *The Biological Basis of Medicine,* Vol. 6, eds. E. E. Bittar and N. Bittar. London and New York: Academic Press, pp. 59-91.

Szabó, G., A. B. Gerald, M. A. Pathak, and T. B. Fitzpatrick. 1969. Racial differences in the fate of melanosomes in human epidermis. *Nature* 222: 1081-82.

Szabó, G., A. B. Gerald, M. A. Pathak, and T. B. Fitzpatrick. 1972. The ultrastructure of racial color differences in man. In *Pigmentation: Its Genesis and Biologic Control,* ed. V. Riley. New York: Appleton-Century Crofts, pp. 23-41.

Thomson, M. L. 1954. A comparison between the number and distribution of functioning eccrine sweat glands in Europeans and Africans. *J. Physiol.* 123:225-33.

Wasserman, H. P. 1974. Ethnic Pigmentation, Historical, Physiological and Clinical Aspects. New York: American Elsevier.

Wolff, K. and K. Konrad. 1971. Melanin pigmentation, an *in vivo* model for studies of melanosome kinetics within keratinocytes. *Science* 174:1034-35.

Wolff, K. and K. Konrad. 1972. Phagocytosis of latex beads by epidermal keratinocytes *in vivo. J. Ultr. Res.* 39:262-80.

4. The Ecology of Work

R. BROOKE THOMAS *

In anthropology, the term "work" has been used in a variety of ways, from a rather specific physiological context to one as general as "making a living." In this chapter, work will be considered, more within an ecological perspective, as those activities performed by a group in order to meet its social and biological requirements—these being essential if a group is to persist. Simply stated, successful interaction with the environment necessitates a continuous process of resource acquisition and utilization. This, in turn, is accomplished by a complex of behavioral and biological responses operating at the individual, group, and intergroup level. The author is aware of the ethnocentric bias introduced by referring to such responses as "work," but he will use the term for lack of a more convenient one.

Whereas physiological and morphological responses to work are a part of such a complex (and are probably of primary concern to the reader), the rather obvious argument will be made that it is difficult to assess their over-all adaptive significance without reference to habitually performed behavior. Adaptiveness of a physiological response, for instance, has frequently been suggested only by comparison to standardized criteria of physiological fitness. In taking a broader and possibly more relevant approach, it is also of interest to evaluate the adaptiveness of a response with regard to the performance of the critical activities that a group must carry

* Department of Anthropology and Section of Ecology and Systematics, Cornell University, Ithaca, New York. Support for this work was kindly provided by the Wenner-Gren Foundation for Anthropological Research.

out if it is to successfully adjust to its environment. Important questions, therefore, become: To what extent is an indicator of physiological fitness meaningful in terms of an ability to perform critical activities?; How does the physiological response under consideration contribute to or interfere with other kinds of adjustment to the environment (i.e., thermoregulation)?; and, finally, What is the relative effectiveness and efficiency of the response compared with other possible biological or behavioral alternatives? These questions appear to be necessary to an assessment of the over-all adaptiveness of either a single response or a response complex, yet they are clearly without simple answers. It seems that such answers will appear only after a conceptual and methodological framework can be developed to deal with adaptation in a general sense. In this chapter, I will therefore attempt (a) to justify the value of considering general adaptation, using work as an example; (b) to point out difficulties with more traditional approaches to the study of work; and (c) to propose a methodological approach for dealing with general adaptation and, hence, the ecology of work.

MAN AS COMPARED TO OTHER ANIMALS

The general adaptive criteria underlying man's utilization of resources remain much the same as for other animals. Human groups must acquire sufficient food for energy and nutrients and, concurrently, buffer serious environmental perturbation if they are to persist. How they do this differs conspicuously from other species in that most requirements cannot be met without prior modification of a large variety of inedible resources and frequently the habitat itself. All human groups, therefore, depend upon an elaborate complex of both edible and inedible resources to interact with and modify their environments successfully.

The presence of human groups in every major terrestrial ecosystem and the large human biomass supported in the biosphere serve as indicators of man's adaptive capacity relative to other mammals. This suggests that human groups have been able to modify components of their abiotic, biotic, and social environment effectively and to compete with other species under widely differing environmental conditions. These include the arctic, desert, tropical and temperate forests, grasslands, and high mountain areas, as well as isolated islands and large urban centers. Such adaptive success is explained primarily through the rather novel species-specific emphasis on both technology and extensive cooperative behavior. This success has permitted the development of flexible adaptive strategies capable of overcoming a variety of environmental constraints. As a result, interpopulational variability in ecological role (niche) within the human species is extremely diverse relative to other animals. Human groups attach themselves to terrestrial, fresh water, and marine food webs as herbivores and predators; they gather, hunt, herd, practice various forms of agriculture, exchange foods with other groups, or perform a combination of these subsistence activities.

Although impressive, such diversity in habitat and ecological niche has added both increased complexity and special conditions to an ecological study of human resource acquisition and utilization. Thus, it has been difficult to demonstrate environment-specific regularities in adaptive strategies to the extent possible for most other animals. Patterns of resource utilization, for instance, are not necessarily consistent among groups inhabiting the same ecozone. Nor do groups practicing similar subsistence patterns rely on the same resource base. Consequently, a search for simple environmental correlates in this area has not been overly rewarding. This suggests either that human groups are so effective in buffering environmental constraints that their biology and behavior are left uninfluenced or that the questions we have asked thus far are not sufficiently sensitive to take into account the significant human environment, as well as the diverse, dynamic, and sometimes atypical adaptive strategies utilized by our species. Working on the well-supported assumption that the environment does exert an influence on the biobehavior characteristics of human groups, I will attempt to show how an adaptive problem of this sort might be approached.

DEFINING THE ADAPTIVE PROBLEM

If generalizations of predictive value concerning human adaptation are to be established, consideration need first be given to what constitutes an appropriate adaptive problem. Ideally, this should deal with an environmental interaction common to a wide range of human groups, where environmental differences would be expected to elicit differences in adjustment. Responses relied upon in making the adjustment should be both behavioral and biological in nature and involve a considerable portion of a group's time and effort. Also, these should affect a large segment of a group's members. From a biological standpoint, it is desirable that morphological and physiological responses be both identifiable and measurable. Finally, the adjustment should be critical in terms of a group's ability to maintain itself.

The application of these criteria to the study of work, in an ecological sense, appears to offer considerable potential as an area of research. Behavior oriented at essential resource acquisition and modification applies universally to human groups and is critical to their persistence. It takes up a substantial amount of time and, in most nonindustrialized groups, effort. Although normally considered a behavioral complex, work, in most instances, exerts a definite influence on the biological organisms performing it. In turn, the biological organisms influence the type of work that can be performed and the nature of the performance. Within a group, for instance, individuals of different sex and age vary considerably in their work capacity. When this is viewed in terms of group size and composition, it reflects the kind and variety of tasks that can be collectively undertaken by that group and, hence, upon its resource utilization potential.

Although anthropologists have long been interested in various aspects of work, the subject has received relatively little attention from human biologists studying contemporary human variability and adaptation. In this regard a question that has often been asked but infrequently tested is: To what extent does performance of habitual subsistence activities influence biological characteristics of group members? In asking this, one is seeking confirmation of an adaptive pattern consistently observed in other animals in which life-support activities are shown to influence biology.

Although man is frequently described as an unspecialized species, Brues (1960), in an insightful paper, points out that a dominant weapon or tool would be expected to alter physical characteristics of groups relying upon it. Conversely, a tool may not be accepted because characteristics that are already present do not allow its effective or efficient use. In speculating as to how this might operate, she proposes that certain forms of agriculture would select for a generally heavy body build capable of sustained labor. Hunting groups highly specialized in the use of the spear and emphasizing linearity would consequently be poorly endowed for performing such tasks. Thus, in giving up hunting, such groups would preferentially have turned to herding, where ecological conditions permitted.

Such speculation is hardly new, but there has been relatively little research in human adaptation oriented at testing associations between dominant work patterns and biological characteristics. This is rather surprising in view of the abundance of studies in work physiology showing that participation in activities of moderate to heavy work loads can lead to changes in physiological function and body composition (fat and muscle tissue) and that body size, type, and composition can influence endurance, level of physiological strain, and metabolic cost in the performance of these activities. These studies have been summarized by Morehouse and Miller (1963), Durnin and Passmore (1967), and Astrand and Rodahl (1970).

Considering these data in terms of human biological variation, one might expect differential selection to favor individuals possessing characteristics better suited for performing critical activities. The idea, for instance, that physical or physiological fitness reflects Darwinian fitness is indeed enticing when studying a species in which it is difficult to measure selective advantage directly, except in retrospect. Sadly, it is evidence of genetic adaptation that the human biologist has been interested in and yet has not been very successful in discovering. Reasons for this interest have arisen, in part, from the emphasis on understanding an adaptive response in terms of causation rather than adaptive function. Although both causation and function constitute legitimate biological questions, the order in which these questions are asked frequently has an important bearing on how well they will be answered.

Take, for example, a group residing at high altitude and showing a significantly greater maximum oxygen consumption (aerobic power) than lowlanders. If the purpose of the investigation is to determine that the difference is attributable to genetic adaptation, a rather sophisticated research design must be employed to control for developmental influences (Harrison, 1966). On the other hand, realizing the function of increased maximal oxygen consumption is considerably easier, and possibly of greater importance, since it serves as one criterion for assessing an individual's or group's ability to utilize the environment. As Astrand (1952) and Christensen (1953) have shown, using lowland samples, adults can work for an entire day (6 to 8 hours) at an oxygen consumption level up to 50% of their maximum. Their data have been confirmed at high altitudes as well (Thomas, 1973). Therefore, this value provides a basis for assessing an individual's capacity to participate in prolonged and strenuous tasks. If, in the course of the investigation, it is discovered that a high level of oxygen consumption is required to perform essential sustained activities, then there is some basis for considering the characteristics adaptive. Labeling it adaptive does not imply causation of any sort, but simply the existence of a functional relationship whereby the success of the living system possessing it is demonstrable. Thus, at this rather fundamental level of analysis, one is not concerned about which adaptive process contributes to its presence, but what its presence means in terms of functioning in the environment.

Should determining genetic adaptation and causation be an investigative goal in analyzing work, it would be useful to have information on essential tasks, their performance requirements, a relevant gauge of physiological fitness, and how differential selection would operate. Such information is, in turn, provided by more functional type questions aimed at (a) the environmental constraints to which adaptation is expected; (b) the interrelationships between biobehavioral adaptive responses employed in making the adjustment; and (c) their relative effectiveness and efficiency in accomplishing this. Unfortunately, such basic information has frequently not been available to investigators searching for causation. The consequences of this are serious, since one is put in a position of trying to explain the presence of a biological response without a complete idea of the conditions under which it operates or even if it is adaptive. This applies especially to contemporary human groups in which genetic adaptation would be expected to be, and, from all we can tell, apparently is, an infrequently utilized adaptive pathway relative to non-genetic biobehavioral alternatives (Lewontin, 1957; Baker, 1966). As Morton (1968) has stated, only when extreme selection coefficients occur is it probable that variations in gene frequencies can be attributed to evolutionary causes. It is rather doubtful that differences in work performance would result in such coefficients. Hence, studies seeking to explain biological characteristics as genetic adaptations to work may well be disappointing and, in any case, premature.

At this stage, a more realistic investigative goal might be to understand how morphological and physiological responses interact with behavioral and technological ones to allow successful resource acquisition and utilization. It has been pointed out that biological responses are important in that they permit increased work performance. The over-all adaptive import, however, is not the work itself, but that it is one means of meeting a group's requirements.

Data pertaining to the interaction between biological and behavioral responses can, in part, be drawn from studies in work physiology. As Astrand and Rodahl (1970) have stated, the objectives of this field are to investigate the effects of both activities and environmental factors on different organ functions; to examine the individual's capacity to meet the demands imposed upon him or her; and to determine how this capacity is influenced by training, acclimatization, etc. Thus, a large portion of research in work physiology has been concerned with factors influencing biological work potential. This is illustrated on the left-hand side of Fig. 4-1, where behavioral, biological, and environmental factors are shown to affect strength, speed, endurance, and efficiency.

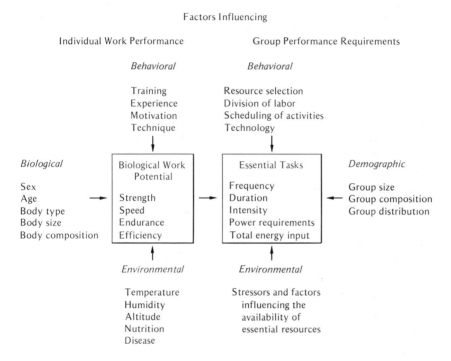

Factors Influencing

Individual Work Performance   Group Performance Requirements

Behavioral   *Behavioral*

Training   Resource selection
Experience   Division of labor
Motivation   Scheduling of activities
Technique   Technology

Biological	Biological Work Potential	Essential Tasks	*Demographic*
Sex		Frequency	Group size
Age	Strength	Duration	Group composition
Body type	Speed	Intensity	Group distribution
Body size	Endurance	Power requirements	
Body composition	Efficiency	Total energy input	

Environmental   *Environmental*

Temperature   Stressors and factors
Humidity   influencing the
Altitude   availability of
Nutrition   essential resources
Disease

Fig. 4-1. Factors influencing individual work performance and group performance requirements. (Modified, in part, from Astrand and Rodahl, 1970.)

Emphasis within work physiology, however, has traditionally been upon the individual organism and not the population. Consequently, adaptation is used in an acclimatizational or training sense and has been based upon standards of physical or physiological fitness. Although this approach has yielded methods and data pertinent to the study of human populations, some caution is required in applying them in an unmodified form to anthropological problems. This is to say that simply comparing maximal oxygen consumption values between groups tells us only that differences exist. As has been recognized by some work physiologists and anthropologists alike, these values need to be first understood (and presented) in terms of a group's ability to interact with its environment successfully. A large, powerful body type, for instance, may not be advantageous in a group where it makes little difference in the performance of subsistence tasks. In fact it could well be disadvantageous if such a group inhabited a region of chronic food energy shortages, since energy expenditure would be expected to correspond to body size (Talbot, 1945; Miller and Blyth, 1955; Durnin, 1965). To enlarge upon this hypothetical example, if the group's subsistence tasks were primarily sedentary (e.g., crafts), and if the group inhabited a cold region, individuals having more subcutaneous fat would be better insulated against the cold. This means they would require less metabolic activity (have less energy loss) to keep warm. On the other hand, if the group members were tested for their ability to perform at moderate to high submaximal work levels, the more obese individuals would be expected to have higher energy expenditure values and a lower endurance than their leaner counterparts (Buskirk and Taylor, 1957; Welch et al., 1958). Hence, they would be regarded as physiologically less fit. These examples are presented simply to underline that, unless we know more about the specific adaptive criteria to which a group must adapt, it is inappropriate to make inter-group comparisons based on a single standard that implies differences in fitness.

It, therefore, is suggested that if the findings and methods of work physiology are to be applied to anthropologically relevant problems, the concepts of work and adaptation should be more in keeping with a population and ecological perspective. In human groups where cooperation is an essential part of the subsistence pattern, the resource procurement or productive unit generally exceeds the individual. Frequently, the majority of resources are produced by young and middle-aged adults, and are distributed to less productive segments of the population. Thus, it becomes important to view work as a series of essential tasks that must be accomplished to meet the group's requirements. These tasks, in turn, have certain performance requirements with regard to frequency, duration, intensity, power, and total energy input. As indicated on the right-hand side of Fig. 4-1, such factors as resource selection, scheduling, division of labor, group demographic characteristics, environmental constraints, along with the biological work potential of group members, influence how effectively and efficiently these performance requirements will be met.

It should be apparent by now that examining work from a population and ecological perspective becomes a rather complex adaptive problem, despite its potential. Furthermore, it is a problem for which the more traditional single-stress approach cannot provide meaningful answers. Work, in an ecological sense, is not a response to one stress or limited factor. Instead it constitutes responses to a wide range of environmental, behavioral, biological, and demographic variables. As such, work influences the exposure pattern to environmental stressors (hunting in the arctic cold, gardening in the tropical heat) to which further adjustment is necessary. This being the case, an approach that can integrate and evaluate a diversity of adaptive responses to multiple environmental constraints is needed. Such an adaptive framework would not only permit inquiry into the ecology of work but would allow the examination of adaptive questions involving responses to several environmental stressors and limiting factors. Since most human groups must adapt to such conditions, an attempt to understand this would seem worthwhile.

A GENERAL ADAPTIVE FRAMEWORK

Confusion and disagreement as to the meaning of adaptation will doubtlessly persist. Despite the traditional biological usage of the term, as synonymous with genetic adaptation, there is a growing tendency by biologists to consider it in a more generic sense, as a process whereby a beneficial adjustment to the environment is achieved (Lewontin, 1957; Prosser, 1958; Eagan, 1963; McCutcheon, 1964; Baker, 1966; Folk, 1966; Harrison, 1966; Dobzhansky, 1968; Slobodkin, 1968; Lasker, 1969; Adolph, 1972). Recently, Mazess (1973) reviewed the various uses of the concept and defined adaptation in the above manner, pointing out its applicability to a wide range of biological and social levels of organization. If this broader usage is accepted, genetic adaptation becomes one of several adaptive pathways or processes that can explain the presence of a particular biological response.

Given such difficulties in terminology, it is, nevertheless, possible to outline some generally agreed upon statements concerning the adjustment of human groups to their environment. Such an adjustment is the result of a complex set of interrelationships between members of a group and the physical, biotic, and social environments that surround them. Since they result from these interactions, biological requirements must be met to the extent that most members are able to survive, function, and reproduce. These then constitute basic adaptive criteria for a group, which are met by a combination of behavioral and biological responses. The degree to which these responses can meet the adaptive criteria will determine the group's continued adaptive success or its failure. In the case of failure, a biobehavioral line becomes unable to effectively interact with its environment and, hence, ceases to exist. Although the above statements are rather elementary, they can serve as a starting point in an examination of the basic adjustments a group must make. These basic adjustments will be defined as "general adaptation" or the ability of a group to maintain itself over time. This meaning is consistent with Lewontin's (1957) usage of the term, to the extent that the persistence of the evolutionary unit depends upon an interaction of morphological, physiological, genetic, and behavioral homeostatic mechanisms. The main point to be emphasized is that, regardless of the specific adaptive responses contributing to over-all adaptation, the ability of a group to continuously adjust to changes in its environment and, hence, persist seems critical to an understanding of biological and cultural adaptation. This is not to say that specific adaptive responses can be disregarded, but only that an effort must be made to integrate them to this end. It has been pointed out that the task is a difficult one. By not attempting it, however, we will continue either to speak of general adaptation in a rather abstract manner or to oversimplify the concept by basing it on responses to a single environmental constraint. Since a more precise knowledge of general adaptation in man appears to be central to the objectives of biological anthropology, and some areas of cultural anthropology, the effort would seem justified. In pointing out a need for a more general approach to adaptation, we can see that there are obvious difficulties in such a general approach. Some are methodological, others arise from not having asked the right questions. Whatever the case, a clearer idea of the problems involved might be obtained by examining the basic interactions between a group and its environment in more detail.

Slobodkin (1968), in discussing a predictive theory of evolution, points out that adaptive responses must not only be assessed with regard to how well they buffer environmental perturbation but also the extent to which they are capable of adjusting to future perturbation as well. In elaborating on this, he "assumes the following properties to be essentially valid for all organisms" (p. 193). (a) Adjustment processes take various amounts of time to engage. Some types of behavior, for instance, respond quite rapidly to perturbation, whereas genetic responses are relatively slow. (b) Any response involves a commitment of an organism's (or a group's) resources or future response capacity to environmental stress. In this respect, he accepts Bateson's (1963) hypothesis that a hierarchy of flexibility restoring mechanisms exists, which operates in such a way that rapid, short-term responses become freed for future use. (c) A reciprocal relation exists between population density and the biological well-being of individuals in that population. Thus, in the case of crowding, individuals would generally be in poorer physiological condition. Though not mentioned by Slobodkin, I would add that too low a population density in human groups can interfere with cooperative behavior, with the same consequences. (d) A change in a population's gene frequency may alter already established responses and generate additional changes in both genetic and other response systems. Using these four assumptions, he offers evidence to support the theorem that "behavioral, physiological, ecological, and genetic mechanisms interact with each other and with the environment to maximize and conserve the homeostatic ability of populations of organisms" (p. 203). If this is correct, adaptiveness can be stated objectively in terms of the probability with which given environmental states would occur and the chances of a population responding adequately to each state. Slobodkin, therefore, concludes that no single measure is sufficient to gauge a population's adaptiveness, except to the extent it reflects homeostatic capacity within a particular environment. In accepting and relying upon the above points as a conceptual base, I will therefore attempt to incorporate them into a general adaptive framework that can be applied to human groups.

Assuming a dynamic interaction between the physical and biotic components of the environment and the human group, one immediately faces a situation too complex for complete analysis. The interactional network, therefore, must be simplified to a manageable set of problems, which focus on the group's adjustment to principal environmental constraints. Considerations in identifying primary environmental stressors have been outlined by Baker (1965). As mentioned, studies in human adaptation have generally taken a single stress approach. As a result we know a great deal about biological responses to individual physical stressors (i.e., cold, heat, radiation, hypoxia). In focusing on biological responses to stress, behavioral responses (including technology) have often been neglected. Hence, it has been difficult to evaluate the over-all buffering effectiveness of a biobehavioral complex of responses to a single stressor, let alone the more realistic situation of several environmental constraints operating on a group. Obviously, behavioral responses are highly relied upon by the human species in adjusting to the environment, and, frequently, they are effective enough to explain the absence of biological ones.

The interdependency of biobehavioral responses is illustrated in Fig.

4-2, which shows the influence of two buffering systems in blocking a single stress and maintaining homeostasis in group members. The term "buffering system" is used to describe functionally similar adaptive responses and, thus, allows generalization as to their mode of operation. Following the figure from left to right, a stress condition is present that must be counteracted if permanent dysfunction or death are to be prevented. In response, two buffering systems (behavioral and biological) presumably could be immediately employed, the primary distinction between the two being

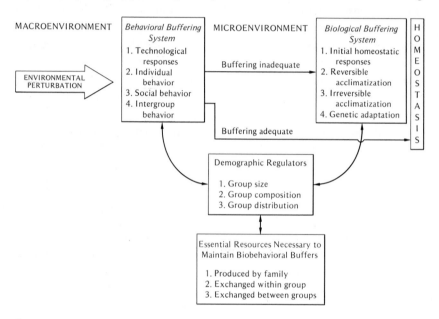

Fig. 4-2. Factors influencing the maintenance of homeostasis.

that, in the case of the behavioral buffering system, the organism (or group) generally attempts to regulate the surrounding environment. The biological buffering system, on the other hand, regulates the internal environment by morphological or physiological means. It should be apparent that both systems are concerned with environmental regulation, but their potentials may be rather different depending on the stress. There are some stressors that can be blocked more effectively by regulating the body's internal environment, as frequently occurs in response to infectious disease. Others, such as cold, are more easily regulated technologically or behaviorally through external environment modification.

In looking at the interaction between the two buffering systems, should a behavioral response be effective in modifying the stressor, a microenvironment is formed, and it is to this that the organism is directly exposed. Stress intensity or duration of course can reach the point where the behavioral buffering system alone is insufficient. Consequently, engagement of the biological system is necessary if homeostasis is to be maintained. Precedence as to which system is engaged first and which serves as a backup would seem to depend on the relative effectiveness and efficiency of individual responses with regard to the aforementioned homeostatic ability.

Briefly, what has been suggested is a biobehavioral approach to stress physiology. With the exception of population genetics, human biologists have relied heavily on physiological concepts in examining questions of human adaptation. As a consequence, relatively little attention has been paid to ecology and, in particular, the concept of limiting factors (or scarce essential resources). Although the physiological and ecological concepts relate to different levels of biological and social organization, there are a number of similarities, which can be profitably combined in an approach to general adaptation. These similarities are reviewed below.

In the case of the physiological "stress concept," when environmental conditions reach the stage where they are capable of disrupting homeostasis, a physiological strain on the organism occurs. This strain must consequently be reduced and a dynamic equilibrium re-established, if permanent dysfunction or death is to be prevented. Thus, the concept is oriented primarily toward the maintenance of homeostasis in the individual organism, although attempts have been made to interpret this at the population level.

The ecological concept of limiting factors, on the other hand, is oriented directly at the population or biotic community level and concerns the biomass that can be supported on a given resource base. Two points are important here: (a) the population characteristics of a group will influence its ability to obtain limiting factors, and (b) if the limiting factors are not obtained in adequate amounts, stress conditions will result. Stated differently, if a group's requirement for a limiting factor is not met, it becomes or contributes to a density-dependent stressor. This is consistent with Slobodkin's third assumption. The point to be made is that adjustment depends upon both types of responses, which do not function independently of each other.

It is worthwhile to distinguish between two types of limiting factors by the manner in which they are linked to density-dependent stress conditions. In the case of resources that are necessary to meet biological require-ments, such as food, the linkage is quite direct. Low intake of a limited nutrient results in a physiological strain and ultimately becomes mani-fested in deficiency-related symptoms. The second type of limiting factor does not directly lead to a stress condition but, instead, influences the op-erational effectiveness of the biobehavioral buffering system. Thus, agri-cultural tools are needed for environmental modification if food resources are to be produced. Should a resource necessary for their construction or maintenance become scarce, the limited resource does not in itself be-come a stressor but, instead, leads to a nutritional one, since the group's ability to regulate aspects of the biotic community is considerably im-paired.

The reason for calling attention to both types of limiting factors is to point out the wide influence they have on producing stress conditions in human groups. Because man depends to a large extent on the material culture to regulate (or buffer) the environment, the list of essential re-sources that must be acquired is quite large compared to other species. Consequently, it is rare for a stressor not to be either directly or indirectly density dependent: hypoxic stress seems to be an exception in this regard. Cold, for instance, which appears to operate as density independent in most other species, does not act this way in the case of man, where groups normally buffer the stress and create a microenvironment largely through their material culture. Thus, most stressors affecting human groups are, to some extent, influenced by an inability to acquire essential limited re-sources in sufficient quantities.

This suggests that, in addition to understanding how the biobehavioral buffering system responds to a given stress condition, consideration must also be given to the continued maintenance of the system's effectiveness and efficiency. In doing so, a third category, labeled "demographic regula-tors" in Fig. 4-2, has been proposed. Although obviously made up of both behavioral and biological responses, its mode of operation is distinct from these two buffering systems, in that population size, density, and/or com-position influence the availability of the essential resources. Thus, a com-plex of resources, technological processes, and work patterns may be op-timally set up for accommodating certain population characteristics. If these demographic parameters are significantly altered, it is then possible that the subsistence pattern would become less efficient. If irrigation agri-culture is used as an example, an optimal range of population density re-lated to the productive capacity of this sociotechnological complex can be hypothesized. Although an increase in density beyond this range would have little effect on productivity, it would definitely increase the group's consumption requirements. Consequently, the availability of food and other resources per individual would decrease. The same result might also occur if population density dropped below the optimal range, since this would influence the effective utilization of irrigation technology and work patterns. Thus, the inability to remove silt from irrigation ditches as a result of insufficient manpower could seriously affect the productivity of the entire system. Functionally, then, demographic regulators influence the buffering capacity of the biobehavioral buffering systems through responses in population characteristics operating on essential resources.

A list of essential resources, even for a technologically simple group, is extensive and, hence, difficult to work with. Fortunately, not all of these resources pose serious problems as limiting factors. Following the aforementioned procedure used to isolate principal environmental stressors, a similar approach can be employed to identify essential limited resources. Important selection criteria would seem to be those resources that (a) are critical in the operation of the adaptive system; (b) are frequently relied upon; (c) are scarce; and (d) have no other alternatives. Thus, from an extensive list of essential resources, one is able to focus upon relatively few limiting factors, which, potentially, could result in or lead to significant environmental constraints.

The identification of these factors is of value in that they provide an additional basis for assessing the adaptiveness of a wide range of responses. Consequently, if a group is to maintain itself, acquisition of limited resources must theoretically equal and, accounting for wastage, actually exceed the total amount utilized by its members. One is, therefore, interested in the relative efficiencies of alternative responses in utilizing a resource. Stated differently, adaptiveness in this sense is directly related to the ratio of units of resource acquired to units expended in the acquisition process.

To return to an earlier example, we can consider the adaptiveness of a variety of biobehavioral responses to an environment in which cold and low availability of food energy are the principal environmental constraints. If adaptation to cold is the only constraint investigated, it becomes difficult to determine which of the several possible responses that effectively buffer the stress is more adaptive. Is clothing a more effective insulator than subcutaneous fat, or is an insulative response more appropriate than a metabolic one? High blood flow to the extremities, for instance, keeps the hands and feet warm, but does so with significant heat loss. Which is more important? Relying on buffering effectiveness to a single constraint as the sole criterion for adaptiveness therefore can result in considerable confusion. When the same phenomenon is viewed in terms of both constraints, this becomes resolvable. A high and sustained level of heat loss through the extremities would ultimately necessitate thermogenesis and might, therefore, be judged maladaptive with regard to energy conservation. If, on the other hand, success in food energy acquisition depended on unimpaired manual dexterity and, hence, high extremity temperatures, the response would be adaptive. The example suggests that energetic efficiency, or, in a broader sense, expenditure-acquisition efficiencies related to essential limited resources, may be used along with buffering effectiveness in evaluating adaptations to a variety of stressors.

Should the proposed guidelines for evaluating the relative adaptiveness of alternative responses prove feasible, they would provide a basis for an investigation of why certain types of responses occur more frequently under given environmental conditions. It is this level of analysis that has permitted biologists studying animals other than man to generalize concerning environment-specific adaptive strategies. Thus far, investigators of human adaptation have focused primarily upon identifying adaptive responses and have not taken this further analytical step. In several regions, such as the Aleutians, Arctic, and Andes, there now exists a sufficient data base to warrant testing of the proposed guidelines to establish such generalizations for man.

If this is to be successful, functionally distinct types of responses must be identified along with their general capabilities and limitations. Although this has already been done in distinguishing between the mode of operation for the buffering systems, considerably more precision is necessary. Thus, within each buffering system, responses sharing functional similarities have been grouped as "adaptive pathways" and are listed in Fig. 4-2. In discussing these pathways, we will attempt to point out differences in their ability to respond to environmental constraints.

Turning to the behavioral buffering system, we include as adaptive pathways oriented at the regulation of the external environment technology, individual behavior, social behavior, and intergroup cooperation. The technological pathway functions in extending the adaptive options of the organism or group beyond its biological potential to modify and regulate the environment. Adaptive advantages and flexibility provided by a high reliance on this pathway are, of course, apparent. Since tools are extrasomatic, their utility can be assessed in terms of costs of manufacture and maintenance relative to benefits derived from use. An obvious condition upon which employment of this technological pathway depends is that the technology must be available when it is needed. Thus, for mobile groups, an additional cost of transporting material culture is to be considered, making bulkier items less practical and the pathway, as a whole, less effective. In contrast, sedentary groups living in environments where needs are quite predictable would be expected to emphasize this pathway. Finally, an important dependence on technological responses would be expected in environments where a combination of nontechnological responses was not sufficient to overcome environmental constraints.

When we turn to other adaptive pathways, individual behavior or actions carried out alone have the advantage of always being present when needed. Social behavior, on the other hand, depends on assembling persons having the necessary potential to accomplish a task. Both pathways have clear limitations and advantages depending on environmental conditions and group capabilities for effective interaction. As Jolly (1972) has summarized from studies on individual and social behavior in birds (Crook, 1965) and mammals (Eisenberg, 1966), environments where essential resources are dispersed in small packets or where they are acquired by stealth are best accomplished by individuals. Social behavior, however, would seem to be more effective where resources were continuously distributed or where they were in large packets at stable sites. Intergroup cooperation has the distinct advantage in gaining access to resources that are either not available to the group or cannot be produced in sufficient quantity by group members. Limitations of this pathway result in a possible rupturing of ties between groups, in which case essential resources would become unavailable. Thus, measures need to be taken to ensure the persistence of such cooperation, whether it be at the intra- or intergroup level. As in the case of technology, definite costs in maintaining these relationships must be considered. The purpose of reviewing the above pathways is simply to point out their different adaptive potentials, not to review the extensive literature available on each.

In the biological buffering system, adaptive pathways that regulate the internal environment include initial homeostatic responses, reversible acclimatization, irreversible acclimatization, and genetic adaptation. Time of response to a perturbation and the resulting adaptive flexibility it offers the individual are used to characterize these adaptive pathways. Many of the statements made concerning these pathways follow those of Bateson

(1963) and Slobodkin (1968), who have dealt with the subject in considerable detail. Initial homeostatic responses refer to the somatic responses of an unacclimatized individual to environmental perturbation. To be effective, these responses must either reduce serious physiological strain for the stress period or, with time, give way to an acclimatizational response. Initial homeostatic responses would therefore be most frequent in environments where perturbations were of short duration and infrequent in occurrence.

Harrison (1966) has characterized two types of acclimatization, which appear to have different consequences for the organism. Reversible acclimatizations are those improvements over the initial homeostatic responses; their state is alterable. That is, should the stress condition cease to exist, the acclimatizational response would likewise ultimately disappear. This is consistent with Bateson's argument that the maintenance of such a response in the absence of a stress impairs the adaptive flexibility of the organism in responding to other stressors. Irreversible (or developmental) acclimatization is a response to the environment that occurs only within the growth and development period. Once established, it cannot be reversed regardless of a shift in environmental conditions. Irreversible acclimatization would, therefore, be most adaptive under conditions of persistent stress throughout the life cycle, whereas reversible acclimatization is best suited to conditions where a stress appears periodically and lasts for several weeks or months.

Thus far, the biological adaptive pathways considered have been responses made by the individual. Viewing this in terms of the population, we assume that if homeostatic and acclimatizational responses are adequate for most members then there is little opportunity for genetic adaptation to take place. If, on the other hand, genetically different members differentially adjust its environmental conditions, then genetic adaptation is to be expected. As Slobodkin (1968, p. 204) stated "In well adapted organisms there is a strong correlation between the probability of environmental events occurring and the probability of responding to these events without any genetic change. That is gene frequency changes are a type of last resort in the process of adjusting to environmental change." Genetic adaptation, therefore, would be expected under fairly severe stress conditions that persisted over generational time, in which other biobehavioral pathways were not sufficient for all members.

Thus, as has been suggested for the behavioral buffering system, biological adaptive pathways differ both in their capacity to respond to environmental perturbation and in their effectiveness on the individual's or group's adaptive flexibility. Since it does seem possible to classify adaptive responses and environmental perturbation into functionally distinct groupings, one might then expect that generalizations concerning environment specific adaptive strategies would follow.

CONCLUSIONS

In summarizing the proposed general adaptive framework, responses of a variety of environmental constraints have been evaluated in terms of their ability to maintain a population over time—this being the most critical aspect of general adaptation and central to evolution. Environmental constraints are considered both as stressors and limiting factors that necessitate the integration of physiological and ecological concepts of adaptation as well as concepts of behavior and genetics. In order to make such an analysis manageable, guidelines have been set for the identification of principal environmental constraints. Adaptive responses to these constraints are divided into two functionally distinct buffering systems. The behavioral buffering system generally consists of responses that regulate the external environment, whereas the biological system is directed at the regulation of the internal environment through morphological and physiological means. The sustained buffering capabilities of these systems are, in turn, influenced by demographic regulators, through which population characteristics exert an influence on availability of essential limited resources.

Within each buffering system, functionally distinct adaptive pathways have been proposed. As was the case for the buffering systems, tentative generalizations can be made as to their relative capabilities and limitations in response to environmental constraints. Evaluation of the adaptiveness of a specific response is based upon the dual criteria of its effectiveness in buffering one or several stress conditions and the efficiency in which essential limited resources are acquired and utilized in this process. Thus, given a range of alternative responses of seemingly equal effectiveness, their relative adaptiveness may be assessed by comparing their efficiencies. Those demonstrating higher efficiencies can be regarded as more adaptive.

The significance of being able to identify a complex of adaptive responses directed at meeting a group's basic requirements is that the interdependency of functionally diverse responses is emphasized. And, from this, a basis for understanding why certain types of adaptive pathways or buffering systems are preferentially employed under given environmental conditions is provided. In applying this adaptive framework to the ecology of work, we, therefore, anticipate that similarities in the utilization of pathways would appear among groups exposed to similar types of environments.

REFERENCES

Adolph, E. F. 1972. Physiological adaptations: Hypertrophies and superfunctions. *Amer. Sci.* 60:608-17.

Astrand, P. O. 1952. Experimental studies of working capacity in relation to age and sex. Ejnar Munksgaard, Copenhagen.

Astrand, P. O. and K. Rodahl. 1970. *Textbook of Work Physiology*. New York: McGraw-Hill.

Baker, P. T. 1965. Multidisciplinary studies of human adaptability: Theoretical justification and method. In *International Biological Programme Guide to the Human Adaptability Proposals*, ed. J. S. Weiner. ICSU Special Committee for the IBP.

Baker, P. T. 1966. Human biological variation as an adaptive response to the environment. *Eugen. Quart.* 13:81-91.

Bateson, G. 1963. The role of somatic change in evolution. *Evolution* 17:529-39.

Brues, A. 1960. The spearman and the archer—an essay on selection in body build. *Amer. Anthropol.* 61:457-69.

Buskirk, E. and H. L. Taylor, 1957. Maximal oxygen intake and its relation to body composition, with special reference to chronic physical activity and obesity. *J. Appl. Physiol.* 11:72.

Christensen, E. H. 1953. Physiological valuation of work in the Nykroppa Iron Works. In *Ergonomics Society Symposium on Fatigue*, eds. W. F. Floyd and A. T. Welford. London: Lewis.

Crook, J. H. 1965. The adaptive significance of avian social organizations. *Symp. Zool. Soc.* (London) 14:181-218.

Dobzhansky, T. 1968. Adaptedness and fitness. In *Population Biology and Evolution, Proceedings of an International Symposium*, ed. R. Lewontin. Syracuse, N.Y.: Syracuse University Press.

Durin, J. V. G. A. 1965. Somatic standards of reference. In *Human Body Composition*, ed. J. Brožek. Oxford: Pergamon.

Durnin, J. V. G. A. and R. Passmore. 1967. *Energy Work and Leisure*. London: Heinemann.

Eagan, C. J. 1963. Introduction and terminology. *Fed. Proc.* 22:930-32.

Eisenberg, J. F. 1966. The social organization of mammals. *Handbuch Zool.* 8,39:1-92.

Folk, G. E., Jr. 1966. *Introduction to Environmental Physiology*. Philadelphia: Lea and Febiger.

Harrison, G. A. 1966. Human adaptability with reference to IBP proposals for high altitude research. In *The Biology of Human Adaptability*, eds. P. T. Baker and J. S. Weiner. Oxford: Clarendon Press.

Jolly, A. 1972. *The Evolution of Primate Behavior*. New York: Macmillan.

Lasker, G. W. 1969. Human biological adaptability. *Science* 166:1480-86.

Lewontin, R. C. 1957. The adaptations of populations to varying environments. In *Cold Spring Harbor Symposia on Quantitative Biology*, vol. XXII, Cold Spring Harbor Laboratory of Quantitative Biology.

Mazess, R. B. 1973. *Biological Adaptation: Aptitudes and Acclimatization*. Paper presented at the SSHB Symposium on Population Adaptation, Detroit.

Miller, A. T., Jr., and C. S. Blyth. 1955. Influence of body type and fat content on the metabolic cost of work. *J. Appl. Physiol.* 8:139.

Morehouse, L. E. and A. T. Miller. 1963. *Physiology of Exercise*, 4th ed. St. Louis: Mosby.

Morton, N. E. 1968. Problems and methods in the genetics of primitive groups. *Amer. J. Phys. Anthropol.* 28:191-202.

Prosser, C. L. 1958. General summary: The nature of physiological adaptation. In *Physiological Adaptation*, ed. C. L. Prosser. Washington, D.C.: American Physiological Society, pp. 167-80.

Slobodkin, L. B. 1968. Toward a predictive theory of evolution. In *Population Biology and Evolution*, ed. R. C. Lewontin. Syracuse, N.Y.: Syracuse University Press.

Talbot, F. B. 1945. Basal metabolism in children. In *Practice of Pediatrics*, ed. J. Brennemann. Hagerstown, Md.: Prior.

Thomas, R. B. 1973. *Human Adaptation to a High Andean Energy Flow System*. Occasional papers in anthropology, No. 7. Department of Anthropology, The Pennsylvania State University, University Park, Pa.

Welch, B. E., R. P. Riendeau, C. E. Crisp, and R. S. Isenstein. 1958. Relationship of maximal oxygen consumption to various components of body composition. *J. Appl. Physiol.* 12:395.

5. Human Adaptation to Heat

RUSSELL W. NEWMAN [*]

In this chapter, we will focus on only those aspects of heat adaptation of interest to anthropologists. In general, these aspects involve genetic adaptations characteristic of groups of mankind, some of which, by natural selection, resulted in phenotypes better suited to a particular environment. The adaptations may coincide with or have been adopted by anthropologists as racial criteria, but it is probable that any group residing long enough in a given environment for natural selection to affect the group may show certain morphological tendencies or response patterns that are adaptive. Our restriction of the discussion to heat stress is, of course, arbitrary since most of the world's population undergoes some cold stress on a diurnal or seasonal basis.

The fundamental problem for man and all other homeotherms in a hot environment is heat dissipation. Although there are differences between different genera and larger taxonomic units in their relative dependence on the various mechanisms for heat loss, man has no unique biological mechanisms for heat dissipation, and no one has ever suggested that there are major racial differences in the physiological mechanisms involved. Therefore, we will be concerned with quantitative differences within a generalized pattern of human responses to heat. There are excellent detailed summaries of these physiological responses available (Fox, 1965; Ladell, 1964; Leithead and Lind, 1964), usually based on young and healthy men. Therefore, this description will be short and as nontechnical as possible. Briefly, man relies on convection and radiation as

[*] U.S. Army Research Institute of Environmental Medicine, Natick, Massachusetts.

avenues of heat loss at least up to the point when the air and surrounding objects become hotter than the skin. Delicate adjustment of such heat loss is accomplished by altering the blood flow through the capillary bed of the skin, expanding the blood flow to increase heat loss (vasodilation), and reducing it (vasoconstriction) to decrease heat loss. In the heat, or when exercising, man supplements these avenues by losing heat from the vaporization of moisture brought to the skin surface by thermal sweating (evaporative heat loss), and, of course, such evaporation is the only avenue of heat loss available when air temperature exceeds skin temperature.

ECOLOGICAL RULE STUDIES

It is obvious that such surface properties as area, reflectivity, and nature (i.e., furred, clothed) are critical for transferring body heat to the environment; subcutaneous insulation and blood supply are equally important. The general characterization of a heat-dissipating surface with a heat-generating mass beneath it is valid. This concept implies a relationship that can be changed by altering the ratio of surface area to mass. Unless there is a major change in shape, increasing body size raises the surface area two dimensionally, while raising the mass three dimensionally. A man who is tall and thin will have a high ratio of surface area to mass, whereas one who is short and stocky will have a low surface to mass ratio. Thus, other things being equal, the tall, thin man should be better able to regulate his body temperature in the heat, since he can lose more heat per unit of body mass, than the short individual, who loses less heat; conversely, the short, stocky man should have an advantage in the cold. Modern man exhibits a remarkable range of sizes and shapes. This led, 20 years ago, to a burst of interest in whether man was geographically distributed in a manner that related surface/mass ratio, or something approximating it, to climatic requirements that emphasized heat dissipation or heat conservation.

The rationale for these studies were the so-called Rules of Bergmann and Allen, both zoologists. Bergmann (1847) observed that within a single, polytypic, warm-blooded species, the body size of the various subspecies usually increases with decreasing habitat temperature. Allen (1877) added the observation that mammals living in cold climates characteristically have smaller extremities and appendages than related forms in warm climates. These generalizations do not apply to all mammalian species; a species must be distributed over a sufficiently wide range of climatic extremes for such observation to be possible. Furthermore, the species must not have differentiated to the point where marked specializations in thermoregulatory response are apparent. Man would seem to fit the geographical requirement; it is less certain, however, that he has not developed technological protection, especially against cold, to a point where we may be comparing responses to very unequal cold stress albeit at a common ambient temperature. In any event, it has been shown by Roberts (1953), Newman (1953, 1956), Schreider (1963), Baker (1958a), Coon (1955), and others that some significant correlations can be found between measures of body size in human adult males and measures of climatic stress in the area in which the group resides. It is possible to question the representativeness of the samples (many were small, and some areas not well covered) and the particular measure of environmental stress that was used, but the associations established are clearly not ascribable to chance.

The question is, to what are they ascribable. Is this a result of natural selection along thermoregulatory lines, or is it caused by other factors not considered in the analyses? It is at this interpretive level that disagreements appear. Since statistical correlation does not in itself prove cause and effect, additional evidence, usually experimentally derived, is necessary, and it has not been forthcoming. In fact, it may never be available in a form to convince the skeptics. Body size or the surface area/mass ratio only can explain a very small fraction of the differences between individuals in heat or cold experiments; there are other more important factors ameliorating temperature stress. The human correspondence between body size and climate has not appealed to physiologists (cf. Wilbur, 1957), perhaps because they are more familiar with the wide range of adaptations found in mammals, and this surface/mass geometric explanation lacks the dynamic qualities of most homeothermic responses to stress.

Schreider (1963) is the only one of the earlier group who has pursued this matter further. He has added a refinement by calculating a ratio of limb length/body weight, since it is known that a disproportionate share of the body's heat exchange is through the extremities. This ratio also corresponds to climatic regions and, in a human heat-stress experiment, showed a low but significant correlation with rectal temperature in the subjects.

I would add some reservations of my own to the climate versus body size and shape controversy. Specifically, the data assembled and presented thus far have been almost entirely on adult males. Roberts (1953) found similar height and weight correspondence with climate in a small sample of females, but Schreider (1963) reported no correspondence at all. There has been virtually no work done on subadults in this matter. Although a height-weight gradient in children from the tropics to temperate climates is well known, the influence of nutrition is so well established in subadult growth that it would be very difficult to correct for inequalities in nutritional background in a size-temperature comparison. Yet it is the subadult portion of a population that would have to be the prime target of selective pressure through differential mortality. Adult males represent a sample that has largely passed the screening process from a genetic standpoint. The emphasis on the adult surface/mass relationship ignores the fact that every individual undergoes a remarkable change in this relationship from birth to adulthood. The ratio of surface area to mass changes threefold over this time frame because the mass increases twenty-fold while the surface area increases only sevenfold (Scammon, 1942). Expressed another way, Schreider (1963), who uses the reverse ratio (mass/surface), shows a total average ratio range of nine units from samples with the least mass per area (Bushman and Semang) to samples with the most mass per area (German and Eskimo); this range is the same as that experienced by most individuals, at least in the United States, while maturing from age 2 to adulthood. The change is from a preponderance of surface area (heat adaptation?) to a preponderance of mass (cold adaptation?). It would seem that childhood is the only time frame that might supply an explanation for the observed differences in final adult size and shape that are statistically associated with climate.

STANDARD HEAT TRIALS

There is another possible way to explore group differences in heat adaptation: expose members of diverse groups to a standardized heat stress and measure and compare the responses (Henschel, 1967). This is termed the "experimental approach," and there is a growing body of data from such studies. The measurements collected and the techniques used are borrowed from the classical approach of examining what happens to a human, or non-human, exposed to heat stress under rigidly standardized conditions to uncover the mechanisms and processes involved. Although such experiments have and are being taken to the field, there remains a need to control as many variables as possible to be sure that the measurements are valid and comparable between studies. A description of several "environmental chambers" designed for field use can be found in Weiner and Lourie (1969).

The measurements used in such studies are those considered to be indicators of the stress response or strain shown by the subjects. The standard studies do not require many different measurements: skin temperature and some measure of internal temperature, rate of sweating, heart rate, and perhaps oxygen consumption as a measure of the metabolic response. The more difficult problem is how often should such measurements be sampled during exposure and whether there are critical periods that should be compared, i.e., the immediate response; that after x minutes, x hours, or x days; or the entire response curve. There is also the problem of setting upper limits for safety beyond which the subjects must not be allowed to go. Most such studies have utilized a combination of work and heat, since this imposes both an external and internal heat load, it shortens the time necessary to achieve a high level of protective response (e.g., sweat production), and it allows testing under conditions not considered more than marginally stressful for an inactive man. This obvious convenience, which may be a practical necessity, has an inherent disadvantage in that it assumes all subjects are equally fit for the exercise exclusive of the heat load. In fact, there are many factors that are known to influence the performance of an individual in a combination of exercise and heat. Wyndham (1969), who has done the most extensive racial testing, lists the following dependent variables: body size, state of heat acclimatization, state of hydration, state of physical fitness, and potential for maximum oxygen uptake; to this we must add age, sex, state of nutrition, and state of health, if we are interested in more than just the young, healthy, adult males in a population. This is an imposing array of problems for any straightforward comparison between samples.

This account will avoid a description of the techniques and apparatus used in such studies and concentrate on the biological significance assigned to the measurements. Skin temperature is generally not an important measurement in these studies, although it is almost always recorded. Either exposure to heat or onset of exercise raises skin temperature by peripheral vasodilation. Once active sweating begins, and in the absence of a high radiant heat load, wet human skin temperature stabilizes at 35-36° C; it remains at that level, or may actually drop with good air motion, as long as sweat production is adequate. A subsequent rise above 36° C is indicative of diminished sweating and is interpreted as a danger signal. Whatever measure of internal temperature is used (rectal, tympanic, oral) is given far more weight in assessing strain, although internal temperature is not a simple measure. Like skin temperature, internal temperature rises sharply with work in the heat. It also rises with exercise, even without heat stress, and this is interpreted as adaptive to achieving a more efficient internal environment for muscular work. With the addition of an ambient heat load, the increase in internal temperature may also represent a perfectly normal inability to eliminate all the body heat generated before evaporative heat loss is operating maximally. If the workload is not too great, and the environmental conditions are favorable for evaporation of sweat, as with dry heat, the internal temperature of a healthy young male will plateau for a long period, representing an equilibrium between environmental heat loss and work heat load. In such a circumstance, the internal temperature becomes an important monitor of safety, and any subsequent rise is indicative of an impending thermoregulatory crisis. The most common deviation from this stabilized pattern is when the ambient humidity is too high to allow sufficient evaporative heat loss to occur. Such a humid condition does not have to be extraordinary; even "moderate" humidities are sufficiently stressful at air temperatures of 38° C or higher to prevent a subject from establishing thermal balance with a moderate work load. Therefore, a continuing rise in internal temperature is to be expected, and the assessment of adaptiveness involves how fast and how far the internal temperature rises, small increments per unit time after the initial spurt being considered optimal.

Since evaporation is the principal and, in some cases, the only avenue of heat loss available in these studies, its measurement and interpretation are understandably important. No one bothers to measure the respiratory heat loss under these conditions because it is very constant and only a small fraction (5% or less) of the total evaporative heat loss in a heavily sweating man. Production of sweat ranges from almost none to 2 liters/hour and may diminish from early peak levels, if the exposure is prolonged. Man's thermally activated eccrine sweat glands do not all begin sweating instantly and simultaneously in heat; recruitment is gradual, asynchronous across the body, and in response to rising internal and skin temperature. Statements that tropical populations or certain racial groups have a greater capacity for sweating, on the basis of their greater density of sweat glands, is a gross simplification of a complex process. Man has a marked capacity to produce more sweat than can be evaporated on the skin in any but the driest of conditions, from which comes the familiar phrase "dripping sweat." Sweat production has a low metabolic cost, but it uses a resource (initially, extracellular fluid) that is difficult to replace as fast as it can be used. From this, it is clear that "dripping sweat" is a maladaptive phenomenon, possibly unique to man. Unfortunately, we don't adjust sweat rate to optimal production, i.e., the maximum that could be evaporated, but instead to the required evaporation, although any increase in sweat rate that cannot increase evaporative heat loss is counterproductive. This is an example of why no single measure should be evaluated in such studies except in terms of its total impact on the individual.

A measure of heart rate is essential both as part of the safety monitoring precautions and as the most accessible measure of the cardiovascular response. Unfortunately, exposure to heat alone causes a slight increase in heart rate. This increase compensates for the increased vascular bed, which results from peripheral vasodilation. Exercise, without heat exposure, also leads to an increased heart rate because of the greater metabolic demand of the skeletal musculature. When heat and exercise are combined, there is an initial dramatic rise in heart rate, followed by a plateau or very slow increase. Any subsequent rise or fall indicates impending collapse. A healthy exercising man under a heat load requires an increased cardiac output, both to satisfy increased tissue oxygen requirements and to transport body heat from its sites of origin to the skin for dissipation. Thus, since the volume per beat (stroke volume) is relatively fixed, accomplishing a given work load with the least increase in heart rate is considered an efficient response provided that heat transport remains adequate. The heat transport potential may always be sufficient, even in an exercising man, and the limiting factor is the evaporation potential. Physical training through repeated exercise does increase stroke volume and allows the training work load to be performed with a smaller increase in heart rate; extensive heat exposure without exercise (i.e., "passive" heat acclimatization) has no effect on heart rate, so this measurement is largely an indication of physical fitness.

HEAT ACCLIMATIZATION

The importance of some of the factors mentioned above in influencing the response to work and heat have been noted in passing, and others, such as avoiding initial dehydration, are self-evident. The state of heat acclimatization, however, is so important that it should be amplified. By definition, "artificial heat acclimatization" is a set of beneficial changes, in response to controlled heat exposures, in the pattern and extent of sweat produced, in changes in heart rate in response to work in the heat, and in changes in endocrine function brought about by loss of sodium contained in the sweat, for example. These changes can be demonstrated in healthy subjects who have undergone even one daily exposure to a heat-work situation, and they approach a maximum for a given heat-work stress after 5 to 10 days. "Natural heat acclimatization" involves the same pattern of response changes upon stimulation by the most stressful heat-work combination performed during the daily routine or, at least, very frequently. Heat acclimatization, although gained quickly, can be lost almost as rapidly and is, therefore, a labile thermoregulatory adjustment or adaptation, which requires frequent stimulation for full maintenance. Although it is possible to assess the level of acclimatization by a standard heat exposure, at least crudely, the unactivated potential of an individual cannot really be measured without a subsequent acclimitization training course.

The changes resulting from heat acclimatization show up in all of the measurements discussed so far. With acclimatization, internal temperature does not show as much initial increase and tends to level off, or rise very slowly, for the remainder of the exposure. Sweat production is initiated sooner, reaches a high point earlier, and is maintained at a reasonably constant rate for a longer period of time. Heart rate does not increase as much, although, as was pointed out, this is primarily a function of the exercise training. Skin temperatures have been reported to be lower in acclimatization involving dry heat (Lee, 1964) but not humid heat (Ladell, 1964). Presumably, this difference depends on whether evaporation is sufficiently effective to create a functionally drier skin with less than optimal sweating. An additional change, which is often emphasized, is the reduced concentration of salts, principally sodium chloride, in each unit of sweat after acclimatization. This is not particularly important for assessing the effects of a short heat exposure because the greater sweat production tends to balance off the decreased concentration.

The principal sources of comparative heat trials in geographical and ethnic groups can be examined: Robinson (1941a,b) and Baker (1958b) on American Negroes versus American whites; Wyndham (1966) on South African Negroes, Bushmen, Saharan Arabs, French soldiers, and South African and Australian whites; Ladell (1964) on West African Negroes and West African whites; and Macpherson (1960) on Asiatics. All reveal very few differences that are not presumably a function of the states of heat acclimatization and physical fitness in each group at the time of the study. Even if the comparison is restricted to those studies involving groups who have undergone a heat acclimatization process, there still are no important differences. Wyndham's (1966) acclimatized Negroes showed lower hourly sweat rates than acclimatized whites, but, when the group averages are corrected for body weight or surface area, the differences disappear. Baker's (1958b) whites and Negroes were matched for body size and showed no significant differences in sweating. Ladell (1964) reported that acclimatized Nigerians sweat exactly the same amount as acclimatized Europeans. Only the study in Singapore (Macpherson, 1960) showed less sweating corrected for body weight in Asiatics than British sailors, but this represents only two Malays and one Indian versus six Europeans. Rectal temperatures and heart rates were not different in any of these studies.

Readers who are familiar with anthropological literature will find that the physiological data are often reordered to increase analytical insight. A common practice is to express values as differences (increases or decreases) from the beginning or time zero to some subsequent time. Rectal temperature is often described in this manner, since it allows two values (e.g., initial and final temperatures) to be expressed as a single number. Unfortunately, the assumption behind this practice is that there were no true biological differences at time zero—only the minor variability that normally occurs between subjects and within the same subject from day to day. Since this may not be an appropriate assumption when diverse groups are being compared, it must be used with caution in the type of studies reported here. An even more esoteric approach is to combine two different measures, such as heart rate increase per degree rise in rectal temperature (centigrade) or any other desired combination, and then plot them against ambient temperature or other measures of stress or for specific time frames. The value of this approach is limited by the precise control exercised by the investigator; it was designed to uncover mechanisms, interactions, etc., with a subtlety not yet entirely appropriate for crude human studies of racial differences.

The chance of ever finding identical backgrounds in small samples from distant and diverse populations is too small for practical consideration. Whenever a comparison is made, a qualitative allowance for any differences between what is observed and what might be observed after a standard work-heat conditioning regimen must be made. Otherwise, assuming the biological potential for adjustment is the same in all men, we actually end up with an estimate of the state of natural heat acclimatization and level of physical fitness in different populations (Fox *et al.*, 1968); if we do not make this assumption of biological identity for adjustment, we have a multifactorial problem.

The work load for most of these trials has been "standardized" for each individual on the basis of body weight, and the results are interpreted in units of body weight. Some adjustment is necessary to correct for differences between large and small men; this may not entirely balance the work load, however, since, for any given weight, we can expect a range of leanness-fatness, especially in the heavier men. This titration of work load by weight probably means that the corpulent subjects were assigned a higher work load for their muscle mass than the lean subjects. This kind of a problem has plagued the few studies using women (Hertig and Sargent, 1963; Bar-Or *et al.*, 1969). Since, for each unit of body weight, women have a greater percentage of fat and, therefore, a smaller percentage of skeletal muscle, the work loads assigned on a total weight basis are not really comparable. In general, women react the same as men in heat-work trials and show comparable changes with heat acclimatization. They have trouble finishing a prolonged heat-work experience, however, becoming exhausted sooner than men probably because of the disparity of work load.

It is difficult to read the results of such heat trials without being struck by how close the subjects fit the ideal pattern of acclimatization: heavy and early sweat production, minimal temperature rise, and slow heart rate. These responses are typically human and rather specialized. There is no other known mammal who produces as much sweat for a given heat stress, and no other large land mammal I know of is so remarkably affected by internal temperature rise. It is a fair generalization to say that our defenses against heat are primarily designed to maintain internal temperature below what many other large mammals can tolerate. Sweating is an efficient mechanism for maintaining internal temperature only when the sweat can be totally evaporated about as fast as it is produced; this is not possible in humid heat, and man's tolerance is greatly reduced in such circumstances. Ideally, it would be advantageous to man if he regulated sweat production to fit the evaporation potential, but, as indicated previously, he does not. Regardless of how much is evaporated and how much drips to the ground uselessly, an increase in internal temperature promotes greater sweating. This is because sweating is regulated primarily by internal temperature and only secondarily by skin temperature, except for such special circumstances as high radiant input or the application of hot water to the skin. Any shift in regulation toward a per-unit-evaporated system would have to emphasize skin temperature at the expense of internal temperature and would involve tolerating higher internal temperatures. Such a shift would conserve sweat (body water), and the accompanying loss of electrolytes, and thus would be a rather unique, water-sparing, thermolabile response. The idea of such a deviation from what might be termed the straight-line, hyper-acclimatization approach is not especially new (Ladell, 1964), but there has been no real research here. It is possible that our species has only one biological response pattern to heat stress. In that case, the chance of establishing true ethnic differences, after proper weighting of personal and group history background, is very low.

CONCLUSION

This presentation has emphasized the uncertainties and complexities that beset any attempt to compare heat adaptations directly in different groups of mankind. This does not mean that there are no differences—only that they have not been demonstrated beyond a reasonable doubt. Part of this problem is the simplistic philosophy inherent in our traditional approach. In essence, we say implicitly (or explicitly) "if all other things are equal, our measurements show . . . ," even when we know that achieving equality in all other independent variables is impossible. This well-known weakness of the comparative approach involves the hope that the biological differences are so important that they override, or at least are visible through, the background noise of the system. One may seriously question whether intra-species differences in heat adaptation have ever been that important to man. Furthermore, the traditional approach, whether it involves extracting heights and weights from the literature or subjecting men to a standardized heat-work exposure, ignores the whole problem of behavioral response. A given population sample may have avoided or buffered the heat stress for generations or, on the other hand, exploited its maximal biological potential as a tradition. Certainly, if there is one area in which the anthropologist can contribute to understanding heat adaptation, it is at the interface between what people can do and what they actually do, starting with the skeptical assumption that these parameters are not necessarily identical.

REFERENCES

Allen, J. A. 1877. The influence of physical conditions in the genesis of species. *Radical Rev.* 1:108-40.

Baker, P. T. 1958a. Racial differences in heat tolerance. *Amer. J. Phys. Anthropol.* 16:287-305.

Baker, P. T. 1958b. The biological adaptation of man to hot deserts. *Amer. Nat.* 92:337-57.

Bar-Or, O., H. M. Lundegren, and E. R. Buskirk. 1969. Heat tolerance of exercising obese and lean women. *J. Appl. Physiol.* 26:403-409.

Bergmann, C. 1847. Über die Verhältnisse der Wärmeökonomie des Thiere zu ihrer Grösse. *Göttinger Studien.* 3:595-708.

Coon, C. S. 1955. Some problems of human variability and natural selection in climate and culture. *Amer. Nat.* 89:257-80.

Fox, R. H. 1965. Heat. In *The Physiology of Human Survival*, eds. O. G. Edholm, and A. L. Bacharach. New York: Academic Press, pp. 53-81.

Fox, R. H., G. W. Crockford, and B. Löfstedt. 1968. A thermoregulatory function test. *J. Appl. Physiol.* 24:391-400.

Henschel, A. (comp.) 1967. Comparative methodology for heat tolerance testing. Techn. Report 44, USPHS, Occup. Health Res. & Tng. Facility, Cincinnati, Ohio.

Hertig, B. A. and F. Sargent. 1963. Acclimatization of women during work in hot environments. *Fed. Proc.* 22:810-13.

Ladell, W. S. S. 1964. Terrestrial animals in humid heat: Man. In *Handbook of Physiology: Adaptation to the Environment*, vol. 4, ed. D. B. Dill. Baltimore: Williams & Wilkins, pp. 625-59.

Lee, D. H. K. 1964. Terrestrial animals in dry heat: Man in the desert. In *Handbook of Physiology: Adaptation to the Environment*, vol. 4, ed. D. B. Dill. Baltimore: Williams & Wilkins, pp. 551-82.

Leithead, C. S. and A. R. Lind. 1964. *Heat Stress and Heat Disorders*. Philadelphia: Davis.

Macpherson, R. K. (comp.) 1960. *Physiological Responses to Hot Environments*. Med. Sci. Council Spec. Rpt. #298. London: HMSO.

Newman, M. T. 1953. The application of ecological rules to the racial anthropology of the aboriginal New World. *Amer. Anthropol.* 55:311-27.

Newman, M. T. 1956. Adaptation of man to cold climates. *Evolution* 10:101-105.

Roberts, D. F. 1953. Body weight, race and climate. *Amer. J. Phys. Anthropol.* 11:533-58.

Robinson, S., D. B. Dill, P. M. Harmon, F. G. Hall, and J. W. Wilson. 1941a. Adaptation to exercise of Negro and white sharecroppers in comparison with northern whites. *Human Biol.* 13:139-58.

Robinson, S., D. B. Dill, M. Nielsen, and J. W. Wilson. 1941b. Adaptation of white men and Negroes to prolonged work in humid heat. *Amer. J. Trop. Med.* 21:261-87.

Scammon, R. E. 1942. Developmental anatomy. In *Morris' Human Anatomy*, ed. J. P. Schaeffer. Philadelphia: Blakiston, pp. 9-52.

Schreider, E. 1963. Physiological anthropology and climatic variations. *Arid Zone Research, Review of Research (UNESCO)* 22:37-73.
Weiner, J. S. and J. A. Lourie. (comp.) 1969. *Human Biology, a Guide to Field Methods*. IBP Handbook #9. Philadelphia: Davis.
Wilbur, C. G. 1957. Physiological regulations and origin of human types. *Human Biol*. 29:329-36.
Wyndham, C. H. 1966. South African ethnic adaptation to temperature and exercise. In *The Biology of Human Adaptability*, ed. P. T. Baker and J. S. Weiner. Oxford: Clarendon Press, pp. 210-45.
Wyndham, C. H. 1969. Human studies. *7th Annual Research Review*. Johannesburg: Chamber of South Africa Research Organization.

6. Environment and Human Adaptation in the Sahara

L. CABOT BRIGGS*

Human activity everywhere is always influenced to some extent by the natural environment. In regions where some of its components are extremely rigorous, environmental influences may assume the proportions of controlling factors in the lives of the inhabitants, both as individuals and as communities. Any environmental factor that limits freedom of action must inevitably have a selective effect, genetically, in the long run, for no two persons will be inconvenienced by it in exactly the same way or to quite the same extent, and so the reproductive potential of one will be somewhat more affected than that of another. Natural selection gradually weeds out less adaptable strains, while others, including any particularly appropriate mutational variants, will find it relatively easy to reproduce their kind. Such, in a word, is the mechanism of environmental adaptation at the level of the ongoing population.

Most of my readers will find these reflections thoroughly familiar and commonplace. Nevertheless, their repetition here helps define the framework of this exploratory chapter.[1] My inquiry will be aimed, first, at establishing the imperatives inherent in the natural environment of the Sahara, those forces of nature that exert a critical influence and, in some cases, peremptory control over human activities. The second step will be to consider certain characteristics of various Saharan peoples, with a view to dis-

* Research Associate, Peabody Museum of Harvard University, Cambridge, Massachusetts.

1 This chapter is an expanded version of a lecture given at the University of Paris on April 23, 1970.

covering how and to what extent they have been shaped by their natural surroundings. These two lines of inquiry together should help throw light not only on the ways in which native Saharans have come to be what they are, but also on the ways in which outsiders can live and function satisfactorily in such a place as the Sahara.

The Saharan environment is distinguished, particularly, by extreme aridity and often very high temperatures, with marked differences between diurnal and nocturnal thermal means. Nevertheless, this singularly inhospitable region has been inhabited since long before the dawn of history by a large, though widely scattered population. It is disconcerting, therefore, to be obliged to recognize that there is still no major study available to tell us just what the effects of the environment may have been on the genotypic and phenotypic physiology of the native Saharan peoples.

The rapid expansion of oil field operations (which began in 1956) inspired a series of studies the value of which is more or less limited for the most part by their restriction to questions of immediate industrial needs (see Lambert, 1968). A few relatively general studies also exist, but most of these are too vague, if not downright fanciful, to be very useful to us. For some authors, the temptation to publish attractive fantasies concerning the Sahara seems to be irresistible when they realize that very few if any of their readers will be able to distinguish between fact and fiction in this area.

The *Archives de l'Institut Pasteur d'Algérie* contains a series of regional studies by French Army doctors who have served in outposts scattered all over the Algerian Sahara. For roughly 80 years, these posts were the operational centers of French military government in the area then known as the *Territoires du Sud*. The doctors in question were mostly young men fresh from their internships in France and still fired by the investigative zeal that is found so often at that stage in a medical career. Since they were in practically constant contact with the entire population of their various regions, their observations are always interesting and usually valuable. If I cite very little of their work directly in the following pages it will be only that most of their findings that interest us here have been included in more general studies that appeared relatively recently and are much more readily available. Among the best of these is the work of Dubief (1960, 1959-1963) on the Saharan climate, and so what I will have to say on that subject is based primarily on his findings and opinions.

SOLAR RADIATION

Dubief has pointed out that, although the Sahara has a multiplicity of regional climates, its chief distinguishing characteristics in general are that it is one of the hottest and also driest places in the world. Its great heat is due partly to the negative factor of very low nebulosity. Clouds are rare, and so the rate of solar radiation reaching the ground is one of the highest recorded anywhere. Nebulosity varies regionally but mainly within the limits of some 100 to 200$^+$ cloudless days a year. In the western central Sahara, the annual range recorded over a period of 25 years was from 100 to 266 completely cloudless days. In terms of daily averages over a full year, these figures show a range of 8$^+$ to 11 hours of sunshine per day, in other words, well over four-fifths of the theoretically possible maximum. The Paris daily average is only one-half as much. Indeed, the annual rate of solar radiation reaching ground level in the Sahara is thought to be the highest in the world.

GROUND RADIATION

A very considerable part of this massive solar radiation is reflected directly from the surface of the ground, and it is this that causes the characteristic effect of blinding glare. Also, its abrupt disappearance at sunset is more responsible than falling air temperature for the equally characteristic sensation of sudden cooling when the Sun first goes down.

Another part of the solar radiation is absorbed by the ground surface and reradiated later. In the hot Summer, this produces a disagreeable feeling of suffocation during the early hours of the night, when it is most apparent. My own experience is that the feeling of a sudden drop in temperature at sunset passes in an hour or so, at which time one becomes aware of what feels like a reheating of the air, gentle and very pleasant in Winter but extremely irksome in Summer. This effect is perceptibly accentuated when the air is charged with dust, the particles of which not only reflect but also absorb and then reradiate the incident solar heat.

AIR TEMPERATURE

Desert air temperature varies greatly in the Sahara, both seasonally and within 24-hour periods. The extreme range of annual variation at ground level in the open is roughly from —15°C (5°F) at night in Winter to a high of 72°C (162°F) in the full heat of a day in Summer. The normal daily range is usually of the order of 40° to 50°C. In the shade, however, the daily range of variation is relatively slight, averaging only some 16° to 18°C; 29°C is the maximum daily variation ever recorded under shelter in the Algerian Sahara. Extreme absolute air temperatures under shelter rarely fall below —5° or rise above 50°C.

It is the relatively narrow daily ranges of thermal variation that make the desert so unpleasant in Summer, when restful sleep becomes nearly impossible. At Ouallen, in the southwest, the mean minimum nocturnal temperature under shelter during July and August is around 30°C, although the extreme hardly ever falls below 25°C (77°F).

Dubief has pointed out that, however fascinating all these figures on air temperature may be to meteorologists and physicists, their practical value for biologists and physiologists is somewhat limited. What these investigators need most in this field is more precise information concerning caloric radiation from ground surfaces and relative temperatures at various levels above but still close to the ground. Nevertheless, the information summarized above does give a good indication of the nature and degree of heat stress to which the inhabitants of the Sahara are subjected.

ARIDITY AND HUMIDITY

The second major characteristic of the Saharan environment is its extreme dryness. Again it is Dubief (1960) who has pointed out that this is not so much a question of low atmospheric water content as of a water content that is always far lower than what it could be in view of the prevalent temperatures. In other words, aridity in this case is not caused by an absolute lack of humidity but rather by a very marked deficiency in the degree of saturation of the air. The extremely high rate of evaporation in the desert is due mainly to the fact that the humidity varies from no more than one-third of the theoretical potential maximum in Winter to as little as one-fifth or even one-sixth in Summer. This, in turn, tends to reduce effective precipitation by progressively increasing the tendency of rain to evaporate as it approaches ground level. Thus, as Dubief has emphasized, the concept of a "saturation deficit" is often more useful in the field of climatology, for us at least, than the more popular ones of relative or absolute humidity. In his words, it is obvious that the effects of 10% humidity in the Sahara and at the Poles are not at all the same or even comparable.

WIND

The very low rainfall in the desert, combined with the extreme dryness, reduces greatly and often eliminates floral cover. As a result, the slightest breeze is felt immediately. Although the Sahara has the reputation of being a very windy place, it is not, in fact, particularly windy, and, indeed, the nights are nearly always calm. Still it is true that here one is most aware of whatever wind there may be; here wind exerts its greatest influence on human beings.

Ladell (1957), in his encyclopedic article on "The Influence of Environment in Arid Regions on the Biology of Man," makes the interesting point that a hot desert wind can increase the body's heat load seriously. In temperatures of 45° to 50°C, increased air movement produces a convective gain from the circulating hot air that outweighs the increase in heat loss by evaporation, especially in nude or lightly dressed individuals. Indeed, under desert conditions, with an air temperature above 38°C, or about 100°F, any wind is likely to increase the heat load rather than reduce it, especially in persons who are very lightly clothed.

According to Buissière (1960), a high and very hot wind lowers the threshold of resistance to dry heat substantially by greatly accelerating the process of dehydration. Then the thermoregulatory system may be quickly overwhelmed, and when this happens the victim simply collapses, loses consciousness, and dies. Hot wind seems to be the main factor in the spectacularly sudden deaths that occur occasionally in sandstorms. And sandstorms blow for a total of from 25 to 30 days each year in most of the Sahara (Yacono, 1968). The effect of a hot wind is also produced, sometimes unwittingly, by artificial means. Buissière (1960) observed this in three cases involving heatstroke in healthy young men, who, with torsos bared or covered only with an open shirt, had driven rapidly across the hot desert in open vehicles for only 2 or 3 hours.

WATER

The chief difficulty with water in the Sahara, aside from its well-known scarcity, is that it often has a high mineral content. Although a few favored spots like the Oasis of El Goléa are blessed with water that would do credit to Poland Springs or Evian, they are very rare exceptions. At Salah, which for centuries and perhaps millennia was one of the most important caravan crossroads in the desert world, the water has such a high mineral content that few visitors can drink it without suffering serious digestive and intestinal disturbances, and even the lucky few who escape these effects find it extremely unpleasant to the taste. But all too often water of this kind is all that is or ever has been available to native inhabitants in much of the desert. Just how precious water of any sort is to them is vividly reflected in Gast's (1968) remark that they "appreciate the savor of water, its odor and its mineral and medicinal qualities in a manner as refined as that of any gourmet judging a fine wine." To them water is so important that it is even more than a matter of life and death.

For the purposes of this chapter I will consider only "ground water" as it is drunk normally by the native population and drawn from wells dug by hand. Usually these wells range from 40 to 80 ft deep, but they may occasionally reach a depth of 200 ft or more. Together with water holes, they were the only source of water supply that was available for the liquid requirements of the native peoples until very recent years, and they are still the only source for most sedentary groups. Nomads often, and, in some cases, nearly always, depend on water holes, either natural or scooped out by hand. Nothing need be said concerning such sources except that natural permanent or semi-permanent water holes are filled mainly with accumulated rainwater, more or less polluted by the excreta of the animals that use them and by the rotting bodies of creatures that have fallen in and died. The nomadic Tuareg sometimes bathe in those that are big enough.

Wells, too, sometimes become polluted, for occasionally a goat will scramble onto their high coping walls and fall in, and small children have also been known to fall in. The bodies of unwanted babies, usually stillborn or illegitimate, and even corpses of murder victims are now and then consigned secretly to these conveniently discreet repositories. But wells that become noticeably polluted are usually cleaned out or abandoned fairly promptly.

Nor will I consider here the recently developed supply of "fossil water" obtained by drilling many hundreds of feet below ground level. Although this is now the major factor in the liquid requirements of Saharan oil field workers and the inhabitants of a very few favored desert towns, such as Ghardaia, it has become so only during the last 15 years or thereabouts, and it is available only in a tiny area of the vastness of the entire desert.

MINERAL CONTENTS OF WATER

Gomella (1960) is the principal general source on drinking water in the Sahara, although a good deal of information on various limited localities is available elsewhere. He states that the maximum mineral content thought to be comfortably tolerable is around 2.7 g/liter, whereas the maximum recorded for ground water in the Algerian Sahara is in the neighborhood of 17.0 g/liter. He has also pointed out that the water in waterholes often attains much higher levels of concentration due to evaporation and/or seepage. For ordinary well water, the average degree of salinity seems to be about 2.0 g/liter, although Gomella emphasized that this is more of a general impression than an established fact. In tests carried out in oil fields in the northern central desert, only six wells out of twenty-two tested yielded water with a mineral content of less than 2.7 g/liter. And, incidentally, the maximum for deep-lying "fossil" water in the same area proved to be only about 2.5 g/liter.

Gomella considered that the high concentrations of iron, magnesium, and hydrogen sulfide make Saharan water unpleasant or even dangerous to drink. Individual tolerance of these minerals varies considerably, however, and so most of the native inhabitants seem able to get along reasonably well on the water of their local habitat, at least partly, no doubt, as a result of many centuries of natural selection.

Newcomers may or may not be able to adapt to local water, physiologically, and, in this connection, it should be noted that ill effects vary in proportion to the quantity ingested. As Gomella pointed out, it is obvious that an inactive man who may drink a liter or so of ground water with a mineral content of 4.6 g/liter will not suffer as severely as a roughneck who, in the course of his day's work, drinks 10 liters or more of "fossil" water with a mineral content of only 1.6 g/liter. He adds, however, that we really have very little precise knowledge of either the dangers or possible benefits arising from the ingestion of waters with a high mineral content. A rather striking example involves the work of Maire and Savelli (1955) at and around In Salah. Their sweeping and meticulous medical survey of the area pointed to the possibility that water with a high magnesium content may, perhaps, act in some way to inhibit cancer, and yet this very interesting suggestion has never been followed up systematically as far as I am aware.

DEHYDRATION

The two vital considerations for our purposes concerning water in the Sahara are that one needs a lot of it to survive at all and that the requirements are raised sharply by any increase in physical activity. In a hot and very dry environment, the greatest natural danger for man, as for all mammals, is dehydration. We often hear of death from thirst in the desert. In these cases, dehydration is usually the main cause, together with the less obvious loss of sodium chloride through sweat. Leithead (1960) noted that even natives of the desert who increase their work load suddenly are often subject to heat illness, as manifested by fatigue and fever, and that this is due to their failure to make an adequate corresponding adjustment of their habitual water intake. Clinical examination of such workers has shown that they were suffering from primary water deficiency. How very serious this condition can be is made clear by Schmidt-Nielsen's (1964) sobering statement that "a man is physically and mentally unable to take care of himself at 10 per cent weight loss, and at about 12 per cent water deficit he is unable to swallow and can no longer recover without assistance."

A significant factor in water loss, which is seldom considered is the discharge of water vapor through the lungs. According to Ladell (1957), this is always considerable and increases in proportion to the dryness of the ambient air. "Under resting conditions," he says, "11 per cent of the metabolic heat is lost through the lungs." And when dry air is breathed, the resulting uptake by water vapor results in a further substantial heat loss, even at temperatures as high as 50°C.

What is known as invisible or insensible perspiration (IP) is another factor in water loss that is seldom taken into account. Again, according to Ladell (1957), this phenomenon is continuous, even when there is no active sweating, and consists of water in the form of vapor passing by osmosis through the skin and off into the ambient air. He reports further that pigmented and nonpigmented skin behave alike in terms of IP rate, although regional differences have been recorded.

Visible sweating is, of course, the principal way in which the body loses both metabolic and absorbed ambient heat in a hot arid environment. In air temperatures of around 35°C and over, all heat loss is by evaporation, with none by radiation or convection, according to Ladell, who emphasizes also that evaporative heat loss increases in a nearly geometrical progression relative to a rising ambient temperature. It has often been suggested that heatstroke is usually preceded and perhaps precipitated primarily by the arrest of sweating, due to the overloading and consequent breakdown of the sweating mechanism. Kuno (1956), however, has presented evidence indicating that the arrest of profuse sweating may well be a consequence rather than a cause of heatstroke.

Contrary to popular belief, an increase in water intake does not increase the sweating rate, nor does a reduced consumption of water cause it to diminish until a serious degree of water deficiency has already occurred. Drinking large quantities of water in advance as a precaution against dehydration is useless, for once the body is fully hydrated no more water can be stored except very temporarily by filling up the stomach.

It is true that heavy sweating reduces the flow of urine and that this is not markedly affected by an increased intake of water as long as sweating continues. Apparently there is some unknown mechanism that inhibits excretion by the kidneys of excess water that is badly needed elsewhere. This reaction, however, does not normally occur in time to save any surplus water stored in the stomach before heavy sweating has occurred. The rule for drinking in hot climates, according to Ladell, is to drink water only in small quantities but often. Making up for water loss by drinking relatively large quantities only while resting results in a small but definite increase in urination and, thus, an increase in water loss.

One curious feature of sweating noted by Ladell is that it seems to begin in the feet and work upward, ending with the face. Another is that women, in general, sweat less than men, although their sweat is also said to be less salty. These sexual differences naturally make one wonder about racial differences. Apparently there are none of any real significance. Australian aborigines may possibly be an isolated exception to this general rule, for there is some evidence that their sweating rate and consequent water loss are less than three-quarters of that found in other human populations (Wyndham, 1964). Although Sergent (1953) said that "the quantity of sweat secreted by a Black is nearly twice that secreted by a European," Baker (1958a) has demonstrated beyond all question that the sweat rates of strictly comparable samples of Negroes and whites exposed to identical conditions are just about the same, when normal ranges of individual variation have been taken into account. Sergent's conclusion, as he told me himself not long before he died, was based only on general impressions, gathered over a period of many years and mainly on hearsay. Baker's study, on the other hand, culminated a long series of similar, though somewhat less tightly controlled investigations by others (Caplan and Lindsay, 1946; Robinson *et al.*, 1941; Wyndham *et al.*, 1952; Ladell, 1957). His findings recall Ladell's (1957) statement, already cited, that pigmented and nonpigmented skin are alike in their IP reaction to a rise in air temperature. Apparently other reactions to a hot desert environment are just about the same for Negroes and whites, too, except in the absorption of heat from solar radiation, which I will come to later.

Ladell (1957) believes that scleroderma reduces IP locally, in the areas affected, and that this reduction is compensated for by an increased IP rate in unaffected areas. On the other hand, the hyperkeratosis that may result from chronic sunburn, for example, increases the IP rate, and this is probably a factor in water loss through sweat in the Sahara.

WATER REQUIREMENTS

The maximum rate of total water loss a healthy human body can support seems to be about 1 liter/hour (Weiner, 1954; Macfarlane, 1964), but this drain can be maintained for only 5 or 6 hours before collapse occurs. And, whenever the sweating rate continues for any considerable length of time above the normal level, a corresponding increase in the rate of water intake must occur. The customary daily water ration of Saharan road gangs is about 8 liters/man, for drinking and the preparation of food only. Many years of experience have shown this to be the practical minimum, an important thing to know in an area where much road maintenance work must be done far from any wells or water holes and where the workers often must be supplied entirely by truck.

Ladell (1957) sounds an ominous note in this connection, remarking that, in Arabia, it has been shown that a man may need as much as 16 liters of water/day, without being at all aware of this need. According to Buissière (1960), an only moderate thirst, in association with heavy sweating, is one of the distinctive symptoms of severe extracellular dehydration in persons who are accustomed to heat. Thirst apparently is not a reliable indicator of water requirement.

Monod (1947) says that desert caravan men can keep going on as little as 5 liters of water/day, but he adds that this should be considered the absolute minimum. These figures all underline the fact that the rate of dehydration is a function not only of environmental conditions but also of the degree of physical activity and that this last factor is an important one. Pond (1956), for example, found that a "normal European" can survive for 2 days in a temperature of $38°C$ to $43°C$ with no water at all, but that, after this, he will need at least 4 liters/day in order to stay alive. As regards physical effort, he found that this same man can cover 24 km in 24 hours, but only if he remains inactive during the day and moves at night. Again the safe minimum daily water ration appears to be 4 liters in hot deserts. Macfarlane (1964), after a more refined analysis of water requirements for "moderately hard work," concluded that 1 liter/day is enough at temperatures no higher than 20°C, but that another liter a day is needed for each 5.5°C of temperature rise above that.

Although it is true that there are reliable records of Camel Corps patrols in the Sahara that have covered as much as 1200 km in 2 weeks with only 60 liters of water for each man and his mount (Monod 1955), these have been most exceptional performances, and no doubt the camels involved suffered permanent physiological damage.

SALT LOSS AND REQUIREMENTS

In hot deserts the problem of water loss through sweat is aggravated by the concomitant loss of salt. As Buissière (1960) said, the loss of water and salt together produces cardiovascular collapse by reducing plasma volume, in other words by extracellular dehydration. According to Ladell (1957), however, performance is adversely affected mainly by a reduction of the intracellular fluid volume, in association with increases in heart rate and rectal temperature. Probably both factors play significant roles in heat illness. The chief symptoms of salt depletion, according to Malhotra (1964), are first lassitude, then headache and dizziness, and finally nausea, vomiting, constipation, absence of thirst, and insomnia.

Raising the rate of salt intake beyond a certain point is inadvisable and may become dangerous, because continued high salt consumption by persons who are fairly well advanced in the process of adaptation can produce a rise in temperature of 1°C or more (Buissière, 1960). Ladell (1957) has pointed out that drinking a strong saline solution, with a salt concentration twice that of sweat, or more, lowers the sweating rate but also increases the rate of salt loss through sweat and raises the rectal temperature. Exaggerated salt intake may also cause edema, especially in the feet (Macfarlane *in* Malhotra, 1964). These observations apply not only to drinking water that has been salted purposely, but also to naturally salty ground water and, incidentally, to urine. Therefore only enough salt should be taken to maintain equilibrium, unless the supply of good drinking water is unlimited.

We know that the body can and does regulate its rate of salt elimination to some extent, although individuals vary considerably in this respect. In those with a moderate habitual salt intake, increased salt elimination is somewhat compensated for by an automatic physiological reduction of the rate of salt elimination. It has been observed, for example, that, in European newcomers to the Sahara, the salt content of sweat diminishes progressively until a balance has been reached between consumption and elimination. According to Weiner (1954), this process is begun by the kidneys, followed after a few days by the sweat glands themselves. Unfortunately, changes in the salt content of sweat are not easy to evaluate, partly because increased salt intake makes the sweat more salty (Ladell, 1957).

I have already mentioned that heavy sweating in humans reduces the flow of urine. The sweat glands of dogs, curiously enough, seem to respond to heat in a different way from those of humans (Aoki and Wada, 1951); they seem to act in response to elevated temperatures in the skin alone rather than in the body as a whole, so that "essentially all dissipation of heat is accomplished from the respiratory tract" (Schmidt-Nielsen, 1964), in other words, by panting. And, in dogs, urine secretion does not drop markedly until a negative water balance has already been established, even when the rate of respiratory water loss is considerable (Ladell, 1957).

HEAT ABSORPTION

As I explained at the beginning of this chapter, it is strong solar radiation combined with low nebulosity that makes the Sahara and its extensions in northeastern Africa and Arabia the hottest and driest desert in the world. I have already outlined Dubief's (1960, 1959-1963) very clear description of the different kinds of solar radiation—direct, reflected, and reradiated—that affect man in this biggest and most dangerous of deserts. For an individual to maintain heat equilibrium, heat loss must equal the sum of the environmental and metabolic heat loads, and the hotter the environment the more difficult this becomes (Consolazio and Shapiro, 1964). Acclimatization is a very important part of the adjustment to such an environment, but it can never be perfect. Even the native inhabitants of the Sahara are by no means completely acclimatized to the atmospheric rigors of their habitat, as witness Leithead's (1960) remarks cited in the first paragraph of my section on dehydration. Ladell (1957) says that "Merely resting in the heat will give some degree of acclimatization but full acclimatization can only be achieved by exercise or by working in the heat." By "full acclimatization" he means presumably only the fullest possible, however, and that is always far from complete. Danger becomes somewhat less immediate, but it is always there. Therefore, the grave effects of overexposure of various kinds must be guarded against constantly, even by the most "fully" acclimatized.

Heatstroke is a fairly common and sometimes spectacular result of overexposure. The chief physiological mechanism here is a sudden cardiovascular upset followed quickly by collapse. Its most striking form will be familiar to those of my older readers who have seen soldiers faint while standing at attention on a sun-baked parade ground. But although this is the most striking manifestation of heatstroke, it is by no means the most typical. Usually the triggering mechanism is a prolonged and fairly strenuous muscular effort, and, although this often ends with fainting, too, the loss of consciousness comes as less of a surprise. Shibolet *et al.* (1964) found that in healthy young men well acclimatized to work in a hot desert, strenuous effort may produce heatstroke even "in the presence of copious sweating and an intact heat dissipating mechanism," and under conditions where the external heat load is not unduly severe, plenty of good water is available, and dehydration is insignificant. Overheating in sunless or relatively sunless conditions produces less spectacular symptoms, but the results can still be very serious. A slightly elevated rectal temperature that continues to rise progressively but without an accompanying loss of consciousness is a characteristic symptom according to Buissière (1960), while Shibolet *et al.* have observed that euphoria and restlessness often foreshadow imminent heatstroke.

Ladell (1957) explains that exposure to heat diverts blood from the viscera to the skin and the muscles of the extremities. Ordinarily, the only notable result is an increased cardiac output, but in extreme conditions there may be "peripheral pooling, a diminished venous return and a lower cardiac output." Then fainting results from hypotension caused by an insufficient vasomotor or cardiac response. Exposure to heat also produced a rise in rectal temperature, and this, in turn, increases the heart rate, but no amount of increase can compensate for a failing venous return. Ladell insists that most of these symptoms occur mainly during erect posture, and that they tend to disappear with acclimatization, although chronic exposure to heat does sometimes lower blood pressure.

Heat exposure often results in a narrowed range of blood pressure, for it tends to lower the systolic pressure in unacclimatized persons and raise the diastolic pressure in acclimatized ones (Ladell, 1957). Buissière (1960) also found marked seasonal variations in blood pressure generally, with readings rising as high as 200/120 not uncommon during the Summer, which then fall off markedly in the closing months of the year. In his series of 317 healthy young adult European males, systolic pressures dropped sharply in the Fall, while diastolic pressures usually fell considerably less. Narrowed ranges persisted in most cases through at least November.

BODY BUILD

The size, shape, and composition of the body are all important factors relative to survival in the Saharan environment, as they must be in any hot desert. Nearly everyone is familiar with the rule of radiation according to which the most efficient radiator is the one with the most surface area in relation to its volume. Other things being equal, a lean person should therefore be relatively favored in the Sahara. In hot dry climates, critical overloads of body heat are reduced mainly by the cooling effect of evaporating perspiration, which drains off excess heat from the skin. In Coon's (1955) words, "The more skin per unit mass, the easier it is to cool the body by perspiration," both visible and invisible. Baker (1958b) has noted that each gram of water evaporated from the skin's surface carries off over one-half a calorie of heat, whereas the ability of the environment to absorb this water depends not only on the absolute atmospheric humidity but also on the skin area over which the water is distributed. In other words, the more skin you have the better off you ought to be in the Sahara. This principle is modified, however, in its practical application, by certain other factors.

WEIGHT

Weight appears to play an important role in an individual's ability to withstand heat strain in a hot desert environment. Newman (1952, 1955) has shown that, in general, there is a negative correlation between obesity and the mean ambient temperature of the natural habitat, whereas Baker (1955) found that fat men suffer more, physiologically, than thin men under hot desert conditions. Fat is a poor conductor of heat, and so a substantial subcutaneous layer of it tends to inhibit radiation from the interior of the body. Fat also is poorly equipped for the circulation of blood and, therefore, also inhibits free circulation just below the skin, where heat exchange takes place between hot arterial blood and the ambient air. Thus, a man who has a large skin surface merely because he is fat is at a disadvantage as compared with one who has the same skin area but little subcutaneous fat. Dupertuis (1948) has found that ecto-morphs have the most blood in relation to body weight, and this, too, may be advantageous in various aspects of heat adaptation. And ecto-morphs are also lean, by definition.

In her investigation of the deaths from heat illness of 147 military trainees in desert areas, Schickele (1947) compared their weights and statures with those of a random sample of 100,000 soldiers. Her findings show a definite positive correlation between body weight and susceptibil-ity to heatstroke. Men whose weights were 35 lb or more above the aver-age for their age and stature were most dangerously susceptible. But even those with only 5 to 14 lb of excess weight were still four times as sus-ceptible as men of only average weight. And these, in turn, were still four times more susceptible than men who were underweight by 16 lb or more, in terms of the means of her enormous random sample.

World-wide geographical distributions bear out Schickele's findings, as my remarks on those of Newman and Baker have already suggested. New-man and Munro's (1955) investigations showed a difference of 20 lb be-tween the mean weights of the inhabitants of the hottest and the coldest states in the U.S.A., whereas Roberts (1953) found a similar correlation between weight and climate in the British Isles. Whatever factors besides climate may be involved here, the weight differences are still so great as to be significant at the very least. In another article, Roberts (1952) pointed out that although weight varies with mean annual temperature, stature does not significantly. In other words, as mean temperature in-creases, the ratio of surface area over weight tends to increase too; and this again emphasizes the adaptive value of a relatively large skin surface.

Roberts's (1952) findings also shed some light on the importance of skin surface area per se, relative to basal metabolism. His findings here suggest strongly that there is usually a negative correlation between mean metabolic rate and the mean annual temperature of the natural habitat, although men living and working in extreme heat apparently have in-creased nutritional caloric requirements (Consolazio and Shapiro, 1964). In his own words, "the output of heat per unit surface area decreases with increasing environmental temperature, while . . . heat production per unit weight scarcely changes." But there are other aspects of the skin besides its surface area that are important factors in adapting to continu-ous dry heat, as I will point out later.

SURFACE AREA AND VOLUME

Unfortunately, the relation between body volume and skin surface area has not been established directly for any Saharan people, but the correlation of weight with volume is high enough so that weight can be used for purposes of rough comparative analyses. Since the form presenting the least surface area relative to its volume is the sphere, a surface area that is relatively small relative to weight indicates a spherical or endomorphic tendency. Thanks to Coblentz (1967), we have the figures necessary to calculate stature/weight and weight/surface-area ratios for the pastoral nomadic Teda, Rguibat, and Shaamba and for the Mekhadma who were once nomadic but have become progressively sedentary over the last 70 years. Pertinent material is available also for the old sedentary Jewish colony at Ghardaia, in the Mzab (Briggs and Guède, 1964) (Table 6-1).

Table 6-1   Stature/weight and weight/surface area ratios
for selected Saharan peoples[a]

	N	Weight/ Surface	Stature/ $\sqrt[3]{Weight}$	Per cent fat
Teda	244	32.8	45.3	3.7
Rguibat	177	35.2	43.1	5.3
Shaamba	130	35.8	42.8	4.5
Mekhadma	35	36.2	42.1	5.4
Jews	36	37.0	41.7	6.1
Jewesses	60	40.0	39.1 (N = 55)	7.2

[a] The first four series are taken from Coblentz (1967); the last two from Briggs and Guède (1964) and unpublished notes.

The first column in the table shows that the weight/surface-area ratio diminishes progressively from the ultrasedentary Jews to the ultranomadic Teda. The second column, showing stature/cube-root-of-weight ratios, strengthens the conclusions suggested in the first. The third column shows fat components, as determined by skinfold measurement, in terms of percentages of weight, and here again a corresponding progression appears. The only divergent figure, in the third column, concerns the surprisingly fat Rguibat, but it is not sufficiently divergent to be seriously disturbing. In any case, I am at a loss to explain it, unless, perhaps, it may be due to sampling error in this still considerable sample. The data as a whole, however, clearly emphasize the fact that the more active one is in a hot desert, the thinner one must be in order to succeed, and so, survive.

AGE

Age is another factor in tolerance to dry desert heat. As Strong (1945) noted, both the very young and very old are at a serious disadvantage upon exposure to heat. It has been established, according to Leithead (1960), that heat tolerance decreases with age, although to just what extent and within what limits of individual variation is not yet clear. As far as older people are concerned, we know very little, although we do know that they are definitely at a disadvantage as compared with the youthful and people in the prime of life. The very young, on the other hand, are in a most precarious position, in any case, partly because their ratio of surface area to volume is only about one-quarter that of adults (Macfarlane, 1964).

Baker (1958b) has noted that the chief mechanisms of physiological adjustment to heat, namely vasodilation, sweating, and increased blood flow, are inadequate, and sometimes fail entirely, during the first few days of life. Further, he has suggested that this may be a significant factor in relation to population size in hot desert areas. In the Mzab region of the northwestern central Sahara, Guède and I (unpublished notes) found that the highest mortality rates for newborn in Ghardaia occurred unquestionably during the Summer. At this season it is extremely hot, and there is almost no movement of the air, for whatever breeze there may be passes over at the level of the surrounding plateau and well above the canyon-like valley in which this oasis city lies. We feel also that Baker (1958b) was right in saying that there is no evidence to suggest that pre-natal environment has played an important role in modifying the mechanisms of adaptation to dry heat. At Ghardaia, the 6-month-old infant seemed to be almost at as much risk as the newborn, for reasons that remain a mystery to us. In general, the seasonal shifts we noted in the annual mortality pattern of the newborn continued only slightly diminished until age 2, when weaning was accomplished. In fact, mortality in all age groups was considerably higher in Summer than during the rest of the year, but, in older adults, heat was usually no more than a complication imposed on some such primary factor as dysentery, with its violent dehydration. For this reason it was not possible for us to obtain any very clear idea of the mortal danger of heat as such to very old persons, most of whom had more or less chronic senescent ailments anyway.

SUNBURN AND TOXEMIA

In a general article on the effects of overheating of the skin, Malméjac (1960) noted that when skin temperature is raised above 41°C, the results include not only local disturbances of the more familiar kinds but also general symptoms resembling those of toxemia. These seem to be caused largely by a spectacular and suddenly increased release of histamine by the overheated skin, for, when skin temperature is raised to 41°C, the rate of histamine release may increase to as much as four times normal. As skin temperature continues to rise above this point, histamine release continues to increase in an almost geometrical progression, producing a sharp drop in blood pressure. The effects of vasodilation are then enhanced by an increase in capillary permeability which, in turn, produces edema. Although Malméjac's conclusions were based mainly on experiments with dogs, it seems likely that his findings are largely applicable to human beings.

SKIN COLOR

Thus far I have been considering physical and physiological factors, which seem to operate independently of racial differences, even though some if not all of them may have influenced racial differentiation in the ways that Coon *et al.* (1950) described so well over 20 years ago. There is, however, one racial trait that plays an important, though complex and still somewhat obscure role in resistance to radiational heat stress and that is skin color.

As Ladell (1957), among others, has pointed out, both skin and hair color are important because the darker the color, the higher the rate of heat absorption. Baker (1958a) finally demolished the myth that Negroes sweat more profusely than Europeans, as I pointed out earlier in this chapter. But in another article (Baker, 1958b), he also reported the finding that Negroes are less tolerant of hot desert conditions because of the greater absorption of heat by their dark skins. Ladell (1957) had already noted that "a white man reflects three times as much direct incident solar radiation as does a black man," although "both Negro and Caucasian absorb the same amount of low temperature radiation from the ground."

Weiner and his associates (1964) found that the skin of black Negroes absorbs more than twice as much light as that of white Europeans. Brown Bushmen, and presumably brown Negroes and other brown-skinned people, too, fall between Blacks and Whites in this respect. Absorbed light is transformed by the body into heat, which, when added to the combined load of metabolic heat and heat absorbed from the environment, increases the total heat excess that must be discharged by radiation, convection, and, particularly, evaporation of sweat. Thus, in the Sahara, a black skin increases heat stress seriously, especially in unshaded areas. On the other hand, the melanin of black skin blocks out much of the most dangerous direct solar radiation (Coon, 1965, citing Luckeish, 1946). This harmful radiation is in the ultraviolet range of frequencies, between 3000 and 4000 Å, the most dangerous of which are grouped around 3400 Å. In brief, a person with a black skin is heated more but burned less than a white person when both are exposed to direct solar radiation in a hot desert. The reverse is true of blond people, for, although they burn much more severely, they are heated very much less than people with dark skins and hair.

Most people with white skins, however, manage to acquire considerable protection by tanning, and some achieve the best of both worlds, so to speak, by tanning to a degree that blocks out most of the harmful range of light without significantly increasing heat absorption. This is, of course, the ideal condition in terms of adaptation and natural selection. Anyone who makes even a brief excursion into the Sahara cannot help but be struck by the remarkable degree to which all but the most sedentary groups among the native population have adapted.

PSYCHOLOGICAL CONSIDERATIONS

Certain other factors of adaptation, or rather nonadaptation, should be mentioned here, even though there is almost no precise information available concerning them. Whatever their true etiologies may be, their manifestations seem to be primarily psychological and psychosomatic in nature. Because so very little work has been done on psychological aspects of adaptation to heat, we know very little about them. One particularly attractive avenue for further investigation is suggested by Cottin's (1964) observation that members of tightly organized and fairly large groups are much less seriously disturbed, psychologically, by prolonged exposure to the Saharan environment than are the relatively independent members of very small groups or large, but only loosely organized groups. Laborit (1960) summed up our current understanding of the over-all problem when he spoke of "agitational psychoses which are often no more than the expression of a disorderly reaction of the individual to his social environment." And I suspect that this may well prove to be the last word on the subject.

But this kind of general psychological reaction is by no means peculiar to Europeans. Miner (Miner and De Vos, 1960), working with Arabs near the northern edge of the Sahara, and the Bleulers (Bleuler and Bleuler, 1935), in their study of Moroccan Berbers, both found levels of "psychological rigidity" significantly higher than among Americans. Rigidity, as defined by Miner, is characteristic "of people who cannot react or adapt freely to a new situation but who tend to react, instead, with set patterns of behavior and ways of thinking developed in the past." In comparisons with the Americans sampled, Miner found that levels of hostility were lower and levels of anxiety higher among native oasis dwellers than among psychologically "normal Americans," but that the levels of both components were higher among migrants from the oasis to the city than in his normal American sample. Both Miner and the Bleulers agree in that their subjects rated significantly higher than Americans on the rigidity scale, but one may wonder just how meaningful any of these differences really are when the differences between the old familiar situation and the new one are so extreme. In any case, the underlying mechanism of psychological maladjustment to a completely strange environment may well be pretty much the same in human beings generally. The high level of anxiety among the native Saharans of Miner's oasis sample possibly reflects the relatively hazardous life these people lead, in places where practically none of the "essential" conveniences and safeguards of Western urban civilization are available.

Fessard (1960) elaborated on Laborit's theme, stressing the disturbing effects of acute nostalgia in new arrivals in the desert, who are subjected to the double strain of strange geographical and social surroundings. In European newcomers, whose families remained at home, he also found that the abrupt break in normal family life often played a seriously disturbing role. He noted that the common features of the resulting syndrome were a disturbed rhythm of sleep together with usually minor affective disturbances, which often took the form of fatigue, irritability, and a slight but prolonged state of depression. Ladell (1957) considered the most characteristic feature to be irritability, accompanied by a rise in rectal temperature. Buissière (1960), in turn, suggested that ectomorphs may be particularly subject to nervous heat fatigue, a conclusion Morton (1944) had already arrived at and Beckman (1948) and others have since accepted as an established fact.

It was Strong's (1945) impression that women suffer psychologically from exposure to dry heat more than men, and he explained this as probably being due to their comparative idleness and lack of exercise rather than to any physiological factors. Although my own observations certainly bear out all of the foregoing conclusions, I still feel that there is sometimes rather more to the problem, which might emerge following more thorough investigation.

Among Europeans who have spent considerable time in the Sahara, and particularly the Ahaggar Mountains, one often hears it said that European women living there feel oppressed and irritable and suffer serious disturbances of their menstrual cycles. Several married female European residents have told me so themselves, and their husbands have confirmed it. Other Europeans, however, including a resident French Army doctor and his wife, have insisted that these phenomena are purely psychosomatic. In any case, I have observed personally over a period of years that the only women who complained seriously were more or less unhappy and distraught for personal reasons, such as neglect or infidelity on the part of their husbands. Those who did not complain, and who treated such complaints as more or less ridiculous, were all leading apparently tranquil and contented lives. Although there is no hard evidence of any kind to go on here, I still feel strongly that Laborit's brief but pithy statement is the most satisfactory explanation of this kind of maladjustment to be offered so far. It is certainly much more convincing, to me, at least, than the explanations commonly given by the complainants who usually attribute their difficulties to excessive electricity or ozone in the atmosphere or mysterious local magnetic forces. I have heard even government school teachers put forward such theories, with a faintly but definitely aggressive insistence, which in itself suggested some degree of psychological disturbance. And these views have been repeated so often and for so many years in the Algerian Sahara that they long ago became almost an article of faith among a very considerable segment of the resident European population.

For many years this problem has been examined and discussed in medical literature, and most investigators seem to have become convinced that a hot climate does cause a very high incidence of menstrual disorders in women coming from more temperate regions (Sargent, 1963). Some of them have definitely concluded that it is these disorders that produce the relatively high incidence of "tropical neurasthenia" in transplanted European women. Cilento (1925), however, felt as I do that the symptoms in question are more often a result than a cause of neurasthenic disturbances, and he added that the victims are the "lazy, inactive and self-indulgent." It must surely be significant that native Saharan women do not differ from women who were born and live in other parts of the world in their menstrual functions. Although it is true that among Tuareg women in the Ahaggar the onset of menstruation is usually delayed considerably in comparison to normal world standards, often by 4 or 5 years, it is true also that once menstruation has begun, it proceeds normally. In the sedentary population of the Mzab, the onset of menstruation usually occurs between the ages of 9 and 11, but here, too, it proceeds quite normally thereafter.

Men living in the desert seem to be at least relatively free from psychological upsets and almost wholly free from psychosomatic disturbances. Lassitude, extreme irritability, mild but persistent depression, and a slight rise of rectal temperature are found occasionally among them, too, but mainly in situations where social intercourse is extremely limited and normal family relations non-existent. Among European workers in the Saharan oil fields, one peculiarly distressing psychosomatic phenomenon did occur quite often. These men usually left their families in northern coastal areas, and then came south alone to work for 3 to 5 weeks before returning north for a week or two. Not infrequently they arrived in the bosom of the family in an extreme state of sexual excitation and then found themselves unable to achieve erection. This often caused overt hysterical reactions in them and also in their wives. All that could be done, however, was to insist that their condition was merely transitory and would pass with rest and relaxation in pleasant surroundings, as I believe it always did.

COLD

Cold is hardly ever a serious problem in the Sahara, but it can sometimes be troublesome. Although freezing or subfreezing temperatures are extremely rare and almost never last through an entire day, they do occur occasionally along the northwestern edge of the desert and in the high mountain massifs of the central area. But even in these regions this usually nocturnal cold is never either severe or prolonged, and would scarcely be worth mentioning except that it is often felt quite keenly because of the great contrast with normal daytime temperatures. Cold is never so severe, however, as to require any more complicated adaptation than simple shelter from the wind, bundling up in extra clothes or blankets, and perhaps a small fire. Except for the very few miserably poor, who have no house or tent and only a few rags of clothing to their name, it produces no effects of consequence on human beings, and so need not be considered further here. From our point of view, it is merely a meteorological curiosity.

OTHER CONSTITUTIONAL FACTORS

Most of the major constitutional factors in adaptation to dry desert heat are fairly obvious, and most have already been discussed in this chapter. A few others have been dealt with so thoroughly elsewhere by various authorities and are already so well known that I have hardly done more than touch on them in passing. The rest are very rare and of only minor importance, numerically, and so are of practical interest only to specialists. The disastrous disadvantages of being born without pigment (albinism) or without sweat glands are too self-evident to require our consideration. That endocrine activity, particularly that of the adrenal cortex, is closely related to heat regulation of the body appears to be an established fact (Ladell, 1957), but the precise nature of this relationship is not yet very clear, and much of the pertinent evidence seems contradictory. Clothing, although anything but physiological in itself, does affect the effectiveness of some physiological processes enough to make it an important factor in heat adaptation anywhere, and especially in a hot desert, so I will consider it now.

CLOTHING

The critical importance of clothing in the Sahara is clearly apparent when one realizes that a nude man attains his maximum sweat rate in an ambient temperature of about 43°C, whereas with "proper clothes" on he reaches his maximum rate only when the temperature has risen to about 52°C (Ladell, 1957). By the term proper clothes, I mean clothing of a type that has certain well-recognized advantageous features, without which they can be almost worse than none at all.

The desirable characteristics of proper clothing are those that insulate against dry desert heat and minimize the effects of heat on the body of the wearer without inhibiting the evaporation of sweat. Clothes should be light in color, so as to absorb a minimum of radiational heat. They should be light in weight, too, and woven loosely enough to allow reasonably free passage of evaporation from the surface of the skin.

Gosselin (in Adolph, 1947) has pointed out that light clothing (by which he apparently meant light in both color and weight) reduces high rates of heat absorption by as much as 100 cal/hour. Strong (1945) and Ladell (1957), among many others, have also emphasized the importance of thin, light-colored clothes. Clothing of this kind can be helpful in yet another way, by acting to some extent as a wick, which transfers liquid sweat and vapor from the skin surface to the outer surface of the cloth where it can evaporate more readily. Water-repellent materials are seriously disadvantageous (Ladell, 1957), because they seal in both moisture and radiational body heat.

Ladell (1957) stressed the point that clothing that covers the body and extremities entirely reduces sweat loss at very high temperatures but increases it at relatively low ones and, so, can sometimes increase dehydration. This underlines the fact that, even in hot deserts, there is no single type of costume that is ideal under all conditions within the normal ranges of thermal variation. But common sense and a reasonable familiarity with the physiology of heat illness should be a sufficient guide in this respect. Buissière's (1960) report on heatstroke in the young men who drove at high speeds in open vehicles across the desert in daytime with their shirts open shows just how crucial this combination of common sense and elementary knowledge can be in the Sahara. For no amount of equipment of the finest quality can possibly protect against the effects of gross thoughtlessness. A man who goes about habitually in shorts and with his shirt open is simply asking for trouble.

Clothing should cover the body well, but it should also fit loosely, so as to maintain a layer of stagnant air between it and the surface of the skin. As long as it remains dry, such clothing affords good protection against both radiational and convectional heat gain, and also against the kind of heat gain from a hot desert wind that prostrated the men whose cases Buissière described. Even the best of clothes, however, retain their insulating effect only as long as they remain dry. Clothing that has become soaked with sweat gives very little or no protection, for the insulating air between it and the skin is then replaced with water which not only is a relatively poor insulator, but also blocks whatever porosity the material may have had and so inhibits evaporation of sweat and perspirational vapor.

Going without shoes or wearing just sandals is very unwise, too. In the section on climate, I described how a considerable amount of solar radiation is absorbed by the ground surface and reradiated later. This kind of latent radiational heat is absorbed directly through the feet by anyone standing or walking on heated ground. And this, in turn, adds to the body's over-all heat load, which must be kept within safe limits by mechanisms that deplete reserves of water and salt. The soles of footgear reduce the absorption of ground heat very considerably. Shoes also have the advantage of preventing sunburn on the upper surface of the feet and toes, which comes so often as a painful surprise to tourists in the Sahara. Shoes or low boots that reach the bottoms of the trousers tend to reduce the absorption of heat from the air just above ground level, which is often considerably hotter than that only a little higher up.

GENERAL CONSIDERATIONS

In closing my consideration of physical and physiological factors that influence human adaptability in the Sahara, I can hardly do better than present, with some slight modifications and additions, two classic statements of Weiner (1954) and Ladell (1957), respectively. The fact that rules for living have to be acquired for desert life, as for all other parts of the world, and that this can be done efficiently, is obvious from the successful survival of the great variety of desert peoples. Provided that men are well fed, properly clothed, and take reasonable precautions, they can remain fit and well in any climate. There is no clear-cut evidence that any major race of mankind is better adapted to hot deserts than any other in terms of over-all genotypic composition, although there are suggestions that some subraces may have become better adapted as a result of natural selection over very long periods of time (Coon *et al.*, 1950; Coon, 1965; Garn, 1965).

NATIVE SAHARAN PEOPLES

I have so far considered, primarily, those natural environmental factors that endanger human beings in the Sahara and the ways in which their undesirable effects can be avoided or at least mitigated. The second step that I proposed at the beginning of this chapter was to consider the native inhabitants of the desert with special attention to their physical responses to these environmental imperatives. Here we are seriously handicapped, however, because the long-term effects of the Saharan environment on human beings have been largely neglected.

Several small and scattered series have indeed been cursorily measured and described during the last 90 years, and nearly all of the results have been published together in comparative tables complete with statistical constants (Briggs, 1958). But only in the six series listed in Table 6-1 have weight, girth, and skinfold measurements been recorded. And, again, only in these series have skin color and the darker shades of hair color been observed with methodical precision. Thus, we are deprived at the start of much of the more important kinds of data necessary to evaluate precisely whatever long-range effects natural selection and genotypic adaptation may have had on desert peoples exposed for many generations to the Saharan environment.

As though this were not bad enough, one of the numerically most important and perhaps the oldest of all Saharan peoples, the sedentary negroid Haratin, has never been the subject of any published study, however modest, except for two early ABO blood-group surveys (Horrenberger, 1933; Kossovitch, 1934). Even the famous and flamboyant Tuareg, whose social, political, and economic structures have been discussed so exhaustively in the literature, have not fared much better in the field of somatological investigation. In the face of this dilemma I will try to make the best of what meager data we do have, fleshed out as much as possible by my own observations.

It can be seen from the figures in Table 6-1 that a fair cross section of the native white population seems to conform reasonably closely to the requirements imposed by the general rules that govern heat equilibrium through the mechanisms of radiation, convection, and evaporation. But the variations within single populations have not yet been considered. Among nomads like the Berber-speaking Tuareg and Arab Shaamba, body form seems to be influenced considerably by social and economic rank. The more important a chief is the less he travels, as a rule, and, when he does, it is often in a vehicle. Important persons in general exert themselves the least, and they are also usually the best nourished. Therefore it is not surprising that major chiefs are often big physically as well as socially. Among the Tuareg, for example, the Amenokal or paramount chief of the Ahaggar is considerably taller than the average for his people; he stands out in a crowd. And he is also the fattest Targui I have ever seen. Except for the very poor, Tuareg women, on the whole, are noticeably plumper than the men, and a very few of the most wealthy and aristocratic become enormously obese in middle age. But these women usually exert themselves much less than do their menfolk, while those of the very highest rank enjoy a sort of *grande dame* status that exempts them from practically all physical exertion. In short, one gets the distinct impression that corpulence among Saharan nomads is not primarily a function of either climatic or genetic factors. On the contrary, it is controlled phenotypically, mainly by the relative degree of muscular exertion, and also probably by differential nutrition. As regards stature among Tuareg men, the situation apparently is not the same as that regarding corpulence. Although they are by no means as gigantic as some popular writers and lecturers would have us believe (Briggs, 1960), they are still among the tallest men in the world, almost as tall as today's white Americans (Newman, 1954, 1956). Most of them are lean and sinewy as well, with somatotypes that tend to cluster near the ectomorphic end of the scale, and this, together with their costume, may be one reason why some observers quite honestly have thought them to be taller than they really are.

Nothing certain is known about the origins of the Tuareg, but the fact that they are basically white Berber speakers suggests strongly that their closest morphological affinities should be sought among the mountain Berbers of the northwestern zone of Africa (Coon, 1931; Linares Maza, 1941, 1946; González Gimeno, 1946; Kidder *et al.*, 1955). This suggestion is apparently confirmed by their ABO blood group patterns, which are typically Berber (Kossovitch, 1934; Mandoul and Jacquemin, 1953; Barnicot *et al.*, 1954), and so differentiate them sharply from all other Saharan peoples whose serology has been studied (Briggs, 1958). Morphologically, however, they differ markedly from other Berber speakers, for their bodies are both taller and relatively more slender. If a normal Berber population from the north were to be transplanted to the Sahara and live there for many generations, one might reasonably expect the morphological result to be a physique much like that of the modern Tuareg. Perhaps one would not expect them to grow quite so tall, but Tuareg stature has certainly been influenced by other factors besides environmental ones, genetic drift, perhaps, or some local nutritional peculiarity.

Among the heavily Arabized Berber Rguibat of the far western desert, one finds again a correlation between rank and corpulence, even though the conditions under which these nomads live are still more rigorous than

those of the Ahaggar. The statures of the Rguibat and of the Arab Shaamba nomads, too, are only moderate, however, slightly less than that of
Parisians (Schreider, 1950), who, in turn, are over 2 inches shorter, on the
average, than Newman's white American mean. Here again is strong
suggestive evidence that stature alone has no primary function in human
adaptation to heat, for otherwise the Tuareg mean stature would surely
be closer to the means of the Shaamba and Rguibat.

The Berber-speaking Mzabites are in striking contrast to the Tuareg
and other nomads, both physically and in their way of life. For over a
thousand years, these people were freight brokers and tradesmen, catering
to the trans-Saharan caravan trade and the nomadic Shaamba who live in
the desert all around them. Since World War II, the caravan trade has
nearly died out, but the industrious Mzabites have adjusted to this
quickly and skillfully by developing services of all kinds for personnel of
the neighboring oil fields and for those who supply them, who are constantly passing through the Mzab on their way to and from the northern
coastal cities of Algeria. In addition, the Mzabites have always been and
still are producers of dates, a little grain, and vegetables, notably onions
and tomatoes. Most of the vegetables are dried and sold to the Shaamba,
whom the Mzabites still supply with goatskin water bags and leather
boots, rugs, clothing, and imported hardware of European manufacture.
In the great market square of Ghardaia, where livestock markets are held
every Friday, nomads and Mzabites trade in goats, sheep, and camels and
secondhand rugs, clothing, and all sorts of delapidated bric-a-brac. Thus
the Mzabites, although always extremely busy, are never very active
physically. Even when moving between the towns of the Mzab, most
of which are less than a mile apart, they rode on tiny donkeys until about
a dozen years ago. Since then automobiles have largely replaced the don-
key, just as trucks had already largely superseded camels for long-distance
freight hauling.

And yet here again there is a general, although less marked correlation
between corpulence and degree of physical activity. In this case the palm
groves have made the difference. These groves are outside the towns, at
distances that vary from 1 to 5 miles; they are always visited regularly and
carefully cared for and watched over. No self-respecting Mzabite can ever
have full confidence that anyone will really take proper care of his affairs
except himself or, perhaps, a brother or adult son. And so it is among
Mzabite families of the middle and upper classes, some of whose members
do this kind of work, that the correlation between weight and activity is

most apparent. Here it is no longer a matter of correlation between corpulence and rank, except insofar as nutrition plays a relatively minor role.

The Jews of Ghardaia used to do nearly all the metalwork in the Mzab, including the working of quite beautiful gold jewelry, and they had a near monopoly of the cloth and grocery trades and tailoring. Their clients were the Mzabites and Shaamba and the small colony of European administrative and military personnel who left with them when Algeria became independent. In other words, the Ghardaia Jews were even less active physically than the Mzabites, and yet there were no obese men among them and very few fat women. Neither wealth nor social rank were factors here, for there were almost as many very rich men among the thousand odd Jews as in the Mzabite population of nearly ten times that number.

The sedentary negroid Haratin, whom I have already mentioned briefly, are oasis gardeners most of whom live in the central and southern desert. Among them, too, wealth and social rank practically never influence corpulence. Socially, these people all fall in the lower lower class (Warner, 1963), and all but an insignificant minority are wretchedly poor and chronically undernourished. Their stature is short to medium, and almost all of them are thin nearly to the point of emaciation. They all work hard physically throughout the year, and, as negroid sharecroppers, they are cut off effectively and permanently from all hope of ever rising on the social scale. In very rare cases, a Hartani may manage to put by enough money or crops to buy a garden plot or two or perhaps even a one-room adobe house. But this is almost impossible unless he marries a prostitute who brings her savings with her or unless he has a daughter who is a prostitute.

Female Negro household slaves who were brought north across the desert from the Sudan used to be standard appurtenances of every self-respecting Mzabite household until some years before French domination began. Even today one may be imported occasionally, but, since the French put an official end to slavery in the Mzab nearly 80 years ago, these slaves have been known officially as "servants," and have been kept almost completely out of sight. They do no hard physical work, and, in fact, are almost more a luxury than a convenience. Consequently they all look healthy and plump and usually become obese in early middle age.

My reason for dwelling at such length on the ultrasedentary Jewish, Negro, and negroid inhabitants of the Sahara is that among them climate seems to have affected physique and physiology only and directly in relation to physical exertion. And this becomes all the more striking when one recalls that the valley of the Mzab is one of the most unbearably hot places in the entire desert during the Summer. The people here live in houses of stone and plaster, to be sure, and these, with their little interior patios and thick and nearly windowless walls, are ideally designed for protection against heat. But even so, when Summer is well under way, they are as hot as ovens. The only reasonable conclusion one can draw from all this seems to be that obesity is not a serious handicap in the Saharan environment as long as muscular exertion is kept to an absolute minimum.

As regards skin and hair color there is not much to be said in terms of the title of this chapter. Nothing remains to be added regarding skin color beyond what has been said already. As for hair color, it is very dark in all Saharan peoples as a rule. Among the nomads one may occasionally see a redhead, but they are extremely rare. I have never seen or heard of a true blond among the Tuareg, whose hair is always very dark brown or black with the exception of an occasional more or less rufous individual. Among the Shaamba, the lightest hair I have seen was a light chestnut brown. Sedentary oasis dwellers are all very dark-haired too, as far as I am aware, except for the Jews among whom blondism and rufosity seem to occur in about the same proportions as they do among most circum-Mediterranean peoples. But all native Saharans, except Jews and, occasionally, Mzabites, wear turbans, and so, with them, hair color is not a factor in the absorption of heat.

Clothing, including head covering, is very important in adaptation to the Saharan environment, as I have already pointed out in some detail. And here again we find that the Saharan peoples universally conform to the established adaptational rules governing costume. Ordinary clothing, including turbans, is always loose and made of lightweight material. That covering the head and body is usually light in color, also, and two or more layers of it are almost always worn. Turbans are made of strips of porous and often almost gauze-like material 7 ft or more long, and they are nearly always twisted into a loose spiral before being wound around the head. Trousers are nearly always black but they are always long and very baggy, with a narrow band around the ankle just big enough in circumference to pass one's foot through. Thus, the air inside them constitutes an almost perfect dead air space and is excellent insulation against both heat and cold. The body is covered with two or more loose shirt-like garments, at least one of which has more or less loose sleeves covering the arms. Only

in chilly weather or on ceremonial occasions do well-to-do Saharan nomads put on a relatively heavy hooded cloak or *burnoos,* which is made of
wool that has not been completely defatted and so is practically impervi-
ous to rain and wind. The feet are always protected in some way, except
among Haratin gardeners, who work their tiny plots barefooted. Sandals
with flexible leather soles that project about an inch all around are the
usual Saharan footwear. Mzabites and Jews, however, wear laceless shoes
with relatively hard soles, now usually cut from old automobile tires.
Shaamba caravan men and the guardians of camel herds use a kind of
bushkin-like half-boot, the top of which is open in front, but no important man or chief would ever think of appearing in such things. In short,
native Saharan clothing in general is just what it should be to best protect
the wearer from the stresses of a hot desert environment.

SUMMARY AND CONCLUSIONS

In discussing the effects of thermal influences on the nervous system,
Schreider (1963) remarked that, although "pioneer work has been done
by physiologists . . . , useful results from the anthropological standpoint
are still non-existent, or almost so." In this chapter I have tried to show
to what extent the same is true of nearly all aspects of human adaptation
to the Saharan environment. The findings of such investigators as Dubief
and Gomella give us a good idea of just what this environment is like
and of the environmental imperatives that human beings cannot hope to
change and so must adjust to or die. Considerable information is available, notably in the publications of *PROHUZA,* concerning nutrition,
rhythms of work and rest, and many other aspects of life in the Saharan
oil fields and other centers of modern commercial exploitation. I have not
gone into these aspects because for us they are irrelevant. The groups they
deal with are transient populations who bring with them insulated housing, air conditioning, pure water, as needed, and many other things with
which to modify their surroundings profoundly. Nor have I considered
native types of shelter in the Sahara, for each of these in its small way
creates an artificial microclimate. We are not concerned with artificial
environments in this chapter.

A good deal of additional information can be deduced from the publications of workers like Baker, Coon, Ladell, Newman, and many others,
but none of this is direct evidence. No matter how useful it may be to us,
the most that we can hope to get from it are hints as to the ways in which

native Saharan populations may have been influenced environmentally.

In the field of anthropological information, including physical and physiological factors of adaptation, our only useful direct evidence consists of the rather meager data gathered by Coblentz and his associates and by Mrs. Guède and myself. Over a period of a dozen years or so, all of us also gathered some suggestive impressions, discussed them with helpful Saharans and administrative officers, and then coordinated our observations. But that is all there is to go on. Thus, it is painfully obvious that Schreider's stricture is fully applicable in the area with which we are concerned here.

In considering the native populations of the Sahara, I have presented and discussed all that is known with any certainty about the ways in which they appear to have responded to their natural surroundings. That they are all reasonably well adapted is self-evident, for otherwise they could never have continued, as they have for many centuries, to maintain themselves in a state of numerical equilibrium. Just how they have achieved this, however, is still far from clear. The physiology of native Saharan groups has yet to be studied in ways that could yield results that would be of much use to us.

Observation has revealed that the more active individuals are relatively lean and sinewy, but there are indications also that there is probably nothing genotypic about this. On the contrary, it seems to be a matter of individual rather than racial or even subracial adaptation, with the probable exception of the Teda and the possible, but more doubtful exception of the Tuareg. Also, it is apparent throughout the Sahara that obesity is no serious disadvantage when physical activity is kept to a minimum. We can say with certainty, however, that no male Saharan group that has been examined anthropometrically so far, not even the ultrasedentary Jews, has a mean weight/surface ratio as high as those of Moroccan or French soldiers or Oxford undergraduates (Schreider, 1963).

Water requirements seem to be about the same as those of all peoples living elsewhere in the world under similar conditions of heat and aridity, and, in fact, native Saharans may perhaps be less well adapted in this respect than Australian aborigines. Here we find no apparent hint of either genotypic or phenotypic adaptation.

The situation is not the same with skin color, however, for the types that are least well suited to exposure to dry heat are strikingly exceptional. Only among sedentary oasis dwellers who are sheltered much of the time by trees and houses does one often find either the darker negroid shades of heat-absorbent skin or the kinds of white skin that tan poorly or not at all. Most Teda and some Saharan Tuareg nomads are more or less negroid, and Negro slaves are always present in most Tuareg camps, but all these people cover themselves so completely that only their faces, hands, and feet are normally exposed. Thus, the adaptational disadvantage of their black or very dark brown skins is largely neutralized by the clothes they wear. The very great majority of white Saharans have skins that develop a deep rich tan with habitual exposure. This is, of course, the ideal kind of skin to have in the desert, and its prevalence there suggests the possibility that here we may have a true case of genotypic adaptation achieved through natural selection.

In summing up, my general conclusion from the meager evidence we do have concerning the adaptational effects of environment on the native peoples of the Sahara is that, on the whole, they seem to have been slight and largely phenotypic. The fact that Arab-speaking nomads of the area do not show the same development of linearity as do the Teda and Tuareg may perhaps be a function primarily of their relatively recent arrival. Arab speakers first came into the Sahara probably in the 7th century, whereas the Berber-speaking Tuareg seem to have been there for at least 2000 years. One can hardly imagine that this time difference is enough for any marked genotypic differences to develop, but it is possible that the Tuareg may have been in place much longer than most people seem to think. On linguistic grounds alone (Greenberg, 1963), there is good reason to believe that the Teda, on the other hand, have occupied their present habitat for an indefinite period, which can probably be described best as "from time immemorial," and so the same objection, even if it is a real one, does not apply to them. But the truth of the matter is that we just do not yet have enough anthropological evidence to justify any firm conclusions in this field. An immense lacuna remains to be explored before it is too late, if indeed it is not too late already.

REFERENCES

Adolph, E. F. 1947. *Physiology of Man in the Desert.* New York: Interscience.
Aoki, T. and M. Wada. 1951. Functional activity of the sweat glands in the hairy skin of dogs. *Science* 114:123-24.
Baker, P. T. 1955. *Body Composition in the Desert.* Technical report EP-7. Natick, Mass.: Office of the Quartermaster General.

Baker, P. T. 1958a. Racial differences in heat tolerance. *Amer. J. Phys. Anthropol.* n.s. 16:287-305.

Baker, P. T. 1958b. The biological adaptation of man to hot deserts. *Amer. Nat.* 92:337-57.

Barnicot, N. A., E. W. Ikin, and A. E. Mourant. 1954. Les groupes sanguins *ABO, MNS* et *Rh* des Touareg de l'Aïr. *L'Anthropologie* 58:231-40.

Beckman, H. 1948. *Treatment in General Practice*. Philadelphia: Saunders.

Bleuler, M. and R. Bleuler. 1935. Rorshach's ink-spot test and racial psychology: Mental peculiarities of Moroccans. *Character and Personality* 4:97-114.

Briggs, L. C. 1958. *The Living Races of the Sahara Desert*. Papers of the Peabody Museum, vol. 28, No. 2. Cambridge, Mass.: Peabody Museum of Harvard University.

Briggs, L. C. 1960. *Tribes of the Sahara*. Cambridge, Mass.: Harvard University Press.

Briggs, L. C. and N. L. Guède. 1964. *No More For Ever: A Saharan Jewish Town*. Papers of the Peabody Museum, vol. 55, No. 1. Cambridge, Mass.: Peabody Museum of Harvard University.

Buissière, J. 1960. Les troubles de la chaleur observés dans le Sahara occidental. *Journées d'information médico-sociales Sahariennes*. Paris: Arts et Métiers Graphiques.

Caplan, A. and J. K. Lindsay. 1946. Experimental investigation of the effects of high temperatures on the efficiency of workers in deep mines. *Bulletin of the Institution of Mining and Metallurgy*, No. 480. London: Institution of Mining and Metallurgy.

Cilento, R. W. 1925. The white man in the tropics, with special reference to Australia and its dependencies. *Department of Public Health, Tropical Division, Service Publications*, No. 7. Melbourne: Commonwealth of Australia.

Cloudsley-Thompson, J. S. (ed.) 1954. *Biology of Deserts*. London: Hafner (Institute of Biology).

Coblentz, A. 1967. *Écologie et Anthropologie de Nomades sahariens*. Thèse de Doctorat d'État ès Sciences Naturelles, présentée à la Faculté des Sciences de Paris.

Consolazio, C. F. and R. Shapiro. 1964. Energy requirements of men in extreme heat. *Environmental Physiology and Psychology in Arid Regions. Proceedings of the Lucknow Symposium*. Paris: UNESCO.

Coon, C. S. 1931. *Tribes of the Rif. Harvard African Studies*, vol. 9. Cambridge, Mass.: Peabody Museum of Harvard University.

Coon, C. S. 1955. Some problems of human variability and natural selection in climate and culture. *Amer. Nat.* 89:257-80.

Coon, C. S. 1965. *The Living Races of Man*. New York: Knopf.

Coon, C. S., S. M. Garn, and J. B. Birdsell. 1950. *Races*. Springfield, Ill.: Charles C. Thomas.

Cottin, H. J. 1964. Comportement psychologique comparé de groupes de jeunes adultes européens en zone aride. In *Environmental Physiology and Psychology in Arid Regions. Proceedings of the Lucknow Symposium*. Paris: UNESCO.

Dubief, J. 1959-63. *Le Climat du sahara*. Mémoires de l'Institut de Recherches Sahariennes (hors série), Vol. 1 (1959); Vol. 2 (1963). Algiers: Université d'Alger.

Dubief, J. 1960. Le Climat saharien. *Journées d'information médico-sociales sahariennes.* Paris: Arts et Métiers Graphiques.

Dupertuis, C. W. 1948. Somatotypes and blood volume. *Amer. J. Phys. Anthropol.* n.s. 6:242-43.

Fessard, J. 1960. L'Adaptation psychologique en milieu saharien. *Journées d'Information médico-sociales sahariennes.* Paris: Arts et Métiers Graphiques.

Garn, S. M. 1965. *Human Races.* Springfield, Ill.: Charles C. Thomas.

Gast, M. 1968. *Alimentation des Populations de l'Ahaggar.* Paris: Arts et Métiers Graphiques.

Gomella, C. 1960. Épuration et conservation des eaux dans les régions désertiques. *Journées d'Information médico-sociales sahariennes.* Paris: Arts et Métiers Graphiques.

de González Gimeno, M. 1946. Antropología de la mujer bereber en Marruecos. *Trabajos del Instituto Bernardino de Sahagún* 2:141-302.

Greenberg, J. H. 1963. The languages of Africa. *Intl. J. Amer. Ling.* 29, no. 1, part 2.

Horrenberger, R. 1933. Recherches sur les groupes sanguins dans le Sahara oranais. *Archives de l'Institut Pasteur d'Algérie* 11:433-44.

Kidder, H. H., C. S. Coon, and L. C. Briggs. 1955. Contribution à l'anthropologie des Kabyles. *L'Anthropologie* 59:62-79.

Kossovitch, N. 1934. Recherches séro-anthropologiques chez quelques peuples du Sahara français. *Comptes rendus des Séances de la Société de Biologie* 116:759-61.

Kuno, Y. 1956. *Human Perspiration.* Springfield, Ill.: Charles C. Thomas.

Laborit, H. 1960. Opinions concernant la fatigue et l'adaptation de l'homme à la chaleur. *Journées d'Information médico-sociales sahariennes.* Paris: Arts et Métiers Graphiques.

Ladell, W. S. S. 1957. The influence of environment in arid regions on the biology of man. *Human and Animal Ecology. Reviews of Research.* Paris: UNESCO.

Lambert, G. 1968. *L'Adaptation physiologique et psychologique de l'homme aux conditions de vie désertiques.* Paris: Hermann.

Leithead, C. S. 1960. Aeteological factors in heat illness. *Journées d'Information médico-sociales sahariennes.* Paris: Arts et Métiers Graphiques.

Linares Maza, A. 1941. Características raciales en mujeres de dos cabilas bereberes puras. *Atlantis* 16:3-24.

Linares Maza, A. 1946. *Estudio para una Antropología del Territorio de Ifni.* Madrid: Instituto Bernardino de Sahagún.

Luckeish, M. 1946. *Application of Germicidal and Erythemal Infrared Energy.* New York: Van Nostrand.

Macfarlane, W. V. 1964. Water and electrolytes of man in hot dry regions. *Environmental Physiology and Psychology in Arid Regions. Proceedings of the Lucknow Symposium.* Paris: UNESCO.

Maire, A. and A. Savelli. 1955. In Salah et le Tidikelt oriental. *Archives de l'Institut Pasteur d'Algérie* 33:367-435.

Malhotra, M. S. 1964. Salt requirements of acclimatized people during summer in the tropics. *Environmental Physiology and Psychology in Arid Regions. Proceedings of the Lucknow Symposium.* Paris: UNESCO.

Malméjac, J. 1960. Rôle de l'hyperthermie cutanée dans le déclenchement des

accidents généraux par la chaleur. *Journées d'Information médico-sociales sahariennes.* Paris: Arts et Métiers Graphiques.
Mandoul, R. and P. Jacquemin. 1953. *Études des groupes sanguins au Tassili n'Ajjer. Mémoires de la Mission Scientifique au Tassili des Ajjer,* Vol. 1, no. 1. Algiers: Institut de Recherches Sahariennes de l'Université d'Alger.
Miner, H. M. and G. De Vos. 1960. *Oasis and Casbah: Algerian Culture and Personality in Change.* Anthropological Papers of the Museum of Anthropology, University of Michigan, No. 15. Ann Arbor: University of Michigan.
Monod, Th. 1947. *Méharées.* Paris: Éditions "Je Sers."
Monod, Th. 1955. Longs trajets chameliers. *Bulletin de Liaison Saharienne* No. 20:38-42.
Morton, T. C. 1944. Heat stroke. *Trans. Roy. Soc. Trop. Med. Hyg.* 37:347-72.
Newman, R. W. 1952. *Measurement of Body Fat in Stress Situations.* EPB Report No. 193. Lawrence, Mass.: Office of the Quartermaster General.
Newman, R. W. 1954. The development and use of anthropometric standards. *Yearbook of Physical Anthropology 1952.* New York: Wenner-Gren Foundation for Anthropological Research, Inc.
Newman, R. W. 1955. The relation of climate and body composition in young American males. *Amer. J. Phys. Anthropol.* n.s. 13:386.
Newman, R. W. 1956. Skinfold measurements in young American males. *Human Biol.* 28:155-64.
Newman, R. W. and E. H. Munro. 1955. The relation of climate and body size in U.S. males. *Amer. J. Phys. Anthropol.* n.s. 13:1-17.
Pond, A. W. 1956. *Afoot in the Desert.* Montgomery, Ala.: Air University.
Roberts, D. F. 1952. Basal metabolism, race and climate. *J. Roy. Anthropol. Inst.* 82:169-83.
Roberts, D. F. 1953. Body weight, race and climate. *Amer. J. Phys. Anthropol.* n.s. 11:533-58.
Robinson, S., D. B. Dill, J. W. Wilson, and M. Nielsen. 1941. Adaptation of white men and Negroes to prolonged work in humid heat. *Amer. J. Trop. Med.* 21:261-87.
Sargent, F., II. 1963. Tropical neurasthenia: Giant or windmill? *Environmental Physiology and Psychology in Arid Conditions. Reviews of Research.* Paris: UNESCO.
Schickele, E. 1947. Environment and fatal heat stroke. *The Military Surgeon* 100:235-56.
Schmidt-Nielsen, K. 1964. *Desert Animals.* Oxford: Clarendon Press.
Schreider, E. 1950. Les variations raciales et sexuelles du tronc humain. *L'Anthropologie* 54:67-81; 228-61.
Schreider, E. 1963. Physiological anthropology and climate variations. *Environmental Physiology and Psychology in Arid Conditions. Reviews of Research.* Paris: UNESCO.
Sergent, E. 1953. Le peuplement du Sahara. *Archives de l'Institut Pasteur d'Algérie* 31:1-45.
Shibolet, S., T. Gilat, and E. Sohar. 1964. Physical effort as main cause of heat stroke. *Environmental Physiology and Psychology in Arid Regions. Proceedings of the Lucknow Symposium.* Paris: UNESCO.
Strong, R. P. 1945. *Stitt's Diagnosis and Prevention of Tropical Diseases,* 7th ed. Philadelphia: Blakiston.

Warner, W. L. 1962. *American Life: Dream and Reality.* Chicago: University of Chicago Press.

Weiner, J. S. 1954. Human adaptability to hot conditions of deserts. In *Biology of Deserts,* ed. J. S. Clousley-Thompson. London: Hafner (Institute of Biology), 193-99.

Weiner, J. S., G. A. Harrison, R. Singer, R. Harris, and W. Jopp. 1964. Skin color in southern Africa. *Human Biol.* 36:294-307.

Wyndham, C. H. 1964. Heat reactions of different ethnic groups. *Environmental Physiology and Psychology in Arid Regions. Proceedings of the Lucknow Symposium.* Paris: UNESCO.

Wyndham, C. H., W. M. Bouwer, M. G. Devine, and H. F. Paterson. 1952. Physiological responses of African laborers at various saturated air temperatures, wind velocities, and rates of energy expenditure. *J. Appl. Physiol.* 5:290-98.

Yacono, D. 1968. Essai sur le climat de montagne au Sahara. L'Ahaggar. *Travaux de l'Institut de Recherches Sahariennes* 27:Fasc. 2.

7. Human Adaptation to Cold

A. T. STEEGMANN, JR. *

Man's capacity to survive in almost any setting of environmental cold is commonly recognized and is not at issue here. One topic of this chapter is, rather, the search for special biological traits or mechanisms that aid people in cold adaptation. The pervasive efficiency of human culture in doing our adapting for us, built upon a biological base of no more than the capacity to carry culture, makes this entire endeavor a search, indeed, rather than a description and quantification of the obvious. Eskimo tailored skin boots, for instance, are obvious, but the functional advantage or biological determinants of the toe temperature inside are more subtle. The second topic, which underlies most research in human cold adaption, involves questions of genetic versus ontogenetic (lifetime) origins of the cold response. The approach has been comparative, especially in reference to variation within our species.

DEFINITIONS AND PERSPECTIVES

If you really want to understand how people cope with life in the cold, you must come to grips with certain problems. Not the least of them are the writers on that subject themselves; they use technical vocabulary inconsistently and their writings are often more descriptive than interpretative. Such terms as "adaptation" or "acclimatization" are employed in various ways, and the disagreements alone add up to an interesting history (Folk, 1966). Adaptation, in the general sense, means any advantageous biological

* Department of Anthropology, State University of New York at Buffalo, Amherst, New York.

adjustment to the environment; an additional and narrower meaning is the adjustment that results from genetic response, which is usually a product of specific natural selection. Since adaptation is a widely used term in both the general and scientific vocabulary, it should be modified to "genetic adaptation" when that is implied. Acclimatization denotes adjustment to the environment limited to the lifetime of the individual. Although this capacity, of course, relies upon genetically based potentials, it is not usually thought of as being genetically directed. The process or state of "acclimation" or "habituation" may develop over a few days, may be seasonal, or may operate over a longer time. Cold impact on the young, developing organism is expected to be greater than on the adult, and some acclimative responses are limited or impossible after growth has stopped (see Little and Hochner, 1973, for an extensive review). The potential for adaptive cold response in developing humans of either arctic and tropic background is not yet well explored; until it is, we shall not reach a satisfactory understanding of differential cold response in *Homo sapiens*.

A second apposition to be noted is between "response" and "adaptive response." We cannot simplistically assume that all biological responses to cold are always adaptive. For instance, allowing the hands to cool under extreme conditions certainly conserves general body heat, since the hands act as efficient radiators when warm. The cooling, however, also impairs hand sensation, movement, and, ultimately, tissue survival itself. A man exposed to cold may lose his hands if his body heat-conservation response is "too adaptive." In the same sense, an adaptive response may not be direct. For instance, raising animals in the cold may slow the growth of limb and body length by direct inhibition of circulation at growth sites (Lee *et al.*, 1969); although growth is consequently "abnormal," the resulting shorter, stouter extremities may incidently aid in heat conservation. There are cultural analogies, too; for instance, the Siberian populations, who successfully developed reindeer herding, opened a new econiche. The resulting economic pattern allowed them to occupy an area of extreme continental cold, but it also required outdoor care of deer herds during severe cold. While they enjoyed a fine cultural adaptation from one perspective, they possibly exposed themselves to a greatly heightened risk of cold injury from another.

A further complexity in the interpretation of cold-associated human traits resides in our tendency to confuse products of cold-selection with products of the broader process of evolution. That is, not all the physical differences between Eskimos and Bantus can be referred to contrasting thermal settings. The distinctive biological configurations of Alaskan Eskimo populations may derive from dietary patterns, effects of genetic drift, sexual selection, and their Asian origin as well as from cold responses. Studies in which traits are tested on a world-wide or continent-wide basis for correlation with environmental variables have been useful in partitioning the various evolutionary processes, and they will be reviewed in the next section.

As a mammal, man is equipped with the remarkable adaptability that marks the class. We find ourselves in a situation, however, not imposed upon seals, caribou, moose, or walrus. Our membership in a widespread species limits our potential for extreme, local, genetically based adaptations (Mayr, 1963). So, our plasticity may be called upon to stretch a little farther than that of other animal groups. Although arctic hunting culture is a classic example of "buffering" man against the environment, the fact is that man comes in one basic physical form—lineal in build, large, meaty, hairless, and sweaty (Newman, 1970). The amount of local climatic modification of that pattern is clearly limited, and the same is true of physiological cold responses. So, we see a picture of man whose culture can sustain him under adversity and who carries a physiology that is normally up to the task since man is indeed ubiquitous. One of the great questions, curiously underplayed in normal cold biology so far, has to do with what happens and to whom when that cultural-physical system fails. There are more studies of cold injury than of cold mortality (Steegmann, 1967), especially among peoples close to nature; there is little information on either that refers these events to individual characteristics. In both physiology and pathology we may have overlooked much available information because we have been inclined to use grouped data analysis instead of, rather than in addition to, data on the individual.

Finally, with the odd exception, few studies of ethnic differences in cold response show more than quite modest sample sizes. There are at least two reasons for this. In a community of one hundred people, the number of adult males (for instance) in good health who can be convinced to undergo unpleasant experiments may not exceed five or ten subjects. Also, physiological experimental apparatus often will accommodate only one or two subjects per trial, and a sizable number of trials may be rejected due to technical or human problems. Consequently, a great deal of time may be consumed in gathering even small samples. Even though these real problems exist, we are, with many studies, forced to hold conclusions suspect due to small sample size. There are obvious statistical limitations with samples of five for comparative uses, even if those five represent 10% of the population.

ASSESSMENT OF COLD RESPONSE AND ADAPTATION

Broadly speaking, two types of approach have been used in attempts to assess biological cold adaptation in man. In the *distributional method*, such human physical characteristics as weight or nose shape are tested for association with natural environmental variables. The geographic range from which samples are drawn is commonly a continental area, hemisphere, or the entire Earth, and, for each datum, a population or climatic mean value is used. Consequently, these studies analyze a great mass of human material over a wide range of man's zone of occupation. Their findings are both convincing and impressive and, in the writer's opinion, constitute most powerful evidence of human environmental response. Results may be stated as clines of human variation, much discussed, yet so hard to find. If associations are proved (between human body weight and Winter temperatures, for example), causation or adaptive advantage (if any) must remain inferential, and herein lies a deficiency. Other factors beyond cold affect human body weight, and even a truly cold-associated trait may be of questionable advantage.

Physiological or *functional* studies, in contrast, place human subjects in actual or simulated cold environments and assay one or more indices of physiological response. Recording of finger temperature during immersion in ice water is an example. The goal in these experiments is to explain variation of response in reference to cold adaptation. When either within-group or between-group analysis is used, various known determinates of cold response can be assessed, including "race," cultural pattern, sex, age, body build and composition, fitness, diet, etc. (Carlson and Thrush, 1960). The deficiency of such studies has mainly had to do with the difficulty in using the data in world-wide comparisons and with the problem of separating multiple cultural and situational factors in cross-group comparisons. They have, nevertheless, allowed some solid conclusions to be drawn; these will be reviewed presently, but only racial or ethnic differences can be adequately covered in the space available here.

Distributional studies: Whole body

Research on the correlational distribution of human physical phenotype may be divided into studies employing whole body traits (e.g., stature) and those concerned with more local or specialized anatomies (e.g., the nose). These broad distributions often encompass human territory not thought of as "cold" (which overlap other chapters of this book), yet the tropic-to-arctic clines cannot be logically separated. Consequently, the summary presented in Table 7-1 includes some material beyond the topic of this review (see pp. 140-43).

Only in three studies have total body traits been considered on a world-wide distribution; even with a scant sample of sixteen male populations, Schreider (1950) concluded that groups native to cold have a relatively smaller amount of skin surface for a given unit of body weight. Although Schreider used no arctic groups, his data did suggest the association of a heat conservation body build with temperate cold. Bergmann's and Allen's "rules" had earlier predicted the association, in widely distributed homeo-therms, of a large, short-extremity body with cold climate. There was now some inferential evidence of conformity in man, and Roberts (1953) strengthened the proof, using a larger sample of indigenous peoples and absolute rather than relative (proportional) dimensions. His regression calculation determined that average human male weight increases by 0.305 kg (about 0.67 lb) for every 1°F fall in mean annual temperature. The −0.600 correlation was raised to a multiple correlation coefficient of 0.813 when both weight and stature were tested relative to the thermal variable, but stature alone was a weak value; the conclusion was that man conforms well to Bergmann's rule, but for weight rather than stature. Roberts suggested a possible heat-saving function for the heavier body, but he also noted that there was no way to demonstrate with his data whether the condition resulted from direct thermal effects or from diet, heredity, and other indirect causes. Roberts's 1973 article, which updates his original paper (1953), presents additional information on body pro-portions. Again using mean annual temperature as the climatic variable, Roberts concluded that natives of cold areas have relatively longer bodies, larger chests, and shorter arms than have natives of warmer areas.

Several phenotype-environment associations have been found for sepa-rate geographic regions, as seen in Table 7-1. Roberts's 1953 report in-cluded sub-samples from four areas, and in 1953 M. T. Newman pub-lished a non-statistical but highly influential pilot study of the aboriginal New World. Roberts's negative correlation of weight to mean annual temperature for native Americans was sustained and increased to a co-efficient of −0.668 by Newman (1960), who used a larger sample. This value improved to −0.729 when mean-coldest-month temperature was used but held at −0.670 when stature was statistically held constant during the weight to mean-coldest-month temperature correlation; two insights were thus provided. First, Roberts's conclusion concerning the primacy of a weight-to-temperature relationship (stature being secondary) was supported, and, second, Newman and Munro's (1955) use of coldest-month temperatures rather than annual temperatures as a better measure of cold environment was confirmed. Newman examined deviations from the New World regression, case by case, concluding that a portion of the weight variance not explained by temperature or stature could be explained by dietary and disease pressures. For the sake of parsimony, Newman's 1960 correlations and regression coefficient (see Table 7-1) are preferable to those from the smaller Roberts sample.

R. W. Newman and Munro (1955) provide insights into whether weight-climate clines are genetically based or primarily acclimatizational. The critical nature of their evidence rests upon their use of white males of European background, born and raised in North America, and the vast sample tested. If north to south body-size clines were products of natural selection, they would not be expected to be seen at all in these recent migrants from Europe. The study, however, showed strikingly high correlations of weight to both annual and coldest-month temperature and, incidently, quite similar slopes of regression to those for ancient inhabitants. Although this does not prove that the aboriginal American clines are largely non-genetic, it does suggest that a sizable part of the native weight variance *could* derive from lifetime response to temperature. We can conclude that there are probably genetic, differential growth, and dietary factors all at work.

Africa is the only other area in which more than one study of body form and climate is available. Roberts (1953) cautioned that his sample of twenty-eight had been hard to find and may not have been an adequately broad spectrum, but Hiernaux's 1968 monograph provided a broader range and more detailed analysis—a model, indeed, for this kind of work. African cold is much less severe than cold in the Northern Hemisphere, potentially reducing values of cold-related phenomena. Sitting height and stature correlate to temperature variables, but, contrary to the American data, the correlations suggest increased body lengths in hotter settings; weight, which is so critical elsewhere, seems unrelated to cold. The relationships between physical traits and both rainfall and heat are interesting in themselves, but they suggest that African aborigines do not conform to Bergmann's rule. Finally, Hernaux did introduce one major conceptual methodology, which is of such potential importance as to merit notice before going on. He not only tested anthropometric data for correlation to simple climatic factors but also to annual *ranges* of the same factors. For instance, whereas the stature to least-humid-month humidity correlation was 0.35, the stature to humidity range (most humid minus least humid) correlation rose to 0.48. The idea that human phenotypes might respond to ranges of conditions (possibly because such variation is stressful) deserves serious attention.

In sum, there is now convincing evidence that human body weight is higher in colder regions, and there is additional evidence, form other species, that a "Bergmann-Allen" body form can be produced in at least two ways. After the cold-selective effects of a $-3°C$ environment on twelve generations of laboratory mice, Barnett (1965) found cold had produced a relatively heavy, but lean strain; furthermore, where lifetime growth was observed in rats, cold produced shorter tails and possibly left other extremities shorter, too (Lee *et al.*, 1969). These results are complicated by the limitation of only twelve generations of selection and the genetic homogeneity of the animals used. Growth in cold also affects craniofacial changes (Steegmann and Platner, 1968; Riesenfeld, 1973).

The most disappointing conclusion we must draw here derives from studies of physiology-body morphology interaction. As of now, of all the physical traits tested, only human body fat has consistently been found to function in thermoregulation, in this case, to conserve heat (Buskirk *et al.*, 1963; Buskirk, 1966). Baker (1959, p. 321) obtained indirect evidence that body build influenced body temperature, and Steegmann (n.d.) showed that the relatively long trunk, short leg physique is associated with higher finger temperature in the cold. Cold research employing variation in body build rather than body weight or fat is urgently needed and would complement Schreider's (1951) heat study, in which physiological findings were congruent with his earlier distributional results.

Distributional studies: The nose, face, and head

Possibly because of its dramatically variable appearance, the human external nose has been subject to several distributional studies (Table 7-1). Indeed, Thomson's opening contribution (1913) and follow-up (Thomson and Buxton, 1923) offered the first systematic proofs of human anatomical-climatic congruence. The earlier work, incidently, employed Amerind data and proposed a warming function for the narrow arctic nose.

Thomson and Buxton's 1923 findings, shown in Table 7-1, were based on nasal index (nose width/nose height) in living populations and were further sustained with additional tests of 98 skeletal populations. They concluded that the human nose becomes relatively narrower (i.e., shows a low nasal index) as the mean annual temperature drops, and this has since been called "Thomson's nose rule." Further analysis convinced these authors that temperature had more effect on nose-shape than had humidity. The article is still worth reading for its anthropological insights, especially in reference to the nose form in fossil man and the now clearly limited utility of the nose as a "racial" marker trait.

Taking hottest-month temperature and humidity, and a larger sample, Davies (1932) confirmed Thomson and Buxton's conclusions, and advanced some new ideas as well. Davies felt that the earlier results were inaccurate at climatic extremes; when nasal indices from four different temperature zones were separately considered, the index-climate regressions were clearly curvilinear; hot climate more strongly affected nose form than did cold and temperature more than humidity. The concept of a threshold level at which severe physiological strain begins (and at which a consequent accelerating anatomical response is induced) is a real contribution but, sadly, has not been pursued since. Davies saw nose form as a longer-term climatic evolutionary end product (hinting at respiratory disease mortality) but reviewed numerous non-climatic sources of nasal variation as well.

Weiner (1954) reasoned that since the nose is partly an organ of humidification, and since humidity is dependent on temperature (cold air being dry absolutely no matter what the relative humidity), that absolute rather than relative humidity should closely relate to nose form. By the use of two measures of absolute humidity derived from Thomson and Buxton's data, he obtained the highest correlations of any yet found (Table 7-1). Although this indicates that humidity more strongly affects nose form than does temperature, Weiner failed to present regression formulas giving the *shape* of the climate-nose association and, consequently, failed to integrate Davies's valuable insights on curvilinearity into his conclusion. If both Davies's and Weiner's results are considered, African nose form clines should produce high correlations, yet Hiernaux (1968) found rather low values (Table 7-1). This is hard to explain unless extensive recent movements of African peoples have disturbed the clines (probable), or unless Weiner is wrong about the importance of humidity, and the African temperature homogeneity is acting to suppress differences.

Two pilot studies of craniofacial feature distributions merit notice,

more for their approach than for the strength of their conclusions. Wal-
poff (1968) found that Alaskan Eskimo nasal breadth (skeletal) decreases in the colder, drier areas; this result agrees with most other data
(Table 7-1). In his opening study of a new area, Koertvelyessy (1972) discovered an association between cold and small frontal sinuses. Since
sinuses have much to do with face shape and with respiratory function, we
look forward to continuation of this research. A third study (Beals, 1972)
comes to firm conclusions based on a world sample of 339 populations.
Round heads (high cephalic index) are associated with cold, and especially with dry cold climates, and long heads with hot climates. This
agrees with Hiernaux's head width statistics from Africa (Table 7-1).

The differential distribution of nose shape with climate is a fascinating
association, but the evolutionary causes have never been systematically investigated. Webb (1951) showed that the nasal chamber both warms in-
haled air and conserves some of the heat upon expiration; the upper
respiratory passage is thus a "counter-current heat exchanger," and Veghte
(1964) found high warming efficiency even in subjects exercising at
$-62°C$. A detailed review (Walker et al., 1961) outlines the water vaporization and conservation functions of the nose, which are similar to and
of course closely related to temperature functions. These workers also
focused on nasal passage *turbulence* as the physical mechanism whereby
such great volumes of heat and vapor can be drawn off and reclaimed by
nasal mucosa. No physiological studies, to my knowledge, have been made
of humidity, temperature, and disease or survival in the context of the
nasal variation in a single population or in the whole species. Once again,
these areas of distributional-physiological integration await simple but un-
completed experimentation. We may eventually find that European Ne-
anderthals and contemporary central Asians both have "turbulence-
producing" or "heat-saving" noses, but of quite different designs. There
is also ample opportunity to study organ function relative to morbidity
and mortality.

Distributional studies: Physiological

One day, we will be able to write a review of human cold adaptation with
the help of distribution studies; at present, however, tests of cold response have been of such diverse technique and style of reporting that
only a less systematic approach is possible, and it will be offered in the
section to follow. To my knowledge, the only cold-associated trait studied

distributionally is basal metabolic rate (BMR). Since cold adaptation is partly a body heat management problem, Roberts (1973) attempted a world-sample correlation between basal calorie production and mean annual temperature, and found that more calories were burned per unit of body surface area by cold climate peoples (calories to $\bar{X}$ Ann. Te. $r = -0.736$). Mason and Jacob (1972) offer a review of progress and problems in the area.

Physiological studies: Introduction

The goal of physiological response studies, as already mentioned, has been to examine those aspects of man's biology that might confer differential cold adaptation. From the onset, it has been apparent that optimum "adaptiveness" of response is not entirely self-evident, nor are many of the experimental settings used to elicit such responses comparable to natural conditions. Nevertheless, a long list of such endeavors can be compiled, and this review will try to summarize the data from a genetic rather than a physiological perspective.

Flexibility is a property common to most physiological responses. Although that condition confers on higher species, particularly, the blessings of minute-to-minute and season-to-season adaptive adjustments (and this is a "buffer" between nature and narrow genetic adaptation), it confers upon researchers a complex problem of defining limits for "phenotype." For most indices of cold response (metabolic rate or skin temperature, for example) any given human may not respond identically, as shown by data from two or more identical experiments. Here is an example from the author's own research. Differences between human facial temperatures (at the ends of two identical 70-minute exposures to moving 0°C air) averaged between 10 and 15% of the total variation within a large sample at the end of one exposure. Such "intraindividual" variation, usually measured over various lengths of time, is reviewed by Sargent and Weinman (1966) and Schreider (1966). The point is this: if individual variation is high, it is, by definition, less predictable when such other variables as diet, body fat, shape, or other factors of anthropological interest are used. There will always remain an irreducible lump of unexplained variation.

As a technical issue, anthropologists are concerned with individual response, but our primary commitment has been to comparisons of different populations. The goal of these "ethnic" studies is simple: it has been to discover whether the ability of diverse groups to successfully exploit so

Table 7-1   A summary of studies relating climatic variables to human physical characteristics

Physical characteristics	Climatic variables	Source of sample	Number of samples (all male)	Correlation coefficient (sig. ≦ 0.05 unless noted)	Regression/comment (weights in kilograms unless noted)	Citation
Weight/surface area ratio	Latitude	World	16	(Not calculated)	Greater relative surface area in tropics	Schreider, 1950.
Weight	$\bar{X}$ Ann. temp.	World	116	−0.600	Wt. = 75.6 − (.305 × temp. in °F): 0.305 kg loss/1°F rise	Roberts, 1953
Weight (Stature const.)	$\bar{X}$ Ann. temp.	World	116	−0.538	Wt. = (0.071 × stat.) − (0.199 × temp) − 48.1 stature, mm.; temp., °F. This suggests this wt. relates more strongly to temp. than does stature	Roberts, 1953
Weight and stature	$\bar{X}$ Ann. temp.	World	116	0.813		
Stature	$\bar{X}$ Ann. temp.	World	116	−0.351		
Weight	$\bar{X}$ Ann. temp.	Sub-Saharan Africa	28	−0.395	Wt. = 87.8 − (0.512 × temp.)	
	$\bar{X}$ Ann. temp.	Americas (aborigines)	16	−0.493 (sig. 0.10)	Wt. = 66.2 − (0.123 × temp.)	Roberts, 1953
	$\bar{X}$ Ann. temp.	East Asia	27	−0.421	Wt. = 60.1 − (0.100 × temp.)	
	$\bar{X}$ Ann. temp.	Europe	20	−0.775	Wt. = 84.4 − (0.414 × temp.)	
Relative sitting height (head and body height, as % of stature)	$\bar{X}$ Ann. temp.	World	300	−0.619	Rel. sitting ht. = 554.9 − (0.639 × temp.): as temp. (°F) decreases, leg length decreases. Several other body traits showed congruent regressions	Roberts, 1973
Relative span (arm span, as % of stature)	$\bar{X}$ Ann. temp.	World	372	+0.470	Rel. span = 996.9 + (0.703 × temp.): hotter climates associated with relatively long arms	Roberts, 1973
Chest girth	$\bar{X}$ Ann. temp.	World	133	−0.575	Chest girth = 951.3 − (1.55 × temp.): smaller chests typical of warmer climates	Roberts, 1973

	Climatic variable	Population	N	Correlation	Notes	Source
Weight/surface area ratio	$\bar{X}$ Ann. temp.	North America (whites)	48 (by state) N = 15,216	−0.535		R. Newman and Munro, 1955
Weight/surface area ratio	$\bar{X}$ July temp. (hottest month)	North America (whites)	As above	−0.384		
Weight/surface area ratio	$\bar{X}$ Jan. temp. (coldest month)	North America (whites)	As above	−0.587		
Weight	$\bar{X}$ Ann. temp.	North America (whites)	As above	−0.460	0.109 kg loss/1°F rise	
Weight	$\bar{X}$ July temp.	North America (whites)	As above	−0.310		
Weight	$\bar{X}$ Jan. temp.	North America (whites)	As above	−0.528		
Surface area	$\bar{X}$ Ann. temp.	North America (whites)	As above	−0.359		
Surface area	$\bar{X}$ Jan. temp.	North America (whites)	As above	−0.436		
Weight and surface area	$\bar{X}$ Jan. temp.	North America (whites)	As above	−0.611		
Weight and stature	$\bar{X}$ Jan. temp.	North America (whites)	As above	−0.612		
Weight	$\bar{X}$ Ann. temp.	Americas (aborigines)	53	−0.668		M. T. Newman, 1960
Weight	$\bar{X}$ Coldest mo. temp.	Americas (aborigines)	60	−0.729		
Weight	$\bar{X}$ Coldest mo. temp., Stature, const.	Americas (aborigines)	60	−0.670	Wt. = 66.07 − (0.176 × $\bar{X}$ cold mo. temp.): 0.176 kg. fall in weight/1°F rise in coldest mo. temp. Stature-temp. relationship non-significant at const. weight	
Stature	$\bar{X}$ Coldest mo. temp.	Americas (aborigines)	60	−0.470		
Stature	Max. temp.	Sub-Saharan Africa	312	0.450	Stature increases with hotter summers. See end of table for Hiemaux's climatic variable definitions	Hiemaux, 1968
Stature	Max. temp., max. humidity, const.	Sub-Saharan Africa	312	0.480		

Table 7-1   A summary of studies relating climatic variables to human physical characteristics (continued)

Physical characteristics	Climatic variables	Source of sample	Number of samples (all male)	Correlation coefficient (sig. ≦ 0.05 unless noted)	Regression/comment, (weights in kilograms unless noted)	Citation
Sitting ht.	Max. temp.	Sub-Saharan Africa	87	0.570	Congruent with stature but stronger. Disagreement may be due to great diurnal temp. range in some areas	Hiernaux, 1968
Sitting ht.	Min. temp.	Sub-Saharan Africa	87	0.500		
Sitting ht.	Altitude	Sub-Saharan Africa	87	−0.480	Shorter bodies in highlands	
Sitting ht.	Min. humidity	Sub-Saharan Africa	87	−0.400		
Weight	Altitude	Sub-Saharan Africa	63	−0.270	Unrelated to temp.?	Hiernaux, 1968
Weight	X̄ Ann. rainfall, stature, const.	Sub-Saharan Africa	63	0.280		
Head width	Max. temp.	Sub-Saharan Africa	189	−0.330	Wider heads with relatively cooler and drier seasons	Hiernaux, 1968
Head width	Max. temp., stature, const.	Sub-Saharan Africa	189	−0.310		
Head width	Min. humidity	Sub-Saharan Africa	189	0.280		
Bizygomatic width	X̄ Ann. rainfall	Sub-Saharan Africa	160	0.410	Wider faces when humidity extreme?	Hiernaux, 1968
Bizygomatic width	Min. humidity	Sub-Saharan Africa	160	0.310		
Nose ht.	Altitude	Sub-Saharan Africa	105	0.370	Nose longer with altitude	Hiernaux, 1968
Nose ht.	Altitude, min. temp. const.	Sub-Saharan Africa	105	0.310		
Nose ht.	Altitude, max. hum. const.	Sub-Saharan Africa	105	0.290		
Nose ht.	Max. humidity	Sub-Saharan Africa	105	0.260		
Nose ht.	Min. temp.	Sub-Saharan Africa	105	0.210		
Nose width	X̄ Ann. rainfall	Sub-Saharan Africa	179	0.490	Nose widens with increased rainfall; possibly with max. temp.	Hiernaux, 1968
Nose width	Max. temp.	Sub-Saharan Africa	179	−0.330		
Nose width	Max. temp., rain const.	Sub-Saharan Africa	179	0.210		

Nose width	X̄ Ann. rainfall, max. temp.	Sub-Saharan Africa	179	0.520	Nose relatively wider with seasonal conditions wetter and hotter. Nasal index defined at end of table	Hiernaux, 1968
Nasal index	X̄ Ann. rainfall	Sub-Saharan Africa	123	0.460		
Nasal index	Min. humidity	Sub-Saharan Africa	123	0.280		
Nasal index	Altitude	Sub-Saharan Africa	123	−0.230		
Nasal index	Min. temp.	Sub-Saharan Africa	123	0.220		
Nasal index	X̄ Ann. temp.	World	153	0.6291	$N.I. = 43.95 + (temp. \times 0.4610)$: nasal index increases 0.46 points/1°F rise.	Thomson and Buxton, 1923
Nasal index	X̄ Ann. rel. hum.	World	153	0.4188	$N.I. = 60.01 + (R.H. \times 2284)$	Thomson and Buxton, 1923
Nasal index	X̄ Ann. temp. and hum.	World	153	0.7238	$N.I. = 24.91 + (temp. \times 0.4834) + (R.H. \times 0.2525)$	Thomson and Buxton, 1923
Nasal index	X̄ Max. hottest mo. temp. and hum.	World	590	0.601	Shape-climate regressions are apparently curvilinear; effects of climate (esp. temp.) strongest in tropics. See Davies's paper for prediction curves	Davies, 1932
Nasal index	As above	World (except India)	442	0.714		Davies, 1932
Nasal index	As above	Africa	170	0.810		Davies, 1932
Nasal index	As above	Europe	53	0.770		Davies, 1932
Nasal index	As above	Americas	61	0.680		Davies, 1932
Nasal index	West Bulb Temp.	World	150	0.770	This suggests that the nose becomes relatively wider as the actual amount of water in the air increases and that absol. hum. has more impact on morphology than temp. has. No regression given	Weiner, 1954
Nasal index	Vapor Pressure (or absolute hum. index)	World	150	0.820		Weiner, 1954

Hiernaux's Climatic Variables (1968)
Maximum temperature: Mean of the highest daily temperatures for the hottest month
Minimum temperature: Mean of the lowest daily temperatures for the coldest month
Maximum humidity: Mean relative humidity of the most humid month
Minimum humidity: Mean relative humidity of the least humid month
Other Definitions
Sitting height: Height of head, neck, and trunk (or stature minus leg length)
Bizygomatic: Greatest face width
Nasal index: Nose width as % of nose height; it rises as nose becomes relatively wider

many contrasting climates is derived in part from specialized physiological patterns, and whether these patterns, once defined, are based on genetic differences. If genetic in origin, they could be considered products of natural selection and, if not, products of simple acclimatization. The most used approaches have been comparisons of different ethnic or occupational population samples under laboratory conditions.

Physiological studies: Extremity cooling

If human groups were to have contrasting responses to cold, these differences should be more obvious at the extremities than at any other site. The hands and feet are situated far from the warm body core, are linear in build (good radiators), and are deficient in "hot" muscle or organ mass. In extreme cold, they are hard to protect, while, at the same time, they are in constant use by the hunter or herder and critical to his welfare and survival. Serious cold injury to hands or feet is a potential source of natural selection, either by death or by reduced efficiency as a provider and, thus, fertility. Native peoples do suffer such cold injury today (Steegmann, 1967) and have doubtless endured equal or more severe injuries far into the past. Consequently, it is possible that different ethnic groups may carry different genetic capacities of hand or foot cold-protection.

The ethnic studies summarized in Table 7-2 (pp. 146-51) are those in which extremity cooling was the primary goal and in which other conditions were, by-and-large, held constant. Although a quantity of additional data on extremity cooling is available from other groups, it derives from situations in which entire body cooling (not just extremity cooling) produced the response. They are neither as direct nor as useful for evolutionary insights as is the former group, but they will be considered presently. The names used for populations in Table 7-2 merit explanation here. Where a group is ethnically definable (Ainu; Eskimo), the customary name is employed, even though there may be some populational diversity within that category. The variation of populations in Europe and North America suggests that this "white" conglomeration from which come so many "control" groups simply be called "European," regardless of nationality. The Lapps are from Europe, geographically and genetically (Lewin, 1971), but their arctic history and life style justify a separate category. Due to the gene flow into American "Black" populations, it seems misleading to call them "African"; we will consequently retain the equally unsatisfactory term "Negro" used elsewhere in this book.

Two basic approaches are seen in Table 7-2; the most common approach is to immerse fingers, hands, or feet of otherwise comfortably warm subjects in a coolant, which is maintained at a stable low temperature. This imposes a constant cooling (greater in water than air) and taxes the hand or foot severely; "response" is usually gauged by how warm the skin remains (and, inferentially, how well tissue integrity and joint function are preserved). The second (calorimetric) procedure consists of letting the extremity warm up cold water for a set period of time, in order to calculate heat loss. In either case, higher tissue temperatures or greater heat loss (from having maintained warmer hands) is taken as an "adaptive" response. "CIVD," meaning "cold-induced vasodilation," is a widely seen cold response. Cooling constricts the blood vessels of the extremity immediately; by cutting down the flow of hot blood, body heat is conserved, but the hands and feet may be dangerously cooled. CIVD is a relatively rapid release of this constriction to allow rewarming.

Conclusions derived from the research outlined in Table 7-2 are discussed below, starting with those which the writer feels are the most firm.

1. *Adult male Negroes compared to adult male Europeans of equivalent background and state of cold acclimatization show inadequate cold response* (Meehan, 1955a; Newman, 1967; Rennie and Adams, 1957; Iampietro et al., 1959). In high percentages of Negro subjects, the finger temperature falls to that of the coolant and shows no rewarming. Since the subjects here are comparable, we are assuming that this is a truly "racial" or genetically based rewarming inhibition. Further and even more convincing evidence rests with the greater rapidity, frequency, and severity of cold injury among American Negro soldiers in Korea and Alaska (Schuman, 1953; Sumner et al., 1971).[1] The rewarming failure, quantified in both the laboratory and the field, can be accepted with assurance, but why it persists is another question.

In the writer's opinion, this clearest-of-all racial contrast in cold physiology derives from an equally clear difference in human distribution; Africans simply never experience freezing cold and have never been "tailored" to cold-tolerance by natural selection. Their tropical-adaptive pattern has been determined by moderate cooling only—the most economical response being peripheral vasoconstriction. Heat conservation is the result and is optimum where one is safe from freezing. Europeans, conversely,

[1] As a fascinating gratuity here, Sumner's team also found those Negroes of blood group O to be more frostbite-susceptible than those of A or B blood groups.

Table 7-2   A summary of ethnic differences in response to hand or foot cooling. See text for definitions and discussion.

Sample compared	Cold testing procedures	Assessment of response ($>$ = warmer; $\cong$ = equivalent)	Results	Citation
28 Adult ♂ Eskimos, N. Alaskan 24 Adult ♂ Indians, N. Alaskan 38 Adult ♂ Negroes, Am., South 168 Adult ♂ Europeans, Am., South 9 Adult ♂ Negroes, with histories of frostbite 12 Adult ♂ Europeans, with histories of frostbite Site: Alaska	Fingers immersed in 0°C water, 30 minutes	Mean finger skin temp.; min. finger temp.	Native Alaskans > Europeans > Negroes, 4% of Alaskans failed to keep finger temp. >0°C; 63% of Negroes failed. Those with cold-injury history generally showed low response	Meehan, 1955a
8 Adult ♂ Negroes, moderately cold habituated 8 Adult ♂ Europeans, moderately cold habituated Site: Alaska	Hands exposed to −12°C air, 90 minutes (environmental room); rest of body exposed but clothed. One Summer, one Winter test	Finger temp.; other skin temp.; core temp.; CIVD; metabolic rate	Europeans > Negroes as to finger temp. Europeans showed more CIVD. This advantage was seen both Summer and Winter. Negro Summer ≅ Negro Winter; European Summer ≅ European Winter	Rennie and Adams, 1957
16 Adult ♂ Negroes, matched for physical characteristics 17 Adult ♂ Europeans, matched for physical characteristics Site: Massachusetts	Fingers immersed in 0°C water, 45 minutes	Yoshimura's and Iida's criteria (see below)	Europeans > Negroes, all criteria	Iampietro, Goldman, Buskirk, and Bass, 1959
17 Adult ♂ Negroes 22 Adult ♂ Europeans Site: Massachusetts	Hands immersed in 5°C water, 30 minutes. Repeated after a 8-week cold acclimatization to 5°C air	Heat loss from hand; finger skin temp.	Europeans > Negroes, heat loss and skin temp. Results similar for post-cold acclimatization tests	Newman, 1967

Subjects / Site	Conditions	Measures	Results	Reference
37 Adult ♂ *Europeans*, students; Site: Central Canadian Arctic; Southern Ontario	...samples. Immersion of hand in 5°, 10°, and 20°C *water* for 2 hours	...tuation of flow; skin temp.	...*Eskimo > Europeans* (white) relative to initial resistance to cooling, volume of extremity blood flow, CIVD, and skin temp.	Brown and Page, 1952
5 ♂ *Arctic Indians*; 3 ♂ *Eskimos*; 2 ♂ *Indian–Scot* mixtures; A group of *European* troops (white), acclimatized; Site: Central Canadian Arctic	Exposure of hands during dexterity tasks to still or moving *air* at between −25° and −40°C (subjects warmly clothed); specifics not reported	Manual dexterity and skin sensitivity; skin temp.; pain	*Native > whites* as to dexterity and pain at any given ambient temp. *Natives > whites* at avoiding frostbite	Coffey, 1954
9 ♂ *Eskimos*, hunters; 4 ♂ *Europeans*, scientists; Site: Eastern Arctic	Exposure of one hand in calorimeter starting with 4°C *water*, warmed by hand during 30-minute exposure. Trials with subjects warm or stripped to waist in 15°C room (chilly)	Heat loss from hand; av. hand temp.; hand volume	The larger the hand, the less heat lost per unit of hand volume. *Eskimo > Europeans* in heat loss (absolute values); more of that heat loss was circulatory in Eskimos	Hildes, Irving, and Hart, 1961
8 Adult ♂ *Eskimo*; 3 Adult ♀ *Eskimo*; 8 *Eskimo Boys*; 4 *Eskimo Girls*; 4 Adult ♂ *European*, cold habituated; Site: Alaska	Hand and face exposed to moving air at between 0° and −9.5°C. Otherwise, seated and warmly clothed. Exposures (minutes): adult ♂, 45; adult ♀, 35; children, 30.	Skin temp.; min. skin temp.; CIVD	*Eskimo adults > Europeans ≅ Eskimo* children, generally, for hand temp. and pain. Habituated Europeans started high but finally "failed" to match Eskimo adults. Europeans showed a clear "adequate/poor" dichotomy in hand cold response. Face temp. of all groups equivalent	Miller and Irving, 1962
4 ♂ *Eskimo*, after 9 months living European style; 5 ♂ *European*, physically fit mountaineers; 20 ♂ *European*, non-fit controls; Site: Alaska	Fingers immersed in 0°C *water*, 10 minutes, and, for a smaller sample, −22°C air	Finger temp.	*Eskimo > Control Europeans ≅* mountaineer *Europeans* in cold water test. All Eskimo finish air test, but only 25% of controls and 40% of mountaineers finished (due to frostbite or danger thereof). There was seemingly a clear dimorphism of response among whites (adequate/poor)	Eagan, 1963

Table 7-2 A summary of ethnic differences in response to hand or foot cooling (continued)

Sample compared	Cold testing procedures	Assessment of response ($>$ = warmer; $\cong$ = equivalent)	Results	Citation
33 Young and adult ♀ Eskimo 39 Young and adult ♂ Eskimo, hunters A group of European lumberjacks Site: Greenland, Norway	Immersion of hand in calorimeter starting with 0.5 to 1.5°C water, warmed by hand during 20-minute exposure	Heat loss from hand to water; blood pressure rise ("cold pressor response"); CIVD as judged by finger temp.	Greenland Eskimo > European (white) lumberjacks in temp. and flow values	Lund-Larson, Wika, and Krog, 1970
8 Adult ♂ Arctic Indians, hunters 6 Adult ♂ Europeans, scientists Site: Alaska	Right hand immersed in calorimeter starting with 4° to 5°C water; hand warms water for 30 minutes. Two runs, one with men warmly clothed; other runs, men nude in chilly room (17° to 19°C ambient)	Heat loss from hand; skin temp.	Indians > Europeans in heat loss and finger temp. under all conditions. Europeans also showed greater vasoconstriction of non-immersed hand	Elsner, Nelms, and Irving, 1960
6 Adult ♂ Indians, hunters 5 Adult ♂ Europeans, scientists Site: Alaska	Right hand immersed in 0°C water for 30 minutes or less. Tested after calorimetry test, above. Subjects comfortably warm	Skin temp.; time to 1st CIVD; ability to endure pain and complete test	Indians > Europeans in finger temp., early CIVD onset, and pain tolerance. Two Europeans (40%) could not finish test due to pain	Elsner, Nelms, and Irving, 1960
6 ♂ Arctic Indians 6 ♂ Europeans, hand cold-habituated 6 ♂ Europeans, not cold-habituated (control) 6 ♂ Europeans, starved 5 days, but cold habituated Site: Alaska	Fingers immersed in 0°C water for 10 minutes	Finger temp.; pain; metabolic rate	Indian > Habituated > Control > Starved for temp. Indian > Others for pain tolerance. Finger temp. relates closely to metabolic rate. Over-all, Indians responded faster with rewarming, but ended only just > habituated	Eagan, 1963

Subjects	Procedure	Measurements	Results	Reference
farmers 23 Adult ♂ *Indians*, students, Peruvians 26 Adult ♂ *Europeans*, students, Peruvians 22 Adult ♀ *Europeans*, students, Americans 22 Adult ♂ *Europeans*, students, Americans Site: Peru, Pennsylvania			*Indian* farmers ≅ *Indian* students. *Peruvian whites* ≅ *American whites. American* ♂ ≅ *American* ♀	(1965) reported by Little, 1968
12 Highland Peruvian *Indians*, farmers 12 *Europeans*, University people Sites: Peru, Pennsylvania	Foot immersed in calorimeter *water*; starting temp. 5°, 10°, and 15°C (each on a different day); water is warmed by foot heat loss during the 30-minute tests. Subjects comfortably clothed	Skin temp.; heat loss from foot; difference between foot and water temp.	*Indians > Europeans* in initial resistance to temp. decrease but differences decreased with time. Indians lost more heat in 15°C and probably in 10°C baths, but *not* at 5°C. Overall Indian response was better impressionistically, not clearly statistically	Little, 1969
30 Adult Highland Peruvian *Indians*, farmers 26 Adult *Europeans*, University people Sites: Peru, Pennsylvania	Foot exposed to 0°C moving *air*. Subjects comfortably clothed, tested twice each—same day, morning and afternoon	Skin temp.; CIVD	*Indians > Europeans* as to temp., unambiguously and throughout exposure. Highly significant statistical differences; CIVD involved, but not the only circulatory contrast	Little, 1969
41 ♂ Highland Peruvian *Indians*, farmers 10 ♂ Lowland Peruvian *Indians*, farmers 8 ♂ *Europeans*, scientists Site: Peru	Hand exposed to 0°C, moving *air*, 60 minutes. Subjects comfortably clothed and tested twice each	Skin temp.	Lowland *Indians* ≅ Highland *Indians*. *Indians > Europeans*, especially as to finger temp., but may have become ≅ had tests been longer	Little, Thomas, Mazess, and Baker, 1971

Table 7-2 A summary of ethnic differences in response to hand or foot cooling (continued)

Sample compared	Cold testing procedures	Assessment of response (> = warmer; ≅ = equivalent)	Results	Citation
19 Young and young adult Orochons 72 Young and young adult Mongols 52 Young and young adult N. Chinese 367 Young and young adult Japanese Site: Local	Immersion of left index finger in 0°C water, 30 minutes	Index based upon timing and degree of CIVD judged by finger temp.; mean finger temp.	Orochons > North Chinese ≅ Mongols > Japanese	Yoshimura and Iida, 1952
98 Young adult Japanese (cool or cold climate) 36 Young adult Japanese (warm climate) 33 Adult Chinese laborers (cold climate) 27 Adult Chinese laborers (warm climate) Site: Local	See above	See above	Cold climate Chinese > Cold climate Japanese. Warm climate Chinese ≅ Warm climate Japanese	Yoshimura and Iida, 1952
14 Adolescent ♂ and ♀ Ainu 35 Adult ♂ and ♀ Ainu 14 Adolescent ♂ and ♀ Japanese 160 Young adult ♂ and ♀ Japanese	Immersion of left index finger in 0°C water, 20 minutes or more	Index based upon timing and degree of CIVD judged by finger temp.	Cold response of Ainu was equivalent to that of the Japanese of north and central Japan. People of north and central Japan showed warmer responses than southern Japanese	Kondo, 1969

Subjects	Procedure	Measures	Results	Reference
...ated 12 Adult ♂ Europeans, fishermen, cold habituated 11 Adult ♂ Europeans, university people, not cold habituated (control) Site: Northern and southern Norway	water, 30 minutes, followed immediately by immersion of hand in calorimeter water (which started at 0° to 1°C and warmed during the 30-minute test due to hand heat loss). Hand cooled by a plethysmograph cuff-cooler at 40°, 20°, 10°, and 2° to 5°C, 30 minutes each, separate test series	... blood flow vol.; dexterity	ably equivalent. Controls, delayed CIVD onset and poorer post-cooling strength of grip. Lapp > fishermen > controls, dexterity with hands chilled, possibly for blood flow. Pain seemed about ≅ over all.	and Andersen, 1960
30 Young and adult ♀ Lapps, cold habituated 26 Young and adult ♂ Lapps, cold habituated Three groups of Norwegians cited above Site: Finland	Immersion of hand in 0°C water, 15 minutes	Skin temp.; CIVD; blood pressure rise (pressor response)	Finnish Lapps ≅ Norwegian Lapps > Norwegian controls only for earlier CIVD onset. Otherwise, all groups about equivalent, confirming earlier work. No sex or age differences in Lapps	Krog, Alvik, and Lund-Larsen, 1969

endured episodes of extreme climatic cold during the Pleistocene and probably up until fairly recent times. Although cold-selective pressure is now relaxed, the gains of thousands of years of genetic adaptation have not been entirely lost. The European adaptation is apparently a specialized inhibition of "normal" tropical heat conservation. It would appear that for man, the Arctic hunter, keeping the metabolic furnace stoked is less of a problem than is freezing of the hands and feet.

2. *In every experiment in which adult Europeans have been compared to adult natives of Asiatic origin (Eskimos; Indians), the natives show a superior cold response.* Such a statement can be made without reservation, but the larger samples provide especially convincing evidence (Meehan, 1955a; Brown and Page, 1952; Little, 1969; Hanna, 1965). Yet, this can be less clearly ascribed to genetic differences, as in the case of Negro/European comparison. That is, since the Europeans were not exposed to extreme cold in childhood, as were the natives, there is a real question as to whether their "cold adaptation" genes produced up to an optimum potential. Furthermore, many of the Europeans had not had any of the benefits of cold acclimation as adults.

There is some evidence that these observations do indeed reflect genuine genetic ("racial") differences in cold response. Little *et al.* (1971) found that non-cold-exposed Indians from the Peruvian coast responded in the same way as highland Peruvian Indians, who were born and raised in a periodically cold climate (implying that both were genetically adapted and that cold acclimatization does not improve that state). In the same area, Hanna (1965) observed that Indian students (unacclimated) did as well on cold-tests as did acclimatized Indian farmers and that Europeans of both Peruvian and American nationality performed equivalently. In another experiment, a group of Eskimos who lived away from home for 9 months in a moderate climate still responded better than a group of highly cold acclimated European mountaineers (Eagan, 1963). Unfortunately, the critical experiment for this question has yet to be done. It requires the comparison, under identical testing circumstances of a group of Europeans to a group of Asians, both groups cold acclimatized since birth. Although nomadic Lapps and Arctic Indians, for instance, have indeed been tested, the two were not compared directly as to extremity cooling alone (Andersen, 1963). Thus, an important evolutionary question rests unresolved.

Another approach has been used to examine the problem of capacity to develop better responses during adulthood. Several workers have compared groups of people whose occupations chronically cold-expose their extremities to unexposed control groups from the same populations. Most studies (LeBlanc *et al.*, 1960; Nelms and Soper, 1962; Tanaka, 1971) indicate that a better cold response can be developed by cold-occupation groups, but Hellstrom and Andersen (1960) did not confirm this. It is at least clear that habituation markedly reduces cold-induced pain, no matter what other contradictions exist (see also Eagan, 1963).

Let us now return to the European/Asian differences in cold response and assume that northern Asians will eventually be shown to possess a genetic-based response superiority. A number of cultural and historical questions and implications would be raised. The first implication would be that the prehistoric north Asian cultural capacity to provide extremity protection was lower than that seen in Europe, permitting more cold injury (selective) and resulting in a superior Asian adaptation to this day. Equally possible, assuming equivalence of cultural cold-protection patterns, would be the implication that the continental cold of Asia was simply more severe than its maritime Western European counterpart and produced a biologically better cold-adapted Asian. The amount of time spent under selective pressure over-all would seem an equally attractive hypothesis; that is, the longer a group endures selection, the better adapted it becomes. This ignores the likelihood that such physiological adaptations probably reach optimal plateaus after a certain period and that this shouldn't take the entire glacial Pleistocene. It also seems that, if anything, Europeans have lived with severe cold longer than have Asians (Chard, 1969, pp. 80, 93) and should consequently be as well adapted. The final obvious evolutionary possibility has to do with the poorly understood phenomenon of "relaxed selection" in which relief from a selective pressure permits a movement of mean response "back down" from an adaptive plateau. Since Europeans have been sedentary food producers for many generations, compared to only recent Eskimo and Indian shifts away from nomadic hunting-trapping, some genetic cold-resistance may have been lost to the Europeans. This might occur if a balancing type of natural selection were involved, but all this is speculative pending solution of the acclimatization problem.

3. *There may be a clinal distribution of cold-resistance or cold-tolerance in east Asia* (Kondo, 1959; Yoshimura and Iida, 1952; see Table 7-2). The northern and central Japanese showed a cold-resistance index higher than that found in the southern Japanese, and the northern Chinese showed a higher cold-resistance index than the northern Japanese. The

climate of northern China is more severe than that of Hokkido. The ethnically and genetically distinct Ainu, incidently, were no different from their Japanese neighbors. In a comparison of non-cold-acclimatized Chinese, So (1973) has found that those of north Chinese origins kept their hands warmer in cold water than did those of south Chinese origins. This research suggests the presence of a possible cline deriving from genetic adaptation and/or from acclimatization. What it shows is that one "race" or large areal grouping of man may show a great intra-race or intra-group diversity in cold response. If this diversity were truly genetic in origin, it might also suggest that there has been less actual movement of populations of different genetic background in east Asia than has been proposed (Hulse, 1971, p. 387) or that genetic cold adaptation can accrue rather rapidly.

4. *If there is a clinal distribution of cold-resistance across Europe, it has not been demonstrated.* Krog et al. (1960) and Krog et al. (1969) tested the assumption that Lapps (who up until recently were nomadic arctic herders) would be better cold-adapted than other northern Europeans. There do seem to be slight differences (Table 7-2), but the evidence for real contrast is unimpressive. Considering the amount of work Europeans have done elsewhere, their own homelands have been neglected. We must await studies comparing northwestern, northeastern, and Mediterranean Europeans before this issue will be clarified. We would expect at least some differences between the south and other areas, but an unpublished comparison of American Italians and Poles (So, personal communication) has failed to confirm this.

I would like to conclude this discussion of extremity cooling with what I consider to be the problems that must be solved before certain genetic conclusions can be drawn. The first problem concerns the validity of comparing data for a man immobilized in a laboratory setting and that same man out in the natural cold, coping with familiar challenges and using long-perfected skills. We badly need studies in which the same subjects are compared for response under laboratory and field conditions; to the writer's knowledge, only one such study has been reported. Hanna (1970) concluded, using a mixed extremity-whole body method on Peruvian Indians, that laboratory and field cold responses were somewhat similar. He pointed out, however, that this was most true where laboratory conditions and tests closely simulated natural circumstances. His techniques were not closely comparable to much of the data reported in Table 7-2, leaving much to be done on this problem.

The second problem concerns developmental acclimatization. There is some evidence that adults in native, cold-exposed groups maintain warmer extremities than do children from these groups, the children's temperatures often being similar to non-native adults (Yoshimura and Iida, 1952; Miller and Irving, 1962; Little *et al.*, 1971). Neither Krog *et al.* (1969) nor Lund-Larson *et al.* (1970) agree, however. If it is eventually shown that native adults are consistently warmer, it would suggest that a lifetime of exposure to cold is necessary for the development of an *optimum* response, even with the optimum genotype; it would not necessarily imply, however, that no genetically based advantage could be seen unless lifetime cold conditioning occurred. The Negro/European differences already noted indicate some "strictly genetic" factor, no matter what. Also, children have smaller hands and their surface area per unit of weight is higher; both could be the critical variables here rather than strictly physiological factors.

Physiological studies: Whole body cooling

The response of the entire body to cooling is more of a total organismic activity than is the reaction to extremity cooling alone, and measurements of that response have been more diverse. The tests normally expose inadequately clothed people to a cooling medium for periods of from 1 to 8 hours; several surface temperatures (including extremities), deep body temperature, metabolic rate, and comfort (often ability to sleep) are the common indices of response.

Several studies of tropical peoples have fairly closely approximated actual native sleeping conditions "in the bush." Nevertheless, test results of this type are much more difficult to integrate into an adaptive-selective evolutionary model than are hand-cooling experiments. Whereas we can prove the potential selective power of freezing cold, the near-freezing cold of the low tropics would be expected to operate at a slower rate, and more subtly, as a selective force on man; indeed, I would like to argue here that it may have had no recent effect at all (since evidence of cold-associated differential fertility and mortality is lacking). It may well be advantageous for the sleeping tropical native to keep metabolism low (energy conservation) and extremities cool (body heat conservation), while still sleeping soundly (fatigue recuperation). These patterns, however, although possibly selection related, could just as well be acclimatization phenotypes deriving from genotypes that are older than fire and possibly older than the hominid line. In other words, perhaps tropical hunters are not recently cold adapted but rather continue to employ very ancient cold-adaptation mechanisms, common to many mammals. Those mechanisms can no longer be employed by Europeans or Asians who have recently experienced severe cold selection, a selection producing new adaptations that have overridden the older conservation pattern of non-cold climates. The northern cold selection was peripheral, anatomically, and scarcely touched the easily protected body. Warm extremities may demand high metabolism and thus could involve metabolism in an adaptation. Therefore, peoples who have adapted to cold recently may have changed from an older pattern; thus, tropical adaptations to cooling are not recent, positive selection outcomes in the usual sense. Neither tropical nor arctic peoples, in short, have recently experienced whole body cooling selection, and whole body studies may be an indirect measure of adaptations better tested directly. Nevertheless, such studies survive and flourish and will be briefly reviewed here.

Australian Aborigines/Europeans. Scholander *et al.* (1958) observed the responses of two small samples during a native-style night on the desert. Not only did the aborigines sleep better, but they did so while their metabolic rate, deep body temperature, and surface temperatures dropped. The investigators concluded that both physiological and cultural patterns were essential to this "conservation" adaptation, a conclusion supported by Hammel *et al.* (1959). Hammel's team also tested a sample of coastal aborigines who had never really been cold exposed. This group increased their metabolic rate to counter the cold but to a lesser extent than the Europeans and in clear contrast to their desert brethren. So, the desert aboriginal pattern was judged to be both genetic and ontogenetic (acclimatizational) in origin.

South African Bushmen/Europeans. In a follow-up project on Wyndham and Morrison's nearly anecdotal observations (1958), Ward *et al.* (1960) came to the following conclusions. Bushmen are lean of body fat and build, and they respond to cold by allowing their body surfaces to cool in conjunction with relatively high metabolic rates and high core temperatures. This is not greatly different from the European pattern, except that the natives were more comfortable sleeping in the cold. Both scientific teams emphasized the importance of the Bushman's leather cloak as a protective microclimate. Ward's conclusions, however, are weakened by the test design (daytime, three short sequential exposures), which may have introduced subject anxiety or annoyance and disturbed the basal metabolic rate. Consequently, the work of Hammel (1964), in which the standard night-long exposure was applied to a larger sample, offers more valid conclusions. Over-all, Hammel's Bushmen subjects responded by peripheral and deep body cooling, without strong metabolic compensation; that is they reacted very much as did the desert Australian aborigine.

South African Bantus/Europeans. The work of Wyndham *et al.* (1964) is one of the most sophisticated and thought-provoking of the whole body studies. South African black and white males were subjected to a range of air temperatures (5°C to 27°C). The objective of the experiment was to determine whether heat production and conservation mechanisms operate similarly in the two races under various temperatures. Some of the conclusions, which follow, have considerable implication for future studies of this sort.

1. Many cold responses are curvilinear, the curves for the two groups often matching over one part of the range but diverging over another part.

2. European extremities were warmer above 17°C ambient temperature, but equivalent between 5° and 17°C; there is also a hint that they might have been warmer at 0°C from the direction of the curve, but no proof of this was obtained. The Bantu metabolic rate was higher at high and low ambient temperatures, but not at moderate ambient temperatures.

3. A number of differences were attributed to the constitution of the smaller, more lightly built, poorly insulated Bantu; the clearest examples were high body skin temperatures and low rectal temperatures of the Bantus in the colder air. This suggests that these tests may have taxed the subjects somewhat, under circumstances simulating a possibly selective stress.

American Negroes/Europeans. Several reports have concluded that American Blacks and whites show few dramatic differences in whole body response to cooling. Adams and Covino (1958) did find, despite equivalent extremity temperatures and body cooling rates, that the metabolic response in Negroes was slower. Iampietro *et al.* (1959) came to similar conclusions but observed that in Negroes there was more over-all surface cooling by the end of the 2 hours at 10°C (nude). Working with Black and white groups matched for per cent body fat, Baker (1959) found that subcutaneous fat was an effective buffer against deep body heat loss and, also, that it worked more efficiently in whites than Blacks (possibly due to a more radiative, linear body build in the latter). Perhaps the 10°C temperature in these experiments was not cold enough to bring out potential differences.

Eskimos/Europeans. It is generally agreed that Eskimos can afford a non-conservation response to body cooling, with an elevation of both metabolic rate and skin temperature compared to Europeans (Rodahl and Rennie, 1957; Adams and Covino, 1958; Hart *et al.*, 1960; Rennie *et al.*, 1962; Milan *et al.*, 1963); with the hotter skin goes a higher sweat rate (Rodahl and Rennie, 1957). Most workers would also agree, however, that these differences are probably attributable to the thermogenic Eskimo diet and his relatively high muscle mass-low subcutaneous fat body build and that Eskimos and Europeans do not differ significantly. There is disagreement between Rennie *et al.* (1963), who do not hold with a special Eskimo total surface circulation adaptation, and Milan *et al.* (1963), who do; either way, it is clear that both Eskimos and Europeans show a biological-cultural pattern that calls for producing and losing quantities of heat. Indeed, Rennie *et al.* (1962) have suggested that this may be a positive adaptation to keep down heat load when working, and it is in clear contrast to adaptation in tropical desert peoples. See Rennie (1963) for a review.

Arctic Indians/Europeans. The differences between Arctic Indians and Europeans appear to be even less marked than those between Eskimos and Europeans. During cooling, Indian surface skin temperatures are equivalent to European, while extremities are warmer. Meehan (1955b) and Milan *et al.* (1963) found higher native metabolic rates, although Irving *et al.* (1960) did not; and, if Indians allowed their deep body temperature to fall (Meehan, 1955; Irving *et al.*, 1960), total agreement was not seen (Milan *et al.*, 1963). At least some of these disagreements may be due to the different tests used; Irving's team was using the most widely comparable "Scholander bag," 8-hour night exposure. It is of interest that outdoor clothing comfortable to the natives was inadequate for the European visitors, once more suggesting the need of more realistic cold-exposure methods.

Other American Indians/Europeans. Hammel (1966) investigated the few surviving Alacaluf peoples of the frigid southern tip of South America; the 8-hour sleeping-bag test was used. Metabolic rate started high (native anxiety?) but declined to European levels ultimately; deep body temperature also declined (0.8°C, an appreciable fall) but only to average European values. At the end of the test, body surface temperatures were lower than and foot temperatures higher than those of the Europeans. In general, this pattern is not unlike that of arctic Indians.

According to Baker *et al.* (1967), a pilot study by Elsner and Bolstad on Highland Peruvian Indians demonstrated warm extremities and lowering deep body temperatures during a "sleeping-bag" cold test. From their own work (employing a 2-hour test period), Baker's team confirmed the higher native peripheral temperatures and concluded that Indians show less "metabolic compensation" (heat production) to balance this loss, ultimately tolerating lower core temperatures than the Europeans. Although reservations were expressed about the final conclusions (due to the shortness of the test), they agreed, in essence, with those of Elsner and Bolstad.

Asian/European. Hanna and Hong (1972) investigated tropical water cold acclimation among Hawaiian swimmers of Japanese and of European backgrounds; the goal was to gain an understanding of insulative mechanisms. The results showed no ethnic differences, but workers concerned with acclimation should read this paper.

Lapps/Norwegians (European). In a limited study, Scholander and his co-workers (1957) were not able to find differences in whole body adaptation between Norwegians and Lapps, but they did conclude that Lappish clothing was quite effective in cold protection. A follow-up effort (Andersen *et al.*, 1960), using the night-long sleeping-bag test, is technically more acceptable. Village Lapps, strongly acclimatized nomadic Lapps, and Norwegian controls all responded with equivalent increases in metabolic rate. That is, all compensated metabolically for heat loss. The nomads also slept better than the other Lapps (who slept better than the controls) and did so with warmer extremities but falling core temperatures. Therefore nomads showed *relatively* less metabolic compensation (due to heat loss), but they still showed the European type of metabolic response.

WHOLE BODY COOLING STUDIES: CONCLUSIONS

No firm, clear conclusions comparable to those for extremity cooling can be drawn. There may be a tendency for natives of the warm tropics to experience decreases of both extremity and deep body core temperatures without responding metabolically, whereas northern peoples tend to produce and "waste" heat for hand and foot warmth. These same tropical peoples, as well as cold-adapted ones, seem to have developed the capacity to sleep well in a chill setting. In the desert Australians and African Bushmen, this is accomplished by tolerating colder tissues, whereas other ethnic groups appear to sleep well because they can keep their extremities warm. We would expect this (see introduction to this section), but we cannot completely accept these results because many of the test protocols cannot be compared and because of the presence of uncontrollable cross-cultural factors of anxiety, diet, body mass and build, variable insulation, and so on.

Physiological studies: Special applications

Rather than seeking answers to traditional problems in biological anthropology, anthropologists have used physiological techniques to study an entirely new branch of the field; the methodology and conclusions of that branch have been outlined above. One exception to this trend, however, is the series of studies in which human facial form has been examined as a possible end product of natural selection by cold. Defining the distribution and adaptive functions of human craniofacial form is one of anthropology's oldest preoccupations.

In 1950, Coon *et al.* proposed dry cold as an evolutionary force that molded northern Mongoloid facial features into their present broad, low-profiled, impressionistically "rounded" form; specifically, frostbite selection would have operated by freezing the sharper noses, thinner cheeks, and smaller cheekbones within groups of paleolithic Asian northerners, to ultimately lead to the present "adapted" phenotype. Steegmann (1965, 1972) tested this adaptive model by measuring human facial temperatures under controlled laboratory conditions, the objective being to see whether people with protrusive noses or narrow faces do indeed experience more cooling at these sites. By comparisons within and between group data (European and Asian), he reached the following conclusions.

1. The larger, more protrusive cheekbones of Asians get *colder* rather than warmer in a o°C breeze.

2. Nose temperature seems to increase with head size, but it is unrelated to nose shape or protrusiveness. Increased thickness of subcutaneous fat also decreases surface temperature.

Therefore, if the head had been tailored for frostbite resistance (warm surfaces), it would not have become the present north Asian head. These observations, plus the low frequency of craniofacial frostbite today (Steegmann, 1967), led to the rejection of the "frostbite" hypothesis; this is not, however, a rejection of other types of cold selection, such as the role of sinus infection in the formation of the human face, and broader interpretations are presented in the literature (Steegmann, 1970, 1972).

We look forward to other applications of local physiology/anatomy tests; Little *et al.* (1971) suggested, for instance, such a special vascular adaptation in the highly cold-exposed Indian foot, and Hildes *et al.*

(1961) noted that hand size (or relative size of warm-tissue mass) may also have a special function.

Physiological studies: An interpretative problem

One of the great accomplishments of evolutionary biology has been the successful promotion of populational thinking over typological; we have at last become convinced that microevolution, especially, can never be understood unless the concept of the group occupies a primary place in our thoughts and analyses as the basic unit of study. A group, however, is not just a mean and a variance, and many authors (this one included) tend to forget this. I raise this issue because physiological studies have, by-and-large, not rested comfortably in the analytic structures of balancing or directional selection. There are many good reasons why that is true.

If directional selection is operating on a group (by freezing feet, for instance), it will, by definition, eliminate or incapacitate individuals who have feet that get cold no matter what they do. There is an enormous amount of undigested data, in the articles reviewed above and others, too, concerning one or more *individuals* in a sample who simply cannot rise to the challenge. In many cases, this "negative response" syndrome dichotomizes the sample, and this may be noted in data from Eagan (1963), Meehan (1955a), and Miller and Irving (1962) among others. Ironically, anthropologists who might see the selective implications tend rather to look at group statistics, whereas the more individually oriented physiologists tend to be less aware of evolutionary mechanics.

Differences of this sort must be plotted to be seen. For instance, if two samples of, say, twenty people are compared, one sample may contain a low "tail" of two inadequate responders. Depending on the shape of the curves, this may be lost in a "*t*-test" analysis, and yet this is the most significant finding. In a selective model, the loss of two people out of twenty would be massive selection, indeed (assuming poor response is genetically caused). This is the place to note rather than pursue this analytic problem, and I can only conclude with the observation that a union of evolutionary genetics and cold response physiology or pathology is long past due.

SUMMARY

Based on a survey of available evidence, *Homo sapiens* shows the following genetic or non-genetic adaptations to environmental cold.

1. People living in cold areas are heavier than those living in warmer areas; this may be a result of both genetic adaptation and dietary influence and may in part function to generate and conserve body heat. Superficial body fat also helps conserve heat.

2. The foregoing adaptation also involves relatively shorter extremities, larger chests, and less body surface area per unit of weight in natives of colder climates.

3. The human nose is narrower and higher (vertically) in cold climates. The strongest evidence suggests that this *may* be due to the low absolute humidity associated with cold air rather than with cold per se. A relatively narrow nose is, apparently, a more efficient air humidifier and heater than a broad one, but this remains to be proved.

4. Cold dry climates are associated with round headedness in man. The functional implications may involve heat conservation.

5. Non-tropical, or perhaps non-African, peoples show a physiological extremity-warming adaptation, which is almost certainly genetic and probably a product of natural selection. In the same sense, north Asians may show a superior warming adaptation to north Europeans.

6. There are no clear racial contrasts in cold response to cooling of the entire body that can be separated from the stronger adaptation noted in point 5, above."

(Damon 7**5**)

REFERENCES

Adams, T. and B. J. Covino. 1958. Racial variations to a standardized cold stress. *J. Appl. Physiol.* 12:9-12.

Andersen, K. L. 1963. Comparison of Scandinavian Lapps, Arctic fishermen, and Canadian Arctic Indians. *Fed. Proc.* 22 (3):834-39.

Andersen, K. L., Y. Loyning, J. D. Nelms, O. Wilson, R. H. Fox, and A. Bolstad. 1960. Metabolic and thermal response to a moderate cold exposure in nomadic Lapps. *J. Appl. Physiol.* 15:649-53.

Baker, P. T. 1959. American Negro-White differences in the thermal insulative aspects of body fat. *Human Biol.* 31:316-24.

Baker, P. T., E. R. Buskirk, J. Kollias, and R. B. Mazess. 1967. Temperature regulation at high altitude: Quechua Indians and U.S. Whites during total body cold exposure. *Human Biol.* 39:155-69.

Barnett, S. A. 1965. Adaptation of mice to cold. *Biol. Rev.* 40:5-51.

Beals, K. L. 1972. Head form and climatic stress. *Amer. J. Phys. Anthropol.* 37:85-92.

Brown, G. M. and J. Page. 1952. The effect of chronic exposure to cold on temperature and blood flow to the hand. *J. Appl. Physiol.* 5:221-27.

Buskirk, E. R. 1966. Variation in heat production during acute exposure of men and women to cold air or water. *Ann. N.Y. Acad. Sci.* 134 (2):733-42.

Buskirk, E. R., R. H. Thompson, and G. D. Whedon. 1963. Metabolic response to cooling in the human: Role of body composition and particularly of body fat. In *Temperature—Its Measurement and Control in Science and Industry* 3, Part 3, ed. J. D. Hardy. New York: Reinhold, pp. 429-42.

Carlson, L. D. and H. L. Thrush. 1960. *Human Acclimatization to Cold. A Selected Annotated Bibliography of the Concepts of Adaptation and Acclimatization as Studied in Man.* Fairbanks: Arctic Aeromedical Laboratory TR# 59-18.

Chard, C. S. 1969. *Man in Prehistory.* New York: McGraw-Hill.

Coffey, M. F. 1954. A comparative study of young Eskimo and Indian males with acclimatized white males. In *Cold Injury*, ed. M. I. Ferrer. New York: Josiah Macy, Jr., Foundation.

Coon, C. S., S. M. Garn, and J. B. Birdsell. 1950. *Races—A Study of the Problems of Race Formation in Man.* Springfield, Ill.: Charles C. Thomas.

Davies, A. 1932. A resurvey of the nose in relation to climate. *J. Roy. Anthropol. Inst.* 62:337-59 (now called *Man*).

Eagan, C. J. 1963. Local vascular adaptations to cold in man. *Fed. Proc.* 22 (3):947-51.

Elsner, R. W., J. D. Nelms, and L. Irving. 1960. Circulation of heat to the hands of Arctic Indians. *J. Appl. Physiol.* 15:662-66.

Folk, G. E. Jr. 1966. *Introduction to Environmental Physiology.* Philadelphia: Lea & Febiger.

Hammel, H. T. 1960. *Thermal and Metabolic Responses of the Alacaluf Indians to Moderate Cold Exposure.* Wright Air Development Division TR# 60-663.

Hammel, H. T. 1964. Terrestrial animals in cold: Recent studies of primitive man. In *Adaptation to Environment*, ed. D. B. Dill. Washington: American Physiological Society.

Hammel, H. T., R. W. Elsner, D. H. LeMessurier, H. T. Andersen, and F. A. Milan. 1959. Thermal and metabolic responses of Australian Aborigines. *J. Appl. Physiol.* 14:605-15.

Hanna, J. M. 1965. *Biological and Cultural Factors in Peripheral Blood Flow at Low Temperatures.* M.A. Thesis, The Pennsylvania State University.

Hanna, J. M. 1970. A comparison of laboratory and field studies of cold response. *Am. J. Phys. Anthropol.* 32:227-32.

Hanna, J. M. and S. K. Hong. 1972. Critical water temperature and effective insulation in scuba divers in Hawaii. *J. Appl. Physiol.* 33:770-73.

Hart, J. S., H. B. Sabean, J. A. Hildes, F. DePocas, H. T. Hammel, K. L. Andersen, L. Irving, and G. Foy. 1962. Thermal and metabolic responses of coastal Eskimos during a cold night. *J. Appl. Physiol.* 17:953-60.

Hellström, B. and K. L. Andersen. 1960. Heat output in the cold from hands of Arctic fishermen. *J. Appl. Physiol.* 15:771-75.

Hiernaux, J. 1968. *La Diversité Humaine en Afrique subsaharienne.* Bruxelles: L'Institut de Sociologie, Université Libre de Bruxelles.

Hildes, J. A., L. Irving, and J. S. Hart. 1961. Estimation of heat flow from hands of Eskimos by calorimetry. *J. Appl. Physiol.* 16:617-23.

Hulse, F. S. 1971. *The Human Species.* New York: Random House.

Iampietro, P. F., R. F. Goldman, E. R. Buskirk, and D. E. Bass. 1959. Response of Negro and white males to cold. *J. Appl. Physiol.* 14:798-800.
Irving, L., K. L. Andersen, A. Bolstad, R. Elsner, J. A. Hildes, Y. Loyning, J. D. Nelms, L. J. Peyton, and R. D. Whaley. 1960. Metabolism and temperature of Arctic Indian men during a cold night. *J. Appl. Physiol.* 15:635-44.
Koertvelyessy, T. 1972. Relationships between the frontal sinus and climatic conditions: A skeletal approach to cold adaptation. *Amer. J. Phys. Anthropol.* 37:161-72.
Kondo, S. 1969. A study on acclimatization of the Ainu and the Japanese with reference to hunting temperature reaction. *J. Faculty Science, Tokyo University* Sect. V, III-4:253-65.
Krog, J., B. Folkow, Jr., R. H. Fox, and K. L. Andersen. 1960. Hand circulation in the cold of Lapps and North Norwegian fishermen. *J. Appl. Physiol.* 15:654-58.
Krog, J., M. Ålvik, and K. Lund-Larson. 1969. Investigations of the circulatory effects of submersion of the hand in ice water in Finnish Lapps, the "Skolts." *Fed. Proc.* 28 (3):1135-37.
LeBlanc, J., J. A. Hildes, and O. Heroux. 1960. Tolerance of Gaspé fishermen to cold water. *J. Appl. Physiol.* 15:1031-34.
Lee, M. M. C., P. C. Chu, and H. C. Chan. 1969. Effects of cold on the skeletal growth of albino rats. *Amer. J. Anat.* 124:239-50.
Lewin, T. 1971. History of the Skolt Lapps. *Snomen Hammaslääkäriseuran Toimituksia* 67 (Suppl. I):13-23.
Little, M. A. 1968. Appendix I. In *Racial and Developmental Factors in Foot Cooling: Quechua Indians and U.S. Whites*. Occasional Papers in Anthropology. No. 1. The Pennsylvania State University, pp. 327-517.
Little, M. A. 1969. Temperature regulation at high altitude: Quechua Indians and U.S. Whites during foot exposure to cold water and cold air. *Human Biol.* 41:519-35.
Little, M. A., R. B. Thomas, R. B. Mazess, and P. T. Baker. 1971. Population differences and developmental changes in extremity temperature responses to cold among Andean Indians. *Human Biol.* 43:70-91.
Little, M. A. and D. H. Hochner. 1973. *Human Thermoregulation, Growth, and Mortality*. Addison-Wesley Module in Anthropology, No. 36. Reading, Mass.: Addison-Wesley.
Lund-Larson, K., M. Wika, and J. Krog. 1970. Circulatory responses of the hand of Greenlanders to local cold stimulation. *Arctic Anthropol.* 7:21-25.
Mason, E. D. and M. Jacob. 1972. Variations in basal metabolic rate responses to changes between tropical and temperate climates. *Human Biol.* 44:141-72.
Mayr, E. 1963. *Animal Species and Evolution*. Cambridge, Mass.: Belnap Press of Harvard University Press.
Meehan, J. P. 1955a. Individual and racial variations in vascular response to cold stimulus. *Military Med.* 116:330-34.
Meehan, J. P. 1955b. Body heat production and surface temperatures in response to cold stimulus. *J. Appl. Physiol.* 7:537-41.
Milan, F. A., J. P. Hannon, and E. Evonuk. 1963. Temperature regulation of Eskimos, Indians, and Caucasians in a bath calorimeter. *J. Appl. Physiol.* 18:378-82.

Miller, L. K. and L. Irving. 1962. Local reactions to air cooling in an Eskimo population. *J. Appl. Physiol.* 17:449-55.

Nelms, J. D. and D. J. G. Soper. 1962. Cold vasodilatation and cold acclimatization in the hands of British fish filleters. *J. Appl. Physiol.* 17:444-48.

Newman, M. T. 1960. Adaptations in the physique of American aborigines to nutritional factors. *Human Biol.* 32:288-313.

Newman, M. T. 1953. The application of ecological rules to the racial anthropology of the aboriginal New World. *Amer. Anthropol.* 55:311-25.

Newman, R. W. 1967. A comparison of Negro and White responses in a 5°C water bath (Abst). *Amer. J. Phys. Anthropol.* 27:249.

Newman, R. W. 1970. Why man is such a sweaty and thirsty naked animal: A speculative review. *Human Biol.* 42:12-27.

Newman, R. W. and E. H. Munro. 1955. The relation of climate and body size in U.S. males. *Amer. J. Phys. Anthropol.* 13:1-17.

Rennie, D. W. 1963. Comparison of nonacclimatized Americans and Alaskan Eskimos. *Fed. Proc.* 22 (part 3):828-30.

Rennie, D. W. and T. Adams. 1957. Comparative thermoregulatory responses of Negroes and white persons to acute cold stress. *J. Appl. Physiol.* 11: 201-204.

Rennie, D. W., B. G. Covino, M. R. Blair, and K. Rodahl. 1962. Physical regulation of temperature in Eskimos. *J. Appl. Physiol.* 17:326-32.

Riesenfeld, A. 1973. The effects of extreme temperatures and starvation on the body proportions of the rat. *Am. J. Phys. Anthropol.* 39:427-60.

Roberts, D. F. 1952. Basal metabolism, race, and climate. *J. Roy. Anthropol. Inst.* 82:169-83 (now called *Man*).

Roberts, D. F. 1953. Body weight, race, and climate. *Amer. J. Phys. Anthropol.* 11:533-58.

Roberts, D. F. 1973. *Climate and Human Variability*. Addison-Wesley Module in Anthropology, No. 34. Reading, Mass.: Addison-Wesley.

Rodahl, K. and D. W. Rennie. 1957. *Comparative Sweat Rates of Eskimos and Caucasians*. Arctic Aeromedical Laboratory PN8-7951, Part 7.

Sargent, F. II and K. P. Weinman. 1966. Physiological individuality. *Ann. N.Y. Acad. Sci.* 134:696-719.

Scholander, P. F., K. L. Andersen, J. Krog, F. V. Lorentzen, and J. Steen. 1957. Critical temperature in Lapps. *J. Appl. Physiol.* 10:231-34.

Scholander, P. F., H. T. Hammel, J. S. Hart, D. H. LeMessurier, and J. Steen. 1958. Cold adaptation in Australian aborigines. *J. Appl. Physiol.* 13: 211-18.

Schreider, E. 1950. Geographic distribution of the body weight/body surface ratio. *Nature* 165:286.

Schreider, E. 1951. Anatomical factors in body heat regulation. *Nature* 167: 823-24.

Schreider, E. 1966. Typology and biometrics. *Ann. N.Y. Acad. of Sci.* 134: 789-803.

Schuman, L. M. 1953. Epidemiology of frostbite, Korea, 1951-1952. In *Cold Injury—Korea, 1951-1952*. U.S. Army Medical Research Laboratory (Ft. Knox, Ky.), Report 113:205-568.

So, J. 1973. *Physiological Response to Extremity Cooling among North and South Chinese* (Abst). American Association Physical Anthropologists Meetings, Dallas, Texas, April 1973.

Steegmann, A. T., Jr. 1965. A study of relationships between facial cold response and some variables of facial morphology. *Amer. J. Phys. Anthropol.* 23:355-62.

Steegmann, A. T., Jr. 1967. Frostbite of the human face as a selective force. *Human Biol.* 39:131-44.

Steegmann, A. T., Jr. 1970. Cold adaptation and the human face. *Amer. J. Phys. Anthropol.* 32:243-50.

Steegmann, A. T., Jr. 1972. Cold response, body form, and craniofacial shape in two racial groups of Hawaii. *Amer. J. Phys. Anthropol.* 37:193-222.

Steegmann, A. T., Jr., and W. S. Platner. 1968. Experimental cold modification of cranio-facial morphology. *Amer. J. Phys. Anthropol.* 28:17-30.

Steegmann, A. J., Jr., n.d. Ethnic and anthropometric factors in finger cooling: Japanese and Europeans of Hawaii. *Human Biol.* (in press).

Sumner, D. S., T. L. Criblez, and W. H. Doolittle. 1971. Host factors in human frostbite (Abst). Amer. Assn. Adv. Science, Alaska Science Conference Proceedings 22, August 1971.

Tanaka, M. 1971. Experimental studies on human reaction to cold. *Bull. Tokyo Medical & Dental University* 18:169-77.

Thomson, A. 1913. The correlations of isotherms with variations in the nasal index. *Intl. Cong. Med. (London)* Section 1, 2:89-90.

Thomson, A. and L. H. D. Buxton. 1923. Man's nasal index in relation to certain climatic conditions. *J. Roy. Anthropol. Inst.* 53:92-122 (now called *Man*).

Veghte, J. H. 1964. Respiratory and microclimate temperatures within the parka hood in extreme cold. *Aerospace Medical Research Laboratory* (Wright-Patterson AFB) *TDR-64-79.*

Walker, J. E. C. and R. E. Wells with E. W. Merrill. 1961. Heat and water exchange in the respiratory tract. *Amer. J. Med.* 30:259-67.

Ward, J. S., G. A. G. Bredell, and H. G. Wenzel. 1960. Responses of Bushmen and Europeans on exposure to winter night. *J. Appl. Physiol.* 15:667-70.

Webb, P. 1951. Air temperatures in the respiratory tracts of resting subjects in cold. *J. Appl. Physiol.* 4:378-82.

Weiner, J. S. 1954. Nose shape and climate. *Amer. J. Phys. Anthropol.* 12:1-4.

Wolpoff, M. H. 1968. Climatic influence on skeletal nasal aperture. *Amer. J. Phys. Anthropol.* 29:405-24.

Wyndham, C. H. and J. F. Morrison. 1958. Adjustment to cold of Bushmen in the Kalahari Desert. *J. Appl. Physiol.* 13:219-25.

Wyndham, C. H., J. S. Ward, N. B. Strydom, J. F. Morrison, C. G. Williams, G. A. G. Bredell, J. Peter, M. J. E. Von Rahden, L. Holdsworth, C. H. Van Graan, A. J. Van Rensburg, and A. Munro. 1964. Physiological reactions of Caucasian and Bantu males in acute exposure to cold. *J. Appl. Physiol.* 19:583-92.

Yoshimura, H. and T. Iida. 1952. Studies on the reactivity of skin vessels to extreme cold. II. Factors governing the individual difference of the reactivity, or the resistance against frostbite. *Jap. J. Physiol.* 2:177-85.

8. Human Adaptation to High Altitude

RICHARD B. MAZESS*

INTRODUCTION

There are two paramount problem areas in dealing with adaptation to environmental stress: (a) delineation of the actual pattern of structural, functional, or behavioral response and (b) evaluation of the assignment of adaptive value to a response based on the relative benefit of that response to the individual or population. The assessment of adaptation in high altitude zones presents an interesting paradigm for approaching this dual problem. As with other environmental stresses, the description of responses to high altitude has advanced to a far greater extent than has sophistication in the evaluation of adaptive value. In fact, descriptions of responses to high altitude, whether pertaining to newcomers, sojourners, or residents, have often omitted explicit consideration of relative benefit, or, even worse, ascriptions of adaptive value have been based on unstated or unsupported assumptions with regard to selective advantage or enhanced performance. This review will not summarize the already abundant data describing responses to hypoxia and high altitude. A recent bibliography on the subject containing 4000 references is available (Wulff et al., 1968). In the past decade, responses to high altitude and to hypoxia have been well documented in a variety of books (Chernigovsky, 1969; Dickens and Neil, 1963; Hart et al., 1969; Hatcher and Jennings, 1965; Hegnauer, 1969; Makarchenko, 1964; Pan American Health Organization, 1966; Porter and Knight, 1971; Van Liere and Stickney, 1963; Vogel, 1970; Weihe, 1969a)

* Cosmic Medicine Laboratory, University of Wisconsin Hospitals, Madison, Wisconsin.

and in numerous major review articles (Hurtado, 1963, 1964a,b; Baker, 1969, 1971; Barbashova, 1967, 1969; Clegg *et al.*, 1970; Dill, 1968; Grover, 1968; Hock, 1970; Hultgren and Grover, 1968; Lahiri and Milledge, 1965; Margaria and Cerretelli, 1962; Mazess, 1970; McFarland, 1969a; Otis, 1963; Robin and Murdaugh, 1967; Timiras, 1965). Instead, in this chapter I will concentrate on the broad categorization of responses to high altitude and with assessment of adaptive value.

As with all ecological zones, the environment of altitude regions may be separated into major bioclimatological components (Prohaska, 1970) and even further subdivided into micro-environmental stresses. The most apparent stresses for man at altitude include:

1. Hypoxia
2. High solar radiation
3. Cold
4. Aridity
5. High winds
6. Limited nutritional base
7. Rough terrain

Of these, the first is of predominant physiological interest, since the other stresses are present to equal or greater degrees in other geographical zones, but hypoxic hypoxia, the low oxygen tension (partial pressure of oxygen) resulting from reduced barometric pressure at altitude, stands alone. It is worth noting here that the stresses on human populations are not directly correlated with elevation above sea level alone; the difficulties at 3000 m in the Alps are far different, and more severe, than are the difficulties at comparable altitudes in the Andes. Even barometric pressure and the degree of hypoxia vary widely at comparable elevations in different geographical areas (Moore, 1968) so that care must be exercised when elevation is used as an index of stress.

Human populations in the course of territorial expansion have met and conquered most environmental stresses, and in the past 10,000 years human populations have even expanded into the hostile highlands where large populations and even such civilizations as the Incan developed. Even so, it is estimated that only 12% of the planet's population live in mountainous zones, and probably no more than a few per cent live above 3000 m where altitude stress becomes apparent (Clegg *et al.*, 1970). It is probably not hypoxia that is responsible for this limited population, but rather other factors, particularly the limited nutritional base, that have hindered expansion.

High altitude hypoxia is interesting to a physiological anthropologist for several reasons, even though it affects only a small segment of the earth's people. First, the hypoxia at altitude is a pervasive and ever-present stress, which can be ameliorated only slightly by altering behavioral patterns or by developing special altitude technologies. All organ systems and physiological functions are affected by hypoxia, often adversely, and these functional modifications can only be studied over time at altitude. In contrast, most environmental stresses, such as thermal stress or high insolation, are not all pervasive, affect limited organ systems, and can be ameliorated by modification of behavior or even by simple technology. The responses of newcomers, sojourners, and residents at high altitudes must be chiefly biological, and the study of these responses could provide a general framework for the evaluation of human adaptation to the climatic environment. Second, although hypoxia is ever present only at altitude, it is encountered commonly though intermittently at sea level. Tissue hypoxia may be a critical element in a variety of clinical conditions, including aging, neurological deterioration, and certain diseases (McFarland, 1969a); it is also a factor in producing training effects for exercise and in certain other conditions. Examination of the "unusual" condition of altitude hypoxia may provide abundant insights into the more usual responses of the organism at sea level to less severe and less continuous hypoxia.

Over the past half-century, major studies have been conducted in most of the mountainous regions of the world, but it is apparent that the greatest amount of work has been done in the Andes. The establishment of the Institute of Andean Studies in Peru and the pioneering work of Dr. Carlos Monge (1948, 1954) and Dr. Alberto Hurtado (1963, 1964a,b) not only provided basic information but led to the establishment of other altitude laboratories in Peru and in Chile, Bolivia, and Argentina. Monge (1948) advanced a major hypothesis that the Andean natives constitute a distinctive race with "genetic adaptations" to altitude, and this hypothesis, however unsupported and misleading, greatly influenced subsequent research on highland peoples (Baker, 1969). Evaluation of the genetic basis for population adaptation to a major environmental stress in a human population is a third reason for high altitude effect studies, and it certainly is of the greatest significance to anthropologists.

ASSESSING ADAPTATION TO HYPOXIA

The fundamental basis for assessing human adaptation involves the evaluation of (a) relative benefit or (b) degree of necessity, relative to an environmental stress (Mazess, 1975a). There are diverse criteria for such an evaluation, and the criteria differ at infra-individual, individual, and populational levels. For the genetically oriented anthropologist, the denotation of characteristics as "adaptive" often implies selective advantage or, perhaps, fitness. More generally, populational adaptation involves evaluation of benefit in one or more of several domains; these include reproductive advantage (selection, fitness), demographic optimality (age-sex structure), spatial-temporal spread (dominance, persistence), and energetic or ecological efficiency (biomass, numbers). There has been almost no direct evaluation of population adaptation in humans, and there is little or no direct evidence that human populations at high altitude are adapted at the population level.

In human and other populations, population adaptation is nearly always evaluated by extrapolation from individual adaptation. The supposed abilities and advantages of highlanders relative to lowlanders, such as an increased work capacity or enhanced ventilatory efficiency, have formed the basis for assuming that altitude populations are adapted (Mazess, 1970; Monge, 1948; Baker, 1969, 1971; Clegg et al., 1970). I will therefore focus on individual adaptation and only secondarily on adaptation at the infra-individual and population levels.

Adaptation at the individual level is assessed by examining relative benefit in one or more of the several key areas of life that may be called "adaptive domains" (Mazess, 1975a,b). These domains include:

1. Physical performance—exercise and motor abilities, skills
2. Nervous system functioning—sensory, motor, and neural function
3. Growth and development—progression in rate and attainment
4. Nutrition—requirements, utilization, efficiency
5. Reproduction—survival, reproductive advantage
6. Health—morbidity, mortality, disease resistance
7. Cross-tolerance and resistance—generalized stress resistance
8. Affective functioning—happiness, tolerance, sexuality
9. Intellectual ability—learning, expression

To assess adaptation to altitude hypoxia, putative responses to that stress must be shown to be of advantage in one or more of these areas. Actually, we are limited in our ability to make such an assessment in the latter two adaptive domains, and this survey of hypoxic adaptation will concentrate on the first seven domains.

Finally, the dominant interest of non-anthropologists has been and continues to be adaptation at the infra-individual level, most typically organ-system adaptations. Just as population or individual adaptation denotes relative advantage to the population or to the organism in some specific domains, so does infra-individual adaptation imply benefit or necessity. At this level, that of physiological changes and acclimatization, the notions of benefit and necessity are translated as (a) homeostasis, or the maintenance of function, and (b) resistance or tolerance. At high altitude the pervasive hypoxia produces a definite stress at the beginning of the oxygen transport chain. The responses at infra-individual levels are usually assessed as adaptive in at least two broad ways: (a) by increasing oxygen transport at any level between the inspired air and the utilizing tissue, thereby aiding or maintaining function (i.e., homeostasis) or (b) by allowing function to continue despite lowered oxygen tension, thereby conferring resistance or tolerance. Western physiologists have been most concerned with oxygen transport and homeostasis, whereas eastern European and Russian physiologists have been most concerned with anoxia resistance, particularly at the cellular level.

It should be noted that the level of adaptation considered pertains to the level at which significance (that is, benefit) is purported to occur. Thus, a cellular change that maintains homeostasis would be an infra-individual adaptation, but, if it benefitted the individual or population, then it would be considered an individual or a population adaptation. The existence of an infra-individual adaptation, such as a homeostatic maintenance of oxygen tension, cannot be construed as individual adaptation, nor can individual differences in, say, exercise performance in hypoxia, be directly construed as a demonstration of population adaptation.

PROBLEMS IN ASSESSING ADAPTATION TO ALTITUDE

The assessment of altitude adaptation involves several specific types of difficulties, which are also characteristic of environmental adaptation in general. First, assessment requires examination of relative benefit or necessity in an adaptive domain. It is not sufficient to show that a response occurs, or that individuals or populations differ in their responses, but rather that some benefit is conferred. It is all too common for the ascription of adaptive benefit to be made without any substantial investigation of actual effects. In altitude research it has been usual for the characteristics of native highlanders, such as a large chest or high hematocrits, to be viewed as distinctive and, hence, beneficial (Monge, 1948). A subtopic of this particular problem is the equivocation so common among adaptive domains. For example, an organ-system response, such as hyperventilation, which increases oxygen transport might be supposed to benefit individuals, or even populations, without any demonstration of advantage in any domains. Similarly, differences among populations in such individual adaptive domains as exercise performance are postulated as being population adaptations even where the inference of population advantage is completely unsupported.

Second, there is a tendency, especially among anthropologists, to define phenotypically stable adaptive characteristics as "genetic adaptations." These stable characteristics I have termed "aptitudes" (Mazess, 1975b), in contrast to phenotypically labile responses, which are "acclimatizations." Thus, the often-quoted relationships between body size, body shape, and thermal extremes are sometimes viewed as examples of genetic adaptation to climate, whereas acclimatizations are viewed as "nongenetic" adaptations. Actually, both aptitudes and acclimatizations have genetic components, and these may differ among ethnic groups and be subject to evolutionary change. Acclimatization responses have appeared to be far more important than aptitudes in altitude hypoxia; the only common example of a hypoxic aptitude, and one often mistakenly thought of as a genetic adaptation, is large chest size and, presumably, large lung size. It is clear that large chests or lungs are no more, or less, genetic than are such ventilatory acclimatizations as hyperventilation. The heritability of aptitudes and acclimatizations to altitude hypoxia and to other environmental stresses is one area where virtually nothing is known and where immediate research is needed. Not only have there not been detailed heritability studies, but there have not even been controlled comparisons among populations of highlanders and lowlanders taking into account differences of exposure, nutrition, training, and disease. Perhaps it would be best to abandon the search for the so-called genetic adaptations, and to begin determination of the genetic basis for infra-individual, individual, and population adaptations.

Finally, it is necessary to note that the adaptive benefit may be temporally, spatially, and populationally specific. For example, those characteristics that occur with long-term exposure may not be advantageous in short-term exposure and, in fact, may be harmful. Take the case of a hyperventilatory response to lowered ambient oxygen tension, which increases the alveolar oxygen tension and aids oxygen transport. Hyperventilation in response to hypoxia is a basic functional characteristic of both lowlanders and highlanders, although the hypoxic drive is considerably diminished in the latter group (Lahiri *et al.*, 1969, 1970). The increased hypoxic sensitivity and hyperventilation that occurs during the first few days to months at altitude exposure is acclimatizational. A diminished hypoxic ventilatory drive occurs with long-term exposure, however, especially during the developmental period (Lahiri *et al.*, 1970; Lenfant and Sullivan, 1971). Smith and Crowell (1963, 1967) have shown with regard to yet another obvious trait, high hematocrits and red blood cell volume, that there is an optimal hematocrit for survival in severe exposure, but that the optima differ for acutely and chronically exposed animals. Some of the advantages of hyperventilation, and high hematocrits, therefore, appear quite exposure specific. Population specificity is easy to imagine. For example, hyperventilation would be of greater advantage to a population with a rightward shift of the hemoglobin-oxygen dissociation curve (where a high alveolar oxygen tension is needed to maximize arterial saturation) than to a population with a leftward shift. Similarly, hyperventilation is advantageous especially if there are no increases in diffusing capacity of the lung, but it is less useful in a population with a high diffusing capacity. It therefore seems important to at least acknowledge the possibility of different adaptive import associated with the nature of the stress exposure (duration, rate, magnitude, and frequency), as well as with age, sex, and other biological factors.

ORGAN-SYSTEM ADAPTATIONS

Effective oxygen transport and tissue resistance to hypoxia and anoxia are the criteria for physiological success in hypoxia and, hence, for adaptation at the infra-individual levels. A variety of characteristics and responses enhance oxygen transport or increase resistance to hypoxia, and these may be viewed as aptitudes and acclimatizations, but chiefly at an organ-system level. The study of these adaptations is the task of environmental physiology, and most of the reviews of hypoxia cited in the introduction deal with them in detail. In the present section, aptitudes and acclimatization responses will be briefly summarized.

The only major aptitude presumed to be of import in altitude hypoxia is a large chest and a large lung. This assumption apparently derives from the finding of large chests in native Andean highlanders (Hurtado, 1931), a finding substantiated by later studies on growth (Frisancho, 1969, 1970). It is not clear if this larger chest is directly associated with larger lungs, nor even if a larger lung volume would be functionally important, since the Andean highlanders differ from lowlanders chiefly in their larger residual volume (Hurtado, 1964a). Moreover, this larger chest size may be responsible in part for the higher oxygen cost of breathing in highlanders (Mazess, 1968). In sum, a large chest does not have a demonstrated relation to increased oxygen transport and, hence, cannot be assumed to be an adaptive aptitude.

Most of the infra-individual adaptations in humans to hypoxia are acclimatizational. These are as follows:

1. *Red blood cells:* there is an increase of red blood cell volume and concentration (hematocrit), and, consequently, total hemoglobin and its concentration increase. This results from an increased erythropoietin output. These changes allow a higher volume of oxygen to be carried per unit of blood, but, at the same time, the increased blood viscosity may affect blood flow and circulatory work.

2. *Hemoglobin-Oxygen Dissociation Curve:* there is a rightward shift of the dissociation curve in newcomers and residents associated with an increased concentration of intra-erythrocytic 2,3-diphosphoglycerate. This shift is toward decreased affinity, so that the release of oxygen to the tissue is enhanced. This also decreases oxygen loading in the lung; however, the import of this shift appears wholly dependent on the altitude on the interaction of such other factors as hyperventilation and acid-base status.

3. *Circulation:* there is a transient increase in cardiac output at rest during the first days' exposure and then a return to normal levels. Maximal cardiac output may be reduced. Increased blood flow may be of transient advantage but involves increased cardiac work. Such circulatory alterations, as reduced flow to the skin, kidneys, and heart occur, with greater flow to muscle and the brain.

There is an increased pulmonary artery pressure, which may enhance perfusion of the upper lung and thereby increase the diffusing capacity of the lung. In persons growing up at high altitude, there are histological alterations of the pulmonary tree and right ventricular hypertrophy.

4. *Capillarity:* there is an increase of tissue capillarity in hypoxia, but it is not clear to what extent this is due to the opening of the many previously non-patent capillaries or to the proliferation of new capillaries. This increase of capillarity is of great importance for it aids diffusion to the tissue. Without increased capillarity the higher flow of more viscous blood would entail a greater peripheral resistance and greater cardiac work.

5. *Ventilation:* there is a major increase in the hypoxic drive resulting in hyperventilation at least during the first year of exposure. This increases the alveolar oxygen tension and thereby increases the arterial tension and saturation. With long sojourn, or in native residents, there is a diminished hypoxic sensitivity and the level of hyperventilation is greatly diminished. This seems compensated for in the residents, at least, by an increased diffusing capacity of the lung. An increased diffusing capacity is not found in sojourners, but only in subjects who have grown up at altitude.

6. *Cellular Metabolism:* Barbashova (1964, 1967, 1969) and Reynafarje (1971) have summarized the numerous cellular changes and their importance. For example, there is a higher muscle myoglobin concentration, the activity of some glycolytic enzymes in various tissues is increased, and there is enhanced anaerobic glycolysis. The concentration of high-energy phosphates is greater in the tissues of altitude animals, and oxidative enzymes show greater activity. One of the major impacts of these cellular changes may be to increase the resistance of the tissues to low oxygen tensions.

The relative effects of the various organ-system adaptations have never been systematically evaluated, but there have been some comparative examinations of oxygen transport (Lenfant and Sullivan, 1971; Torrance *et al.,* 1971). These investigators, using mixed venous oxygen tension as an operational criterion for oxygen delivery to the tissues, found that increased hemoglobin and the rightward shift of the hemoglobin-oxygen dissociation curve had much less effect than hyperventilation had in sojourners and residents. The shift of the dissociation curve was of more benefit to newcomers than to residents. The increased cost of hyperventilation at altitude was estimated to be within 3% of the increased oxygen transport achieved by hyperventilation, and hence it is an effective mechanism.

As noted at the beginning of this section, organ-system adaptation pertains to the field of environmental physiology. When the study of these adaptations goes beyond a definition of the mechanism and its effect, and includes the implications for the individual and the population, then human biology and adaptive anthropology become involved. With regard to the preceding half-dozen adaptive mechanisms, one anthropological question, of obvious importance, is the extent to which population differences occur and to what extent such differences are genetic. At present data are incomplete even on these relatively well-defined responses. For example, it is clear that native highlanders differ from lowlanders and sojourners, but the relative influence of genetics, degree of exposure, and background factors has not been demonstrated. A second major question is how the organ-system adaptations relate to the effects of hypoxia on the various individual adaptive domains.

INDIVIDUAL ADAPTATION

The effects of hypoxia in the individual adaptive domains are reviewed in this section.

Physical performance

It is widely recognized that altitude exposure impairs physical abilities; this topic has been summarized in several symposia (Jokl and Jokl, 1968; Goddard *et al.*, 1967; Margaria, 1967). The maximal work capacity of newcomers decreases, and submaximal work becomes far more stressful, entailing high heart rates and rapid breathing, which decrease endurance time. Native highland residents appear to tolerate work much better, and their performance, which would be normal by sea level standards, appears supernormal at altitude.

There is an acceleratingly progressive decline in the maximal work capacity (aerobic capacity or maximal oxygen intake) above 2000 m (Balke, 1960, 1963; Pugh *et al.*, 1964), so that at 4000 m the typical newcomer has a 25% decrease and 40% at 5000 m. A decrease in maximum heart rate is often seen after several days' exposure, but this disappears after several months; heart rate is not depressed at all in residents. The decrease in aerobic capacity is proportional to the extent of training; athletes show the greatest decrease, sedentary individuals the least, and active subjects an intermediate decrease (Buskirk *et al.*, 1967; Mazess, 1969a). The anaerobic capacity, which is not dependent on oxygen transport, is not reduced by hypoxia, and, in fact, there may be a slight elevation in the ability for high-intensity work of short duration.

The metabolic cost of standard submaximal work is relatively unaffected by altered oxygen pressures over a wide range of work loads (Bason *et al.*, 1971; Billings *et al.*, 1971; Velasquez, 1970; Mazess, 1969a). As a consequence, submaximal work at altitude uses a greater percentage of the reduced total work capacity; this percentage is called the "relative work load." Ordinary activity at altitude involves a greater relative work load, and, at extreme altitudes, even moderate activity may involve the maximal capacity. Above 80% relative work load, a physiological steady state is not obtained, but, at lower work loads, the time to attain a steady state is the same at high and low altitudes (Bason *et al.*, 1973).

Comparisons of such native highlanders as the Himalayan Sherpas and Andean Quechuas, who have lived at altitude for many generations, suggest that they have an aerobic capacity comparable to that of sea-level dwellers (Lahiri, 1966; Mazess, 1969a,b; Pugh, 1968; Frisancho *et al.*, 1973a). Highlanders increase their aerobic capacity only slightly on going to sea level (Velasquez, 1970), indicating that they have only a slight reduction in maximal performance at altitude. Diet, training, growth, and development at altitude, or possibly some genetic component, may be responsible for this lesser deterioration in highlanders. There are virtually no performance differences between Quechua newcomers and white newcomers, nor between Quechua residents and white residents, although there is a 20% difference between residents and newcomers (Mazess, 1969a,b; Frisancho *et al.*, 1973a). Higher aerobic capacity was associated with growth and development at altitude.

Relative work load is particularly important in a comparison of submaximal work in highlanders and lowlanders. For example, altitude newcomers show greater hyperventilation upon exercise relative to their own ventilation values at sea level or to the values of highlanders. If the relative work load is considered, the magnitude of altitude-induced hyperventilation is seen to be less, thus reducing the differences between newcomers and residents. Similarly, the high endurance for submaximal work in highlanders reflects in part their higher maximal capacity and, consequently, the lower relative work load at a fixed oxygen intake. The outstanding endurance of these highlanders is no doubt associated with other factors as well. First, the highlanders are small in body build, and, consequently, most of their usual activities, which involve moving body weight, entail a lower oxygen cost. Second, the highlanders have a life of vigorous activity and tolerance of discomfort in work, which enables them to endure. Finally, high carbohydrate diets, like those of most highland peoples, are well known to enhance endurance of hard work through their increase of muscle glycogen (Karlson and Saltim, 1971).

Altitude has a severe effect on the maximal and submaximal performance of highlanders, sojourners, and newcomers. Some adjustments appear
to occur through the period of growth and development. In this respect,
highlanders fare better than newcomers, but their attainments are still below those they themselves would achieve at sea level, so adjustment is not
complete.

Nervous system: Sensory and psychological performance

It is a well-known fact that nervous tissue is highly susceptible to oxygen
deprivation, and sensory, motor, and mental functioning is impossible at
extreme altitudes (Van Liere and Stickney, 1963). The immediate effects
of moderate altitudes are less severe, due to the almost complete vascular
compensation for reduced oxygen tension. Cerebral blood flow increases
reversibly in hypoxemia, as in exercise (Russek and Beaton, 1967), and
there is an exquisite regulation of flow in relation to the interaction of
hypoxia and hypocapnia (Kogure *et al.*, 1970; Shapiro *et al.*, 1966). Although biochemical and metabolic changes do not occur in mild hypoxia, impairment of tryptophan hydroxylation and altered serotonin synthesis does occur and may account for some symptomatology (Davis *et al.*,
1973).

Reversible increases of synaptic delay, conduction time, and excitability occur at moderate altitudes (Woolley *et al.*, 1963; Woolley and Timiras,
1963, 1965; Williams *et al.*, 1966). Central nervous system development
is markedly delayed at altitude (Castillo and Timiras, 1964; Heim, 1965;
Heim and Timiras, 1964), and neurochemical and structural alterations,
including cellular decreases and defective myelinogenesis, characteristic of
impairment, occur (Timiras and Woolley, 1966; Petropoulos *et al.*, 1969,
1970, 1972; Shivers and Roofe, 1966).

Severe intermittent hypoxia may be more severe than chronic moderate
hypoxia and occurs frequently at altitude. Brief fetal anoxia causes brain
damage and retardation, with late appearance of developmental behaviors
(Sechzer *et al.*, 1971; Ingalls *et al.*, 1952). Andean Quechua infants are
retarded in motor development and growth (Baker, 1969), which could
reflect perinatal anoxia or chronic mild hypoxia.

Sensory and psychological functions at altitude have been reviewed
(Tune, 1964; McFarland, 1952, 1969b; Cahoon, 1972; Stamper *et al.*,
1970). Performance in many tasks deteriorates at altitude in those involving cognitive and psychomotor ability. Visual performance and color

sensitivity decrease even at moderate altitude (Kobrick, 1970; Kobrick and Appleton, 1971; McFarland, 1969b; Ohlbaum, 1969), but there may be partial recovery with extended exposure. Carbone *et al.* (1971), however, demonstrated a greater reduction in corneal sensitivity with chronic compared to acute exposure. Auditory function is not greatly affected.

These results overwhelmingly indicate nervous system impairment as a result of hypoxic exposure. There are physiological adjustments, especially with regard to blood flow, but individuals most likely suffer some impairment, especially with chronic exposure and development at altitude. Marginal caloric and protein intakes in many altitude zones may exacerbate nervous system difficulties.

Growth and development

Nearly all the evidence from the wide variety of animals studied shows that hypoxia retards over-all growth and reduces cellular and organ development. There are, however, different magnitudes of retardation in different organs and under different conditions (Clegg, 1971; Delaquerriere-Richardson *et al.*, 1965; Glauser, 1966; Naeye, 1966; Pepelko, 1970; Timiras, 1963; Timiras *et al.*, 1957). Many organs, such as the heart, lung, and spleen, although reduced in weight, are not reduced proportional to the lower body weight, whereas others, such as the thymus and kidney, appear to be so reduced. As a consequence the heart, lung, spleen, liver, and adrenals are large relative to the reduced body weight. Apparently the reduction in hypoxia is due to a reduced number of cells, with normal or large cell size; in contrast, malnutrition tends to produce reduction to cell size but normal cell numbers (Naeye, 1966).

Clegg *et al.* (1970) reviewed the evidence on human growth and suggested a retarding effect of altitude, presumably due to hypoxia, on body size and maturation. In some geographical regions, such as Ethiopia, altitude hypoxia may be counterbalanced by a lower incidence of disease. In Ethiopia, the growth of genetically similar peoples is relatively advanced in mountainous zones compared to the more disease-prone lowlands (Clegg *et al.*, 1972), whereas high-altitude Peruvian natives show a marked retardation of growth and delay in development (Frisancho, 1969, 1970; Hurtado, 1932; Frisancho and Baker, 1970). Despite the over-all diminution, there is a relative increase in the growth rate of the chest in the altitude native. This increase, however, appears to be without functional importance to ventilatory function. The larger chest does contain a larger lung, but most of this increase in size is due to an increased residual volume (Hurtado, 1964a); the larger chest may simply increase the work of breathing in altitude natives (Mazess, 1968) and not be of any benefit. In Peru, in contrast to Ethiopia, there is little evidence of reduced childhood disease at altitude; disease and malnutrition in the Peruvian highlands may interact with the hypoxia in retarding growth.

Several authors (Frisancho *et al.*, 1973b; Stini, 1972) have followed Thomas (1972) in suggesting that the diminished body size of altitude natives may be relatively beneficial in regard to (a) chronic food shortage, (b) sporadic famine, and/or (c) the energetics of work. This illustrates the complexity of evaluating adaptation. Here evidence for the lack of individual adjustment to hypoxia (poor growth) may be taken as evidence of adjustment to a different stress and at a different level of complexity (nutritional stress on the population in the biomass domain).

It is worth noting, however, that exposure to hypoxia during growth and development does apparently result in some alterations, particularly in the cardiopulmonary system, which may increase oxygen transport (organ-system adaptation) and may account for the somewhat better physical performance (individual adaptation) of highlanders. Bartlett (1970) showed that somatic growth in rats slowed in hypoxia, but the rats had normal lungs. Burri and Weibl (1971) showed that alveolar, tissue, and capillary volumes of the lung were increased in altitude-reared rats, whereas Tenney and Ou (1970) showed only an increase in capillary density. These changes might increase the diffusing capacity of the lungs.

The diffusing capacity of the lung may be limiting to oxygen transport in hard work at altitude, and arterial desaturation does occur (Banchero *et al.*, 1966; Pugh, 1964; West *et al.*, 1962); a high diffusing capacity is obviously advantageous. There appear to be, at best, minimal increases of diffusing capacity in newcomers, even after several months' exposure (Degraff *et al.*, 1970; Weiskopf and Severinghaus, 1972; Kreuzer and van Lookeren Campagne, 1965; West, 1962), whereas native highlanders in both the Andes and Colorado have increased capacities (Velasquez, 1966; Velasquez and Florentini, 1966; Degraff *et al.*, 1970). Apparently growth and development in hypoxia are necessary for increased lung diffusion.

Growth and development in hypoxia also appear responsible for decreasing the hypoxic ventilatory drive responsible for the adaptive hyperventilation of newcomers. Studies by several groups (Lahiri, 1968; Byrne-Quinn *et al.*, 1972; Lahiri *et al.*, 1969, 1970; Lefrancois *et al.*, 1968; Severinghaus *et al.*, 1966; Sorenson and Severinghaus, 1968a,b,c) have shown that permanent altitude residents have a hypoxic chemoreceptor insensitivity, a result also found in sea-level subjects with hypoxemia of various origins (cyanotic heart disease, obstructive lung disease). This insensitivity is not reversed by transfer to sea level. This relative hypoventilation is not adaptive and would definitely be harmful were it not for the increased diffusing capacity of altitude residents, which occurs concomitantly during growth. Accentuation of this hypoventilation, together with polycythemia, apparently results in the high pulmonary artery pressures and other signs and symptoms of chronic mountain sickness (Penaloza and Sime, 1971).

Growth at altitude also profoundly affects the pulmonary circulation (Penaloza and Sime, 1971; Grover, 1965; Heath, 1966; Hultgren *et al.*, 1965; Vogel *et al.*, 1962; Arias-Stella, 1966; Sime *et al.*, 1963; Penaloza *et al.*, 1964; Banchero *et al.*, 1966; Cruz-Jibaja *et al.*, 1964). Hypoxia elevates pulmonary artery pressure in both newcomers and residents, and right ventricular dominance and hypertrophy of the right ventricle also occur. Histological differences are seen in the pulmonary trunk of altitude-reared individuals, suggesting a retention of fetal and infant characteristics into adult life. Pulmonary hypertension may be advantageous in providing a better ventilation perfusion ratio in the lung. Accentuation of the hypertension, however, is seen in chronic mountain sickness. Such hypertension can be reversed by several days at sea level.

The diminution of over-all growth and retardation of development that occurs in hypoxia indicates that adjustment, even with chronic exposure, is not complete or even very evident. Alterations of growth do occur in particular organ systems, and the result may be beneficial (increased diffusing capacity of the lung), harmful (diminution of hypoxic ventilatory drive and nervous system deterioration), or uncertain (alteration of pulmonary circulation). There is little controlled evidence of differences among human populations in either the extent of hypoxic influence on growth and development or the magnitude of developmental responses to hypoxia.

Nutrition

Altitude regions are often quite cold, and this, together with aridity and hilly terrain, makes agricultural production precarious. In many areas, agriculture is supplemented or replaced by pastoralism, but, in any event, the nutritional base for altitude regions is at best marginal, and persons growing and living at altitude are probably far more subject to at least seasonally deficient caloric and nutrient intakes than would be the case in lower zones. These facts make the influence of altitude hypoxia on nutritional status particularly important.

Acute exposure to hypoxia usually is associated with large losses of body weight over days and even weeks, including both water and tissue loss (Consolazio *et al.*, 1968, 1972). Hypohydration and anorexia occur to varying degrees and with varying persistence. It is, therefore, not unusual to see negative nitrogen and caloric balances, as well as negative balances of other nutrients, in acute exposure (Johnson *et al.*, 1969). These problems may be exacerbated by an apparent large reduction in the efficiency of food utilization (Chinn and Hannon, 1969; Schnakenberg and Burlington, 1970); in particular, the utilization of fats may be most adversely affected, and there is at the outset of exposure fat mobilization from body stores resulting in increased serum free fatty acids (Whitten and Janoski, 1969). Protein utilization also is adversely affected, probably by an increased protein catabolism (Surks, 1968; Whitten *et al.*, 1968; Klain and Hannon, 1970). It is not clear, however, to what extent these problems are associated with the anorexia and hypohydration of acute exposure versus hypoxia itself. In any event, it appears that the period of the first days and weeks of hypoxic exposure are a period of nutritional stress.

The effects of longer-term hypoxic exposure on nutritional parameters are less clear. Picon-Reategui (1962) has demonstrated alterations of carbohydrate metabolism in high altitude natives. Blume and Pace (1969) indicated that there was a slower oxidation of glucose and a greater formation, and perhaps turnover, of glycogen in hypoxic animals. There is a slight hyperproteinuria in altitude residents (Rennie *et al.*, 1971, 1972), which suggests that the increased protein catabolism seen in acute exposure occurs in chronic exposure. Animals raised at high altitude may grow less on high protein diets (Schnakenberg and Burlington, 1970), but there are findings that diet does not interact with hypoxia in growth (Chinn and Hannon, 1970). As in acute exposure, there is great uncertainty as to the actual effects of hypoxia versus other factors; in acute exposure hypohydration and anorexia are complications, whereas in longer exposure probably the prevailing diet has a great influence. The low-protein, low-fat, high-carbohydrate diets prevalent in many altitude zones (see Collazos *et al.*, 1960) probably influence nutritional findings with chronic exposure. On the other hand, such diets may be of benefit in hypoxia, since it has long been reputed that high carbohydrate diets were both desired and beneficial at altitude, and recent evidence suggests that such diets diminish clinical symptoms of acute exposure and increase the endurance in heavy physical work (Consolazio *et al.*, 1969). At the same time, even moderate amounts of fat (12%) in the diet of rats are detrimental to survival in severe hypoxia (Hove *et al.*, 1945).

Reproduction

One of the commonest notions about high altitude is that it has profoundly deleterious effects on animal fertility and reproduction. This idea gained wide support as a result of Monge's (1948) classic study on altitude. Monge examined the records of the Spanish chroniclers in early colonial Peru, which suggested that subnormal reproduction of animals and man was a major factor in the Spanish preference for settlement along the coast rather than in the highlands. It was even reputed, following the exaggeration of some of the chroniclers, that no children of Spanish descent were born in the highlands; at the same time it was observed that the native altitude dwellers had no difficulties with reproduction. It should be recognized that no specific evidence of reduced fecundity, fertility, or reproduction was scientifically documented in these anecdotal reports and that there has not been enough emphasis on the observations of normal reproduction after initial acclimatization (Cobo, 1892). The more recent literature has shown, almost without exception, very little effect of moderate altitude (up to 4000 m) on reproduction (Van Liere and Stickney, 1963; Weihe, 1963b, 1965; Swain, 1970), leaving aside disturbances occurring during the first days or weeks of exposure. It is also clear that exposure to extreme altitudes (more than 5000 m) does have marked effects on gonadal function, success of pregnancy, litter size, birth weights, lactation, and litter survival (Printz, 1972; Altland and Highman, 1968; Van Liere and Stickney, 1963).

In the male animal, there seems to be transient effects on sexual characteristics and functioning at moderate altitudes and some damage and impaired fecundity at extreme altitudes. Clegg (1968) found few differences in the secondary sexual characteristics of male mice exposed to moderate hypoxia compared to controls when adjustment was made for the lower body weight of the hypoxic animal. There are minor testicular changes, with consequent effects on fertility, until rats are exposed to 6500 m and mice to 7500 m (Altland and Highman, 1968). In man reduced sperm count, increased sperm abnormalities, and a fall in urinary testosterone have been observed in acute exposure to 4300 m, but these seem to be temporary phenomena and are not observed in the altitude resident (Donayre, 1966; Donayre et al., 1968).

Female gonadal function seems adversely affected by hypoxia, in a way analogous to the male, in that there are only transient effects at moderate altitude and no real damage except at extreme altitudes. In acute exposure, there is a brief increase of anestrus days followed by an increase of estrus days. Donayre (1966, 1969) found at 4300 m an increase of estrus days in rats, decreased ovulation in mice, and some minor menstrual disturbances in human females. At an extreme altitude (7000 m) female hamsters were found to become acyclic; the ovaries were polyfollicular, suggesting that ovulation had been blocked by a failure to release or synthesize luteinizing hormone (Printz, 1972). As in males, there is no evidence of deterioration with chronic exposure to moderate altitudes and no evidence of reduced fecundity in altitude residents.

Metcalfe (1970) in his review of the topic showed the importance of an adequate uterine oxygen supply on fetal growth and survival. Even at low altitudes, fetal oxygen tension is relatively low, a condition which has been described as "Everest in utero," and, as a consequence, the mammalian fetus has a limited margin of safety which, no doubt, is even further diminished at high altitudes. Despite the lower maternal arterial tension at altitude a series of adjustments, which occurs within a week or two after altitude exposure of the pregnant animal, ensure that the fetal oxygen tension is very similar to that at sea level (Barron et al., 1963; Makowski et al., 1968). Sobrevilla et al. (1971) showed that human neonates at 4300 m had oxygen tensions only slightly lower than those encountered at sea level, whereas Howard et al. (1957a) found normal arterial saturation in neonates at 3000 m. Adjustments leading to maintenance of oxygen tension in the altitude neonate include increased placental size and vascularity and increased oxygen capacity of the fetal blood due to an increased red blood cell and hemoglobin mass (Johnson and Roofe, 1965; Barron et al., 1963; Metcalfe, 1970; McClung, 1969). Despite these adjustments, and apparent homeostasis, the fetus at high altitude seems to grow at a lower rate during late pregnancy, and the neonate at altitude is almost invariably of lower weight than the normoxic neonate (Lichty et al., 1957; Howard et al., 1957b; McClung, 1969). This is certainly the case in experimental animals exposed to extreme altitudes (Johnson and Roofe, 1965; Delaquerriere-Richardson et al., 1965). There is some interference with lactation in the unacclimatized animal, which may account for part of the poor growth, morbidity, and mortality (Weihe, 1963b, 1965; Timiras, 1963). It seems more likely, however, that the shift in the distribution of birth weights to lower values, and the consequent greater mortality risks associated with reduced weight, is responsible for the far higher perinatal and neonatal death rate at high altitudes (Grahn and Kratchmann, 1963; Mazess, 1965; Swain, 1970). Better care of the neonate at altitude in the United States has resulted in a recent secular trend toward lower mortality (Frisancho and Cossman, 1970).

In summary then, moderate altitudes, up to the maximum levels of permanent human habitation, seem to have only a mild effect on fecundity and reproductive performance and only during the period of initial exposure. Reproduction is affected, however, by the lower birth weights and increased mortality evident in even permanently resident animals.

Morbidity and mortality

The lack of medical facilities in many high altitude regions causes a two-fold problem in assessing health status in relation to hypoxia: (a) there is a lack of adequate data on disease incidence and causes of death, and (b) the statistics that do exist are biased by this very lack of medical care, as well as by poor sanitation, malnutrition, and related factors. This limits the utility of epidemiological data from broad geographical areas. At the same time, there has been a paucity of intensive medical studies of more limited geographical zones, such as that of Buck *et al.* (1968), and hence our knowledge of illness in hypoxia derives more from clinical and physiological studies than from those emphasizing epidemiology.

Infectious diseases at altitude may differ markedly from those at lower elevations (Buck *et al.*, 1968). The very high death rates in the Andean region, especially among infants, appears related to infectious diseases (Baker and Dutt, 1972; Alers, 1965; Cruz Coke, 1966). On the other hand, the moderate altitudes of Ethiopia seem less disease prone than the surrounding lowlands (Harrison *et al.*, 1969). Epidemics occur commonly in the Andean region, and diseases affecting the lungs, such as pneumonia, tuberculosis, and influenza, are common. Altitude is known to have some debilitating effect on the lungs and can damage pulmonary capillaries thereby exacerbating pulmonary disease (Nayak *et al.*, 1964).

Several studies have suggested that antibody titers are increased in animals at altitude and that there is a greater proliferation of antibody-producing cells in response to an immune challenge (Trapani, 1963, 1966,

1969; Tengardy and Kramer, 1968). Antibody decay time is unaffected by hypoxia, so a greater production must account for whatever elevation occurs (Trapani and Campbell, 1959). The actual fate of the pathogen and the host may be far more complex. For example, Trapani (1966) found enhanced host survival to the challenge of an influenza virus, but others have found no effect of altitude on viral resistance (Schmidt, 1969). Trapani (1969) suspected that resistance to bacterial infection might not be increased as much at altitude as the resistance to viral infection and hypothesized a preferential increase of 7 S antibodies at altitude to account for this. Still, it has been shown (Trapani and Cohn, 1963) that there is a lesser growth of tubercle bacilli in animals at 4300 m. Weihe and Hurni (1963) found that, in mice at 3450 m, the genotype of the mouse strain was the most important factor in resistance to bacterial infection, with some strains showing increased and others decreased resistance. These sometimes conflicting results necessitate cautious evaluation (Schmidt, 1969).

Little detail is available for the common non-infectious diseases. There is reputedly a very low incidence of cardiovascular disease at higher elevations, and the blood pressure of some altitude residents is quite low (Baker, 1969; Galvez, 1966; Zapata and Marticorena, 1968). This may well be a result of dietary and genetic factors rather than of hypoxia; observations on Tibetans, for example, showed a low blood pressure, but the figures were similar to the low values found in many Asian populations (Sehgal, 1968). At moderate elevations in Colorado, Morton *et al.* (1964, 1966) found no effect of altitude on the incidence of arteriosclerotic and hypertensive or rheumatic heart disease. One vascular problem is varicose veins, which occurs with high frequency at altitude in association with the higher hematocrits and greater blood viscosity (Quinones-Moreno, 1968). Some cancers may be affected by altitude. Mori-Chavez *et al.* (1970, 1974) have shown that mice exposed to 4500 m have, in addition to growth impairment, shortening of life-span, decreased incidence of lymphoid neoplasms, increased incidence and severity of pulmonary neoplasms, increased frequency of endocardial thrombosis and myocarditis, increased incidence of pneumonia, and decreased incidence of nephrosclerosis.

The epidemiological picture in relation to hypoxia is unclear, but there are several clinical entities specific to altitude that are debilitating, although not very common, in which hypoxia is clearly implicated (Hurtado, 1955, 1960; Monge and Monge, 1966; Velasquez, 1972). Acute mountain sickness is the most widely known of these sicknesses (Bhatta-charjya, 1964; Carson *et al.*, 1969; Darling, 1963; Hall *et al.*, 1965; Singh *et al.*, 1969) because of its common occurrence, to varying degrees, in nearly all persons during the first days or weeks at altitudes above 3000 m. The most common symptoms are headache, malaise, dizziness, shortness of breath, difficulties with sleep, and stomach upset. Apparently the sus-ceptibility to sickness, and its severity, vary among individuals, but the symptoms are highly reproducible in a given person (Robinson *et al.*, 1971). Cardiovascular fitness does not protect against sickness, but a gradual ascent to altitude over several days does alleviate difficulties (Han-sen *et al.*, 1967). It had been thought that some of the symptoms might be associated with the body dehydration that often occurs during initial altitude exposure (Krzywicki *et al.*, 1971), but this now seems not to be the case (Aoki and Robinson, 1971). Usually symptoms disappear with-out treatment.

Chronic mountain sickness, in contrast, is a severely debilitating dis-ease associated with long sojourn at altitude (Monge, 1943; Monge *et al.*, 1965; Monge and Monge, 1966). Although the disease affects the circu-latory and respiratory systems, the chief symptoms are in the nervous system. The disease is characterized by an excessive hypoxemia and poly-cythemia. Of course, at altitude, there is always some hypoxemia together with elaboration of red blood cells. In chronic mountain sickness, this "physiological" response is accentuated, perhaps because of a relative hypoventilation with a consequent increase of alveolar carbon dioxide tension, decrease of alveolar oxygen tension, and altered acid-base balance (Monge *et al.*, 1964). Elimination of polycythemia by blood-letting does not eliminate the excessive hypoventilation, suggesting that the latter is the chief cause of the problem (Monge *et al.*, 1965). At high elevations there may be less of a margin before polycythemia becomes excessive. Whittembury and Monge (1972) have shown that hematocrits increase with age and that the slope of the increase is dramatically elevated with greater altitude. At 4500 m, a hematocrit of 75% is expected in "normal" man at age 30, whereas at 4200 m this hematocrit is not reached until age 63. A hematocrit of 75% is seen in chronic mountain sickness, and, even if not contributory to the clinical disease, it must increase circulatory work. At such high altitudes, similarly, there will be less of a margin be-tween the normal relative "hypoventilation" of the resident and that of the diseased individual. Dramatic relief is usually conferred by transfer to low altitude. Numerous other diseases, particularly those of the cardiorespiratory system that affect oxygen transport, may interact with what would normally be subclinical mountain sickness to present distinctive varieties of "altitude" diseases.

The most severe altitude disease is pulmonary edema (Arias-Stella and Kruger, 1963; Marticorena *et al.*, 1964; Singh *et al.*, 1965); it can be rapidly fatal if the patient is not given oxygen or moved to a lower elevation. Even in subclinical cases, the disease process may greatly restrict physical activity (Cosio, 1969). Hultgren *et al.* (1971) found persons susceptible to this disease to have developed an excessive pulmonary hypertension and impaired pulmonary oxygen exchange. Other contributory factors may be abnormalities of blood coagulation (Singh and Chohan, 1972) and lesions of the pneumocyte (Valdivia *et al.*, 1966) that occur in hypoxia. Pulmonary artery pressure increases with increased altitude and is associated with a right ventricular predominance (Cruz-Jibaja *et al.*, 1964; Grover, 1965; Grover *et al.*, 1965; Penaloza *et al.*, 1963, 1964). In altitude sojourners, this hypertension is reversed by oxygen administration, transfer to lower altitudes, and certain drugs, but in permanent residents, who have resided since birth at altitude, there is not complete reversal (Hultgren *et al.*, 1965). In such residents, there are profound histological alterations of the pulmonary vessels that represent a prolongation of the normal sea-level histology of infants into adult life (Penaloza *et al.*, 1964; Arias-Stella, 1966; Heath, 1966). This is accompanied by a right ventricular hypertrophy. These changes may account for the apparently greater susceptibility of altitude residents to pulmonary edema when they return to altitude after a short stay at sea level (Arias-Stella and Kruger, 1963; Marticorena *et al.*, 1964). Ordinarily, however, these changes in the cardiopulmonary circulation do not create problems and may even enhance the ventilation-perfusion ratio of the lung (Dawson and Grover, 1974).

Finally, it appears that congenital abnormalities of several types are more common at high altitudes, probably since these are markedly affected by fetal anoxia (Ingalls *et al.*, 1952). Patent ductus arteriosus occurs 20 to 40 times more frequently at altitude than at sea level, and the incidence is directly correlated with elevation; pulmonary hypertension, again, is contributory to this abnormality (Penaloza *et al.*, 1964).

It is difficult to evaluate the net effect of hypoxia on health because the epidemiological pattern is not well defined. Any diminution of cardiac disease is probably offset by increased pulmonary disease. There are several altitude-related diseases, some quite severe. As Monge (1966) pointed out, many of the contributory factors to altitude disease (relative hypoventilation, excessive polycythemia, and pulmonary hypertension) are accentuations of the normal responses to hypoxia. In this sense, altitude sojourn narrows the margin between health and disease.

Cross-tolerance and resistance

Much of the literature on "cross-adaptation" or general resistance to stress has been reviewed recently (Fregly, 1971; Hale, 1969, 1970). It is, of course, understandable that animals exposed continuously, or even intermittently, to hypoxia would show enhanced responses and survivability in more severe hypoxic stress, and this, in fact, has been observed in both humans and lower animals (Balke and Wells, 1958; Velasquez, 1965). The reasons for an enhanced response to unrelated stresses, such as heat or wounds, are less obvious. There are the possibilities of (a) specific cellular, neural, and humoral alterations in hypoxia that by happenstance confer benefit to other stress situations (Barbashova, 1967, 1969) and of (b) more general responses mediated by the sympathoadrenal system (Selye, 1950, 1952, 1956).

Numerous studies have demonstrated an increased adrenal activity and increased catecholamine output during the initial period of altitude exposure (Cunningham *et al.*, 1965; DeBias, 1966; Klain, 1972; Myles, 1972; Richtarik *et al.*, 1966; Van Liere and Stickney, 1963). Tolerance and survivability in hypoxia is reduced by inhibition of adrenal activity or by adrenalectomy (Poupa *et al.*, 1966; Myles and Ducker, 1973), but tissue resistance is not obliterated. Moreover, in chronically exposed animals and man, even in severely stressful conditions like mountain climbing, adrenal activity and catecholamine levels appear normal (Moncloa *et al.*, 1965; Myles and Ducker, 1973; Siri *et al.*, 1969). Therefore, it is more likely that the cross-tolerance and general resistance occurring in hypoxia result from specific hypoxic responses rather than from increased sympathoadrenal activity and the "general adaptation syndrome."

Altitude-exposed animals are more resistant to a variety of stress including hemorrhagic shock (Zapata-Oritz *et al.*, 1967) and hyperoxia (Zhironkin, 1964). Zapata-Oritz *et al.* (1966) found that altitude animals had better survival from surgery, greater tolerance of tourniquet shock, and even survived better in severe heat stress. Barbashova (1967, 1969) found that exposure to hypoxia increased resistance to strychnine poisoning, ionizing radiation, thermal extremes, burns, and anemia. Meerson *et al.* (1973) showed increased resistance to myocardial ischemic necrosis. Ex-

posure to moderate altitudes may increase subsequent exercise performance at sea level slightly (Balke *et al.*, 1965; Dill and Adams, 1971), but
exposure to extreme altitudes has a debilitating effect (Altland *et al.*,
1969).

It has been widely observed that muscle, and, in particular, the myocardium, has an increased tolerance to a variety of stresses, in particular,
anoxic stress, if the animal has been previously exposed to altitude (Mc-
Grath *et al.*, 1969, 1973; Poupa *et al.*, 1966; Souhrada *et al.*, 1971; Barbashova, 1967, 1969). Several factors are thought responsible for this
enhanced tissue resistance, and, since tissue resistance is the most likely
cause of the general resistance of the intact animal, these same factors
are of extreme importance.

An increased vascularity affecting both capillary and larger vessels occurs in response to hypoxia (Valdivia, 1958; Valdivia *et al.*, 1960; Tenney
and Ou, 1970; Anthony and Krieder, 1961). Higher capillary densities
result from the opening of previously underperfused capillaries, but there
may be some capillary proliferation as well during growth. An increase in
capillarity enhances diffusion of oxygen to the cells, particularly in hypoxia where such diffusion may become a limiting factor in oxygen transport (Forster, 1966). An increase of myoglobin is also seen in animals
exposed to hypoxia (Anthony *et al.*, 1959; Reynafarje and Morrison, 1962;
Reynafarje *et al.*, 1966; Reynafarje, 1961, 1962, 1966), but there is not a
change in the equilibrium constant or reaction rate of oxygen and myoglobin (Strickland *et al.*, 1959; Strother *et al.*, 1959). The increased myoglobin content may be of some advantage in working muscle, but does not
seem to be critical for tissue resistance (Poupa *et al.*, 1966). An increase in
mitochondrial number, but not size, has also been observed (Ou and Tenney, 1970) but has a minimal effect on oxygen transport. Alterations of
cellular metabolism in hypoxia may be of greater importance than the
above factors. There is an increase in the capacity for both oxidative and
anerobic metabolism in animals chronically exposed to hypoxia that is
made possible by an increased activity of oxidative and glycolytic enzymes
(Reynafarje, 1961, 1966, 1971; Reynafarje *et al.*, 1966; Chenykayeva, 1964;
Barbashova, 1967, 1969). Under normal conditions of hypoxia, cellular
respiration is not altered (Frehn and Anthony, 1961; Strickland *et al.*,
1961; Dedukhova and Mokhova, 1971), but an increased capacity for
respiration must be of utility in stress situations. Anerobic glycolysis is enhanced in hypoxia-exposed animals (McGrath *et al.*, 1969). A shift occurs
in the complement of lactic dehydrogenase (LDH) isozymes (Andersen

and Bullard, 1971; Reynafarje *et al.*, 1965), but, as Huckabee (1965) pointed out, there is already abundant enzyme available in the sea-level animal, and, hence, the effect of an increase in LDH at altitude is uncertain. In any event it appears that an increased capacity for oxygen transport and for cellular metabolism occur in chronically exposed animals; the chief factors in resistance probably vary with the stress imposed, but increased diffusion, resulting from capillarity, and augmented glycolytic capacity seem of the greatest importance.

POPULATION ADAPTATION

As noted, population adaptation is assessed in relation to reproductive success, demographic optimality, spatial-temporal spread, and energetic or ecological efficiency. Unfortunately, there has been far more speculation than investigation of population adaptation at altitude. Monge (1948) presented a detailed, and highly articulate, argument for considering the native Andean inhabitants as a distinctive human population based on their altitude responses. In proposing that Andeans were an altitude-adapted race, however, he not only failed to demonstrate the extent and origin of their characteristics but failed to show that these characteristics were of relative benefit compared to those of other populations. The ease with which infra-individual adaptations to hypoxia may be demonstrated in highlanders has caused many other investigators to view the altitude native as an adapted individual and to consider the population as also adapted.

In this section, the domains of population adaptation are examined in greater detail. The available data on reproduction suggest that humans and other mammals have a mildly impaired fertility in hypoxia that is associated chiefly with an increase in perinatal mortality; there is not a persistent reduction of fecundity at moderate elevations. Census data seem to support the physiological findings (Clegg *et al.*, 1970). Stycos (1963) found lower fertility in highland than lowland Peru. Heer (1964) tried to explain these differences, and those in Bolivia and Ecuador, on the basis of labor-force participation, adult sex ratio, and possible voluntary birth control. James (1966) found altitude to be the most significant factor. Whitehead (1968) criticized the variables used in these studies, and suggested that high infant mortality gave a spurious impression of decreased fertility. DeJong's cautious review (1970) outlined the complexities of the issue, whereas Baker and Dutt (1972) indicated that controlled comparisons of populations, rather than examination of census data, would provide a better indication of fertility. In any event, the census data do not show an enhanced reproductive success for native highlanders and, in fact, suggest the reverse.

An enhanced reproductive success of native highlanders compared to sojourners might be taken as an indication of selective advantage for the former group. Selection, however, has never been directly observed in a human population, and there is no evidence for selective advantage of particular genotypes within altitude populations or between highlanders and other populations. Cruz-Coke *et al.* (1966) felt that selective forces were of minimal import but demonstrated a dramatic increase in Crow's index of opportunities for selection with elevation. The higher mortality of the altitude region creates an opportunity for selection, particularly if hypoxic stress were a significant factor in mortality. Selection has undoubtedly occurred in some species, for example, poultry. Chickens are highly susceptible to hypoxia as adults (Olander *et al.*, 1967). The initial exposure of the adult to hypoxia results in a high mortality, and fertilized eggs show a very poor hatchability (Smith *et al.*, 1969; Burton and Smith, 1969; Timiras, 1965). In successive generations at altitude, the adult mortality is greatly reduced (from 80 to 25%) and hatchability increased from 3 to 30%). Selection in avian species, with the embryo unprotected by maternal systems, must certainly occur rapidly. In mammals, the intensity and speed of selection would be greatly reduced, and its import relative to that of acclimatization, through either short- or long-term exposure, appears minimal (Hock, 1970).

Demographic optimality is even more difficult to assess than reproductive success, since the criteria for "optimality" are not agreed upon. The analyses of census data cited above have shown an unusual sex and age composition for highland populations compared to the structure of lowland groups. Altitude populations show an unusually high proportion of males, except where there is a selective out-migration of males (Alers, 1965). Also there appears to be a relative deficit of older people (Clegg *et al.*, 1970), but this may be advantageous in a nutritionally marginal population where non-productive adults are a burden.

There is no concrete evidence for the preferential spread of altitude peoples into other zones, although the Inca empire did establish, for a brief moment in the history of Andean populations, a widespread political and economic integration. It must be noted that the Incaic attempts to physically colonize other zones were marked failures. The Incas were obliged to use a system of rotating expeditionary forces to maintain control over lowland areas because they were viewed as very unhealthy for highlanders. In contrast, there appears to be fair evidence for temporal permanence of altitude peoples. Andean, and other altitude populations, have not only maintained population numbers over the centuries but have been able to recover from the massive depopulation brought about by European contact (Clegg *et al.*, 1970; Baker, 1969). Too much cannot be made from these observations as other native populations have survived the centuries, particularly if they occupy undesirable, uncomfortable, and marginal lands.

Finally, there is the domain of energetic or ecological efficiency. The rigors of the altitude zone would suggest a reduced energy base, which would, in turn, limit the biomass and diversity of any species. Dorst (1972), however, found a substantial biomass and diversity of rodents at 4000 m, equivalent to that in temperate lowlands, and these rodents, in turn, supported an abundance of predators. Population densities of humans at altitude are very low compared to the lowlands, even when expressed per unit arable land. Of course this reflects the prevailing cultural and technological patterns rather than fundamental biological characteristics. Altitude populations of other than native descent, for example, Europeans in the Andes, are concentrated in cities and have a different cultural pattern than the natives in which productivity is minimal and utilization maximal. Perhaps they are at a different trophic level, much like the predators described by Dorst. In any event, controlled comparisons are not possible; one can only conclude that humans at altitude generally do less well than rodents.

The preceding discussion indicates that there is no direct evidence of population adaptation to high altitude hypoxia in man. There does seem to be some indirect evidence based on inferences from individual and infra-individual adaptation. High altitude natives show an enhanced exercise performance relative to newcomers (greater endurance, high aerobic capacity, relative hypoventilation, and higher diffusing capacity of the lung). They also show a somewhat distinctive pattern of infra-individual adaptations compared to newcomers and to long-term sojourners. If these differences had a genetic basis, one might infer that selection had been operating on the altitude population to produce a distinctive variety of man (Monge, 1948; Baker, 1969). The differences that do exist, however, seem to result from long-term exposure, particularly during the period of growth, and reflect genetic plasticity common to all humans rather than distinctive genetic attributes of the altitude populations (Guleria *et al.*, 1971; Brauer, 1965; Mazess, 1970; Hock, 1970). Even if such differences have a genetic basis, it must be realized that the inference with regard to selection is unsubstantiated. Further, even if selection were operating to enhance organ-system functioning or performance in a single adaptive domain, this is not tantamount to population adaptation. In fact, the stress of high altitude hypoxia seems to be generally deleterious to the individual; adjustments may be possible for man only on a temporary basis and only in certain domains; prolonged sojourn is suspected of leading to both individual and species deterioration (Timiras, 1963, 1965). Our limited understanding of the extent, and etiology, of differences between highlanders and other populations, together with the massive difficulties of assessing population adaptation directly in man, prohibits even tentative conclusions.

ADAPTATION OF HUMAN POPULATIONS
TO ALTITUDE HYPOXIA

The study of adaptation to altitude hypoxia provides a paradigm for the evaluation of human adaptation to the climatic environment. Adaptations can be examined at different levels of the biological hierarchy (organ system, individual, and population) relative to the adaptive domains germane to each hierarchy. The results of this examination are important not only in altitude studies but in studies of other conditions in which tissue hypoxia occurs.

The questions of greatest anthropological import here are (a) the manner in which adaptation occurs at different levels of the biological hierarchy in this specific environmental stress and (b) the extent and etiology of adaptive differences among human populations. This analysis has concentrated chiefly on the first question, and the results may be summarized as follows:

1. *Infra-individual level:* a variety of adjustments assure homeostasis (maintain oxygen transport) or resistance (increase hypoxia tolerance). Hyperventilation and increased tissue capillarity are the two major adaptive responses; increased hypoxic tolerance, associated with cellular changes, is probably of import only where there is failure of the primary homeostatic responses or where the stress is very severe and the primary responses are insufficient.

2. *Individual level:* physical performance, the nervous system, and

growth and development all appear to deteriorate, but, at least in the case of physical performance, longer exposure increases the individual's ability to compensate. Caloric and protein utilization are adversely affected by hypoxia; the prevailing high-carbohydrate, low-fat diet of altitude regions may be the most suitable for these zones. Some abnormalities in reproduction also occur; the primary defect involves fetal growth, development, and survival, rather than fecundity. The margin between health and disease is narrowed at altitude, and common diseases may be exacerbated by physiological alterations occurring in response to hypoxia. The only beneficial effort of hypoxia seems to be an enhancement of resistance and cross-tolerance produced by increased capacity for oxygen transport and cellular metabolism. In sum, hypoxia is a severe stress since it affects nearly all the individual adaptive domains adversely. In this sense, Barcroft's astute observation that altitude is a deteriorating stress is supported (Barcroft, 1925; Barcroft *et al.*, 1922). The adjustments that occur at the infra-individual level do not provide full adaptation to the individual; the nature and extent of partial, or relative, adaptation provided by those adjustments in the various adaptive domains remains to be investigated.

3. *Population level:* there is little or no evidence of any relative benefits at altitude for any population, although some populations may be at a marked disadvantage. High altitude populations have deviant demographic structures, but their significance is unclear. Altitude populations have survived in their own regions, but have not shown other evidence of relative advantage.

With regard to all of the above levels, there is almost no evidence for population differences of any significance from studies with adequate control for extraneous variables, and there is no basis to infer, nor any direct evidence for, populational adaptation to high altitude hypoxia. Differences that do occur among human populations appear to be a result of the nature and extent of stress exposure. Newcomers to altitude have different characteristics than have sojourners, who, in turn, differ from permanent residents. Growth and development at altitude, and the interaction of hypoxia, nutrition, and vigorous physical activity, appear to be responsible for much of the differences that do exist between individuals and between populations. In view of this, there is little reason to speculate on the possible genetic/evolutionary basis of unsubstantiated population adaptation.

One humanistic, or perhaps anthropological, caveat is in order here, for the designation of adaptation is only operational, and the criteria of benefit and the relationships among adaptive domains are subject to both individual and cultural variance. This, however, is not sufficient to prevent systematization or to forgo documentation of those communalities that do exist.

Hypoxia is only one of the numerous environmental variables in the altitude ecosystem. Both the pattern of responses and the adaptive value of these responses will be modified by the interaction of the many environmental variables and the culture of the population. It is the understanding of this formidable interrelated complex that is the task of human adaptability studies. Altitude hypoxia, one hopes, may serve as a useful model for this exciting focus of scientific endeavor.

REFERENCES

Alers, J. O. 1965. Population and development in a Peruvian community. *J. Intl.-Amer. Studies* 7:423-48.

Altland, P. D. and B. Highman. 1968. Sex organ changes and breeding performance of male rats exposed to altitude: Effect of exercise and physical training. *J. Reprod. Fert.* 15:215-22.

Altland, P. D., B. Highman, and M. P. Dieter. 1969. Reduced exercise performance of rats at sea level after altitude acclimatization: Changes in serum enzymes, glucose, corticosterone and tissue structure. *Intl. J. Biometeorol.* 13:173-81.

Andersen, G. L. and R. W. Bullard. 1971. Effect of high altitude on lactic dehydrogenase isozymes and anoxic tolerance of the rat myocardium. *Proc. Soc. Exptl. Biol. Med.* 138:441-43.

Anthony, A. and J. Krieder. 1961. Blood volume changes in rodents exposed to simulated high altitude. *Amer. J. Physiol.* 200:523-26.

Anthony, A., E. Ackerman, and G. K. Strother. 1959. Effects of altitude acclimatization on rat myoglobin. Changes in myoglobin content of skeletal and cardiac muscle. *Amer. J. Physiol.* 196:512-16.

Aoki, V. S. and S. M. Robinson. 1971. Body hydration and the incidence and severity of acute mountain sickness. *J. Appl. Physiol.* 31:363-67.

Arias-Stella, J. 1966. Morphological patterns: Mechanism of pulmonary arterial hypertension. In *Life at High Altitudes*. Publ. 40. Washington, D.C.: Pan American Health Organization.

Arias-Stella, J. and H. Kruger. 1963. Pathology of high altitude pulmonary edema. *Arch. Pathol.* 76:147-59.

Baker, P. T. 1969. Human adaptation to high altitude. *Science* 163:1149-56.

Baker, P. T. 1971. Adaptation problems in Andean human populations. In *The Ongoing Evolution of Latin American Populations*, ed. F. Salzano. Springfield, Ill.: Charles C. Thomas, pp. 475-507.

Baker, P. T. and J. S. Dutt. 1972. Demographic variables as measures of biological adaptation: A case study of high altitude human populations. In *The Structure of Human Populations*, eds. G. A. Harrison and A. J. Boyce. Oxford: Clarendon Press.

Balke, B. 1960. Work capacity at altitude. In *Science and Medicine of Exercise and Sports*, ed. W. R. Johnson. New York: Harper & Bros.

Balke, B. 1963. Work capacity and its limiting factors at high altitude. In *The Physiological Effects of High Altitude*, ed. W. H. Weihe. Oxford: Pergamon.

Balke, B. and J. G. Wells. 1958. Ceiling altitude tolerance following physical training and acclimatization. *J. Aviat. Med.* 29:40-47.

Balke, B., F. J. Nagle, and J. Daniels. 1965. Altitude and maximum performance in work and sports activity. *J.A.M.A.* 194:646-49.

Banchero, N., F. Sime, D. Penaloza, J. Cruz, R. Gamboa, and E. Marticorena. 1966. Pulmonary pressure, cardiac output, and arterial oxygen saturation during exercise at high altitude and at sea levels. *Circulation* 33:249-62.

Barbashova, Z. I. 1964. Cellular level of adaptation. In *Handbook of Physiology. IV. Adaptation to the Environment*, eds. D. B. Dill, E. F. Adolph, and C. G. Wilber. Washington, D.C.: American Physiological Society.

Barbashova, Z. I. 1967. Studies on the mechanisms of resistance to hypoxia: A review. *Intl. J. Biometeorol.* 11:243-54.

Barbashova, Z. I. 1969. Dynamics of adaptive reactions at the cellular level during training of rats to hypoxia. Review of research. *Intl. J. Biometeorol.* 13:211-17.

Barcroft, J. 1925. *The Respiratory Function of the Blood. I. Lessons from High Altitudes.* Cambridge: Cambridge University Press.

Barcroft, J., C. A. Binger, A. V. Bock, J. H. Doggart, H. S. Forbes, G. Harrop, J. C. Meakins, and A. C. Redfield. 1922. Observations upon the effect of high altitude on the physiological processes of the human body, carried out in the Peruvian Andes, chiefly at Cerro de Pasco. *Phil. Trans. Roy. Soc.* B211:351-480.

Barron, D. H., J. Metcalfe, G. Meschia, W. Huckabee, A. Hellegers, and H. Prystowsky. 1963. Adaptations of pregnant ewes and their fetuses to high altitude. In *The Physiological Effects of High Altitude*, ed. W. H. Weihe. Oxford: Pergamon.

Bartlett, D., Jr., 1970. Postnatal growth of the mammalian lung: Influence of low and high oxygen tensions. *Resp. Physiol.* 9:58-64.

Bason, R., C. E. Billings, E. I. Fox, R. J. Gerke, and H. S. Turner. 1971. Energy sources during muscular work under normoxic and hypoxic conditions. *J. Appl. Physiol.* 31:392-96.

Bason, R., C. E. Billings, E. L. Fox, and R. Gerke. 1973. Oxygen kinetics for constant work loads at various altitudes. *J. Appl. Physiol.* 35:497-500.

Bhattacharjya, B. 1964. *Mountain Sickness.* Bristol, England: John Wright & Sons.

Billings, C. E., R. Bason, D. K. Mathews, and E. L. Fox. 1971. Cost of submaximal and maximal work during chronic exposure at 3,800 m. *J. Appl. Physiol.* 30:406-408.

Blume, F. D. and N. Pace. 1969. Changes in the tissue distribution of glucose radiocarbon at altitude. *Fed. Proc.* 28:933-36.

Brauer, R. W. 1965. Irreversible effects. In *The Physiology of Human Survival*, O. G. Edholm and R. Bachrach. London: Academic Press.

Buck, A. A., T. T. Sasaki, and R. I. Anderson. 1968. *Health and Disease in Four Peruvian Villages.* Baltimore: Johns Hopkins Press.

Burri, P. H. and E. R. Weibel. 1971. Morphometric estimation of pulmonary diffusion capacity. II. Effect of PO_2 on the growing lung. *Resp. Physiol.* 11:247-64.

Burton, R. R. and A. H. Smith. 1969. Induction of cardiac hypertrophy and polycythemia in the developing chick at high altitude. *Fed. Proc.* 28: 1170-77.

Buskirk, E. R., J. Kollias, E. Picon-Reategui, R. Akers, E. Prokop, and P. Baker. 1967. Physiology and performance of track athletes at various altitudes in the United States and Peru. In *The Effects of Altitude on Physical Performance*, ed. R. F. Goddard. Chicago: The Athletic Institute.

Byrne-Quinn, E., I. E. Sodal, and J. V. Weil. 1972. Hypoxic and hypercapnic ventilatory drives in children native to high altitude. *J. Appl. Physiol.* 32: 44-46.

Cahoon, R. L. 1972. Simple decision making at high altitude. *Ergonomics* 15: 157-64.

Carbone, F., B. G. Morales, H. D. Haro, and V. H. Zegarra. 1971. Querato-estesiometria sectorial en las grandes alturas. *Arch. Inst. Biologia Andina* 4:19-25.

Carson, R. P., W. O. Evans, J. L. Shields, and J. P. Hannon. 1969. Symptomatology, pathophysiology, and treatment of acute mountain sickness. *Fed. Proc.* 28:1085-91.

Castillo, L. S. and P. S. Timiras. 1964. Electro-convulsive responses of rats to convulsant and anticonvulsant drugs during high-altitude acclimatization. *J. Pharm. Exptl. Ther.* 146:160-66.

Chenykayeva, Ys. Yu. 1964. Investigation of oxidative metabolism enzymes (succinoxidase and cytochrome oxidase) in the cerebral cortex and myelencephalon in hypoxia-acclimated rats. In *Oxygen Insufficiency*, ed. A. F. Makarchenko. Trans. from Russian, Foreign Technology Division, Wright-Patterson AFB, Ohio.

Chernigovsky, V. N. (ed.) 1969. *Problems of Space Biology. 8. Adaptation to Hypoxia and the Resistance of an Organism*. NASA Technical Translation TT F-580. Washington, D.C.: National Aeronautics and Space Administration.

Chinn, K. S. K. and J. P. Hannon. 1969. Efficiency of food utilization at high altitude. *Fed. Proc.* 28:944-47.

Chinn, K. S. K. and J. P. Hannon. 1970. Effects of diet and altitude on the body composition of rats. *J. Nutrition* 100:732-38.

Clegg, E. J. 1968. Some effects of reduced atmospheric pressure on the secondary sexual characters of male mice. *J. Reprod. Fert.* 16:233-42.

Clegg, E. J. 1971. Weight changes in different organs of the mouse at two levels of reduced atmospheric pressure. *J. Appl. Physiol.* 30:764-67.

Clegg, E. J., G. A. Harrison, and P. Baker. 1970. The impact of high altitudes on human populations. *Human Biol.* 42:486-518.

Clegg, E. J., I. G. Pawson, E. H. Ashton, and R. M. Flinn. 1972. The growth of children at different altitudes in Ethiopia. *Phil. Trans. Royal Soc.* (*London*) 264:403-37.

Cobo, B. 1892. *Historia del Nuevo Mundo*. Seville.

Collazos, C. C., F. I. Moscoso, Y. Bravo de R., C. Castellanos, C. Caceres de F., A. Roca, and R. B. Bradfield. 1960. *La Alimentacion y El Estado de Nutricion en el Peru*. Lima, Peru: Ministerio de Salud Publica, Instituto de Nutricion.

Consolazio, C. F., L. O. Matoush, H. L. Johnson, and T. A. Daws. 1968. Protein and water balances of young adults during prolonged exposure to high altitude (4,300 meters). *Amer. J. Clin. Nutr.* 21:154-61.

Consolazio, C. F., L. O. Matush, H. L. Johnson, H. J. Krzywicki, T. A. Daws, and G. J. Isaac. 1969. Effects of high-carbohydrate diets on performance and clinical symptomatology after rapid ascent to high altitude. *Fed. Proc.* 28:937-43.

Consolazio, C. F., H. L. Johnson, H. J. Krzywicki, and T. A. Daws. 1972. Metabolic aspects of acute altitude exposure (4,300 meters) in adequately nourished humans. *Amer. J. Clin. Nutr.* 25:23-29.

Cosio, G. 1969. Mining work in high altitude. *Arch. Environ. Hlth.* 19:540-47.

Cruz-Coke, R., A. P. Cristoffanini, M. Aspillaga, and F. Biancani. 1966. Evolutionary forces in human populations in an environmental gradient in Arica, Chile. *Human Biol.* 38:421-38.

Cruz-Jibaja, J., N. Banchero, F. Sime, D. Penaloza, R. Gamboa, and E. Marticorena. 1964. Correlation between pulmonary artery pressure and level of altitude. *Dis. Chest* 46:446-51.

Cunningham, W. L., E. J. Becker, and F. Kreuzer. 1965. Catecholamines in plasma and urine at high altitudes. *J. Appl. Physiol.* 20:607-10.

Darling, R. C. 1963. High altitude sickness. In *Textbook of Medicine*, eds. Beeson and McDermott. Philadelphia: W. B. Saunders.

Davis, J. N., A. Carlsson, V. MacMillian, and B. K. Siesjo. 1973. Brain tryptophan hydroxylation: Dependence on arterial oxygen tension. *Science* 182:72-73.

Dawson, A. and R. F. Grover. 1974. Regional lung function in natives and long-term residents at 3,100 m altitude. *J. Appl. Physiol.* 36:294-98.

DeBias, D. A. 1966. Thyroid-adrenal relationship on altitude tolerance. *Fed. Proc.* 25:1227-29.

Dedukhova, V. I. and Y. N. Mokhova. 1971. Cellular respiration during high-altitude adaptation of rats. *Space Biol. Med.* (*Moscow*) 5:31-38.

DeGraff, A. C., Jr., R. F. Grover, J. W. Hammond, Jr., J. M. Miller, and R. L. Johnson, Jr. 1965. Pulmonary diffusing capacity in persons native to high altitude. *Clin. Res.* 13:74.

DeGraff, A. C., R. F. Grover, R. L. Johnson, J. W. Hammond, and J. M. Miller. 1970. Diffusing capacity of the lung in Caucasians native to 3100 m. *J. Appl. Physiol.* 29:71-76.

DeJong, G. F. 1970. Demography and research with high altitude populations. *Social Biol.* 17:114-19.

Delaquerriere-Richardson, L., S. Forbes, and E. Valdivia. 1965. Effects of simulated high altitude on the growth rate of albino guinea pigs. *J. Appl. Physiol.* 20:1022-25.

Dickens, F. and E. Neil (ed.). 1963. *Oxygen in the Animal Organism.* New York: Macmillan.

Dill, D. B. 1968. Physiological adjustments to altitude changes. *J.A.M.A.* 205:747-53.

Donayre, J. 1966. Population growth and fertility at high altitude. In *Life at High Altitudes.* Washington, D.C.: Pan American Health Organization.

Donayre, J. 1969. The oestrus cycle of rats at high altitude. *J. Reprod. Fert.* 18:29-32.

Donayre, J., R. Grerra-Garcia, F. Moncloa, and L. A. Sobrevilla. 1968. Endocrine studies at high altitude. IV. Changes in the semen of men. *J. Reprod. Fert.* 16:55-58.

Dorst, J. 1972. Premieres recherches sur la densité, la biomasse et la specialisation ecologique de quelques Rongeurs des hautes Andes du Perou. C.R. Acad. Sc. Paris 274:940-42.

Forster, R. E. 1966. Diffusion as a limiting factor in oxygen transport in cells. In Proceedings of the International Symposium on Cardiovascular and Respiratory Effects of Hypoxia, eds. J. D. Hatcher, and D. B. Jennings. New York: Hafner.

Fregly, M. J. 1971. Cross-adaptations and their significance. Rev. Can. Biol. 30:223-37.

Frehn, J. L., and A. Anthony. 1961. Respiration of liver slices from normal and altitude-acclimatized rats. Amer. J. Physiol. 200:527-29.

Frisancho, A. R. 1969. Human growth and pulmonary function of a high altitude Peruvian Quechua population. Human Biol. 41:365-79.

Frisancho, A. R. 1970. Developmental responses to high altitude hypoxia. Amer. J. Phys. Anthropol. 32:401-407.

Frisancho, A. R. and P. T. Baker. 1970. Altitude and growth: A study of the patterns of physical growth of a high altitude Peruvian Quechua population. Amer. J. Phys. Anthropol. 32:279-92.

Frisancho, A. R. and J. Cossman. 1970. Secular trend in neonatal mortality in the mountain states. Amer. J. Phys. Anthropol. 33:103-106.

Frisancho, A. R., C. Martinez, T. Velasquez, J. Sanchez, and H. Montoye. 1973a. Influence of developmental adaptation on aerobic capacity at high altitude. J. Appl. Physiol. 34:176-80.

Frisancho, A. R., J. Sanchez, D. Pallardel, and L. Yanez. 1973b. Adaptive significance of small body size under poor socio-economic conditions in southern Peru. Amer. J. Phys. Anthropol. 39:255-62.

Galvex, J. 1966. Presion arterial en el sujeto de nivel del mar con residencia prolongada en las grandes alturas. Arch. Instit. Biol. Andina 1:238-43.

Glauser, E. M. 1966. Chronic exposure of young rats to hypoxia and hypercapnia. Arch. Envir. Hlth. 13:597-600.

Goddard, R. F., B. Balke, and U. C. Luft (eds.). 1967. The Effects of Altitude on Physical Performance. Chicago: The Athletic Institute.

Grahn, D. and J. Kratchman. 1963. Variation in neonatal death rate and birth weight in the United States and possible relations to environmental radiation, geology, and altitude. Amer. J. Human Genet. 15:329-52.

Grover, R. F. 1965. Pulmonary circulation in animals and man at high altitude. Ann. N.Y. Acad. Sci. 127:632-39.

Grover, R. F. 1968. The high altitude resident of North America. Scientia 103:1-28.

Grover, R. F., J. T. Okin, H. R. Overy, A. Treger, and F. H. N. Spracklen. 1965. Natural history of pulmonary hypertension in normal adult residents at high altitude. Circulation 32 (Suppl. II):102.

Guleria, J. S., J. N. Pande, P. K. Sethi, and S. B. Roy. 1971. Pulmonary diffusing capacity at high altitude. J. Appl. Physiol. 31:536-43.

Hale, H. B. 1969. Cross-adaptation. Environ. Res. 2:423-34.

Hale, H. B. 1970. Cross-adaptation. In Physiology, Environment, and Man, eds. D. H. K. Lee and D. Minard. New York: Academic Press, pp. 158-69.

Hall, W. H., T. G. Barila, E. C. Metzger, and K. K. Gupta. 1965. A clinical study of acute mountain sickness. Arch. Environ. Hlth. 10:747-53.

Hansen, J. E., C. W. Harris, and W. O. Evans. 1967. Influence of elevation of origin, rate of ascent and a physical conditioning program on symptoms of acute mountain sickness. Military Med. 132:585-92.

Harrison, G. A., C. F. Kuchemann, M. A. S. Moore, A. J. Boyce, T. Baju, A. E. Mourant, M. J. Godber, B. G. Glasgow, A. C. Kopec, D. Tills, and E. J. Clegg. 1969. The effects of altitude variation in Ethiopian populations. *Phil. Trans. Roy. Soc. (London)* 256:147-82.

Hart, J. S., J. P. Hannon, J. L. Shields, and R. Em. Smith (eds.). 1969. Proceedings of the International Symposium on Altitude and Cold. *Fed. Proc.* 28 (3):933-1321.

Hatcher, J. D. and D. B. Jennings (ed.). 1966. *Proceedings of the International Symposium on the Cardiovascular and Respiratory Effects of Hypoxia.* New York: Hafner.

Heath, D. A. 1966. Morphological patterns: The structure, composition, and extensibility of the pulmonary trunk at sea level and high altitude in Peru. In *Life at High Altitudes.* Publ. 140. Washington, D.C.: Pan American Health Organization.

Heer, D. M. 1964. Fertility differences between Indian and Spanish speaking parts of Andean countries. *Pop. Studies* 18:71-84.

Hegnauer, A. H. (ed.). 1969. *Biomedicine of High Terrestrial Elevations.* Natick, Mass.: US Army Research Institute of Environmental Medicine.

Heim, L. M. 1965. Spinal cord convulsions in the developing rat at altitude (12,470 ft., 3,800 m). *Nature* 207:299-300.

Heim, L. M. and P. S. Timiras. 1964. Brain maturation measured by electroshock seizures in rats at high altitude (12,470 ft., 3,800 m). *Nature* 204: 1157-59.

Hock, R. 1970. The physiology of high altitude. *Sci. Amer.* (Feb.):53-62.

Hove, E. L., K. Hickman, and P. L. Harris. 1945. The effect of tocopherol and of fat on resistance of rats to anoxic anemia. *Arch. Biochem.* 8:395-404.

Howard, R. C., P. D. Bruns, and J. A. Lichty. 1957. Studies of babies born at high altitude. III. Arterial oxygen saturation and hematocrit values at birth. *Amer. J. Dis. Child.* 93:674-78.

Howard, R. C., J. A. Lichty, and P. D. Bruns. 1957. Studies of babies born at high altitude. II. Measurement of birth weight, body length, and head size. *Amer. J. Dis. Child.* 93:670-74.

Huckabee, W. E. 1965. Metabolic consequences of chronic hypoxia. *Ann. N.Y. Acad. Sci.* 121:723-30.

Hultgren, H. N. and R. Grover. 1968. Circulatory adaptation to high altitudes. *Ann. Rev. Med.* 19:119-52.

Hultgren, H. N., J. Kelley, and H. Miller. 1965. Effect of oxygen upon pulmonary circulation in acclimatized man at high altitude. *J. Appl. Physiol.* 20:239-43.

Hultgren, H. N., R. F. Grover, and L. H. Hartley. 1971. Abnormal circulatory responses to high altitude in subjects with a previous history of highaltitude pulmonary edema. *Circulation* 44:759-70.

Hurtado, A. 1932. Respiratory adaptation in the Indian natives of the Peruvian Andes. Studies at high altitudes. *Amer. J. Phys. Anthropol.* 17:137-65.

Hurtado, A. 1955. Pathological aspects of life at high altitudes. *Military Med.* 117:272-84.

Hurtado, A. 1960. Some clinical aspects of life at high altitudes. *Ann. Intern. Med.* 53:247-58.

Hurtado, A. 1963. Natural acclimatization to high altitudes. In *The Regula-*

tion of Human Respiration, eds. D. J. C. Cunningham and B. B. Lloyd. Oxford: Blackwell.

Hurtado, A. 1964a. Animals at high altitude: Resident man. In *Handbook of Physiology, IV. Adaptation to the Environment*, eds. D. B. Dill, E. F. Adolph, and C. G. Wilber. Washington, D.C.: American Physiological Society.

Hurtado, A. 1964b. Some physiologic and clinical aspects of life at high altitudes. In *Aging of the Lung*, ed. L. Cander. New York: Grune & Stratton.

Ingalls, T. H., F. J. Curley, and R. A. Prindle. 1952. Experimental production of congenital anomalies. Timing and degree of anoxia as factors causing fetal deaths and congenital anomalies in the mouse. *New Engl. J. Med.* 247:758-68.

James, W. H. 1966. The effect of altitude on fertility in Andean countries. *Pop. Studies* 20:97-101.

Johnson, D. and P. D. Roofe. 1965. Blood constituents of normal newborn rats and those exposed to low oxygen tension during gestation; weight of newborn and litter size considered. *Anat. Rec.* 153:303-10.

Johnson, H. L., C. F. Consolazio, I. O. Matoush, and H. J. Krzywicki. 1969. Nitrogen and mineral metabolism at altitude. *Fed. Proc.* 28:1195-98.

Jokl, E. and P. Jokl (ed.). 1968. *Medicine and Sport. Vol. I. Exercise and Altitude*. Basel: Karger.

Karlsson, J. and B. Saltin. 1971. Diet, muscle glycogen, and endurance performance. *J. Appl. Physiol.* 31:203-206.

Klain, G. J. 1972. Acute high altitude stress and enzyme activities in the rat adrenal medulla. *Endocrinology* 91:1447-49.

Klain, G. J. and J. P. Hannon. 1970. High altitude and protein metabolism in the rat. *Proc. Soc. Exptl. Biol. Med.* 134:1000-1004.

Kobrick, J. L. 1970. Effects of hypoxia and acetazolamide on color sensitivity zones in the visual field. *J. Appl. Physiol.* 28:741-47.

Kobrick, J. L. and B. Appleton. 1971. Effects of extended hypoxia on visual performance and retinal vascular state. *J. Appl. Physiol.* 31:357-62.

Kogure, K., P. Scheinberg, O. M. Reinmuth, M. Fugishima, and R. Busto. 1970. Mechanisms of cerebral vasodilatation in hypoxia. *J. Appl. Physiol.* 29:223-29.

Kreuzer, F. and P. van Lookeren Campagne. 1965. Resting pulmonary diffusing capacity for CO and O_2 at high altitude. *J. Appl. Physiol.* 20:519-24.

Krzywicki, H. J., C. F. Consolazio, H. L. Johnson, W. C. Nielsen, and R. A. Barnhart. 1971. Water metabolism in humans during acute high-altitude exposure (4,300 m). *J. Appl. Physiol.* 30:806-809.

Lahiri, S. 1966. Muscular exercise in the Himalayan high-altitude residents. *Fed. Proc.* 25:1392-96.

Lahiri, S. 1968. Alveolar gas pressures in man with life-time hypoxia. *Resp. Physiol.* 4:373-86.

Lahiri, S. and J. S. Milledge. 1965. Sherpa physiology. *Nature* 207:610-12.

Lahiri, S., F. F. Kao, T. Valasquez, C. Martinez, and W. Pezzia. 1969. Irreversible blunted respiratory sensitivity to hypoxia in high altitude natives. *Resp. Physiol.* 6:360-74.

Lahiri, S., F. F. Kao, T. Valasquez, C. Martinez, and W. Pezzia. 1970. Respiration of man during exercise at high altitude: Highlander vs. lowlander. *Resp. Physiol.* 8:361-75.

Lefrancois, R., H. Cautier, and P. Pasquis. 1968. Ventilatory oxygen drive in acute and chronic hypoxia. *Resp. Physiol.* 4:217-28.

Lenfant, C. and K. Sullivan. 1971. Adaptation to high altitude. *New Engl. J. Med.* 284:1298-1309.

Lichty, J. A., R. Y. Ting, P. D. Bruns, and E. Dyar. 1957. Studies of babies born at high altitude. I. Relation of altitude to birth weight. *Am. J. Dis. Child.* 93:666-69.

Makarchenko, A. F. (ed.). 1964. *Oxygen Insufficiency.* (Trans. from Russian.) Foreign Technology Division, Wright-Patterson Air Force Base, Ohio.

Makowski, E. L., F. C. Battaglia, G. Meschia, R. E. Behrman, J. Schruefer, A. E. Seeds, and P. D. Bruns. 1968. Effect of maternal exposure to high altitude upon fetal oxygenation. *Amer. J. Obst. Gynecol.* 100:852-61.

Margaria, R. (ed.). 1967. *Exercise at Altitude.* Amsterdam: Excerpta Medica Foundation.

Margaria, R. and P. Cerretelli. 1962. Physiological aspects of life at extreme altitudes. In *Biometeorology,* ed. S. W. Tropm. Oxford: Pergamon.

Marticorena, E., F. A. Tapia, J. Dyer, J. Serino, N. Banchero, R. Gamboa, H. Kruger, and D. Penaloza. 1964. Pulmonary edema by ascending to high altitudes. *Dis. Chest* 45:273-83.

Mazess, R. B. 1965. Neonatal mortality and altitude in Peru. *Amer. J. Phys. Anthropol.* 23:209-14.

Mazess, R. B. 1968. The oxygen cost of breathing in man: Effects of altitude, training and race. *Amer. J. Phys. Anthropol.* 29:365-76.

Mazess, R. B. 1969a. Exercise performance at high altitude in Peru. *Fed. Proc.* 28:1301-1306.

Mazess, R. B. 1970. Cardiorespiratory characteristics and adaptation to high altitudes. *Amer. J. Phys. Anthropol.* 32:267-78.

Mazess, R. B. 1975a. Adaptation: A conceptual framework. In *Evolutionary Models and Studies in Human Diversity.* The Hague: Mouton & Co.

Mazess, R. B. 1975b. Biological adaptation: Aptitudes and acclimatization. In *Biosocial Interrelations in Population Adaptation* (in press).

McClung, J. 1969. *Effects of High Altitude on Human Birth. Observations on Mothers, Placentas and the Newborn in Two Peruvian Populations.* Cambridge, Mass.: Harvard University Press.

McFarland, R. A. 1952. Anoxia: Its effect on the physiology and biochemistry of the brain and on behavior. In *The Biology of Mental Health and Disease.* New York: Hoeber.

McFarland, R. A. 1969a. The problems of aging at altitude. *Yale Sci. Mag.* 43:20-28.

McFarland, R. A. 1969b. Review of the experimental findings in sensory and mental functions at high altitude. In *Biomedicine of High Terrestrial Elevations,* ed. A. H. Hegnauer, Natick, Mass.: U.S. Army Research Institute of Environmental Medicine.

McGrath, J. J., R. W. Bullard, and G. K. Komives. 1969. Functional adaptation in cardiac and skeletal muscle after exposure to simulated high altitude. *Fed. Proc.* 28:1307-11.

McGrath, J. J., J. Prochazka, V. Pelouch, and Ostadal. 1973. Physiological responses of rats to intermittent high-altitude stress: Effects of age. *J. Appl. Physiol.* 34:289-93.

Meerson, F. Z., O. A. Gomzakov, and M. V. Shimkovich. 1973. Adaptation to high altitude hypoxia as a factor preventing development of myocardial ischemic necrosis. *Amer. J. Cardiol.* 31:30-34.

Metcalfe, J. 1970. Uterine oxygen supply and fetal health. *Yale J. Biol. Med.* 42:166-79.

Moncloa, F., M. Gomez, and A. Hurtado. 1965. Plasma catecholamines at high altitude. *J. Appl. Physiol.* 20:1329-31.

Monge, C., 1966. Natural acclimatization to high altitudes: Clinical condition. In *Life at High Altitudes.* Washington, D.C.: Pan American Health Organization.

Monge, C. C., R. Lozano, and A. Carcelen. 1964. Renal excretion of bicarbonate in high altitude natives and in natives with chronic mountain sickness. *J. Clin. Invest.* 43:2303-2309.

Monge, C. C., R. Lozano, and J. Whittembury. 1965. Effect of blood-letting on chronic mountain sickness. *Nature* 207:770.

Monge, M. C. 1943. Chronic mountain sickness. *Physiol. Rev.* 23:166-84.

Monge, C. 1948. *Acclimatization in the Andes.* Baltimore: Johns Hopkins Press.

Monge, C. 1954. Men, climate, and changes of altitude. *Meterol. Monog.* 2:50-60.

Monge, M. C. and C. C. Monge. 1966. *High Altitude Diseases.* Springfield, Ill.: Charles C. Thomas.

Moore, T. 1968. The world's great mountains: Not the height you think. *Amer. Alpine J.* 109-16.

Mori-Chavez, P., A. C. Upton, M. Salazar, and J. W. Conklin. 1970. Influence of altitude on late effects of radiation in RF/Un mice: Observations on survival time, blood changes, body weight, and incidence of neoplasms. *Cancer Res.* 30:913-28.

Mori-Chavez, P., A. C. Upton, J. M. Salazar, and J. W. Conklin. 1974. Influence of transitory, as compared with permanent, high-altitude exposure on the pathogenesis of spontaneous and X-ray induced neoplasms in RF/Un mice. *Cancer Res.* 34:328-36.

Morton, W. E. 1966. Altitude and rheumatic fever in Colorado. *Amer. J. Epidemiol.* 83:250-53.

Morton, W. E., D. J. Davids, and J. A. Lichty. 1964. Mortality from heart disease at high altitude. *Arch. Environ. Hlth.* 9:21-24.

Myles, W. S. 1972. The excretion of 11-hydroxycortico-steroids by rats during exposure to altitude. *Intl. J. Biometeorl.* 16:367-74.

Myles, W. S., and A. J. Ducker. 1973. The role of the sympathetic nervous system during exposure to altitude in rats. *Intl. J. Biometeorl.* 17:51-58.

Naeye, R. L. 1966. Organ and cellular development in mice growing at simulated high altitude. *Lab. Invest.* 15:700-706.

Nayak, N. C., S. Roy, and T. K. Narayanan. 1964. Pathologic features of altitude sickness. *Amer. J. Pathol.* 45:381-91.

Ohlbaum, M. K. 1969. The effects of hypoxia on certain aspects of visual performance. *Amer. J. Optometry* 46:235-49.

Olander, H. J., R. R. Burton, and H. E. Adler. 1967. The pathophysiology of chronic hypoxia in chickens. *Avian Dis.* 11:609-20.

Otis, A. B. 1964. Some physiological responses to chronic hypoxia. In *Oxygen in the Animal Organism*, eds. F. Dickens and E. Neil. Oxford: Pergamon.

Ou, L. C. and S. M. Tenney. 1970. Properties of mitochondria from hearts of cattle acclimatized to high altitude. *Resp. Physiol.* 8:151-59.

Pan American Health Organization. 1966. *Life at High Altitudes.* Publ. 140. Washington, D.C.: Pan American Health Organization.

Penaloza, D. and F. Sime. 1971. Chronic cor pulmonale due to loss of altitude acclimatization (chronic mountain sickness). *Amer. J. Med.* 50:728-43.

Penaloza, D., F. Sime, N. Banchero, R. Gamboa, J. Cruz, and E. Marticorena. 1963. Pulmonary hypertension in healthy men born and living at high altitudes. *Amer. J. Cardiol.* 11:150-57.

Penaloza, D., J. Arias-Stella, F. Sime, S. Recavarren, and E. Marticorena. 1964. The heart and pulmonary circulation in children at high altitudes—physiological, anatomical, and clinical observations. *Pediatrics* 34:568-82.

Pepelko, W. E. 1970. Effects of hypoxia and hypercapnia, singly and combined, on growing rats. *J. Appl. Physiol.* 28:646-51.

Petropoulos, E. A., A. Vernedakis, and P. S. Timiras. 1969. Nucleic acid content in developing rat brain after prenatal and/or neonatal exposure to high altitude. *Fed. Proc.* 28:1001-1005.

Petropoulos, E. A., A. Vernadakes, and P. S. Timiras. 1970. Neurochemical changes in rats subjected neonatally to high altitude and electroshock. *Amer. J. Physiol.* 218:1351-56.

Petropoulos, E. A., K. B. Dalal, and P. S. Timiras. 1972. Effects of high altitude on myelinogenesis in brain of the developing rat. *Amer. J. Physiol.* 223:951-57.

Picon-Reategui, E. 1962. Studies on the metabolism of carbohydrates at sea level and at high altitude. *Metabolism.* 11:1148-54.

Porter, R., and R. Knight (ed.). 1971. *High Altitude Physiology.* Edinburgh: Churchill Livingstone.

Poupa, O., K. Krofta, J. Prochazka, and Z. Turek. 1966. Acclimation to simulated high altitude and acute cardiac necrosis. *Fed. Proc.* 25:1243-46.

Printz, R. H. 1972. The effects of high altitude on the reproductive cycle and pregnancy in the hamster. *Anat. Rec.* 173:157-72.

Prohaska, F. 1970. Distinctive bioclimatic parameters of the subtropical-tropical Andes. *Intl. J. Biometerol.* 14:1-22.

Pugh, L. G. C. E. 1964. Cardiac output in muscular exercise at 5800 m (19,000 ft). *J. Appl. Physiol.* 19:441-47.

Pugh, L. G. C. E. 1968. Muscular exercise on Mount Everest. In *Medicine and Sport. I. Exercise and Altitude,* eds. E. Jokl and P. Jokl. Basel: Karger.

Pugh, L. G. C. E., M. B. Gill, S. Lahiri, J. B. Milledge, M. P. Ward, and J. B. West. 1964. Muscular exercise at great altitudes. *J. Appl. Physiol.* 19: 431-40.

Quinones, M. E. 1968. La enfermedad varicosa en la altura. *Arch. Inst. Biol. Andina* 2:274-75.

Rennie, D., E. Marticorena, C. Monge, and L. Sirotzky. 1971. Urinary protein excretion in high-altitude residents. *J. Appl. Physiol.* 31:257-59.

Rennie, D., R. Frayser, G. Gray, and C. Houston. 1972. Urine and plasma proteins in men at 5400 m. *J. Appl. Physiol.* 32:369-73.

Reynafarje, D. B. 1961. Pyridine nucleotide oxidases and transhydrogenase in acclimatization to high altitude. *Amer. J. Physiol.* 200:351-54.

Reynafarje, B. 1962. Myoglobin content and enzymatic activity of muscle and altitude adaptation. *J. Appl. Physiol.* 17:301-305.

Reynafarje, B. 1966. Physiological patterns: Enzymatic changes. In *Life at High Altitudes.* Washington, D.C.: Pan American Health Organization.

Reynafarje, D. B. 1971. Mecanismos moleculares de la adaptacion a la hipoxia de las grandes alturas. *Arch. Inst. Biologia Andina* 4:1-14.

Reynafarje, B., and P. Morrison. 1962. Myoglobin levels in some tissues from wild Peruvian rodents native to high altitude. *J. Biol. Chem.* 237:2861-64.

Reynafarje, B., A. Rodriguez, and F. Yen. 1965. Influencia de la altura y el ejercicio fisico sobre la dehidrogenasa lactica del suero y la catalasa sanguinea. *Arch. Inst. Biologia Andina* 1:25-31.

Reynafarje, B., E. Marticorena, J. Guillen, and Arratte. 1966. Contenido pigmentario y enzymatico del musculo esqueletico humano a nivel del mar y en la altura. *Arch. Inst. Biologia Andina* 1:170-78.

Richtarik, A., H. Hift, and E. Valdivia. 1966. Catecholamines in tissue of guinea pigs subjected to hypoxia. *Arch. Intl. Pharmacodyn.* 159:44-47.

Robin, E. D., and H. V. Murdaugh, Jr. 1967. Some general aspects of oxygen depletion. *Intl. Anesthesiol. Clinic* 5 (2):345-58.

Robinson, S. M., A. B. King, and V. Aoki. 1971. Acute mountain sickness: Reproducibility of its severity and duration in an individual. *Aerospace Med.* 42:706-708.

Russek, M., and J. R. Beaton. 1967. Effect of acute exercise on cerebral blood flow in man. *Proc. Soc. Exptl. Biol. Med.* 125:341-78.

Schmidt, J. P. 1969. Resistance to infectious disease versus exposure to hypobaric pressure and hypoxic, normoxic or hyperoxic atmospheres. *Fed. Proc.* 28:1099-1103.

Schnakenberg, D. D. and R. F. Burlington. 1970. Effect of high carbohydrate, protein, and fat diets and high altitude on growth and caloric intake of rats. *Proc. Soc. Exptl. Biol. Med.* 134:905-908.

Sechzer, J. A., M. D. Faro, J. N. Barker, D. Barsky, S. Gutierrez, and W. F. Wondle. 1971. Developmental behaviors: Delayed appearance in monkeys asphyxiated at birth. *Science* 171:1173-75.

Sehgal, A. K. 1968. Observations on the blood pressure of Tibetans. *Circulation.* 37:36-49.

Selye, H. 1950. *The Physiology and Pathology of Exposure to Stress.* Montreal: Acta.

Selye, H. 1952. *The Story of the Adaptation Syndrome.* Montreal: Acta.

Selye, H. 1956. *The Stress of Life.* New York: McGraw-Hill.

Severinghaus, J. W., C. R. Bainton, and A. Carcelen. 1966. Respiratory insensitivity to hypoxia in chronically hypoxic man. *Resp. Physiol.* 1:308-34.

Shapiro, W., A. J. Wasserman, and J. L. Patterson, Jr. 1966. Human cerebrovascular response to combined hypoxia and hypercapnia. *Circ. Res.* 19: 903-10.

Shivers, R. R. and P. G. Roofe. 1966. Cerebral cell population under hypoxia. *Anat. Rec.* 154:841-46.

Sime, F., N. Banchero, D. Penaloza, R. Gamboa, J. Cruz, and E. Marticorena. 1963. Pulmonary hypertension in children born and living at high altitudes. *Amer. J. Cardiol.* 11:143-49.

Singh, I., and I. S. Chohan. 1972. Abnormalities of blood coagulation at high altitude. *Intl. J. Biometeorl.* 16:283-97.

Singh, I., C. C. Kapila, P. K. Khanna, R. B. Nanda, and B. D. P. Rao. 1965. High-altitude pulmonary edema. *Lancet* 7379:229-34.

Singh, I., P. K. Khanna, M. C. Srivastava, M. Lal, S. B. Roy, and C. S. V. Subramanyam. 1969. Acute mountain sickness. *New Engl. J. Med.* 288: 175-84.

Siri, W. E., A. S. Cleveland, and P. Blanche. 1969. Adrenal gland activity in Mt. Everest climbers. *Fed. Proc.* 28:1251-56.

Smith, A. H., R. R. Burton, and E. L. Besch. 1969. Development of the chick embryo at high altitude. *Fed. Proc.* 28:1092-98.

Smith, E. E. and J. W. Crowell. 1963. Influence of the hematocrit ratio on survival of unacclimatized dogs at simulated high altitude. *Amer. J. Physiol.* 205:1172-74.

Smith, E. E. and J. W. Crowell. 1967. Role of an increased hematocrit in altitude acclimatization. *Aerospace Med.* 38:39-43.

Sobrevilla, L. A., M. T. Cassinelli, A. Carcelen, and J. M. Malaga. 1971. Human fetal and maternal oxygen tension and acid-base status during delivery at high altitude. *Amer. J. Obstet. Gynecol.* 111:1111-18.

Sorenson, S. C. and J. W. Severinghaus. 1968a. Respiratory sensitivity to acute hypoxia in man at sea level living at high altitude. *J. Appl. Physiol.* 25:211-16.

Sorenson, S. C. and J. W. Severinghaus. 1968b. Irreversible respiratory insensitivity to acute hypoxia in man born at high altitude. *J. Appl. Physiol.* 25: 217-20.

Sorenson, S. C. and J. W. Severinghaus. 1968. Respiratory insensitivity to acute hypoxia persisting after correction of tetralogy of Fallot. *J. Appl. Physiol.* 25:221-23.

Souhrada, J., B. Mrzena, O. Poupa, and R. W. Bullard. 1971. Functional changes of cardiac muscle in adaptation on two types of chronic hypoxia. *J. Appl. Physiol.* 30:214-18.

Stamper, D. A., R. A. Kinsman, and W. O. Evans. 1970. Subjective symptomatology and cognitive performance at high altitude. *Percept. Motor Skills* 31:247-61.

Stini, W. 1972. Reduced sexual dimorphism in upper arm muscle circumference associated with protein-deficient diet in a South American population. *Amer. J. Phys. Anthropol.* 36:341-52.

Strickland, E. H., E. Ackerman, and A. Anthony. 1959. Effects of altitude acclimatization on the equilibrium constant of rat oxymyoglobin. *Amer. J. Physiol.* 197:211-13.

Strickland, E. H., E. Ackerman, and A. Anthony. 1961. Effects of hypoxia on heart and liver mitochondrial respiration and phosphorylation. *Aerospace Med.* 32:746-50.

Strother, G. K., E. Ackerman, A. Anthony, and E. H. Strickland. 1959. Effects of altitude acclimatization on rat myoglobin. Effect of viscosity and acclimatization on myoglobin reaction rates. *Amer. J. Physiol.* 196:517-19.

Stycos, J. M. 1963. Culture and differential fertility in Peru. *Pop. Studies.* 16: 257-70.

Surks, M. I. 1968. Metabolism of human serum albumin in man during acute exposure to high altitude (14,000 ft). *J. Clin. Invest.* 45:1442-51.

Swain, C., 1970. Sea level and high altitude breeding colonies of *Peromyscus maniculatus sonoriensis. Amer. J. Physiol.* 218:1263-66.

Tengerdy, R. P. and T. Kramer. 1968. Immune response of rabbits during short exposure to high altitude. *Nature* 217:367-69.

Tenney, S. M. and L. C. Ou. 1970. Physiological evidence for increased tissue capillarity in rats acclimatized to high altitude. *Resp. Physiol.* 8:137-50.

Thomas, R. B. 1972. *Human Adaptation to a High Andean Energy Flow System.* Ph.D. Thesis in Anthropology, Pennsylvania State University.

Timiras, P. S. 1963. Comparison of growth and development of the rat at high altitude and at sea level. In *The Physiological Effects of High Altitude,* ed. W. H. Weihe. Oxford: Pergamon.

Timiras, P. S. 1965. High-altitude studies. In *Methods of Animal Experimentation,* vol. 2. Academic Press, pp. 333-67.

Timiras, P. S. and D. E. Woolley. 1966. Functional and morphologic develop-
    ment of brain and other organs of rats at high altitude. *Fed. Proc.* 25:
    1312-20.
Timiras, P. S., A. A. Krum, and N. Pace. 1957. Body and organ weights of rats
    during acclimatization to an altitude of 12,470 feet. *Amer. J. Physiol.*
    191:598-604.
Torrance, J. D., C. Lenfant, J. Cruz, and E. Marticorena. 1971. Oxygen trans-
    port mechanisms in residents at high altitude. *Resp. Physiol.* 11:1-15.
Trapani, I. L. 1963. Immunophysiological considerations of antibody forma-
    tion at high altitude. In *The Physiological Effects of High Altitude*, ed.
    W. H. Weihe. Oxford: Pergamon.
Trapani, I. L. 1966. Altitude, temperature and the immune response. *Fed.
    Proc.* 25:1254-59.
Trapani, I. L. 1969. Environment, infection, and immunoglobulin synthesis.
    Fed. Proc. 28:1104-1106.
Trapani, I. L. and D. H. Campbell. 1959. Passive antibody decay in rabbits
    under cold or altitude stress. *J. Appl. Physiol.* 14:424-26.
Trapani, I. L. and M. L. Cohn. 1963. Environmental effects on experimental
    aerogenic tuberculosis in BCG-immunized and non-immunized guinea
    pigs. *Proc. Soc. Exptl. Biol. Med.* 113:571-74.
Tune, G. S. 1964. Psychological effects of hypoxia: Review of certain literature
    from the period 1950 to 1963. *Percept. Motor Skills* 19:551-62.
Valdivia, E. 1958. Total capillary bed in striated muscle of guinea pigs native
    to the Peruvian mountains. *Amer. J. Physiol.* 194:585-89.
Valdivia, E., M. Watson, and C. M. Dass. 1960. Histologic alterations in mus-
    cles of guinea pigs during chronic hypoxia. *Arch. Pathol.* 69:199-208.
Valdivia, E., J. Sonnad, J. D'Amato. 1966. Fatty change of the granular
    pneumocyte. *Science* 151:213-14.
Van Liere, E. J. and J. C. Stickney. 1963. *Hypoxia.* Chicago: University of
    Chicago Press.
Velasquez, M. T. 1965. Resistencia del nativo de la altura a la anoxia pro-
    funda. *Arch. Inst. Biol. Andina* 1:1-13.
Velasquez, T. 1966. Actividad fisica y cambios de altura. *Arch. Instit. Biol.
    Andina* 1:189-212.
Velasquez, T. 1970. Aspects of physical activity in high altitude natives. *Amer.
    J. Phys. Anthropol.* 32:251-58.
Velasquez, M. T. and E. Florentini. 1966. Maxima capacidad de difusion del
    pulmon en nativos de la altura. *Arch. Instit. Biol. Andina* 1:179-87.
Velasquez, L. L. 1972. Cardiopatias de altura. *Rev. Inst. Boliviano Biol. Altura*
    4:16-24.
Vogel, J. H. K. (ed.). 1970. *Hypoxia, High Altitude and the Heart.* Basel:
    Karger.
Vogel, J. H. K., W. F. Weaver, R. L. Rose, S. G. Blount, Jr., and R. F.
    Grover. 1962. Pulmonary hypertension on exertion in normal man liv-
    ing at 10,150 feet (Leadville, Colorado). *Med. Thorac.* 19:269-85.
Weihe, W. (ed.). 1963a. *The Physiological Effects of High Altitude.* Oxford:
    Pergamon.
Weihe, H. (ed.). 1963b. Some examples of endocrine and metabolic functions
    in rats during acclimatization to high altitude. In *The Physiological
    Effects of High Altitude*, ed. W. Weihe. Oxford: Pergamon.

Weihe, W. H. 1965. Influence of altitude and cold on pregnancy and lactation of rats fed on two different diets. *Intl. J. Biometeorl.* 9:43-52.

Weihe, W. H. and H. Hurni. 1963. The resistance of three inbred strains of immunized and nonimmunized mice to *E. coli* infection at low and high altitude. In The *Physiological Effects of High Altitude*, ed. W. H. Weihe. Oxford: Pergamon.

Weiskopf, R. B. and J. W. Severinghaus. 1972. Diffusing capacity of the lung for CO in man during acute acclimatization to 14,246 ft. *J. Appl. Physiol.* 32:285-89.

West, J. B. 1962. Diffusing capacity of the lung for carbon monoxide at high altitude. *J. Appl. Physiol.* 17:421-26.

West, J. B., S. Lahiri, M. B. Gill, J. S. Milledge, L. G. C. E. Pugh, and M. P. Ward. 1962. Arterial oxygen saturation during exercise at high altitude. *J. Appl. Physiol.* 17:617-21.

Whitehead, L. 1968. Altitude, fertility and mortality in Andean countries *Pop. Studies* 21:71-73.

Whittenbury, J. and C. C. Monge. 1972. High altitude, hematocrit and age. *Nature* 238:278-79.

Whitten, B. K. and A. H. Janoski. 1969. Effects of high altitude and diet on lipid components of human serum. *Fed. Proc.* 28:983-86.

Whitten, B. K., J. P. Hannon, G. J. Klain, and K. S. K. Chinn. 1968. Effect of high altitude (14,100 ft.) on nitrogenous components of human serum. *Metabolism* 17:360-65.

Williams, B., D. E. Woolley, and P. S. Timiras. 1966. Synaptic delay and conduction time in brain during exposure to simulated high altitudes. *Nature* 211:889-90.

Woolley, D. E. and P. S. Timiras. 1963. Changes in brain glycogen concentration in rats during high altitude (12,470 ft) exposure. *Proc. Soc. Exptl. Med.* 114:571-74.

Woolley, D. E. and P. S. Timiras. 1965. Prepyriform electrical activity in the rat during high altitude exposure. *Electroenceph. Clin. Neurophysiol.* 18: 680-90.

Woolley, D. E., S. M. Herrero, and P. S. Timiras. 1963. CNS excitability changes during altitude acclimatization and deacclimatization in rats. *Amer. J. Physiol.* 205:727-32.

Wulff, L. Y., I. A. Braden, F. H. Shillito, and J. F. Tomashefski. 1968. *Physiological Factors Relating to Terrestrial Altitudes: A Bibliography.* Publ. 3. Columbus, Ohio: Ohio State University Libraries.

Zapata, B. and E. Marticorena. 1968. Presion arterial sistemica en el individuo senil de altura. *Arch. Instit. Biol. Andina* 2:220-28.

Zapata-Ortiz, V., R. Castro de la Mata, E. Fernandez, A. Geu, and L. Batalla. 1966. Experimental shock in animals adapted to high altitude. *Acta Physiol. Lat. Am.* 16:66-67.

Zapata-Ortiz, V., R. Castro de la Mata, E. Fernandez, L. Batalia, and A. Geu. 1967. Experimental hemorrhagic shock in animals adapted to high altitudes. *Acta Physiol. Lat. Am.* 17:194-99.

Zhironkin, A. G. 1964. Increasing the resistance of animals to the toxic action of excess oxygen by acclimatization to hypoxia. In *Oxygen Insufficiency* (Trans. from Russian.), ed. A. F. Makarchenko. Wright Patterson Air Force Base, Ohio.

9. Nutritional Adaptation in Man

MARSHALL T. NEWMAN*

INTRODUCTION

Human biologists have been slow to recognize the tremendous importance of nutrition as a key environmental factor affecting man's evolution and variability. When they finally entered the nutritional field, they tended to do so by the back door—without the requisite background in biochemistry, clinical medicine, and food sciences. They first entered principally because the so-called "plasticity" studies, brought to focus by Boas (1911), strongly suggested that postnatal growth and maturation and adult morphology were strongly influenced by diet. Later, their interests expanded to such an extent that by 1966 Garn could say that "primate nutrition, both human and infrahuman, is closely connected to many of the key problems and traditional interests of physical anthropology."

Basic to these interests is the emphasis of modern human biology upon the intimate and complex feedback relationships between man's evolution and his environments. But of increasing moment is the current involvement with the quality of human life throughout the world and its ecological and cultural correlates as they are reflected in man's biological processes and health. These emphases have increasingly invited the attention of a considerable cadre of human biologists to man's nutrition, principally as covered by the following four topics:

1. Biological and cultural evolutionary aspects of human nutrition, with the view to sharpening the focus on man's current dietary dilemmas

* Department of Anthropology, University of Washington, Seattle, Washington.

2. The world's food supply and related problems of quantity and quality of food

3. The effects of nutritional inadequacies upon health and quality of life, with special reference to growth processes and resulting adult morphology in the people of the underdeveloped four-fifths of the world

4. The influence of overnutrition upon the growth, adult morphology, and health of the economically more privileged people in the industrialized, developed one-fifth of the world

BIOLOGICAL AND CULTURAL EVOLUTIONARY ASPECTS OF HUMAN NUTRITION

The hunting phase of man

Man's history as a consummate hunter with a strong dependence upon animal foods goes back at least one million years. Doubtless, there were temporal and regional variations in the amounts of animal food versus collected wild vegetable food consumed during man's long hunting phase. Detailed paleonutritional studies in archeological sites, especially in dry caves where vegetable remains may be preserved, would help elucidate the proportions of hunter-gatherer food sources. Butzer (1971) states that, from the variety and volume of food animal bones found in *Homo erectus* living sites in the Old World, Pleistocene megafauna was apparently hunted on a large scale, possibly eclipsing the importance of vegetable foods in many areas. Of modern hunter-gatherers, however, Service (1966) says "in only a few instances (the Eskimo, particularly) is the hunting of animals as productive as the gathering of seeds, roots, fruits, nuts, and berries." He cites Meggitt's (1964) estimate that in aboriginal Australia—even on the north coast where game and fish are said to have been abundant—vegetable foods, collected principally by women, made up 70 to 80% of the diet. Such estimates are based upon bulk or quantity, rather than quality, and clearly reflects the biota mass of the region. For native Australia, the biota mass (kilogram of game animals per square kilometer) was probably low in Bourliere's (1963) terms. Anyway, it could be argued that most if not all surviving hunter-gatherer populations had been squeezed out of game-rich territories, so, perforce, they would depend heavily upon collected wild vegetables for their food supply.

In any case, man's long hunting phase indubitably brought a high proportion of animal food into his diet and appears to have wrought notable changes in both his social life and his metabolically controlled growth and constitutional patterns. As the next to the last link in the complex food chain leading to man (who may, himself, be consumed by predators), the flesh of game animals is packed with nutrients. Meat is a handy, portable, concentrated food and, in the terminal Mousterian and Upper Paleolithic, appears to have been "harvested" twice annually from migratory herds and possibly stored by smoking or drying (Binford, 1970).

Yet this sort of dependence upon the fruits of the chase means that alterations in the available biota mass could and probably did place hunting populations on periodic short rations. The legends and more contemporary accounts of such technologically well-adapted hunters as the Eskimo (Weyer, 1932) are replete with themes of famine and starvation. Under a "feast or famine" mode of life, McKusick (1963) has suggested that the ability to more efficiently metabolize food and build bodily energy reserves would confer selective advantages. There are several possibilities for favorable genotypes under conditions of severe food deprivation: (a) those determining hypercholesterolemia, which could relate to the extraordinary ability of some hunting people like the Eskimo to metabolize the plentiful fats in their diet; (b) the "thrifty" genotypes (Neel, 1962) with exceptional metabolic efficiency, which, in industrialized civilizations, may lead to diabetes mellitus; and (c) the apparently related genotypes in the sense of those "strange bedfellows" diabetes and obesity predisposing to greater fat storage. The ontogenetic foundation of fat accumulation is actually laid down perinatally and in early childhood in the form of excessive numbers of fat cells, which, once formed, do not disappear even with carefully controlled dieting. Clearly, this early timing of fat build-up could be advantageous to the very young in hunting societies, and conceivably may constitute a temporal aspect of the genetic programming. All three of these hypothetical genotypes become disadvantageous in a high calorie, high carbohydrate, underexercised modern way of life. There may be essentially non-genic accommodations to periodic famine as well, since Grande (1964, p. 931) indicates that "the ability of the body to adapt itself to caloric deficit seems to be enhanced by repetition of the fasting periods."

Prime dependence upon animal food during the million-year hunting phase may very well have altered, through evolution, the amount and especially the kind of man's protein requirements. Infant and early childhood protein requirements are high, as much as four times per unit body weight as adult requirements. Moreover, only the amino acid balance of animal protein provides for the optimum human utilization. The FAO (1957) reference pattern for the proportions of the eight essential amino acids (plus histidine for growth) is closely approached only by proteins of animal derivation. Lederberg (1969, pp. 10-11) has recently described protein malnutrition in man as a rather peculiar kind of genetic deficiency disease. Arguing that "man has evolved from precursors which had the capacity to synthesize all of the essential nutrients from rather simple sources in the diet," Lederberg maintains that man now lacks whole sets of genes needed for the manufacture of the eight essential amino acids. Although Lederberg does not say so, it would seem that it is no coincidence that man derives these amino acids, in best complement, from animal protein. Stone (1965) has also suggested that man and the few higher primates tested may lack the gene(s) controlling the final step in synthesizing ascorbic acid.

For vegetable proteins, Dubos (1965, p. 66) states that those derived from green leaves, algae, and some microbial species "seem to be fairly satisfactory from the viewpoint of amino acid composition, but unfortunately some are not readily digested." Man cannot derive primary sustenance from leaves, although Jolly (1967) suggests that the earliest Old World monkeys were specialized leaf-eaters. There is some evidence that modern human populations subsisting on bulky vegetarian fare have developed elongated intestinal tracts (Steiner, 1946). But, for man, the protein from seeds, tubers, and other storage parts of plants are usually deficient in one or several of the eight essential amino acids. Except for legumes and especially soybeans, seed and tuber protein is in low concentration (Dubos, 1965). It would seem clear that for protein and the dietary metals, at least, modern man is simply not well adapted to an almost exclusively vegetable diet. Indeed, as shall be seen, human populations have had less than 500 generations of evolutionary time, and some very much less, to cope with this drastic forced dietary change.

The agricultural revolution and sequelae

The domestication of certain plants and animals goes back some 10,000 years in the Near East, possibly several millennia earlier in Southeast Asia (Solheim, 1972), and as early as 9000 years ago in Mesoamerica (Meggers, 1972). In most of the world, the transition to a preponderantly vegetable diet was slow but inexorable. At the same time, the burgeoning populations made possible by food production encroached on the territories of wild game and reduced subsidiary hunting yields in many areas. Much later, the pressure for agricultural lands squeezed out pastures for domestic animals except where aridity permitted only the fast-growing grasses.

Archeological evidence for the reduction of animal foods and the increasing predominance of vegetable diets is limited. But, in the Mexican Highlands, MacNeish (1967) has shown that during the early incipient agricultural period, from about 9000-6000 years B.P., the percentage of plant to animal food remains in dry cave refuse and, by implication, in the diet increased from 30 to 66%. As Meggers (1972) states, 14% of this increase was in domesticated plants, principally maguey, squash, avocado, and maize. By about 6000 years B.P., domestication of the bean notably increased the contributions of domesticated plants to the diet. The proportion of plant foods in the diet increased to about 83% by late prehistoric times. Currently, the diet of Mesoamerican Highland villagers, largely of American Indian origin, is of the order of 95% plant-derived. Thus, in less than 9000 years (450 generations), the approximate contribution of animal foods in the diet has shrunk from about 70 to 5%.

Reduction of animal foods, especially protein of high biological value, in other parts of the underdeveloped agricultural world has been of this approximate order. Down through time, the clear trend has been toward increased dependence upon one of the five great staple crops of the world: rice, wheat, maize, manioc, and millet. With increasing technological sophistication, these seed or tuber crops have been bred for high yield, climatic tolerance, and disease resistance, with the possible lowering of nutrient content in consequence. Moreover, mono-crop agriculturalists often have "hungry months" dictated by the growing season and inadequate yield or storage. These annual periods of food deprivation are broken only by the high energy expenditures needed to harvest and process new crops, creating an obvious health dilemma. Through time, food processing has become increasingly commercial and maladaptive, with excessive milling and bleaching for better keeping qualities, at the expense of essential nutrients. Furthermore, increasing dependence upon any one staple has elevated that staple to the position of a cultural "super-food," with magico-religious connotations encouraging its even more exclusive consumption.

Most staples can supply adults with enough protein if large enough amounts are consumed, but their near-exclusive use is clearly maladaptive during the critical periods of enhanced needs: infancy, early childhood, and pregnancy and lactation. The principal staples differ enough in their protein content and amino acid balance for Jelliffe (1968a) to say that people with a relatively high protein super-food such as millet "are at an automatic, base-line advantage with regard to infant feeding and are likely to avoid kwashiorkor, compared with those eating a predominantly low-protein staple, such as plantain or cassava [manioc]." But with most super-foods, which are culturally over-valued and used extensively from weaning on, it may be physically impossible for an infant or young child to consume enough of the super-food to satisfy its protein needs. This point is dramatically illustrated by Behar (1968a) for the modern Maya, where, if maize were the exclusive food for a 2-year-old child, the child would need to eat about 800 g of tortillas a day to secure the requisite 36 g of protein to maintain nitrogen balance. Even if a 2-year-old could eat that much, the caloric intake would be much more than either necessary or desirable. Among the Guatemala Maya, however, it would be expected that maize would be supplemented with black beans and other vegetables and fruits, although the demand for them by Ladinos may deny them to poorer Indians (Behar, 1968a). A saving grace for the younger Maya Indian children is prolonged nursing, but in societies where early weaning has become fashionable, this source of protein supplementation is denied the young (for Chile, see Monckeberg, 1968). At whatever time weaning occurs, feeding practices for infants and young children tend to restrict them to the poorer, high carbohydrate and low protein sector of the adult diet. Similar prohibitions of better nutrients are often applied during pregnancy as well. In fact, within the almost world-wide cultures of poverty, animal foods are largely sold to the more wealthy and what is retained for home consumption tends to go to the adult men.

Whatever the benefits of the Agricultural Revolution, the enormous population explosions it stimulated have put animal foods out of economic reach of most of the world's people, who are now forced to be vegetarians. Those living to adulthood appear to have accommodated themselves to vegetable foods, usually by quantity consumption. But the nutrient quality of the vegetable foods, especially in protein content, deleteriously affects crucial gestational and postnatal growth processes in man, suggesting that he has had insufficient evolutionary time to permit metabolic adaptations to this very recent drastic shift in diet. Moreover, neither niacin nor such minerals as iron and zinc are as absorbable in these vegetable foods.

THE WORLD'S FOOD SUPPLY AND RELATED
PROBLEMS OF QUALITY AND QUANTITY

In 1932, Haldane suggested that since the Agricultural Revolution the strongest selective force impinging upon man has been infectious disease. Man's almost infinite capacity for self-contamination came into full expression with settled life in the villages, towns, and cities made possible by agriculture. Polgar (1964) has outlined five stages in the disease history of man: hunting/gathering, settled villages, pre-industrial cities, industrial cities, and hyperurban conditions. In his opinion, the infectious diseases took their worst epidemic toll during the pre-industrial cities stage. It seems likely that since then their ravages have been to some degree blunted by "herd" immunity reactions, aided in some areas by empirical medical and public health practices. Equally probable is an increase in the incidence and severity of nutritional diseases, especially in such stress groups as the very young and the pregnant and lactating. This probable rise of nutritional disease may coincide with the time of transition between the pre-industrial and industrial cities. If so, this increased nutritional stressing may be the very factor that Tanner (1968) thinks depressed stature and delayed sexual maturation in Western Europe and thus formed the basis of the secular increases evident for at least a century and a half. Conceivably, this dietary deterioration went back further than that, but the historical evidence for this is deficient. There were other indications of nutritional deficiencies at this time period: the wide occurrence of scurvy two or more centuries ago, which was particularly devastating in its infantile form, and rickets as the first major disease triggered by urban air pollution (Loomis, 1970). More historical evidence might also tie in the *protein shift*, which Sherman (1943) had occurring 20 to 40 generations ago, but which may have been grossly delayed in rural areas of Europe where growth and maturation are still retarded (Laska-Mierzejewska, 1970).

The hyperurban stage of human disease history signals the rise of the eco-metabolic disease in the cities, partly replacing and partly augmenting the eco-pathogenic ones. With the world's population so swelled that over 24% of it is urban, the stage was also set for the modern nutritional crisis that Borgstom (1967) aptly describes. "Basically," he states, "there are not many oases left in the vast, almost world-wide network of slums; about 450 million well-fed people living in comparative luxury . . . against

2,400 million undernourished, malnourished, or in other ways deficiently fed and generally poor."

Since poor nutrition usually renders a bad infectious disease worse, and since infection exacerbates nutritional diseases (Scrimshaw *et al.*, 1968), their influence on mortality rates have been and are inextricably intertwined in reported vital statistics and are separable only by intensive longitudinal studies. An example is the 9-month study of Scrimshaw *et al.* (1957) in four highland Guatemalan villages, where the prime cause of infant and child mortality for census purposes was said to be gastroenteritis. But their on-the-spot clinical investigations revealed that at least 50% of the 1- to 4-year-old deaths was attributable to nutritional deficiencies—predominantly protein-calorie malnutrition. If there is a broader, close to world-wide pattern of infectious diseases masking nutritional ones in the official reporting, than the 10 to 20 million famine-induced deaths estimated for the world out of a total annual death toll of 60 million (Dumont and Rosier, 1969) probably represent gross under-registration.

Country-wide nutritional surveys tend to distort the actual situation because of regional, class, and family differences in food intake. An average daily individual intake of 2600 calories could well mean that three people out of ten consumed 4500 calories, while the rest only consumed 1800. In Chile, the poorest one-quarter of 278 families with incomes below $64.00 a month consumed less than 1770 calories and 50 g protein/person/day, whereas the wealthiest one-quarter with over $95.00 a month consumed an average 2650 calories and 86 g protein (ICNND, 1961). In Brazil, with a mean estimated daily individual intake of 2700 calories, the all-class calorie average in the impoverished northeastern sector was 1886. Among these Nordestinos, the poorest averaged 1600 calories and the well-to-do 2323 calories (ICNND, 1965). Individual food intakes within families have not been adequately appraised, but it is clear from p. 216 that the differential can be great.

Food intake data by themselves are clearly inadequate, especially if appraised by only 24-hour recall and other rapid methods. As repeatedly emphasized in ICNND and other reports, food intakes must be cross-checked by clinical examinations and biochemical assays. The various recommended daily allowances (RDA) were not originally formulated to serve as yardsticks for appraising the nutritional status of populations (Goldschmidt, 1953), but they are frequently used for just that. There is a distinct, but untested possibility that even when the standard age, sex, body size, work load, and ambient temperature adjustments are made in the RDA, they may not be appropriate for many non-Western populations with very different nutritional histories and life styles. After all, it is still only an assumption that, after the sort of adjustments cited above, all human populations have essentially the same nutritional requirements. That this is doubtful is suggested by Bailey's (1963) observation that the very low protein intakes of New Guinea highlanders vis-à-vis their considerable stamina and heavy work loads indicate quite special adaptations. Since incomplete data suggest large individual variations in nutritional requirements (Thirumurthi and Longenecker, 1966), there is no reason to suppose comparable variation cannot occur populationally. Moreover, it would be expected that the closest adaptations to a nutritional regimen occur over the greatest time periods as with South Algerians from Ahaggar and a millet-sorghum diet (Gast and Adrain, 1965), whereas the recent shift of the Zulu from millet to maize as a prime staple has had notably deleterious effects on their health (Cassel, 1955).

Other difficulties in appraising the extent of nutritional deprivation in the world arise outside of science. Administrative leaders of countries may consider it politically expedient to hide hunger and malnutrition in their people. It was only recently that upwards of 14 million hungry were "discovered" in that wealthiest of nations, the United States (Citizens' Board of Inquiry, 1968; Kotz, 1969). In other cases, conscious or unconscious selection of study samples can paint a rosier picture than is actually the case. A likely example is the ICNND (1960) report on Ecuador.

Finally, since the margin between health and illness is so thin, and the balance is so delicate, studies more intensive than the quite rapid surveys of the ICNND type, which are usually confined to but one season, are needed to detect the full extent of mild-to-moderate undernutrition and malnutrition. This is another reason why the reports of the FAO, WHO, and others on world nutrition and world health may often be underestimates.

It is in this light that we should view the frequently quoted FAO Third World Survey (1963), which used admittedly limited data to estimate that at least 20% of the underdeveloped four-fifths of the world's population was *undernourished* in the hypocaloric sense. Using a different and probably less realistic scale, Brown's (1963) estimate for the early 1960's was that 79% of the underdeveloped world had caloric intakes below minimum recommendations. The wide range between these two estimates suggests that appraisals of caloric adequacy on a world basis is shaky at best. At that, both estimates were made before Consolazio *et al.* (1961)

demonstrated that for a heavy work load in ambient temperatures over 30°C (86°F), more calories rather than less may be required. Prior procedure had been to reduce caloric recommendations for people in warmer climates. Moreover, the work load in some sectors of some underdeveloped countries may be greater than that of the "reference man," who walks 10 km a day on level ground and performs manual work for 8 hours.

The Third World Survey also estimates that about 60% of the underdeveloped world is on diets insufficient in one or more essential nutrients and, thus, *malnourished*. Nutrient deficiencies are often multiple, and a recitation of them from one underdeveloped country to another has a monotonous quality rather like the click-click-click of a broken record. This is because most vitamins and some minerals vary directly with caloric intake, although there are also clear qualitative differences in foods. But, as Borgstrom (1965) indicates, protein, as the most serious deficit in the world's food intake, follows "the law of the minimum" in being the best single gauge of nutritional adequacy. This would seem to be particularly the case since protein is the only major nutrient with enhanced requirements per kilogram body weight in infants and young children (Mertz, 1959). And as previously noted on p. 216, the post-agricultural shift away from animal protein (whether or not there is a reverse trend, as suggested by Sherman, 1943) is the most drastic dietary alteration man has undergone in the last 500 generations. Again, on limited evidence, the joint FAO/WHO Expert Group on Protein Requirements (1965) suggested that at least one-quarter and perhaps one-third of the underdeveloped country people have a protein-deficient diet. The Paddocks (1967) provide a differently oriented, but probably comparable all-world estimate that "over half the world lives in countries which do not have a protein intake that meets minimum acceptable standards."

No comparable all-world or underdeveloped world estimates have been made for vitamins and minerals, and indeed these may not be feasible. The closest approaches are in the form of sample ranges provided by a Joint FAO/WHO Expert Group for vitamin A and the several B vitamins (see Table 9-1). For comparison, the NAS (1968) recommended daily allowances for 16- to 18-year-olds are included on the grounds that about 40% of any sample will include children under 15. The lowest vitamin A intakes are in the Near East and in Asia and the Far East. African and Latin American intakes are higher; yet, in the latter, a fifteen-country compilation from 7095 families shows an over-all mean intake of 2692 IU/person/day (PAHO, 1970). The PAHO Technical Group con-

Table 9-1   Majority ranges (80% of samples) of daily per capita intake of vitamin A, thiamine, riboflavin, and niacin

Area	Number of population samples	Vitamin A (IU)	Thiamine (mg)	Riboflavin (mg)	Niacin (mg)
United States	1	9000	2.2	2.6	25.5
Europe	47	3000–7000	1.3–1.8	1.0–1.8	11–18
Latin America	49	1500–3000	0.5–1.8	0.4–1.0	9–18
Asia and the Far East	91	1000–2500	0.5–1.0	0.3–0.7	6–15
Near East	76	500–2000	1.5–2.5	0.4–1.2	12–20
Africa[a]	52	1500–4000	0.5–1.8	0.5–0.7	9–15
NRC, RDA (16- to 18-year-olds)		5000	1.2	1.5	17

[a] Only 55% of samples.

siders about 3500 IU an approximately acceptable level and states that hypovitaminosis A is sufficiently prevalent to constitute a public health problem in Latin America—especially in the young children of poorer families. An indication of the extent of the problem is seen in Escapini's (1968) examination of 2532 children in eleven Latin American and Caribbean countries: 14.7% showed signs of malnutrition, and 1.4% had the eye ulcers of keratomalacia. Moreover, a recent law passed in Guatemala requires that vitamin A be added to commercial sugar (Reynaldo Martorell, 1973, personal communication).

The three B vitamins all function in energy metabolism and, hence, vary directly with caloric intake. Their intakes are lowest in Asia and the Far East, where rice is the main staple, although it provides more thiamine when parboiled and undermilled. The Near East, Africa, and Latin America are intermediate in all three, but still far below European and U.S. intakes. No across-the-board figures are available for the incidence of beriberi (due to thiamine deficiency), ariboflavinosis, or pellagra (due to niacin deficiency). ICNND and other reports from the Philippines, South Vietnam, Thailand, and Burma indicate that beriberi is still an important health problem (FAO/WHO Expert Group, 1967). Moreover, the absence of such clinical signs as the knee and ankle jerk and the presence of calf tenderness suggested to the Expert Group common, but moderate thiamine deficiencies in these countries. The high mortality of 2- to 5-month-old, exclusively breast-fed infants in these countries also suggested a low thiamine content of maternal milk.

The FAO/WHO Expert Group (1967) states that clinical signs of ariboflavinosis (principally in the mucous membranes) are widespread in south and east Asia and have been reported for Africa and Latin America as well. But even when severe, ariboflavinosis is not incapacitating and, accordingly, has received scant attention. Niacin-deficiency disease, or pellagra, is still endemic in parts of the Near East, Africa, and southeastern Europe, where it is associated with maize as a dietary staple. In Central America, where maize may supply up to 80% of the calories and 70% of the protein (Behar, 1968a), soaking and cooking it in limewater enhances its calcium, tryptophan, and available niacin content, and, hence, pellagra is rare there.

The ICNND Summary (1966) indicates that vitamin C deficiencies constitute health problems among lower socioeconomic classes in a few countries, but even in such impoverished countries as Bangladesh, country-wide intake levels were considered acceptable (ICNND, 1965).

The President's Science Advisory Committee (1967) states that rickets from vitamin D deficiency has not been reported as a major world health problem in recent years, but it is still a sunless slum affliction of children in North Africa (May 1967) and elsewhere.

The moderator of the PAHO (1969) Symposium on Iron Metabolism and Anemia states that "It would be safe to say, without any statistics on hand, that 1,000 million people in the world are iron deficient and many of them actually have anemia. The problem is most acute in tropical areas, and anemias, particularly iron deficiency anemias, are rampant in all the tropical and subtropical zones of the Americas." Indeed, it is likely that iron-deficiency anemia ranks next to protein deficiency as a critical nutritional problem in the world. A good part of the problem is that, except for soybeans, iron from vegetable foods is poorly absorbed (Layrisse, 1969). Plant proteins are thought to bind metals more avidly than animal proteins, and other organic compounds, such as phytate and phaeophytin, interfere with metal absorption—especially zinc. It is important to note that, in isotopic-absorption studies using food mixtures with and without meat, iron absorption is at least twice as great in meals with some meat in them (Cook and Finch, 1973). As we have seen (pp. 214-15), there appears to be a progressive reduction in consumption of animal foods since the advent of the Agricultural Revolution to the point where the majority of the world's people rarely eat animal foods. Could this be a major reason why man has been termed "an iron-deficient species" (Cook and Finch, 1973, p. 2)?

Endemic goiter has now become a culture of poverty disease due to uncompensated deficiencies of iodine in the soil and, despite easy prevention, still affects some 200 million people in the world (Gillie, 1971).

With these proportions of undernutrition and malnutrition in man, some rather clearly on the increase, it is significant that a WHO Expert Group (1968) stated that "on a world-wide basis, nutritional disorders and their consequences constitute the most serious single threat to the health of children." Those surviving to adulthood accommodate better to nutritional insult, as King (1970) notes:

> In most parts of the tropical belt where large numbers of people live
> on a subsistence agriculture, we are confronted with reasonably well-fed
> adults in homes where about half of the children die of malnutrition
> and its sequelae during the first five years of life.

During most of the 1960's, the informed world was treated to a worsening spectacle of its population increasing by about 2% annually, whereas over-all food production was only increasing by about 1% (Dumont and Rosier, 1967). Thus, even in the official FAO reports (see Boerma, 1970), the food gap between demand and supply was projected as widening from base line 1962 to horizons 1975 and 1985. Increased food needs in the underdeveloped regions of the world for the same time period are projected for Asia and the Far East at 154%; the Near East and Northwest Africa, 143%; Subsaharan Africa, 122%; and Latin America, 120%. Relatively poor crop years between about 1965 and 1969 provided a discouraging prospect of meeting these needs. In addition to these poor food prospects for the future, the world's population moved toward an ominous doubling the next 35 years. These circumstances led to a rash of books and articles in the late 1960's that the media would tag as "doomsday," an example of which is the Paddocks' closely reasoned 1967 book, *Famine 1975!*—amazingly prophetic of the mid-1970's situation. Dumont and Rosier (1969) state in *The Hungry Future*:

> *If nothing is done and present trends continue*, there is serious danger
> that famine, which has already taken hold in India in 1966, will spread
> over most of the Third World. After India, the most vulnerable areas are
> East Pakistan, Java, Egypt (where there is starvation already), the
> Maghreb, the Middle East, the Sahel of the West Sahara (where harvests
> are scanty), and the Andes from Chile to Mexico; and after that the
> Caribbean, the Sertao in Brazil, and perhaps even Anatolia in Turkey.
> The situation in China has been dangerous, as it has been in Vietnam,
> but it is now being regulated, after immense efforts, by population con-
> trol. [Italics mine.]

Efforts, of course, are being made to curb the present trends. For 1970, the FAO reported harvests on the upturn in contrast to the poor crop year of 1969 where the index of 150 (1952-56, 100) was unchanged from 1968. The slowed rate of gain in 1969 actually reduced the per capita food supply in the underdeveloped countries. But food production in the Far East, usually the greatest deficit area, rose 5% in 1970, comfortably ahead of population growth, and due largely to the increasing use of improved seed (Editorial: Science and the Citizen, 1971). But that year showed only enough food production increase in Latin America to keep pace with its population, and in Africa and the Near East the per capita decline continued. The crop year 1971 was predicted as the largest harvest in recent years—4% over 1970, which, in turn, was 2% over 1969. Much of the 4% increase was attributed to the developed market-economy countries, whereas the Third World's food production increases of 2 to 3% generally kept pace with the population increases (Editorial: Sciences and the Citizen, 1972). The FAO has consistently warned that the Green Revolution is not with us yet, and, in 1971, Eric Ojala, FAO assistant director general, stated that "the fabric of this progress [the Green Revolution] in the developing world remains fragile and its base narrow, both geographically and in terms of commodities." This appears to be small respite at best. Moreover, since 1971, the Northern Hemisphere has been more heavily afflicted with droughts in the north and floods in the south, and this may relate to shiftings in climatic zones caused by the average 1.3°C drop in temperature since 1940. In the Sahel and Ethiopia, an apparent southern shift of the subtropical anticyclonic rain belt has caused reductions in precipitation since about 1957 and now spells disastrous famine for the pastoral people there.

There is a tendency in population control vis-à-vis the food production experts to say that "Our progress is slow, but the better hope lies with the progress of the other group." But most know they must go hand in hand, and the view is taking hold that rises in standards of living are necessary preludes to effective population control. The NAS/NRC (1971) committee is optimistic that "making reasonable allowances for reductions in fertility . . . the world's population can be held to 7 billion by A.D. 2000." They point out that sharp changes in fertility occur rapidly, as with the 50% drop in birthrate between 1948 and 1960 in Japan, with almost as much of a drop in Taiwan and South Korea.

Currently, in the underdeveloped countries, there are grave cultural, economic, and sometimes religious impediments to persuading people to have fewer children. Moreover, an equally severe limiting factor lies in the weaknesses of our basic knowledge of human reproduction, thus far slow-ing the development of more effective means of population control.

It also seems clear that food production increases do not occur where they are most needed, either. Thus, the subtitle of the Paddocks' 1967 book is very real—*America's decision: Who will survive?* James Reston (*New York Times*, Nov. 9, 1971) writes of "the emerging tragedy of world inequality." And Myrdal (1972) argues that "the global downward trend of economic assistance in and from the rich countries to the poor countries can be reversed only by stressing the moral argument."

While moral and economic issues are being settled in the developed world, the 269 million malnourished Third World children under 14 years, out of 667 million in 1966 (President's Scientific Advisory Com-mittee, 1967), rose to about 300 million in 1971 and is predicted by the U.S. AID (1966) to reach 329 million in 1975. Ihsan A. Dogramaci, President of the International Pediatric Association, was reported by the Associated Press (Aug. 30, 1971) as stating that currently only one-half of the world's children are treated by modern medicine, and 75% of all below 6 years of age are insufficiently or wrongly fed. And this is essen-tially the nutritional status we must deal with as we move to the next section.

EFFECTS OF NUTRITIONAL INADEQUACIES UPON HEALTH AND QUALITY OF LIFE: GROWTH PROCESSES AND RESULTING ADULT MORPHOLOGY

Fetal retardation

The effects of inadequate nutrition upon fetal development need not start with the maternal diet during pregnancy. Read (1970) has suggested that "the nutrition of the mother prior to pregnancy, perhaps years or over a lifetime, may have a significant influence on fetal and/or infant de-velopment." Within cultures of poverty, the effects of nutritional depri-vation during the mother's early life upon her fetus could extend for gen-erations, as Drillien (1964) has noted. More precise data on the effect of maternal nutritional status upon fetal development are difficult to obtain, especially in view of the other factors involved. But such information is critically needed if indeed fetal health is to be the new goal of obstetrics (Falkner, 1969, p. 45).

Thus far, the approaches to better understanding of human maternal-fetal relationships in nutrition have been largely threefold: (a) the clear relationship of inadequate maternal food intake to poor placental growth and development (fewer cells, altered nutrient levels), and the relationship of the latter two to fetal growth retardation (Winick, 1967, Dayton *et al.*, 1968); (b) autopsies of stillbirths from poor and nonpoor families (Naeye *et al.*, 1971); and (c) the rich data on low birthweights in underdeveloped countries (Meredith, 1970), lower socioeconomic classes (WHO, 1965; also contained in but not emphasized by Meredith, 1970, Naeye *et al.*, 1971, Ademowore *et al.*, 1972), and very young mothers whose nutritional needs are high (Burke *et al.*, 1943).

One of the principal difficulties in elucidating the effects of maternal nutrition on fetal development is the lack of exact information on food intake and utilization during pregnancy. Another is the paucity of late fetal specimens, and a third is that full-term weight is only a small fraction (5.7%, according to Leitch *et al.*, 1959) of maternal body mass, with relatively small variation thereto (Smith, 1962). Accordingly, many of the assumptions concerning human maternal-fetal malnutrition has been interpolated from controlled research on experimental animals (Winick, 1971), and much of the knowledge of late fetal malnutrition in man has been subsumed from neonatal studies. An exception is the work of Naeye *et al.* (1971) on 469 stillbirth autopsies averaging 29 weeks gestation from poor and nonpoor New York City families. The poor mothers were significantly shorter in stature than the nonpoor ones; body weight of their stillbirths was 13-17% less, and body length and all organ weights were also lower. In the stillbirths of the poor, weights of thymus, spleen, liver, and adrenals were disproportionately smaller than weights of other organs; thickness of abdominal subcutaneous fat was also significantly less; but brain-weight differences were small and not significant. The lower organ weights and fat thicknesses were due to reduced cytoplasm in individual parenchymal and adipose cells, the number of cells being much the same in poor and nonpoor stillbirths. This particular ranking of relative organ growth has been repeatedly observed in placental and uterine disorders restricting flow of nutrients to the fetus, and its pattern has been frequently reported in children and young animals with chronic postnatal undernutrition. The total pattern of slowed growth and development in the poor stillbirths of this study is more likely due to inferior maternal nutrition, since there was no evidence that uterine or placental disorders were responsible for the retardation. What is not known is the precise nature of the inadequacies of maternal food intake that most affects fetal development.

In any case, on a more gross basis, it is well established that the body size of adult men and women, and the latter's newborn, show clear socioeconomic gradients, irrespective of ethnic affiliation (p. 27; WHO, 1965). In some populations, at least (Baird *et al.*, 1958; Bresler, 1962), women of shorter stature have poorer reproductive histories—more frequent premature deliveries and/or more difficult labor, higher perinatal mortality, and more infants with birth defects. In the Aberdeen, Scotland studies led by Baird, if inability to effect delivery through the vagina is taken as poor reproductive performance, this inability was four times more frequent in women under 153 cm in stature than in those over 162.5 cm. Jelliffe's (p. 109, György and Kline, 1970) field impression in Uganda was that the small pelvis of many of the women observed there was responsible for the considerable obstetrical mortality, and might relate to protein-calorie malnutrition in their own early life. These points emphasize the two maternal nutritional problems usually associated with poverty: long-term dietary inadequacies and, particularly, those occurring during pregnancy, especially in the third trimester when about 67% of fetal growth is said to take place (Greenhill, 1965). At least during the temporary poverty of World War II, women in the northwestern Netherlands (Smith, 1947) and Japan (Gruenwald *et al.*, 1967) produced babies more than 0.2 kg below their national averages, and babies born during the long siege of Leningrad (Antonov, 1947) 0.5 kg less. In the Dutch and Soviet studies, however, amenorrhea frequently prevented conception.

As Naeye *et al.* (1971) say, "it is widely agreed that birthweights are lower in the poor and that such low birthweights are associated with their high perinatal mortality." Neonates with birthweights below 2.5 kg clearly have more birth defects and a reduced chance of survival, the more so if they are small because of prematurity. In developed countries, at least, it is claimed (Churchill *et al.*, 1966; Niswander *et al.*, 1968) that higher incidences of infant (0-1 year) mortality, morbidity (cerebral palsy), and low IQ are related to low birthweights. The impact of research of this sort is such that the Committee on Maternal Nutrition of the U.S. National Research Council (Editorial, 1970) now recommends that pregnant women not be restricted to a 10-14 lb gain, which would tend to reduce birthweight, and suggests an average 20-24 lb gain.

Low birthweights are clearly more prevalent in underdeveloped countries. The incidence of those below 2.5 kg in Ceylon about 1960 was 28%, as against 9% for the United Kingdom. Deaths in the first week were 7.7% and 14.1% for Ceylon and Britain, respectively, in those under 2.5

kg, and a comparable figure for India was 9.1% (deSilva *et al.*, 1962). But the contribution to neonatal (0-27 days) mortality by the low birthweight Ceylonese was greater, since they occurred in three times as high a proportion as in the United Kingdom (WHO, 1965). Yet, in the Exeter study (Falkner, 1969, p. 10) of County Devon, England, in 1965, only 7% of the live births were under 2.5 kg; yet, they accounted for about 50% of the total perinatal mortality. The U.S. National Institute of Child Health and Human Development states that currently "the incidence of low birth-weight infants is from two to five times greater in families living in poverty, the population [in the United States] in which malnutrition is known to exist."

Infant malnutrition

Mortality rates during the first year of life range from a high level of about 200/1000 live births to some twenty countries with less than 25 (F. Rosa, WHO, *in* Falkner, 1969). Rosa states that, even with poor reporting, a fairly large number of countries have rates about 200/1000, and some depressed socioeconomic groups run up to 500/1000 live births. During the neonatal period (0-27 days), the principal causes of death are stated to be low birthweight, which has already been shown here to be very strongly nutrition-related, and tetanus. A useful developed/underdeveloped country contrast is afforded in the infant mortality rate breakdowns provided by Gordon *et al.* (1967) (Table 9-2).

Table 9-2   Infant mortality rates per 1000 live births (1960)

Time (days)	United States	Guatemala	India
0–6	16.4	37.9	50.6
0–27	18.2	64.4	77.0
28–330	7.0	83.4	84.2

(From Gordon et al., 1967)

Assuming a sufficient supply of breast milk, it is usually calculated that this milk will adequately sustain an infant for its first 6 months. Modern pediatric practice suggests food supplements in the 5th month, assuming a sufficient milk supply. But this may not be forthcoming, especially from mothers in poverty cultures. An average yield from well-nourished mothers is said to be 850 ml/day (NRC, 1968, p. 8), whereas, in Nigeria, Endozien (1970) found that well-fed women produced 850-1200 ml/day. In Nigeria, wives of Nigerian members of the academic staff at the University of Ibadan produced an average of 975 ml/day, whereas village women 20 miles outside Ibadan, on a protein-deficient diet (40-60 g/day low-quality protein) were reduced to an average 350 ml/day. Bailey (1965) cites an average breast milk yield in South India as 430 ml/day, and 384± 20 ml/day was his own figure for New Guinea Highland women from the Upper Chimbu. With the protein content of human milk at 1.0-1.2 g/100 ml, 500 g/day this in theory is barely enough to prevent protein deficiency in a 4 kg infant, and thus would do little more than carry it through its 1st month. Or a sort of adaptation we know little about could occur. Its end products are reduced growth and development, to husband the inadequate available stock of calories, protein, and other nutrients—in a sense, a mild marasmutic reaction to calorie-protein scarcity bordering on starvation. Although the problem remains uninvestigated, it is likely that there is individual, or even populational, variation in accommodation to this sort of nutritional inadequacy that probably begins in the third intrauterine trimester. Endozien (1965a,b) has noted the onset of critically slowed growth and even actual weight loss in Nigerian infants after the 2nd month, due to reduced maternal milk supply.

If the inadequacies of calorie and protein intake are too great, marasmus or extreme growth failure (Jelliffe, 1968, pp. 81-83) sets in. Although antibodies to disease-causing organisms have been coming to the infant across the placental barrier, and then by way of maternal milk, it is likely that infectious diseases act to hasten the downward spiral of the marasmus patient. Artificial feeding can be extraordinarily maladaptive, and the milk in bottle feeding in underdeveloped countries is often both dilute and contaminated. If, as has often been stated, the latrine in underdeveloped countries is a sorry sop to *Hygeia*, the nursing bottle is a similar one to *Nutrea*. Jelliffe (p. 32, György and Kline, 1970) emphasizes "the changing pattern of breast-feeding that is seen all around the world. As breast-feeding is reduced, there is a moving to the left—an earlier occurrence of protein malnutrition in infants. The marasmus-diarrhea syndrome, and even kwashiorkor is seen at 7 to 9 months, particularly in urban communities." He states further that "the use of artificial feeding plainly opens the door to increased avitaminosis A, with the use of skimmilk powder, and also infantile-scurvy may be expected," and concludes that "we cannot expect most mothers in tropical areas to use artificial feeding safely."

This earlier onset of nutritional diseases also occurs with supplemental feeding of adult foods of low nutrient quality—usually high in carbohydrates and low in protein. A second and rather less common protein-calorie deficiency disease can result, and this is kwashiorkor—the malnutrition of the "knee baby" who has been displaced at the breast by a newer family arrival. Jelliffe (1968, p. 76) considers kwashiorkor "a disease principally due to an unbalanced, largely carbohydrate diet, but is always in part caused by infections and parasites, which make still worse the basic nutritional inadequacy." It is a standard enough picture to have been repeatedly noted in the literature: a quite well-nourished infant at the breast, and clinging to the mother's knee, trying vainly to reach the breast, is a poorly nourished older child.

More siblings in a family with limited food resources and a mother overstressed by almost continual pregnancy and lactation makes survival more difficult for later arrivals. Newcombe's (1965) broad survey of underdeveloped countries shows that early mortality increases with birth order. Parity is an important factor, as Gopalan's (1968) investigations of major South Indian pediatric hospitals show: 61% of the protein-calorie malnutrition patients belonged to parity 4 and above. And, with high birthrates outstripping food supplies in underdeveloped countries, the broader picture painted by King (1970) (see p. 222) for infants and children alike in the Dominican Republic is most relevant here.

Child malnutrition

The Jamaican research of Wills and Waterlow (1958) suggested to them that the 1- to 4-year-old death rate of a country constitutes a serviceable index of its nutritional status. Monckeberg (1970) followed this lead by placing the 1- to 4-year mortalities of American countries in a ratio relationship with the 0- to 1-year mortalities and then aligned these ratios with a relative index of living conditions to form a near-linear regression from Guatemala at the bottom to the United States at the top. The earlier part of this 1- to 4-year-old period is sufficiently distinctive and crucial for Jelliffe (1969) to suggest the neologism "Secotrant" for it, namely, "second year" + "transitional." This is usually the year of the "knee baby" and involves particularly difficult nutritional, disease, and psychological transitions from infancy. Gordon *et al.* (1967) provide Secotrant (1- to 2-year) mortality data (Table 9-3) comparable to those in Table 9-2.

The Secotrant period sees the continuation of the marasmus-diarrhea

*Table 9-3   Secotrant (1- to 2-year) mortality rates per 1000 population
(1960)*

United States	Guatemala	India
1.6	62.1	72.2

(From Gordon et al., 1967)

syndrome, which, according to Gopalan's (1968) theory, can lead the
same child into kwashiorkor, where even more functional integrity of the
organ systems is lost. But as the Jelliffes (1969) make clear, marasmus
and kwashiorkor are the easily detectable, clinically apparent manifestations of a much larger number of mild-to-moderate cases of protein-
calorie-malnutrition—subclinical and hidden to view in underdeveloped
countries. Edozien (1970) believes that "the bottom of the iceberg" is
such that

> growth and development studies in children around the world show
> that 50-80% of all preschool children in the developing countries
> suffer from protein/calorie malnutrition of sufficient degree to cause
> retardation of physical growth and development and, by inference, also
> disturbances of learning capacity and behavior.

This is also the time when the mother-offspring unit can begin to rupture, due partly to the birth of a new baby and partly to the sort of emotional alienation described by Gardner (1972) as leading to "deprivation
dwarfism." So this phenomenon of psychologically oriented "deprivation
dwarfism" can be added to the term of "nutritional dwarfism" already entering the literature, which in itself has specific protein and zinc deprivation entities. Chromosomal abnormalities, as well, appear to increase in
protein-calorie malnutrition (Armendares et al., 1971) as well as the considerable likelihood of irreversible brain damage (Frisch, 1970).
    Finally, it is in this crucial transitional period from infancy to child-
hood, that acute diarrheal episodes begin to strike heavily. In many parts
of the world, deaths from diarrheal disease outnumber any other single
cause—at least those diagnosed (WHO, 1961). In Guatemala, where
acute childhood diarrhea has been intensively studied, it commonly pre-
cipitates full clinical expression of protein-calorie malnutrition in already
nutritionally deprived children (Mata et al., 1967). It is not clear whether
childhood diarrhea itself need always be caused by such infectious agents
as *Shigella*, coxsackie viruses, and enteric pathogenic bacteria, but one or

another is significantly more frequent in the sufferers. Sources of infection by mouth are clearly multiple—through contaminated food, crawling about, and playing in the dirt, etc. Jelliffe (1968b) states, in addition, that it is common pediatric opinion in many parts of the tropics that ascariasis, picked up the same way, is often an important accessory to childhood malnutrition, especially the kwashiorkor-nutritional edema syndrome.

The ultimate in the entire maladaptive syndrome of malnutrition, gastrointestinal infections, and contraindicated folk medical practices is dramatically wrapped up in Williams's (1938) description of younger children in the Gold Coast

> Their intestines were so irritated by worms, inflamed by enteritis,
> excoriated by peppers and by purgatives, assaulted by enemata, and
> distended by coarse, bulky carbohydrate food, that they altogether lose
> the power of assimilating the evasive nutrition of their contents.

Retarded growth and development in younger children (1–5 years)

It is generally true that, unless lactation is severely curtailed in underdeveloped country mothers (as noted above), infants adhere closely to a developed country growth curve their first 3 months and fall off somewhat the second 3 months. From 6-12 months, however, weaning period maladaptations due to improper and contaminated food supplementation and infection usually reduce growth and development drastically. Tanner's (1966) suggestion that different populations, in this instance, blacks, may have different growth and maturation velocities that are genetically programmed has not been examined further, largely because of a lack of research models for disentangling genetic and environmental effects. But Garn (1966) has noted that children of certain Indian families living in the protein-poor western Guatemalan Highlands were on a par with U.S. white standards of sketelal maturation. He suggests that this may be genetic, and perhaps related to enhanced protein economy, but very precise data on feeding practices in such families would be needed to prove this.

On the average, however, the astute generalization of Scrimshaw and Gordon (1968) is one of the most important ones made on the subject of growth in underdeveloped countries:

> Guzmán documents the striking universality of retarded physical growth
> among lower socioeconomic groups of developing countries: the concen-
> tration of the condition in early childhood and the similar growth pat-

terns in different underprivileged populations at ages of less than 5 years. The more satisfactory growth of middle- and upper-class children in these same countries is strong evidence that genetic factors are minor determinants compared with those of the environment. The findings are of the same general order, irrespective of racial differences between lower- and upper-income groups of a country, has similar significance.

A graphic confirmation of the preponderant influence of the environment on growth in underprivileged populations is provided in Cravioto and DeLicardie's (1968) finding that the statures of middle- to upper-class urban Guatemalan children tended to reflect those of their parents, whereas, in the lower-class rural children, there was no association in parent-child stature. It is clear that, in the lower-class rural people, environmental factors tended to override in any genetic expression of body size. It would be important to know whether the greater nutritional deprivation of higher parity in both parents and children was a prime factor, as it was in Goldstein's (1971) parity 3$^+$ children in the lowest socioeconomic class covered in Britain's National Child Development Study.

According to Frisancho *et al.* (1970a), however, the statural retardation in preadolescent children from lower socioeconomic levels in Central America is not more than 10% below U.S. standards, but there is a more than 30% delay in skeletal maturation judged by X-rays of the hand and wirst. In a sample of over 10,000 children of both sexes, retardation in statural growth and skeletal maturation is reversed in adolescents and post-adolescents: statural growth is retarded over 30%, and skeletal maturation 10% or less. In younger rural Guatemalan children healthy enough to be active, the degree of retardation in skeletal maturation is on a par with that of protein-calorie malnutrition patients of approximately the same ages (Garn, 1966), a clear indication of the widespread nutritional deprivation of the young in these countries. Statural growth is not as depressed in these younger children, possibly because chronic protein deficiency appears to raise human growth hormone levels (Pimstone *et al.*, 1968). On a world-wide basis, however, Behar (1968b) presents a conservative estimate that 75% of underdeveloped country preschoolers are underweight for their age, and it is likely that there are even greater reductions in muscle tissue mass (Waterlow and Mendez, 1957). In fact, limb circumferences have long been noted as the best indicators of nutritional status in the traditional anthropometric battery, and the upper arm circumference is widely used for this purpose (Arnhold, 1969). Subcutaneous fat thicknesses and bone densities are also depressed in the poorly nourished, but the timing of dental eruption seems little affected (Friedlaender and Bailit, 1968).

The depression of mental performance with grossly inadequate nutrition is an almost universal finding in experimental animals and children alike (Scrimshaw and Gordon, 1968). The principal and as yet incompletely answered question is currently whether the brain damage attributed largely to protein-calorie malnutrition is irreversible in humans. Frisch (1970) has warned against permitting the possibility of irreversibility to become fact in the lay press. Part of the problem in developing a more definitive answer lies in the follow-up studies of mental performance of dietarily rescued protein-calorie malnutrition patients extending over a sufficiently long time-period to ensure that no "catch up" will occur. But a greater problem concerns the multiplicity of factors that affect protein-calorie malnutrition (Cravioto, 1970). As it now stands, a good part of the question depends upon how early in life protein-calorie malnutrition begins. It would appear, from the summaries provided by Birch and Gussow (1970), that if it strikes after 15 months of age, irreversible brain damage is most unlikely to occur. It may be *simpliste* to suggest that the earlier the period in which it strikes (including the prenatal period), the more likely permanent brain damage, but that is about the current stage of the research. A larger question is whether mild-to-medium protein deprivation so common in children of the world appreciably depresses mental performance, and INCAP research (Klein *et al.*, 1973) does show moderate correlations between physical growth in Guatemalan children and their mental-emotional development, with both tied in to nutritional status.

During early childhood, there are indications that not all populations follow the same general nutrition- and disease-mediated growth and development curves. The most striking example of this infantile precosity beginning at birth is in blacks of both the Old and the New World, especially in skeletal maturation and motor performance, followed by deceleration in growth and maturation after 1 to 3 years relative to white standards (see Marshall *et al.*, 1970, for summary and for Jamaican data). Tanner (1966) states that this probably reflects a hormonal difference, beginning in the late fetal period, but Hiernaux (1968a) prefers a largely nutritional explanation:

> The reversal in tempo of skeletal development and physical growth between Africans and Americans closely parallels that of their environ-

mental history: the African enjoys superior nutritional and emotional conditions in infancy, but after this time the American has the greater environmental advantage.

On this particular question of ethnic differences in growth and maturation rates, as well as Asian-white and other differences ably summarized by Tanner (1966), it is clear that sufficient control of a detailed, quantified nature over inherited versus environmental factors is lacking. Even the striking differences between Hutu and Tutsi growth rates by body segment (Hiernaux, 1968b), which result in very different bodily proportions in later childhood and adolescence may indeed be genetically programmed as claimed. But among other things we cannot be sure of is the effect of the extra high-quality protein the Tutsi subadults get. Nevertheless, a valid generalization would seem to be that body proportions are considerably less ecosensitive than body size.

Later childhood and adolescence

A major question for which there is as yet no full answer is whether, or to what extent, children nutritionally deprived during earlier life can catch up and appear to regain their more normal growth track. Cross-sectional data from such developed countries as Germany (Howe and Schiller, 1952) and Japan (Takahashi, 1966) clearly show growth depressions during wars and other times of nutritional stressing, followed by catch up in stature and weight by age in better times. Thus, Tanner (1966) is able to state that "unless the starvation is severe, all that happens is that the child's growth and development slow down, and when food is again available speed up to a rate above normal until the child has quite caught up again to its previous growth curve." This return to a genetically predetermined growth track, as though nothing has happened, can be questioned if the nutritional deprivation goes on long enough to affect the timing of differential growth patterns. As Scrimshaw and Behar (1961) maintain, the parts of the body most influenced by nutritional deprivation are those growing most rapidly at the time. Again, we lack sufficiently detailed and quantified data to discern such alterations.

The very sort of food surplus making dietary rescue commonplace in developed countries is rare in the lower socioeconomic levels in underdeveloped countries, so catch-up phenomena are seldom observed in the latter. When there is the rare case of nutritional intervention, the responses of low socioeconomic class children seem slower and less definitive. Falkner (1966) cites Canosa's unpublished findings in Guatemala to the effect that whereas well-fed, privileged children threw off the effects of perinatal deprivation and illness by 2 years of age and regained their predetermined growth track, low-class rural children took much longer, often up to 6 years, to do this, despite rescue from a malnourished state. Moreover, there may even be no catch up as Collis and Janes (1968) postulated for Western Nigerian children afflicted by a protein-calorie deficit and severe exposure to infectious diseases. As Edozien (1965) shows, adult men from this region reflect this stunting effect seen in the children. Yet, Nigerian children from the Northern region, who are severely exposed to infectious diseases but who do not suffer from protein-calorie deficits in early life, subsequently caught up to Collis's "optimum" Ibadan group in stature and weight.

Part of the slowed catch up in the children of the poor may depend upon the age at which dietary rescue occurs. At Vicos, in the northern Peruvian Sierra, the effects of a 4-year school lunch program were rather minimal in the 7- to 12.9-year-old boys, although they averaged only 25 fewer lunches a year than the 13- to 17.9-year-old boys who showed dramatic improvements in all major aspects studied (Newman *et al.*, unpublished). Table 9-4 shows that the younger boys showed barely significant weight increases at the 5% level, and improvements significant at the 1% level only in trunk dimensions and bone density (cortical thickness). They failed to show the significant increases in stature, trunk and limb circumferences, and skeletal maturation so evident in the older boys. The reasons for the incomplete catch up in the younger boys is not altogether clear. There may be important cultural factors operative in this Quechua Indian community. It seems likely that younger children in these households are the most underprivileged of all age grades: they are assigned the least attractive and most menial of jobs, receive cast-off clothing insufficient for the ambient temperature, and may receive considerably less than their share of the family food. Clinically, they showed more positive signs of nutritional deficiencies before the school lunches began than did the older boys. It also seems likely that younger children are less able to forage for extra food than older ones, who might well out-compete them anyway. Nevertheless, these are only the barest of suggestions of differential treatment of family or household members, and clearly merit careful study to see if they have any validity in different societies.

More broadly applicable than intra-family differential treatment studies is the hope of distinguishing nutritional effects from disease effects upon

Table 9-4   Comparison of body characteristic and skeletal development means in age-matched Vicos boys before and after a 4-year lunch program

Age group/ No. of pairs	7–12.9 Yr. (34–35)			13–17.9 Yr. (36–37)		
Series	Before	After	p <	Before	After	p <
Stature	122.52	122.93		135.93	140.73	0.01
Weight	23.53	24.52	0.05	31.72	36.22	0.01
Sitting height	64.61	66.41	0.01	71.11	73.51	0.01
Biachromial br.	26.40	27.33	0.01	29.22	31.13	0.01
Biiliac br.	20.13	20.21		22.83	23.40	0.05
Chest circum.	65.82	65.60		73.52	74.92	0.05
Waist circum.	60.23	59.41		64.51	66.31	0.01
Upper arm circum.	17.90	18.03		20.33	21.32	0.01
Upper arm diam.	45.11	45.02		51.71	53.71	0.05
Calf circum.	24.01	24.13		27.03	28.12	0.01
Chronol. age	10.63	10.59		14.74	14.86	
Skeletal age	8.50	8.84		11.35	12.03	0.01
Medullary area	9.09	7.60	0.01	13.04	11.17	0.05
Cortical area	20.88	23.71	0.01	28.30	29.47	
Total area	29.96	31.30		41.34	40.64	
Cortical area (%)	69.88	75.60	0.01	69.01	73.24	0.01
Cortical vol. (est.)	969.04	1126.37	0.01	1501.40	1619.96	0.01
Hetacarpal l.	45.40	47.00		52.40	53.70	0.05

(Courtesy of A. R. Frisancho.)

growth and maturation, through the tremendously detailed data collected and being collected by such field research as that of INCAP in Guatemala (R. Martorell *et al.*, 1973), where diarrheal diseases were shown to impede growth. It is possible there, and probably elsewhere, that the impact of infectious diseases upon growth and maturation is decidedly greater in younger children. Those surviving early childhood may indeed have done so partly by developing good immune responses.

Then there is the minority view, according to Scrimshaw and Gordon (1968, p. 29), that in populations hard pressed for food over a number of generations, those individuals with more rapid growth potentials are selectively weeded out, whereas slow growth is advantageous in that minimal food intake is required for survival (Thomson, 1968; Malcolm, 1970). This thesis has not been properly demonstrated, but it has all sorts of tangentially supporting evidence, and, in theory, if it is true for individuals or families as Garn (p. 231) has suggested, it could be true for long-stressed populations. The statural increases with the breakup of the breeding isolates in France (Schreider, 1967) strongly suggests that endogamy and poor nutrition alter a population's range of growth potentialities. The same phenomenon may have taken place in the increased teen-age statural growth in a strongly exogamous Peruvian mestizo community compared to the strongly endogamous Vicos Indian community next door, where nutritional status is much the same (Newman *et al.*, 1963). It is conceivable, although not demonstrable from present data, that the earlier part of the genetically programmed range of growth potentials could be more restricted in a selective sense than the latter part. If true, this would partly explain the lack or incompleteness of catch up in younger children, such as those at Vicos. It could also explain, in part, why Canosa's poor rural children in Guatemala had such a slow catch up, since the Maya Indian villages are likely to be highly endogamous. In the village of Sumpango, Dpto. of Sacetepeque, 97.5% of the Indian spouses were born there, and a similar situation was said to pertain to other villages. Moreover, Behar (1968a) has made clear the dietary deterioration of the Guatemala Maya since their conquest.

It is a commonplace observation that children at lower socioeconomic levels in the underdeveloped world do not show the early and dramatically rapid growth spurt of puberty seen in the privileged, developed-country children. Moreover, Frisch and Revelle (1969a) have shown that the maximum yearly increments of growth in stature and weight of children in six Asian and six Latin American countries are closely geared to mean country-wide caloric intakes. All are delayed in time, relative to developed country standards (Frisch and Revelle, 1969b), and all are also reduced in intensity. The timing of maximum statural growth is closely correlated with sexual maturation. In developed-country samples, Simmons and Greulich (1943) have shown that menarche always occurs after the greatest increment in stature. The proximity in time of the two phenomena may be different, and possibly less, in lower socioeconomic level underdeveloped-country girls, but this has not been studied.

In most developed countries, the last century's secular increase in stature and progressively earlier menarche (Tanner, 1968) is considered to be due to improved diet and public health. The genetic effects of increased outmarriage has been critically reviewed by Chung *et al.* (1966). Where more detailed data are available, as in Slovakia, the question is raised whether those able to marry outside their immediate community are economically better off than those who do not. If so, then the children resulting from such outmarriages would probably enjoy better nutrition and health care, and, in consequence, would grow and mature more rapidly.

The close relationship of menarche to stature has lead to the semi-facetious "Malcolm's Law": the later the menarche, the shorter the adults. If studied by socioeconomic level, this very useful principle seems equally operative in underdeveloped and developed countries. For the latter, the most detailed and spectacular work has been carried on between wealthier town girls and poorer rural girls in Poland (Wolanski, 1966), and the latter even show significant differences in mean menarche, according to details of family occupation (Laska-Mierzejewska, 1970). Kralj-Cercek's (1956) researches on Slovenian girls showed earlier menarche to be closely related to higher animal protein intake. In fact, he hypothesizes that a high carbohydrate diet delays menarche, which may be true, although the nature of his samples and his means of determining both dietary intake and time of menarche raise some questions (Tanner, 1962). Subsequent studies in both developed and underdeveloped countries (Wilson and Sutherland, 1960; Burrell *et al.*, 1961) leave little question that protein intake is a critical factor, as Tanner himself indicated (1966).

It was stated on p. 232 that, in lower-class Central American adolescents and postadolescents, Frisancho *et al.* (1970a) found statural growth to be retarded over 30% and skeletal maturation 10% or less as compared to U.S. standards. The many underdeveloped-country growth curves published in the ICNND studies clearly show adolescent decelerations in statural growth, except when upper-class children are studied. And it would seem likely, as Frisancho *et al.* (1970b) show for Central America and Chamla (1964) for 19th-century France, that the period of growth is extended, about 7% for the former. As for the degree of catch up in skeletal maturation, the Central American findings are not likely to equal standard values elsewhere. Catch up would appear to depend upon the degree of nutritional deprivation. More probable in the more deprived populations is an *increase* in the skeletal maturation lag, much as that seen at Vicos before the feeding program, where the younger group showed a mean 2.13-year retardation and the adolescents and post-adolescents are 3.39 years retarded, slightly more percentage-wise. Nutritionally more deprived adolescents and post-adolescents, such as Malcolm's (1970) Highland New Guinea Bundi, are about 4 years behind U.S. skeletal maturation standards, and menarche may actually be delayed until after epiphyseal union.

Another factor limiting growth and maturation in poor subadults from underdeveloped countries appears to be the availability of zinc in the diet. The pioneer researches in this field were carried out by Prasad *et al.* (1963) on 16- to 19-year-old rural Egyptian males, who showed retarded growth and hypogonadism. In a follow-up study, Sandstead *et al.* (1967) were successful in dietary rescue of those boys placed on a hospital diet, with zinc supplementation; moreover, part of the sample fed the same food, but with iron therapy, did not respond as well. Both statural growth and skeletal age were strikingly retarded, the latter somewhat less so. Only two boys had body weights less than 90% of age-height standards, supporting the clinical impression that gross caloric deprivation was not part of this particular pattern. Whereas zinc interacts with many other nutrients, and intestinal parasitosis, schistosomiasis, malaria, and other diseases are clearly contributing factors, the following maladaptive nutritional pattern seems clear. Sandstead *et al.* (1967) estimate that an average rural Egyptian adult diet contains about 15 mg of zinc/day, but it is probably much less available for absorption for several reasons: (a) the all-vegetable diet is bulky, and much of the material is not digestible; (b) incomplete cooking and/or mastication may fail to adequately break down plant tissues for action by digestive enzymes; (c) plant proteins may bind metals more avidly than animal proteins; and (d) other vegetable organic compounds may also block zinc availability, especially the high levels of phytic acid in wheat bread.

In Iran, Halsted (1970) found the same syndrome in teen-age girls, along with geophagy. As Sandstead *et al.* (1967) strongly suggest, broader studies may find mild growth and maturational retardation due primarily to zinc deficiency to be a common phenomenon in lower socioeconomic levels of the tropics and subtropics. In view of widespread iron deficiency in the world, it would be equally important to determine its effect as well on growth and maturation.

Adult body morphology

Mean adult body weights in native peoples, and mean statures because they are so closely related, show quite regular clinal reductions with higher environmental temperatures. These body-size clines have been interpreted in terms of the 135-year-old Bergmann's "rule" (Roberts, 1953; Newman, 1953), which is based on the principle that larger bodies are advantageous in the retention of internally generated heat in the cold, whereas smaller bodies are advantageous in the dissipation of heat in the heat. The application of Bergmann's rule to man has been criticized mainly on two counts: (a) body size differences in man are insufficiently great to provide appreciable selective advantage, especially in very cold climates (Scholander, 1955), and (b) there are a number of exceptions where certain populations are too large or too small in body size to fit the body weight/ambient temperature regression (Comas, 1968), and, indeed, Subsaharan Africa stands out as a nearly continent-sized exception (Hiernaux, 1968c).

It now appears, however, that the explanation for the remarkably close correlation between mean adult body weights of native peoples and mean annual temperatures of their locations lies less in the body heat retention-dissipation principle and more in the food consumed. It is no accident that the temperate zones of the world include most of the developed countries, and the subtropical and tropical zones most of the underdeveloped countries. Richer soils, adequate growing seasons, and the proper amount and seasonal distribution of precipitation favor temperate-zone crops, as well as pasturage for animal husbandry. This bountiful food base has been largely instrumental in rendering developed countries what they are. Subtropical crops often suffer from poor soils, too much or not enough rain, indigent agricultural technology, food spoilage, and a plethora of hungry insects and other crop pests. Accordingly, higher environmental temperatures spell less efficient food economies for underdeveloped countries, and their largely uncontrolled population increases further diminish the quantity of food per capita. The caloric deficits of the bulk of the underdeveloped-country people have already been covered on pp. 216-17. It is further notable that, whereas in developed countries the lower socioeconomic classes consume enough calories, and especially carbohydrates, to foster several times the incidence of obesity seen in the upper classes, it is the reverse in underdeveloped countries (see pp. 244-45). There, the upper classes show virtually all the obesity there is; lower-class people are likely to be lean; they are rarely obese, which is also due to a much heavier work load.

Food quality, especially in terms of protein, has even closer relationships to climatic temperatures, as Borgstrom (1967) indicates:

> The most extensive [protein] deficiency regions are primarily to be found in warmer latitudes. This is no coincidence. High temperatures bring about a rapid degradation of the organic nitrogen reserves in the soil. The heavy rainfalls common in the wet tropics leach the soil and diminish to a considerable degree the protein return from nitrogen fertilizers.

We have already seen that adequate high quality protein is a prime mover in promoting optimal growth, so it only remains to be demonstrated that the supply of calories, protein, and other nutrients relate to adult body size.

This demonstration is afforded for calories by Frisch and Revelle's (1969a) Asian and Latin American regression of mean male body weights upon estimated caloric intakes for six countries in each group (Fig 9-1). To an extent, these weight-on-calorie regressions also reflect environmental temperatures, but this relationship cannot be further refined from the present data since the body weights are derived from a number of regions within each country and the USDA/FAO estimates were intended to refer to each country as a whole. Where regional studies have been done,

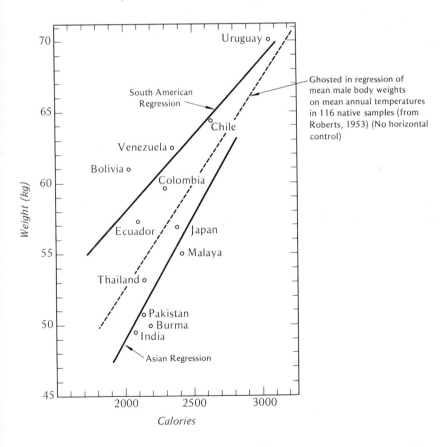

Fig. 9-1. Mean adult male body weights (ICNND) versus estimated calorie supplies (USDA). (From Frisch and Revelle, 1969.)

as in Brazil (ICNND, 1964), the most impoverished northeastern region has the highest ambient temperatures, the lowest caloric and protein intakes, and the lowest adult body weights. The average daily caloric intake of 1888 calories for the Nordestinos is far below the national average of about 2600. Moreover, in 56 Nordestino families divided into socioeconomic classes, per capital daily caloric intakes were as follows:

Very poor,	1606 calories
Poor,	1862 calories
Middle,	2028 calories
Well-to-do,	2323 calories

The very poor consumed 15% less than the average protein intake of 51 g/day, whereas the well-to-do consumed 51% more than this average. Although the sample sizes are very small, body weights clearly follow suit (ICNND, 1964).

Dealing with regional relationships in India between adult male stature and caloric and protein intake, Malhotra's (1966) data show clear increase relationships from the poorer south to the better-off north (Fig. 9-2). Rat assay data cited by Arthur (1969) on the typical foods of these regions show that rats as well as people grow poorly on a south Indian diet and do progressively better on northerly diets. To a considerable degree, there is a climatic regression from the hotter, wetter south to the cooler, drier north. Malhotra (1966) also shows that Indian Air Force personnel from the south (Madras/Kerala) recruited at 15-17 years of age undergo a quite dramatic catch up on the 3960 cal, 130 g protein daily fare provided in the military service, whereas those recruited from central and north India only registered modest statural gains.

In the more temperate zone, better nutrition permits growth and maturation to proceed at rates near the top of the adaptive plasticity range, achieving greater adult body size. The use of such developed countries as Uruguay and Japan in Fig. 9-1 is illustrative of this. It is also notable that the many studies of secular increases in body size that have been reported (Kaplan, 1953, Tanner, 1968) have all involved temperate-zone, developed countries. This seldom happens in underdeveloped countries because of the rarity of dietary rescue. Such rescue may have been commenced through the feeding program, freedom from peonage, and a more ample diet at Vicos, Peru (pp. 235, 237, and Table 9-1), but, if so, this was only accomplished through foreign intervention.

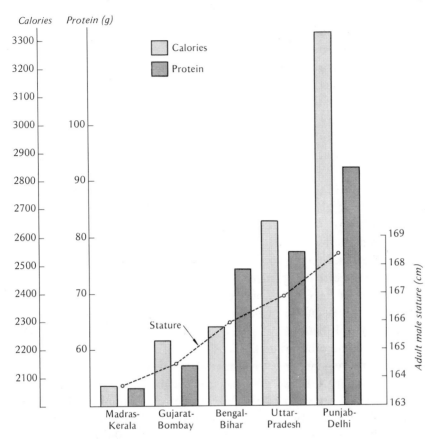

Fig. 9-2. Effects of nutrition on stature in different regions of India. (From Malhotra, 1966.)

In areas of nutritional dwarfism in the Sierra de Perijá, Venezuela among the Yupa Indians, in much of the New Guinea highlands, and, to a more limited degree, in southwestern France (the 19th-century "taches noires"), the stunting effect hits some individuals harder than others. It is likely that, as with the rural Guatemalans (pp. 235-36), there is little or no significant relationship to parental body size, since nutritional impoverishment suppresses genetic continuities. There are, of course, cases of individual dietary rescues with dramatic results, as Gadjusek (1970, personal communication) has noted for New Guinea highlanders whose small body size is attributed to a diet low in proteins, amino acids, fats, and sugars and high in fiber and potassium. When teen-age boys go down to the coast to work, their diet there is reversed in several respects. In several years, they burgeon into approximately 65-kg physiques, with something of the order of 45 kg expectable had they stayed home. When they return to the highlands, it is said that their relatives hardly recognize them. Something of this sort may also happen to the south Indian recruits in the Indian Air Force (p. 242).

There are indications that adult body proportions change with nutritional improvement during growth. In Shapiro's (1939) Japanese reared in Hawaii, most of the statural increase over the sedentes was in leg length. In the study of Harvard fathers and sons dating from 1870 to 1917, Hunt (1958) states that the greatest elongation of body regions probably occurs in the upper leg and lower arm. Hiernaux (1968b) found relatively longer legs after about 6 years of age in the pastoral and presumably better protein-nourished Tutsi than in the agricultural Hutu in Rwanda and Burundi, which he attributes to genetic rather than nutritional influences. Moore (1968) notes in U.S. blacks that there has been a significant increase in leg length with little or no change in sitting height since the turn of the century, but he states that it cannot be definitely determined if this is due to progressive increases in protein and other nutrients during this period.

From these and other studies, it would seem that the main effect of nutritional improvement on body proportions lies in relatively longer legs, but several other studies suggest that it is not that simple. In Hiernaux's (1968b) two Hutu samples, the better nourished sample had slightly longer trunks for the same stature. Thieme's (1959) Puerto Rican sample was divisible into several nutritional classes, wherein the best fed were clearly taller, but their greatest relative gain lay in trunk length. In view of these differences, the allometric timing of growth relative to the diet at different ages may be the critical factor. In any case, it is generally thought that there is more genetic control over body proportions than body size. It should be recalled in this connection that, in comparing U.S. black and white fetuses, Schultz (1926) found that shorter trunks and longer limbs characterized the former at a quite early stage.

EFFECTS OF OVERNUTRITION: GROWTH, ADULT MORPHOLOGY, AND HEALTH OF ECONOMICALLY MORE PRIVILEGED PEOPLE

The stillborn and newborn of financially better-off New York mothers had higher accumulations of subcutaneous fat and larger adipose cells than those of poor mothers (Naeye *et al.*, 1971). There are, moreover, massive accumulations of data, and both of these parameters relate closely to higher socioeconomic levels. Since larger newborns have enhanced chances of survival, the current removal of most restrictions on maternal weight gain during pregnancy (*Hospital Practice* Editorial, 1972) will undoubtedly increase birthweights in economically privileged families. Higher birthweights are strongly associated with greater stature at 7 years of age in the British National Child Development Study (Goldstein, 1971), suggesting a largely nutritional continuity from late fetal life into childhood. The chances are that, in a nutritional environment of plenty, a well-nourished or overnourished fetus will grow into a child of the same ilk. In terms of Dubos's (1968) concept of biological Freudianism, programming for overeating starts early in life.

There is a pediatric dilemma here: whereas a large newborn can better survive the neonatal period, its postnatal growth must be curbed, since it is seriously questioned whether a big baby is indeed a healthy baby (MacKeith, 1963). In the period of infancy and early childhood, overfeeding produces the infantile obesity syndrome, which is often accompanied by lowered resistance to disease. Formula feeding in early infancy often leads to overweight. Taitz (1971) cites individual cases where, at 6 weeks of age, the daily caloric intake was 700-800 kcal: milk + cereal + rusk, etc. Lightwood (1972) has stated that the introduction of cereal into an infant's diet is unphysiological before about 5 months, but most pediatricians permit it earlier. He also believes that the cereal should be as unrefined as possible and that iron supplementation is needed at 5 months since up to that time, the infant has been utilizing largely fetal iron stores.

In treating obesity originating in early infancy, dieting is almost completely unsuccessful, since fat cells are not lost but only shrunk. In obesity, there is a true hypertrophy of fat cells with increases of 300 to 400% in fat cell nuclei. Lightwood views the pediatric problem as one of actually programming an infant or a child to overeat. It is a matter of common observation that a mother will stick a bottle in her baby's mouth to stop its crying. There is a pediatric opinion (Lightwood, 1972) that less intelligent mothers tend to have fatter babies, and this may reflect a formal education differential by socioeconomic class. At even early ages, overeating encourages underexercise—which may become a lifelong pattern, especially since the requisite amount of exertion to compensate for a heavy diet may be uncompatible with the mode of employment of most higher socioeconomic-class, developed country people.

In that most developed of countries, the United States, some 30% of the children are considered obese (Forbes, 1957). A recent study of 3300 U.S. white children from three eastern states showed a maximum socio-economic differential at the age of 6 years: 40% and 29% of lower-class boys and girls were considered obese, as against 25% and 3% of their up-per-class counterparts. These differences became minimal at the age of 12 years but continued to age 18 and doubtless beyond (Stunkard *et al.*, 1972). It is likely amongst the lower socioeconomic classes in developed countries for a considerable proportion of the children to be obese, below mean stature for their ages, and essentially malnourished. Obese, high-class children are taller, have advanced skeletal maturation, and, in fe-males, earlier menarche (Forbes, 1957). As a Hagerstown, Maryland study with a 20-year interval shows (Abraham and Nordsieck, 1960), over-weight children with thick layers of trunk fat usually become overweight adults. It follows that some 25% of U.S. adults are obese (Mayer, 1967), and there is a pronounced differential by socioeconomic class. Stunkard's (1968) Manhattan study found 30% of lower-class women to be obese, with 16% middle class and 5% upper class also obese. This is a 6 : 1 lower- to upper-class ratio. In Manhattan men, 32% lower class and 16% upper class were considered obese. Similar trends are seen by socioeco-nomic class in the British, but, in Germany, the lower-class women and the upper-class men show the greatest obesity. The last finding is trying to tell us something about the life of being *Herrenvolk*. The relationship of obesity to circulatory disorders is multiple. By exerting pressure on the capillaries, excess fat may cause peripheral resistance to blood flow and a tendency toward hypertension. The same overeating-underexercising syndrome, given high polysaturated fat intake, makes for fatty sclerotic deposits on the inner walls of arteries and narrows their bore. Heart func-tion may be impaired by fat infiltration. And, since fat is a metabolically inactive tissue, it is just that much more excess baggage to carry around, and to do so places added strain on an already impaired circulatory system.

There is mounting evidence in overdeveloped countries that circulatory disorders strike earlier and earlier in life. In a sample of about 400 U.S. soldiers averaging under 23 years old at the time of death in the Korean War (1950-1953), about 70% showed at least beginning sclerotic proc-esses in their aorta and coronary arteries. But it is in later life that de-generative circulatory diseases reach epidemic proportions in the U.S. pop-ulation, and they largely account for the fact that this country has slipped from 10th to 40th place in male longevity for the world (Mayer, 1968). Indeed as Mayer (1967) states,

We do have a high mortality rate from violence; several times the death rate from automobile accidents, home accidents, and industrial accidents than in leading developed countries, and 10 to 20 times the rate from homicide. We also have a high and growing death rate from lung cancer. Still, as compared to our main cause of death, cardiovascular disease over 39%, other factors are minor. The fact that half of American men in the 40 to 60 age range die of cardiovascular disease, with coronary heart disease preponderant, means that we have returned unwittingly to the days of the great pandemics where one quarter or a half of the population died of one disease. This time, the pandemic is a degenerative rather than an epidemic disease.

Being overweight has long been recognized by insurance actuaries as contributing strongly to reduced life expectancy. The Metropolitan Life Insurance Company (1959) records increased death rates over normal of 30% and 42% for U.S. women and men classed as 30% overweight for their age and stature. As Cheek (1968) states, "overnutrition with overgrowth may advance cell multiplication and biologic age." Overweight clearly has harmful effects on already existing renal, joint, and respiratory diseases, and has a "strange bedfellow" relationship with diabetes mellitus. Besides obesity, other conspicuous causal agents for cardiovascular disease are hypercholesterolemia, hypertension, cigarette smoking, psychic stress, and lack of exercise. Most are interrelated; for example, a study cited by Davidson and Passmore (1963) that, on the average, an adult of normal weight walks 34.3 miles a week, whereas an obese adult only walks 14.4 miles. But, according to the U.S. Public Health Service study at Framingham, Massachusetts, the results of multivariate analysis show that "above age 50 for constant levels of other risk factors, the coefficient for relative weight to stature is only one-third that for cigarettes and only one-fourth that for cholesterol or blood pressure." Taken together, hypercholesterolemia, hypertension, and cigarette smoking increase the risk of coronary heart disease 563%. Withal, neither physical activity nor psychic stress (both difficult to quantify) were tipped into the Framingham multivariate analysis. Physical activity of sufficient degree to engender *physical fitness* appears to be a key factor in reducing the severity of circulatory and other diseases of industrialization and urbanization. But psychic stress looms as perhaps the single most ominous (and experimentally most intractable) factor.

SUMMARY

It is suggested here that man's million-year hunting phase so narrowed his nutritional requirements, especially in the amino acid balance of animal proteins, that the accelerative shift to vegetable foods occasioned by the Agricultural Revolution some 10,000 years ago has placed him in an increasingly difficult dietary dilemma. In contrast to the amino acid content of animal protein, which closely approximates the FAO optimal pattern, seed and tuber proteins are usually deficient in one or several of the amino acids. Increasingly, human societies have concentrated upon one of the major staple crops—rice, wheat, corn, millet, and manioc, have imbued them with super-food magic, and have developed maladaptive food habits concerning them. Generally, adults can get enough protein from plant sources if they eat large quantities, but the enhanced needs of infancy, gestation, and lactation may be impossible to satisfy in this way. Moreover, plant proteins bind such minerals as iron and zinc more avidly, making them less available for absorption.

Accordingly, although the Agricultural Revolution made possible a settled life, population growth, and technological progress, in both an epidemiological and a nutritional sense it has constituted a very mixed blessing. Villages became towns and towns cities, and man's almost infinite capacity for self-contamination opened the Pandora's Box of the infectious, "crowd-type" diseases. Increasingly restrictive diets have made the nutritional diseases as great a threat to human quality of life as the infectious diseases in the underdeveloped four-fifths of the world's population. Indeed, infectious diseases and nutritional deprivation usually aid and abet each other in a synergistic relationship to exacerbate human misery. Without well-controlled, intensive studies, it is generally impossible to separate pathogenic from nutritional insult as the prime cause of death, although Dumont and Rosier (1969) estimate that of the 60 million deaths in the world each year, 10 to 20 million are due to dietary deprivation.

It may well be that the figures of the FAO Third World Survey (1963) and others underestimate the international food problem and only represent the tip of the dietary iceberg. Admittedly the data for such estimates are limited, but the usually quoted FAO figure is that at least 20% of the world's people are undernourished calorically, and about 60% are malnourished in one or more essential nutrient. A FAO/WHO Expert Group (1965) estimated that at least one-quarter and perhaps one-third of the underdeveloped-country people of the world have a protein-deficient diet, with protein intake the most significant single indicator of nutritional adequacy.

Until 1970, the gloomy picture was one of an inexorable 2% annual increase in the world's population as against about 1% annual food supply increases. But that year the world harvest exceeded that of 1969 by 2%, including a 5% increase in the Far East. These increases are due to the improved seed and agricultural technology of the Green Revolution, but the fabric of this progress is considered fragile and its base narrow in the underdeveloped four-fifths of the world. By the mid-1970's, droughts and floods exacerbated widespread starvation.

In the culture of poverty, the culture of most of the world's people, there is growing evidence that a mother's nutritional history, including her early life as well as her nutritional status during pregnancy, have profound effects upon the growth and development of her fetus. Mothers whose reduced body size is due largely to dietary deprivation have poorer reproductive histories—more difficult labor, more premature births, more birth defects, and a higher perinatal mortality. In one carefully controlled study in New York City, the late stillborn of the poor had disproportionately small organ weights for the thymus, spleen, liver, and adrenals and reduced subcutaneous fat.

It seems to be well established that body size of adults and newborn show clear socioeconomic gradients irrespective of ethnic affiliation. Low birthweights are clearly more prevalent in underdeveloped countries than in developed ones, and neonatal mortality rates are several times higher. Lactation is likely to be halved in quantity by inadequate maternal nutrition, especially protein, and this contributes to slowed growth and even weight loss within the first 6 months—a period when milk production of well-nourished mothers is fully adequate for the proper growth and development of their infants. Either before or upon weaning, the shift to often-contaminated, high-carbohydrate, low-protein solid foods is a critical time when either the marasmic or the kwashiorkor varieties of protein-calorie-deficiency disease sets in. The full clinical manifestations of these diseases occur earlier when breast feeding is reduced, and the mismanaged nursing bottle is substituted. In families with limited food resources, early mortality increases with birth order, and estimates for some underdeveloped tropical and subtropical countries suggest that about one-half of all liveborn die of malnutrition and its sequelae during the first 5 years of life.

Surviving the first year places the young child born to poverty in an even more hazardous age-grade. It has been suggested that the 1- to 4-year-old death rate provides a useful single indicator of a country's nutritional status. Jelliffe's (1969) neologism "Secotrant" (*seco*nd year + *trant*itional) identifies the particularly critical second year of life, when, in all likelihood, a child is displaced at the breast by a newer family arrival. Infectious diseases, especially the diarrheas, act synergistically with poor nutrition, maladaptive food habits, and psychic deprivation to make the mortality and morbidity rates of earlier childhood even higher. Retarded growth and development are the near-universal responses to the insults of inadequate nutrition and infectious disease. The nutritional programming of growth and development under these deprived circumstances appears to override much of the genetic control usually exercised over them; hence, the near-universal retardation patterns. These patterns include small body size, retarded skeletal maturation, low bone densities, and some degree of mental and emotional handicap. The question of irreversible brain damage through protein-calorie malnutrition has not been fully settled, but it would appear at the present writing that the earlier in life the nutritional insult, the more likely the permanency of the damage.

It seems clear that the parts of the body most affected by nutritional deprivation are those programmed to grow most rapidly at the time. Apparently, full catch up, upon dietary rescue, seems to occur after the deprivations of war and other catastrophes in developed countries, but becomes a largely academic question in underdeveloped ones, where such rescue is rare. There is evidence from Guatemala that, even in the rare cases of rescue, lower-class rural children take several times as long to catch up as those from better-off, urban families. The usual picture in cultures of poverty is that during growth there is never sufficient food to constitute dietary rescue, and the slowed physical development results in adults of small body size. Sexual maturation is closely related, so that the semi-facetious Malcolm's Law—the later the menarche, the smaller the people—is of broad applicability. Although the question of mineral availability in plant foods is still underinvestigated, zinc deficiency in poor rural children on almost exclusively vegetable diets appears to retard both growth and sexual development greatly.

Further, there is evidence from Peru that dietary rescue has a reduced effect on younger 7- to 12-year-old boys than on essentially adolescent 13- to 18-year-olds. The reasons for the incomplete catch up in the younger boys are far from clear, but may reflect low social status and all that goes with it in their households, or more restricted growth potentials in earlier life engendered by long-term genetic selection against more rapid growth. In large Central American samples from lower socioeconomic strata, Frisancho *et al.* (1970a) discerned an age-related pattern of retardation, wherein pre-adolescent children showed statural retardation 10% or less below U.S. standards but an over 30% delay in skeletal maturation. In adolescents and post-adolescents, retardation was reversed, with statural growth lagging over 30% and skeletal maturation 10% or less. It is apparent that the pubertal growth spurt is not only milder but delayed as well in cultures of relative poverty, and, as Frisch and Revelle (1969a) have shown, the timing is closely related to caloric intake figures.

It has been clear for 20 years that adult body size is reduced on the average with increasing environmental temperatures. This has been considered fair evidence that Bergmann's rule, developed for other homeotherms, is also operative in man. It now appears that this body size-temperature relationship is due less to the Bergmannian body heat retention-dissipation principle than to the lower food-producing potential of most hotter regions of the world. Some demonstration that body size in man is strongly mediated by nutrition is afforded by the steep regressions of mean adult male body weights or mean caloric intakes for the six Asian and six Latin American countries studied by Frisch and Revelle (1969a). Confirmatory are the clear increases of mean male stature with increased calorie and protein intake from the south to the central and then to the northern parts of India (Malhotra, 1966). There are probably differences in body proportions as well, in that taller and probably better-fed people are relatively longer in the leg, but, generally, body size is considerably more ecosensitive than body proportions.

If, indeed, most of the world is underfed, the better-off socioeconomic strata of the developed countries are clearly overnourished. The "overdeveloped" country counterpart of protein-calorie malnutrition is the infantile obesity syndrome. On the basis of Dubos's (1968) biological Freudianism concept, nutritionally overprivileged individuals can be programmed early in life for overeating. Overweight children become overweight adults. Putative genetic programming for superior metabolic efficiency so adaptive to man as a hunter have become extraordinarily maladaptive in the overfed, underexercised urban life style of developed countries. Largely because of their higher carbohydrate diets, the lower socioeconomic classes in most developed countries show higher incidences of obesity than the upper ones. As obese babies are characteristically lower in resistance to infectious disease, so are obese adults more susceptible to the assaults of metabolic diseases, especially of the circulatory system. Moreover, obesity has a "strange bedfellow" relationship to diabetes. The risks of premature mortality and morbidity from overeating and underexercising are complex and multiple, involving hypercholesterolemia, hypertension, cigarette smoking, overuse of alcohol, and less tractable factors of psychic stressing.

REFERENCES

Abraham, S. and M. Nordsieck. 1960. Relationship of excess weight in children and adults. *Pub. Hlth. Repts.* 75:263-73.

Ademowore, A. S., N. G. Courey, and J. S. Kime. 1972. Relationships of maternal nutrition and weight gain to newborn weight. *Obstet./Gynec.* 39: 460-64.

Antonov, A. N. 1947. Children born during the siege of Leningrad in 1942. *J. Pediat.* 30:250.

Armendares, S., F. Salamanca, and S. Frank. 1971. Chromosome abnormalities in severe protein calorie malnutrition. *Nature* 232:271-73.

Arnhold, R. 1969. Arm circumference as a public health index of protein-calorie malnutrition of early childhood. XVII. The Quak Stick: A field measure used by the Quaker Service Team in Nigeria. *J. Trop. Pediat.* 15:4.

Arthur, D. R. 1969. *Man and His Environment.* New York: American Elsevier.

Bailey, K. V. 1963. Nutrition in New Guinea. *Food Nutr. Notes Rev.* 20:89-112.

Behar, M. 1968a. Food and nutrition of the Maya before the conquest and at the present time. In *Biomedical Challenges Presented by the American Indian.* Pub. 165. Washington, D.C.: Pan American Health Organization, pp. 114-19.

Behar, M. 1968b. Prevalence of malnutrition among preschool children of developing countries. In *Malnutrition, Learning, and Behavior*, eds. N. E. Scrimshaw and J. E. Gordon. Cambridge, Mass.: MIT Press, pp. 30-41.

Binford, S. R. 1970. Late Middle Pleistocene adaptations and their possible consequences. *Bio Science* 20:280-88.

Birch, H. and J. D. Gussow. 1970. *Disadvantaged Children: Health, Nutrition, and School Failure.* New York: Harcourt Brace Jovanovich.

Boerma, A. H. 1970. A world agricultural plan. *Sci. Amer.* 223:54-69.

Borgstrom, G. 1967. *The Hungry Planet.* New York: Collier Books; London: Collier-Macmillan.

Boas, F. 1911. *Changes in Bodily Form in Descendants of Immigrants. Final Report.* Washington, D.C.: U.S. Government Printing Office.

Bourliere, F. 1963. Observations on the ecology of some large African mammals. *Viking Fund Pub. in Anthropol.* 36:43-54.

Bresler, J. B. 1962. Maternal height and prevalence of still-births. *Amer. J. Phys. Anthropol.* 20:515-17.

Brown, L. R. 1963. *Man, Land, and Food.* Foreign Agr. Econ. Report no. 11, USDA.

Burke, B. S., V. A. Beal, S. B. Kirkwood, and H. C. Stuart. 1943. Nutrition studies during pregnancy. *Amer. J. Obstet. Gynecol.* 46:38-52.

Burrell, R. J. W., M. J. R. Healy, and J. M. Tanner. 1961. Age of menarche in South African Bantu schoolgirls living in the Transkei Reserve. *Human Biol.* 33:250.

Butzer, K. W. 1971. *Environment and Archeology*, 2nd ed. Chicago: Aldine.

Cassel, J. 1955. A comprehensive health program among South African Zulus. In *Health, Culture, and Community*, ed. B. D. Paul, New York: Russell Sage Foundation, pp. 15-41.

Chamla, M. C. 1964. L'accroissement de la stature en France de 1880 à 1960: Comparison avec les pays d'Europe Occidentale, *Bull. Soc. Anthropol. (Paris)* 6:201-78.

Cheek, D. 1968. *Human Growth: Body Composition, Cell Growth, Energy and Intelligence.* Philadelphia: Lea & Fabiger.

Chung, C. S., N. E. Morton, and N. Yasuda. 1966. Does isolate-breaking explain the increase in body size in modern populations? *Annals N.Y. Acad. Sci.* 134:666-87.

Churchill, J. D., J. W. Neff, and D. F. Caldwell. 1966. Birthweight and intelligence. *Obstet./Gynecol.* 28:425.

Citizens Board of Inquiry into Hunger and Malnutrition in the United States. 1968. *Hunger, U.S.A.* Boston: Beacon Press.

Collis, W. R. F. and M. Janes. 1968. Multifactorial causation of malnutrition and retarded growth and development. In *Malnutrition, Learning, and Behavior*, eds. N. S. Scrimshaw and J. E. Gordon. Cambridge, Mass.: MIT Press, pp. 55-71.

Comas, J. 1968. Biological subdivisions of the Indian on the basis of physical anthropology. In *Biomedical Challenges Presented by the American Indian.* Publ. 165. Washington, D.C.: Pan American Health Organization, pp. 22-34.

Cook, J. D. and C. A. Finch. 1973. Iron deficiency in man, Miles Symposium Proceedings, Quebec. Ottawa: Department of National Health and Welfare.

Consolazio, C. F., R. Shapiro, J. E. Masterson, and P. S. L. McKinzie. 1961. Energy requirements of men in extreme heat. *J. Nutrition* 73.

Cravioto, J. 1970. Complexity of factors involved in protein-calorie malnutrition. In *Malnutrition is a Problem of Ecology*, eds. P. György and O. L. Kline, Basel: Karger.

Cravioto, J. and E. R. De Licardie. 1968. Intersensory development of school-age children. In *Malnutrition, Learning, and Behavior*, eds. N. S. Scrimshaw and J. E. Gordon. Cambridge, Mass.: MIT Press, pp. 252-68.

Davidson, S. and P. Passmore. 1963. *Human Nutrition and Dietetics.* London: E. and S. Livingstone, Ltd.

Dayton, D. H., L. J. Filer, and C. Canosa. 1968. *Placental Cellular Changes in the Placentas of Undernourished Mothers in Guatemala.* NAS/NRC, Oct. 18.

de Silva, C. C., P. V. D. Fernando, and C. D. H. Gunaratne. 1962. The search for a prematurity level in Colombo, Ceylon. *J. Trop. Pediat.* 8:29.

Drillien, C. M. 1964. The growth and development of the prematurely born infant. *J. Pediat.* 7-8:73-95.

Dubos, R. 1965. *Man Adapting.* New Haven: Yale University Press.
Dubos, R. 1968. *So Human an Animal.* New York: Scribners.
Dumont, R. and B. Rosier. 1969. *The Hungry Future.* New York: F. P. Praeger.
Editorial: News of Hospital Interest. 1972. Weight, salt intake curbs held pregnancy risks. *Hospital Practice* Sept. 1. 23.
Editorial: Science and the Citizen. 1971. *Sci. Amer.* 224:41-42.
Editorial: Science and the Citizen. 1972. *Sci. Amer.* 226:45-46.
Edozien, J. C. 1965a. Establishment of a biochemical norm for the evaluation of nutritional status in West Africa. *J. West Afr. Sci. Assoc.* 10:1.
Edozien, J. C. 1965b. Biochemical evaluation of the state of nutrition in Nigeria. *J. West Afr. Sci. Assoc.* 10:22.
Edozien, J. C. 1970. Malnutrition in Africa—need and basis for action. In *Malnutrition is a Problem of Ecology*, eds. P. György and O. L. Kline. Basel: Karger, pp. 64-71.
Escapini, H. 1968. Ocular manifestations of hypovitaminosis A. (Unpublished thesis cited in PAHO 1970.)
Falkner, F. 1966. General considerations in human development. In *Human Development*, ed. F. Falkner. Philadelphia: Saunders, pp. 10-39.
Falkner, F. (ed.). 1969. *Key Issues in Infant Mortality.* Bethesda: National Institute of Child Health and Human Development.
FAO (Food and Agricultural Organization). 1957. *Protein—at the Heart of the World Food Problem.* Rome: FAO.
FAO. 1963. *Third World Survey.* Freedom from Hunger Campaign. Basic Study No. 11.
FAO/WHO. 1965. *Protein Requirements, Report of a Joint FAO/WHO Expert Committee.* WHO Tech. Report Series No. 301.
FAO/WHO. 1967. *Requirements of Vitamin A, Thiamine, Riboflavin, and Niacin. Report of a Joint FAO/WHO Expert Group.* WHO Tech. Report Series No. 362.
Ferák, T. 1968. Endogamy, exogamy, and stature. *Eugen. Quart.* 15:273-76.
Forbes, G. 1957. Overnutrition for the child: Blessing or curse? *Nutrit. Rev.* 15:195.
Friedlaender, J. S. and H. L. Bailit. 1968. Eruption times of the deciduous and permanent teeth of natives on Bougainville Island, Territory of New Guinea: A study of racial variations. *Human Biol.* 40:51-65.
Frisancho, A. R., S. M. Garn, and W. Ascoli. 1970a. Population differences in skeletal maturation and its relationship to growth in body size (Abst). *Amer. J. Phys. Anthropol.* 33:130.
Frisancho, A. R., S. M. Garn, and W. Ascoli. 1970b. Childhood retardation resulting in reduction of adult body size due to lesser adolescent skeletal delay. *Amer. J. Phys. Anthropol.* 33:325-36.
Frisch, R. E. 1970. Present status of the supposition that malnutrition causes permanent mental retardation. *Amer. J. Clin. Nutrit.* 23(2):189-95.
Frisch, R. E. and R. Revelle. 1969a. Variation in body weights and the age of the adolescent growth spurt among Latin American and Asian populations in relation to calorie supplies. *Human Biol.* 41:185-212.
Frisch, R. E. and R. Revelle. 1969b. The height and weight of adolescent boys and girls at the time of peak velocity of growth in height and weight: Longitudinal data. *Human Biol.* 41:536-59.
Gardner, L. I. 1972. Deprivation dwarfism. *Sci. Amer.* 227:76-83.
Garn, S. M. 1966a. Nutrition in physical anthropology. *Amer. J. Phys. Anthropol.* 24:289-92.

Garn, S. M. 1966b. Malnutrition and skeletal development in the pre-school child. In *Preschool Child Malnutrition,* Publication 1282, ed. W. H. Sehrell. Washington, D.C.: NAS/NRC.

Gast, M. and J. Adrian. 1965. *Mils et sorgho en Ahaggar. Étude ethnologique et nutritionelle.* Mem. Centre Recherches Anthrop., Prehist., et Ethnog. IV.

Geber, M. and R. F. A. Dean. 1957. Gesell tests on African children. *Pediatrics* 20:1055-65.

Gillie, R. B. 1971. Endemic goiter. *Sci. Amer.* 224(6):92-101.

Goldsmith, G. A. 1953. Human nutritive requirements and recommended daily allowances. *J. Amer. Diet. Assoc.* 29:109-15.

Goldstein, H. 1971. Factors influencing the height of seven year old children —results from the National Child Development Study. *Human Biol.* 43: 92-111.

Gopalan, C. 1968. Kwashiorkor and marasmus: Evolution and its distinguishing features. In *Calorie Deficiencies and Protein Deficiencies,* eds. R. A. McCance and E. M. Widdowson. Boston: Little, Brown, pp. 49-58.

Gopalan, C. 1968. Nutrition and family planning. (to be published)

Gordon, J. E., J. B. Wyon, and W. Ascoli. 1967. The second year death rate in less developed countries. *Amer. J. Med. Sci.* 254:357-80.

Grande, F. 1964. Man under caloric deficiency. In *Handbook of Physiology,* Sec. 4, ed. D. B. Dill *et al.* Washington, D.C.: American Physiology Society, pp. 911-37.

Greenhill, J. P. 1965. *Obstetrics Textbook,* 13th ed. Philadelphia.: Saunders.

Gruenwald, P., H. Funakawa, S. Mitani, T. Nishimura, and S. Takeuchi. 1967. Influence of environmental factors of foetal growth in man. *Lancet* 1:1026.

György, P. and O. L. Kline (eds.). 1970. *Malnutrition is a Problem of Ecology.* Basel: Karger.

Haldane, J. B. S. 1932. *The Causes of Evolution,* London: Longmans Green.

Halsted, J. A. 1970. Human zinc deficiency. *Trans. Amer. Clin. Climat Assoc.* 82:170-76.

Hiernaux, J. 1968a. Ethnic differences in growth and development. *Eugen. Quart.* 15:12-21.

Hiernaux, J. 1968b. Body shape differentiation of ethnic groups and of the sexes through growth. *Human Biol.* 40:44-62.

Hiernaux, J. 1968c. *La diversité humaine en Afrique subsaharienne.* Bruxelles: l'Instit. de Soc., Univ. Libre.

Howe, P. E. and M. Schiller. 1952. Growth responses of the school child to changes in diet and environmental factors. *J. Appl. Physiol.* 5:51-61.

Hunt, E. E. 1958. Human growth and body form in recent generations. *Amer. Anthropol.* 60:118-31.

ICNND (Interdepartmental Committee on Nutrition for National Defense). 1960. *Ecuador, Nutritional Survey.* Washington, D.C.: U.S. Government Printing Office.

ICNND. 1961. *Chile, Nutritional Survey, March-June 1960.* Washington, D.C.: U.S. Government Printing Office.

ICNND/Office of International Research, Nutrition Section. 1965. *Nutrition Survey of East Pakistan. March 1962-January 1964.* Bethesda: National Institutes of Health.

ICNND. 1965. *Northeastern Brazil. Nutritional Survey March-May, 1965.* Washington, D.C.: U.S. Government Printing Office.

ICNND. 1966. Summary of reports of ICNND 1956-64. National Institutes of Health. Bethesda: Nutrition Section, Office of International Research.

Jelliffe, D. B. 1968a. *Child Nutrition in Developing Countries*. Washington, D.C.: U.S. Dept. Health, Education, & Welfare.

Jelliffe, D. B. 1968b. *Infant Nutrition in the Subtropics and Tropics*, 2nd ed. Geneva: WHO.

Jelliffe, E. F. and D. B. Jelliffe. 1969. The arm circumference as a public health index of protein-calorie malnutrition of early childhood. *J. Trop. Pediat.* 15:179.

Jolly, C. J. 1967. The evolution of the baboons. In *The Baboon in Medical Research*, vol. 2.

King, K. W. 1970. Malnutrition in the Caribbean. In *The State of Our Species*. New York: American Museum of Natural History, pp. 64-67.

Klein, R. E., J. Kagan, H. E. Freeman, C. Yarbrough, and J. P. Habicht. 1972. Is big smart? The relation of growth to cognition. *J. Hlth. Soc. Behav.* 13:219-25.

Kotz, N. 1969. *Let Them Eat Promises. The Politics of Hunger in America*. Englewood Cliffs, N.J.: Prentice-Hall.

Kralj-Čerček, L. 1956. The influence of food, body build, and social origin on the age at menarche. *Human Biol.* 28:393-406.

Laska-Mierzejewska, T. 1970. Effect of ecological and socio-economic factors on the age of menarche, body height and weight of rural girls in Poland. *Human Biol.* 42(2):284-92.

Layrisse, M. 1969. Iron absorption from food. *PAHO, Iron Metabolism and Anemia*, Sci. Pub. no. 184. Washington, D.C.: Pan American Sanitary Bureau.

Lederberg, J. 1969. Health in the world of tomorrow. In *3rd PAHO/WHO Lecture on the Biomedical Sciences*. Washington, D.C.: Pan American Health Organization.

Leitch, I., F. C. Hytten, and W. Z. Billewicz. 1959. The maternal and neonatal weights of some mammalia. *Proc. Zool. Sci.* (London) 31:11.

Lightwood, R. 1972. CDMRC, Univ. of Wash. Lecture, Feb. 25.

Loomis, W. F. 1970. Rickets. *Sci. Amer.* 223(6):77-91.

MacKeith, R. 1963. Is a big baby healthy? *Prac. Nutrit. Soc.* 22:128-34.

MacNeish, R. S. 1967. *The Prehistory of the Tehuacan Valley*. Austin: University of Texas Press.

Malcolm, L. A. 1970. Growth and development of the Bundi child of the New Guinea highlands. *Human Biol.* 42:293-328.

Malhotra, M. S. 1966. People of India including primitive tribes—a survey on physiological adaptation, physical fitness, and nutrition. In *The Biology of Human Adaptability*, eds. P. T. Baker and J. S. Wiener. Oxford: Clarendon Press, pp. 329-55.

Marshall, W. A., M. T. Ashcroft, and G. Bryan. 1970. Skeletal maturation of the hand and wrist in Jamaican children. *Human Biol.* 42:419-35.

Martell, R., C. Yarbrough, J. P. Habicht, and R. E. Klein. 1973. Diarrheal diseases and incremental growth in Guatemalan children. Preliminary draft (INCAP Guatemala).

Mata, L. J., J. J. Urrutia, and J. E. Gordon. 1967. Diarrheal disease in a cohort of Guatemalan village children observed from birth to age two years. *Trop. Geogr. Med.* 19:247-57.

May, J. M. 1967. *Ecology of Malnutrition in Northern Africa: Libya, Tunisia,*

Algeria, Morocco, Spanish Sahara Ifani and Mauretania. New York: Hafner.

Mayer, J. 1967. Nutrition and civilization. *Trans. N.Y. Acad. Sci.* II:29:1014-32.

Mayer, J. 1968. *Overweight, Causes, Cost, and Control.* Englewood Cliffs, N.J.: Prentice-Hall.

McKusick, V. A. 1963. Natural selection and contemporary cardiovascular disease. *Circulation* 27:161-63.

Meggers, B. J. 1972. *Prehistoric America.* Chicago: Aldine-Atherton.

Meggitt, M. J. 1964. *Aboriginal Food-gatherers of Tropical Australia.* Morges, Switzerland: International Union for Conservation of Native and Natural Resources.

Meredith, H. V. 1970. Body weight at birth of viable human infants: A worldwide comparative treatise. *Human Biol.* 42:217-64.

Mertz, E. T. 1959. *Recent Research on Human Protein Requirements and the Amino Acid Supplementation of Foods.* Proc. 11th Res. Conference. Chicago: American Meat Institute Foundation.

Metropolitan Life Insurance Company. 1959. The new weight standards for men and women. *Statist. Bull.* 40:3.

Monckeberg, F. 1970. Factors conditioning malnutrition in Latin America, with special reference to Chile. Advice for a volunteers program. In *Malnutrition is a Problem of Ecology,* eds. P. György and O. L. Kline. Basel: Karger, pp. 23-33.

Moore, M. W. 1968. *The Secular Trend in Physical Growth of the North American Negro.* 8th Internat. Congr. Anth. & Ethnol. Sci., Kyoto, Japan.

Myrdal, G. 1972. Political factors in economic assistance. *Sci. Amer.* 226(4): 15-21.

Naeye, R. L., M. W. Diener, H. T. Harcke, and W. A. Blanc. 1971. Relation of poverty and race to birthweight and organ and cell structure in the newborn. *Pediat. Res.* 5:17-22.

NAS (National Academy of Sciences). 1968. *Recommended Dietary Allowances,* 7th ed. Publ. 1694, Washington, D.C.: National Academy of Science.

NAS/NRC Committee. 1971. *Rapid Population Growth: Consequences and Policy Implications.* Baltimore: Johns Hopkins Press.

Neel, J. M. 1962. Diabetes mellitus: A "thrifty" genotype rendered detrimental by "progress." *Amer. J. Human Genet.* 14:354-62.

Newcombe, H. B. 1965. Environmental versus genetic interpretations of birth-order effects. *Eugen. Quart.* 12:90-101.

Newman, M. T. 1953. The application of ecological rules to the racial anthropology of the aboriginal New World. *Amer. Anthropol.* 55:311-27.

Newman, M. T., C. Collazos, and C. de Fuentes. 1963. Growth differences between Indians and Mestizos in the Callejon de Huaylas, Peru. (Abst). *Amer. J. Phys. Anthropol.* 21(3):407-408.

Niswander, K., M. Westphall, and J. E. Singer. 1968. Relationship of weight gain during pregnancy to birthweight and infant growth and development during the first year of life. A report from collaborate study of cerebral palsy. *Obstet./Gynecol.* 31:417.

Paddock, W. and P. Paddock. 1967 *Famine 1975!* Boston: Little, Brown.

PAHO (Pan American Health Organization). 1969. *Iron Metabolism and*

Anemia. PAHO Sci. Publ. No. 184. Washington, D.C.: Pan American Sanitary Bureau.

PAHO. 1970. *Hypovitaminosis A in the Americas. Report of a PAHO Technical Group Meeting.* Washington, D.C.: Pan American Sanitary Bureau.

Pimstone, S. M., W. Wittmann, J. D. C. Hansen and P. Murray. 1966. Growth hormone and kwashiorkor. *Lancet* II:777.

Polgar, S. 1964. Evolution and the ills of mankind. In *Horizons of Anthropology*, ed. S. Tax. Chicago: Aldine.

Prasad, A. S., A. Miali, Z. Farid, H. H. Sandstead, and A. R. Schubert. 1963. Zinc metabolism in patients with the syndrome of iron deficiency anemia, hepatosplenomegaly, dwarfism, and hypogonadism. *J. Lab. Clin. Med.* 61:537-49.

President's Science Advisory Committee. 1967. *The World Food Problem.* II. *Report of the Panel on the World Food Supply.* Washington, D.C.: The White House.

Read, M. S. 1970. Nutrition and ecology: Crossroads for research. In *Malnutrition is a Problem of Ecology*, eds. P. György and O. L. Kline. Basel: Karger, pp. 202-18.

Roberts, D. F. 1953. Body weight, race and climate. *Amer. J. Phys. Anthropol.* 11:533-58.

Sandstead, H. H., A. S. Prasad, A. R. Schubert, Z. Farid, A. Miale, S. Bassilly, and W. J. Darby. 1967. Human zinc deficiency, endocrine manifestations and response to treatment. *Amer. J. Clin. Nutrit.* 20:422-42.

Scholander, P. F. 1955. Evolution of climatic adaptation in homeotherms. *Evolution* 9:15-26.

Schreider, E. 1967. Body-height and inbreeding in France. *Amer. J. Phys. Anthropol.* 26:1-4.

Schultz, A. H. 1926. Fetal growth of man and other primates. *Quart. Rev. Biol.* 1:465-521.

Scrimshaw, H. S., M. Behar, F. Viteri, G. Arroyave, and C. Tejada. 1957. Epidemiology and prevention of severe protein malnutrition (kwashiorkor) in Central America. *Amer. J. Pub. Hlth.* 47:63-72.

Scrimshaw, H. S. and M. Behar. 1961. Protein malnutrition in young children. *Science* 133:239-47.

Scrimshaw, N. S. and J. E. Gordon (eds.). 1968. *Malnutrition, Learning, and Behavior.* Cambridge, Mass.: MIT Press.

Scrimshaw, N. S., C. E. Taylor, and J. E. Gordon. 1968. *Interactions of Nutrition and Disease.* WHO Monograph Series No. 57.

Service, E. R. 1966. *The Hunters.* Englewood Cliffs, N.J.: Prentice-Hall.

Shapiro, H. L. 1939. *Migration and Environment.* New York: Oxford University Press.

Sherman, H. C. 1943. *The Science of Nutrition.* New York: Columbia University Press.

Simmons, K. and W. W. Greulich. 1943. Menarchal age and the height, weight, and skeletal age of girls 7-17 years. *J. Pediat.* 22:518-48.

Smith, C. A. 1947. Effects of wartime starvation in Holland upon pregnancy and its product. *Amer. J. Obstet. Gynecol.* 53:599.

Smith, C. A. 1962. Prenatal and neonatal nutrition. *Pediatrics* 30:145-56.

Solheim, W. C. 1972. An earlier agricultural revolution. *Sci. Amer.* 226:34-41.

Steiner, P. E. 1946. Necropsies on Okinawans. *Arch. Pathol.* 42:359-80.

Stone, I. 1965. Studies of a mammalian enzyme system for producing evolutionary evidence on man. *Amer. J. Phys. Anthropol.* 23:83-86.

Stunkard, A. 1968. Environment and obesity: Recent advances in our understanding of regulation of food intake in man. *Fed. Proc.* 27:1367-73.

Stunkard, A., E. d'Aquili, S. Fox, and R. D. L. Filion. 1972. Influence of social class on obesity and thinness in children. *J.A.M.A.* 221:579-84.

Taitz, L. S. 1971. Overnutrition among artificially fed infants in Sheffield regions. *Brit. Med. J.* 1:315-16.

Takahashi, E. 1966. Growth and environment in Japan. *Human Biol.* 38: 112-30.

Tanner, J. M. 1962. *Growth at Adolescence*. Oxford: Blackwell.

Tanner, J. M. 1966. Growth and physique in different populations of mankind. In *The Biology of Human Adaptability*, eds. P. T. Baker and J. S. Weiner. Oxford: Clarendon Press, pp. 45-66.

Tanner, J. M. 1968. Earlier maturation in man. *Sci. Amer.* 218:21-27.

Thieme, F. P. 1959. *The Puerto Rican Population. A Study in Human Biology.* Anthropol. papers No. 13, Mus. of Anthropol., Univ. of Michigan.

Thirumurthi, H. R. and J. B. Longenecker. 1966. Nutritional considerations of biological variation, *Annals N.Y. Acad. Sci.* 134:873-84.

Thomson, A. M. 1968. Historical perspectives of nutrition, reproduction, and growth. In *Malnutrition, Learning, and Behavior*, eds. N. S. Scrimshaw and J. E. Gordon. Cambridge, Mass.: MIT Press, pp. 17-28.

Waterlow, J. C. and C. B. Mendes. 1957. Composition of muscle in malnourished human infants. *Nature*, 1361:2.

Weyer, E. 1932. *The Eskimos: Their Environment and Folkways.* New Haven: Yale University Press.

Williams, C. D. 1938. Quoted by D. B. Jelliffe 1968 in *Infant Nutrition in the Subtropics and Tropics*, WHO Monograph Series.

Wills, V. G. and J. C. Waterlow. 1958. The death rate in the age group one to four years old as an index of malnutrition. *J. Trop. Pediat.* 3:167.

Wilson, D. C. and I. Sutherland. 1950. Further observations on the age of the menarche. *Brit. Med. J.* 2:862.

Winick, M. 1971. Cellular changes during placental and fetal growth. *Amer. J. Obstet. Gynecol.* 109:166.

Wolanski, N. 1966. Environmental modification of human form and function. *Ann. N.Y. Acad. Sci.* 134(2):826-40.

WHO Expert Group. 1961. *Maternal and Child Health.* WHO Tech. Report Series No. 217.

WHO Expert Group. 1965. *Nutrition in Pregnancy and Lactation.* WHO Tech. Report Series No. 302.

WHO Expert Group. 1968. *Nutrition in Pregnancy and Lactation.* WHO Tech. Report Series No. 400.

10. Anthropology and Infectious Disease

BARUCH S. BLUMBERG*

JANA E. HESSER**

INTRODUCTION

Infectious diseases are the major causes of death in many parts of the world; prior to the development of antibiotics and chemotherapeutic agents, they were an even larger factor in mortality rate. A necessary condition for these diseases is, obviously, infection with the organism. For most infectious agents, however, there is an enormous difference in the response of the infected human host including (a) fatal outcome; (b) acute disease with recovery; (c) chronic illness; or (d) carrier state, in which the chronically infected person is not apparently ill but can transmit the infectious agent to other individuals, directly or indirectly.

The nature of the response to infection may depend upon intrinsic host factors. There is reason to believe, particularly from studies on lower animals, that some of these factors are inherited. If this is true, then the genetic makeup of a population would determine the nature of its response to epidemics, and infectious agents could, through evolutionary means, determine the frequencies of part of the gene pool of a population. Host factors other than genetic would also influence the outcome of infection, for example, intercurrent illness, the state of nutrition, age, sex, etc. In addition, environmental factors could have a marked influence. A

* Associate Director for Clinical Research, The Institute for Cancer Research, Fox Chase Cancer Center, and Professor, Department of Anthropology, University of Pennsylvania, Philadelphia, Pennsylvania.
** Medical Anthropologist, The Institute for Cancer Research, Fox Chase Cancer Center, and Department of Anthropology, University of Pennsylvania, Philadelphia, Pennsylvania.

large infective dose may be more disadvantageous than a small one; the strain of the infecting agent (and this can vary from location to location) may determine its pathogenicity; and, frequency of infection may have an effect.

The major interaction with the environment, however, is related to the probability of becoming infected at all. With good sanitation, people are less likely to be exposed to infectious agents present in the feces and other excreta of their neighbors. Eradication of insects that carry infectious agents interrupts the life cycle of many diseases and eliminates them from the environment. Immunization of potential hosts can markedly decrease the susceptible pool and can lead to the complete control of some diseases. Most public health activities have been directed toward decreasing opportunities for infection and have had a major influence on the behavior of populations of developed countries.

Many cultural practices have a profound effect on the probability of infection. In some cases, cultural practices protecting a population against the consequences of infection have developed over the course of many epidemics and generations. Some of these may be incorporated into and maintained by religious or other institutionalized behaviors.

In this chapter, rather than discuss the topic of anthropology and infectious disease in a general fashion, we will discuss one infectious agent in detail, and then describe cultural practices in different populations that relate to it. This will suggest testable hypotheses designed to determine whether an infectious agent's spread by way of cultural practices can be detected. In addition, we will discuss genetic susceptibility to the agent and the effect it may have on the gene pool of a population.

Australia antigen (abbreviated Au), a substance found in human blood, which is intimately related to the etiological agent of hepatitis, will be our focus. It has many characteristics that make it useful for the study of anthropological problems. In the first part of the paper, the characteristics of this unusual agent will be discussed in detail, and, in the second part, anthropological examples will be given. There have been recent reviews of Au containing detailed references (Sutnik *et al.*, 1972; Blumberg, 1972; London *et al.*, 1972b). Only selected references will be cited here.

Hepatitis

"Acute hepatitis" is an inflammation of the liver long thought to be viral in origin. Patients have high fever, striking loss of appetite, and a grave feeling of malaise; they may develop profound jaundice. Damage to liver cells results in the release of a variety of abnormal (or larger than normal amounts of) constituents into the blood and urine. The symptoms usually persist for days, weeks, or months, and most cases proceed to a complete recovery. Abstinence from alcohol is often recommended for the convalescent period, which may be prolonged. Some patients may not recover but develop a chronic or persistent liver disease, with recurrent attacks of symptoms or persistent disability. There are also some chronic cases that start without an apparent acute episode. Occasionally, an acute or chronic case may end fatally.

The acute cases may occur sporadically. There may be a history of exposure to another person with the disease or to some form of contaminating material. A common method of transmission has been by transfusion of blood from asymptomatic carriers of hepatitis or from a person with an incipient or occult form of the disease. The disease may occur in epidemic form and has been a major cause of morbidity in crowded encampments and military units. In these cases, it is probably primarily spread by fecal-oral routes. This kind of spread is possible where water and food supplies are contaminated by the waste from either patients with hepatitis or from asymptomatic carriers of the infectious agent.

Australia antigen

Australia antigen was discovered during the course of a systematic study of the blood of transfused patients (Blumberg *et al.*, 1965). This study had been initiated to find blood constituents, either inherited or acquired, present in the serum of some individuals but absent in others. It was reasoned that some of these inherited or acquired traits would be antigenic and elicit antibodies in the transfused patients who did not have them. To find these reacting materials, the technique of immunodiffusion was used. The serum of a transfused patient was placed in the center well of a pattern of seven wells cut into a thin agar gel. The sera of other patients were placed in peripheral wells surrounding the well containing the serum from the transfused patient. If an antibody were present in the transfused patient's serum of the same specificity as an antigenic constituent in the peripheral well, it would migrate into the gel until it met the specific antigen migrating toward it from the peripheral well. Precipitation would occur, and a fine line would develop between the two wells. In this way, specific antigens and antibody in sera could be detected.

Using this system, we initially found an antibody that was discovered to have a rich polymorphism of the low density lipoproteins of human (and other primate) sera. This was called the "Ag system," and it has been of interest in population and genetic studies and may be of importance in several diseases, such as heart disease, diabetes, etc., which are in some way related to lipid metabolism.

The search for additional antibodies in the transfused sera was continued, and a precipitin was found in the serum of a transfused hemophilia patient that reacted, in the first studies, with the serum of an Australian aborigine. This antigen in the serum was termed "Australia antigen" (Au), and the antibody in the hemophilia patient anti-Au.

THE NATURE OF Au

On the basis of studies, initially from our laboratory and subsequently from other laboratories, a picture is beginning to emerge of the nature of Au. Some of these features are consistent with the definition of a virus, others appear not to be, but none rules out the possibility that Au acts as an infectious agent causing (some) cases of hepatitis in man (Blumberg *et al.*, 1971). In this section, we will attempt to summarize these results in the form of a general description of the properties of the agent.

Infectious agents are always associated with the disease they cause, although the reverse is not necessarily true, i.e., infectious agents may be associated with diseases they do not cause, and, in addition, the agent may be found in apparently normal individuals who do not have the disease (or diseases) caused by the agent. Australia antigen is found in higher frequency in patients with acute viral hepatitis (both infectious and serum) and in some form of chronic hepatitis than in patients with other diseases and normal in subjects. It is also found in the blood of many individuals who are apparently not ill and who appear to be asymptomatic carriers. The frequency of carriers varies from very low values, about 0.1% in North American and North European communities, to about 20% in some Oceanic, Asian, and tropical communities. In this respect, its distribution is similar to that of a serum protein polymorphism with a frequency that may vary from population to population, presumably depending on local ecological and selective factors. There is a striking difference in host reaction to "infection" with Au. The same agent that does not have a noticeable effect on some individuals—the carriers—will cause acute, chronic, and sometimes fatal hepatitis in others. One man's meat is another's poison; "normal flora" in a carrier is a pathogen in another person. This dichotomy between carriers and affected individuals holds true for many, and conceivably most, infectious agents.

Australia affinity group

Australia antigen is also associated with a group of diseases other than hepatitis; that is, it occurs in higher frequency in these diseases than in controls. These diseases, termed the "Australia affinity" group, are characterized by impairments in the immune mechanisms of the host. They include the lymphocytic leukemias, Down's syndrome ("mongolism"), lepromatous leprosy (as opposed to tuberculoid leprosy), chronic renal disease, and hepatoma.

In some of these diseases (i.e., Down's syndrome), the presence of Au is accompanied, in general, by chronic anicteric hepatitis. It is possible that Au is related to the etiology of some of these diseases (i.e., hepatoma, Down's syndrome). Another possibility is that individuals who are susceptible to persistent infections by the agents responsible for these illnesses are also susceptible to persistent infection with Au; that is, these agents are related in that they have an affinity for a common susceptibility factor. If the genetic hypothesis is correct (see below), this susceptibility factor may be inherited. If this is true, they may also have other features in common and, as a consequence, knowledge on Au may help in the identification and understanding of the mode of action of other agents related to the Australia affinity diseases.

For example, there is an increased frequency of Au in lymphocytic leukemia patients who have received blood transfusions, some of which contain Au. The frequency is higher in the transfused leukemia patients than in other patients not in the Australia affinity group who have also received transfusions. The leukemia patients, when exposed, are more likely to develop a persistent infection with Au. The agent responsible for lymphocytic leukemia may have other characteristics of Au, and these characteristics can be used as a basis for formulating hypotheses about leukemia and its etiological agent.

In the electron microscope, the appearance of Au is compatible with that of a small virus. It is 220 Å in diameter and has fine structure detail. Larger diameter units (420 Å) called "Dane particles" and elongated 220 Å units may also be seen, and their relation to the smaller unit and to the biology of Au is under study. The large particles contain an outer coat, antigenically identical with the small particles, and an inner core.

Recently, several investigators have reported the presence of DNA polymerase and small amounts of DNA in the large (Dane) particles. In addition, small amounts of RNA have been reported in the small particles. If these findings are confirmed it could provide important clues on the possible viral nature of Au.

Ability to grow in tissue culture is a characteristic of many viruses. Liver tissue taken from a hepatitis patient who has Au in his blood and liver appears to produce Au in the cells and tissue fluid following many passages of the tissue. It has also been claimed that Au may be grown in fetal liver tissue. Cultures of this type are difficult to maintain, however, so this has not been widely confirmed. This again scores against, but does not rule out, the viral hypothesis. Some viruses, apparently, have not been grown on tissue culture or have been grown only with difficulty.

Cellular localization of Au

Infectious agents that cause disease might be expected to be found within the cells affected in the illness; Au fulfills this criterion. In our initial studies, using fluorescent anti-Au, we found material with the antigenic specificity of Au in the liver cells of patients with Australia antigen in their blood and/or with hepatitis (Millman *et al.*, 1972). This has now been widely confirmed. The fluorescence has been reported to be present in the nucleus in some reports, in the cytoplasm in others. These differences could be due to differences in technique, the kinds of disease studied, or, perhaps, the times after infection at which the cells were sampled. The presence of Au in the nucleus has been confirmed by electron microscope studies using ferritin-labeled anti-Au. These findings are compatible with the notion that the agent can spend some of its time in the nucleus and some in the cytoplasm; that it can don nuclear or cellular coats; and, presumably, that it can interact with the cellular genetic material of the host.

Transmission of Au to non-human primates

An important criterion for determining whether an agent is or is not infectious is its transmission to an experimental animal. In order to find a suitable animal for such studies, many animal species were surveyed for the natural occurrence of Au. It was found only in certain primate species. London (1970) was able to transmit isolated and partially purified Au to infant African green monkeys and passage the material twice. The amount of antigen present in the final monkey was greater than would have been expected by simple dilution. The possibility of transmission to primates was, in part, confirmed some years later by London and his colleagues (1972a). (This second London is not the same person who reported the original primate studies.) They were able to transmit to rhesus monkeys a material that effected the production of antibodies to Au. Transmission to chimpanzees has also been reported (Meynard *et al.*, 1972). The primate studies, therefore, imply that Au can be transmitted to experimental animals in the manner of an infectious agent.

The "Icron"

All the studies taken together do not rule out the possibility that Au is an infectious agent similar in many ways to a virus.

Australia antigen differs enough from viruses, and some of these differences have already been discussed, to warrant its consideration as an infectious agent distinct from a virus. If this consideration is true, then there are probably other infectious agents that could fit into this classification, and, for heuristic reasons, the term Icron has been suggested. The name is an acronym of the Institute for Cancer Research. This concept is discussed elsewhere (Blumberg *et al.*, 1971).

Australia antigen as a blood polymorphism

The term "blood polymorphism" is used in the sense introduced by E. B. Ford. It means that there are two (or more) inherited forms of a blood constituent (i.e., protein) and that the frequency of the less (least) common form is so large that it could not be maintained in the population by recurrent mutation alone. Examples of polymorphism are sickle cell hemoglobin, red blood cell antigens, haptoglobins and gamma globulins (Gm, InV) (serum proteins), and low density lipoproteins (Ag). Implied in the definition of polymorphism is the concept that there is differential selection with respect to different phenotypes and that this is related to differential mortality and fertility.

Australia antigen viewed as a serum protein

In our initial isolations of Au, we were able to show that, although Au was clearly distinct from serum low-density lipoprotein, it had many of the characteristics of the latter. Later Millman *et al.* (1971) isolated Au from blood and purified it to a point where they could not detect serum proteins by immunological methods. When this purified material is treated with Tween 80, it partially disassociates into soluble components. These soluble components include what appear to be serum proteins—gamma globulin (IgG) (both heavy and light chain), complement, beta-lipoprotein, albumin, and, possibly, others. More recently, Sukeno *et al.* (1972), using optical rotary dispersion and circular dichroism methods, found that Au has characteristics that are more similar to human lipoproteins than to a normal virus. The studies on Au and nucleic acid are discussed above. Hence, Au may be made up of serum components that have antigenic characteristics related to those of the hosts, present or previous, many of which may be occult under most circumstances but may be revealed under others.

Genetics of Au

The striking differences in the response of putative hosts exposed to infection with Au has been apparent from the time of the earliest clinical studies. On the basis of the family distribution of Au in a Samaritan family, the hypothesis that persistent presence of Au (as in asymptomatic carriers) is inherited as a simple autosomal recessive trait was proposed (Blumberg *et al.*, 1965). Several studies have supported this model, and it has been independently confirmed. [The data have recently been summarized (Blumberg, 1972).] These original data are consistent with the view that there is a gene (designated Au^1) that, when present in the genotype Au^1/Au^1, renders the bearer more susceptible to persistent infection with the infectious agent associated with Au, if the bearer is appropriately exposed to infection. Many of the carriers will be asymptomatic. In some populations, the susceptibility gene may actually represent an advantage to the host in that the agent assumes the role of normal flora. A further hypothesis may now be made that hosts with alternate genotypes may respond by the development of acute hepatitis, by the formation of antibody, or, one may conjecture, by the development of "complex disease" if both antigen and antibody coexist. Recently, the simple genetic hypothesis has been ruled out, but it is still possible that there is some form of genetic control (see below).

The existence of genetic control implies that there are inherited differences between people, which lead to variations in the consequences of

infection. Inherited antigenic differences in the hosts that make interactions with the Au agent possible could account for these differences.
This interaction could take place at one or more locations, i.e., tissue cell,
formed elements of the blood, serum proteins. That is, if a person is infected with Au particles that contain constituents that are antigenically
very similar to his own, then he will have little immunological response
(he will recognize them as "self") and will tend to develop a persistent
infection with Au. On the other hand, if the constituents of the agent are
antigenically different from his, he will develop an immune response to
the agent (anti-Au and possibly other antibodies) and will have a transient infection. One can also picture an intermediate situation in which
some of the host/agent specificities are shared, and some are not. The result could then be intermediate; some degree of infection will occur, but
antibodies will also develop and this could lead to antigen/antibody complexes and, possibly, another form of disease. During the course of infection in a person, A, new Au particles would be synthesized, which contain
his proteins, lipids, and carbohydrates. He, in turn, can infect another
person, B, and the same alternatives present themselves. If the relevant
proteins, etc., of B are antigenically similar to those contained in A's Au,
then B will develop a persistent infection; if different, he will develop a
transient infection. These considerations lead to interesting kinds of epidemiological studies. The spread of disease is dependent not only upon
the antigenic makeup of the agent and the genetically determined makeup
of the host but also upon the genetics of the human or other hosts from
which the infection came, i.e., the infecting donor (previous host) of the
infectious agent.

Modifications of the genetic hypothesis. Sex and age

In the initial genetic studies, there was a good fit between expected and
observed ratios. Despite this, in the very first study, it was clear that effects
other than genetic had a bearing on the presence of persistent Au; as
noted, in subsequent studies the simple genetic hypothesis has been ruled
out. As is often the case, deviations from a simple hypothesis may be the
most interesting aspects of a phenomenon.

There is a striking sex difference in the frequency of Australia antigen.
In every disease group we studied there is a higher frequency of Au in
males than in females. This is also (nearly) true for all the carrier populations tested. There are some interesting observations on sex that may be
related to this finding. In many of the affinity diseases (i.e., lymphocytic

leukemia, Hodgkins disease, lepromatous leprosy, Down's syndrome—see below) there is a similar predominance of males. Further, the Au agent appears to involve the testes. We have identified Au (by immunofluorescence) in autopsy specimens of human and primate testes. Leukemia involvement of the testes is apparently more common than of the ovaries. Male Down's syndrome patients appear to be sterile, whereas females are not.

There is a higher frequency of Au in younger males than older, except that the frequency appears to be lower in very young people. In the populations in which we have been able to obtain extensive data, there is a peak in frequency in the 6- to 9-year-old group. This change with age is more common in some populations than others. In the genetic study of Sardinians by Ceppellini and his colleagues (1970), it was necessary to correct for penetrance in the older individual in order to have an adequate fit of the observed segregation from that predicted from the genetic model, whereas this was not necessary in the Cebu and Bougainville studies.

Maternal effect

One of the potentially most interesting studies on Australia antigen concerns maternal effects. In addition to the strictly biological features, it also has interesting implications for the study of differences in female behavior in different cultures (see below).

In the genetic family studies, the matings in which one parent is positive (i.e., has persistent Au) are considered separately from the negative by negative matings. In the initial calculations, using these matings, the families in which the mother was positive and the father negative were considered together with matings in which the father was positive and the mother negative; these fit the segregation ratios well. Subsequently, these matings were considered separately. When the mother is positive and the father negative many more offspring have Au than when the opposite is true (i.e., father positive and mother negative). This is statistically significant in several of the populations and highly significant in the total study.

In another study, Mazzur and Blumberg (1974) used data on the complex specificities of Au to investigate the family distribution of Au. In the initial family studies, it was first shown that there is a family aggregation of Au. Family aggregation is characteristic of an inherited trait, but it is also characteristic of an infectious one. In the genetic studies, it was shown that the family data were compatible with a simple genetic model. If infectious transmission were the cause of the family aggregation, then it would be expected that all members of the family group would have the same "strain" of the organism, i.e., Au with the same specificities. It was possible to test this hypothesis using the families in the Bougainville genetic study. In eleven of the thirty-two families tested, there were mixed subtypes of Au in the family members. This finding appears to rule against a simple family infection explanation.

When the data were examined by the sex of the positive parent in matings in which one of the parents was positive, an interesting pattern was seen. In families in which the mother was positive (nearly) all the children had the same specificities as the parent, whereas this was not true when the father was positive. This suggests that transmission can occur directly from the mother to the offspring either before conception, *in utero,* at the time of birth, early in life, or later. It would not appear to rule out the genetic hypothesis, but rather it suggests that both forms of vertical transmission may occur, i.e. (a) persistent infection (or transmission) controlled by a gene segregating as a Mendelian trait and (b) maternal transmission.

There is now considerable information on other aspects of transmission from mothers to their offspring. In a study in California, it was shown that if a mother has hepatitis at the time her child is delivered, it is highly likely that her offspring will develop persistent Au within weeks or months. In a detailed Japanese study of pregnant mothers who were asymptomatic carriers of Au, Okochi and his co-workers (1972) demonstrated, using a sensitive detection method, that Au was found in the child's blood within days or weeks of delivery. A particularly important finding, again from Japan (Nishioka *et al.,* 1973), was the demonstration of a maternal influence in families in which there was clustering of hepatoma and chronic liver disease and Au carriers.

Two recent observations may be of particular importance in that they may have detected an effect on fertility related to the presence of Au, and this could have a bearing on differential selection in relation to the Au polymorphism concept.

Kukowski *et al.* (1972), in a study in northern India, found that the gestation time of mothers with Au is increased and that they are younger compared to mothers who do not have Au in their blood. It will now be necessary to test this hypothesis in other populations. If supported, it indicates that there is a measurable effect of Au on the biology of parturition.

In another study of (mostly) completed families in Bougainville, Solomon Islands, we found that in matings in which the fathers had Au and the mother did not, there were significantly more children (p <0.0001) than in matings with either the mother positive for Au, or neither parent positive. A difference of about 1.2 in the mean number of children per family was observed. In addition, an increased proportion (0.56) of females was observed in the offspring of matings with the mother Au(+), although this was not significant.

In a subsequent study in a Greek village, a significant (p <0.04) increase in the proportion of males (0.64) was observed in the offspring of parents positive for Au. No differences in fertility were detected (Hesser *et al.*, 1974). These observations suggest maternal and paternal effects associated with the Au carrier state.

Modes of transmission of Au

It appears, therefore, that there may be at least three general modes of transmission of Au. It can be transmitted "horizontally" from person to person. This is seen, for example, in the transmission of hepatitis and/or Au by blood containing Au, and this forms the basis for the widespread use of the "Au test" for the detection of hepatitis carriers. Other forms of horizontal transmission are also probable, for example, fecal-oral, by blood-biting insects, etc. The agent may also be spread by two forms of "vertical" transmission. If the results of the genetic studies described above continue to be sustained, then there is the implication that the ability to become persistently infected is controlled (at least in part) as a Mendelian trait. The data are also consistent with the notion that the agent is transmitted with the genetic material in a lysogenic form, but there is no direct evidence for this.

The data also indicate that there is a maternal effect. It cannot be deduced at what time during the maternal-child interaction the infection occurs: in the ovum, *in utero*, at the moment of birth, or at some time afterwards. Further direct studies will be needed to determine this.

ANTHROPOLOGICAL IMPLICATIONS

Au as a balanced polymorphism

The prototype for balanced polymorphism in humans is the sickle cell hemoglobin system. In this system, the sickle homozygote is at a selective disadvantage, since homozygotes usually die before the child-bearing age. The polymorphism is maintained in the population because the sickle/ normal heterozygote is more resistant to malaria than the normal homozygote and, thus, is advantageous. Surprisingly, it has not been possible to apply this concept to many other human biochemical polymorphisms, primarily because the selective factors associated with the different genotypes, if they exist, have not been easy to identify.

The data on Au suggest it can be viewed as a polymorphism and that this concept can yield some interesting hypotheses.

According to the simple genetic concept, individuals who are homozygous for the Au^1 gene will, when exposed to the Au infectious agent, develop a persistent Au infection. In many of these individuals, perhaps the majority, this is not accompanied by any obvious symptoms of illness; they appear to be asymptomatic chronic carriers. It could be construed that in areas of the world where transmission of Au is common, it would be a distinct advantage to live in symbioses with an agent that is omnipresent and difficult to avoid. In this instance, the Au^1/Au^1 genotype is at an advantage, and this would act to increase the frequency of the gene in populations where the Au agent is common.

What, then, would counterbalance the advantageous effects of the gene? According to the interpretations generated by the "Australia affinity" group concept, there are, in addition to the Au agent, other infectious agents related to the Au^1 locus. When individuals of Au^1/Au^1 genotype are exposed to these agents, they may also develop a persistent infection, but, in this case, the effect may not be advantageous. For example, individuals appropriately exposed to the etiological agent of leprosy, Hansen's bacillus, may not become ill or may develop one of several clinical forms of the disease. There are two polar forms of the disease, lepromatous and tuberculoid. The former is more chronic, more extensive, more difficult to treat, and more likely to shorten life than the latter. There is an increased frequency of Au in the lepromatous cases, but not in the tuberculoid. This has been interpreted to mean that Au^1/Au^1 homozygotes are more likely to develop persistent infection with Hansen's bacillus, i.e., develop the lepromatous form of the disease, than are the alternate genotypes. In this case, the genotype Au^1/Au^1 would be at a selective disadvantage. The highest frequencies of lepromatous leprosy occur in young males, and there is evidence that the fertility of afflicted males is decreased. (Hansen's bacillus preferentially invades the testes as well as other peripheral parts of the body.) The disease would have an effect on the genetic composition of the next generation if it were, in fact, related to the Au^1 locus.

In addition to Hansen's disease, there are probably other diseases that are members of the Australia affinity group. Lymphocytic leukemia appears to be one of these, but, because of its low frequency, it is unlikely that it could have a major population effect. Candidates for inclusion in the Australia affinity group would include diseases in which there is a higher frequency of Au than in an appropriate control group, and these diseases can be identified by appropriate studies in areas of the world where Au is common. Hepatoma is another candidate, and, in some areas, it is a major cause of death due to cancer.

From this it is conceivable that the polymorphism could be balanced by different survival values for the homozygote with respect to different diseases. For hepatitis, the homozygote asymptomatic carriers are at an advantage, and the ubiquity of the agent in many tropical countries would maintain the gene at a high frequency. For Hansen's bacillus and probably other as yet unknown infectious agents, the homozygotes are at a disadvantage in that persistent infection can be a more serious disease and can affect reproduction. The relative frequency of "advantageous" and "disadvantageous" infectious agents in the population would, then, determine (at least in part) the frequency of the postulated Au^1 gene.

There is very little known concerning the possible selective factors relating to the postulated genotypes. It is not possible to identify the heterozygotes, except by inference from family studies. There is some evidence that individuals who are not persistent carriers are more likely to develop anti-Au if infected or to develop acute hepatitis, but there is little information on this. It is known that even persistent carriers may have anti-Au, and various forms of complexes can be formed, which may, in turn, be associated with pathological conditions.

This genetic model, in which the major selective effect is on the homozygote, is an interesting problem for theoretical study. The validity of this concept of Au is, of course, dependent on the validity of its various components (the genetic data, Australia affinity group, etc.), but, independent of any final "proof," it can generate some interesting studies.

The status of Au carriers

Screening of potential blood donors for Au is now widely practiced in many parts of the world. Millions of blood specimens are tested to identify carriers, and their blood is not used for transfusions. It has been estimated that screening for Au may eliminate about one-third of the carriers from the donor population. The introduction of more sensitive detection methods may result in the identification of even more hepatitis carriers and lead, it is hoped, to the elimination of post-transfusion hepatitis.

In the past, paid ("commercial") blood donors were sometimes recruited from the ranks of low-income groups, including alcoholics, drug addicts, and others who were forced to lead a life characterized by poor sanitation. It was a common practice to locate the stations where blood was bought for re-sale to hospitals and processors in the section of a city frequented by the "down-and-outs" of the community. There is a high frequency of hepatitis carriers (and Au) in these populations. By one of the strange ironies that characterize much of human behavior, the donors were selected from just those people most likely to spread disease.

The increasing illicit abuse of drugs in recent years has resulted in another major cause of hepatitis. The hepatitis agent is readily spread from person to person by the unsterilized needles used to inject heroin and other drugs, and there is a high frequency of persons with hepatitis as well as carriers of hepatitis among habitual users of these drugs.

The use of the Au test has led to the identification of large numbers of people who are asymptomatic carriers. In the United States and most "developed" countries, the frequency of identifiable carriers would be about 1 or 2/1000. In Japan, the figure is about 1 or 2/100, and, in some tropical and Asian locations, as many as 15 to 20% of apparently normal people are carriers. When more sensitive methods are used, even larger numbers of carriers are found.

There is very little systematic information about what happens to these carriers when they are identified. In some blood collection programs, putative donors are informed that something abnormal has been found in their blood and they are referred to a physician, who is informed of the finding. These people will be advised not to donate blood, but, again, there is little knowledge on what further recommendations can be made to carriers. There is some evidence that carriers do infect other members of their families (Cazal *et al.*, 1972), but additional studies will be required to know how infective such persons are by means other than transfusion. Any rational handling of the carriers will have to await the accumulation of information on the risk they present to uninfected people.

Despite this lack of knowledge, the extensive testing programs have resulted in the delineation of an identifiable and special class of apparently normal people who may be capable of spreading disease. This may represent a unique situation in contemporary social relations. The problems may not be very great for most carriers, but it may have important consequences for people in such occupations as food handling. Consideration must be given to the question of prohibiting carriers from assuming the role of food handlers (London *et al.*, 1969). If this is done, what will become of those who are already in this trade and are found to be carriers?

An even more pressing question is the position of health care personnel. Again, there is little systematic information on the manner in which this problem is being handled. There have been cases, however, in which physicians and dentists who are known carriers have changed their activities so that they no longer are in intimate contact with people. It is important to emphasize again that the extent of the hazard the carriers represent is not known, and precipitous changing of jobs of highly trained professionals who have a great deal to offer to medical consumers should not be undertaken until more is known about the nature of the risk they impose.

A special situation has arisen in renal dialysis (artificial kidney) units. A large number of patients in some of these units become infected with Au and develop chronic hepatitis; they also become persistent carriers of the antigen. There have been some catastrophic epidemics in which many patients and staff have become seriously ill and/or died from hepatitis. Renal dialysis patients with Au may be isolated from other renal patients, and special efforts have been made to protect the staff. A percentage of the medical staff may become carriers either after an acute attack of hepatitis, or, more likely, without any history of disease. Individuals who are carriers are presumably unlikely to develop acute disease, and, in some units, they are used to treat patients who are infected. In this circumstance, carriers are seen to have a special role in administering health care to a select group of patients.

It may be instructive to see how one human population has defined and dealt with a class of persons considered to be "polluting."

The ancient caste system in India, which survives today in the somewhat modified form of the jati, is illustrative. Jati, or the group into which a person is born and within which he marries, is usually associated with occupation. Relations between jati are ruled by the concept of pollution, i.e., the jatis of highest ritual status (which can be associated with the ancient Brahmin caste) are non-polluting, but in danger of being polluted by lower-ranking castes. The untouchables, conversely, may pollute any higher-ranking caste. The rules concerning pollution through contact apply to activities relating to sex, eating, drinking, and smoking. Descent in the caste system is associated with increasing contact with feces, blood, and corpses, which are sources of "pollution." The occupations of lower castes—washing clothes, cutting hair, dressing leather, removing offal—enable the higher castes to be free of body impurities. Contact during such an activity as agricultural labor is not considered polluting. Individuals with high caste ranking, and therefore non-polluting, are in demand in such occupations as water dispensers or cooks. The untouchables, on the other hand, are confined to tasks as disposers of refuse, excrement, and (since blood is considered to be polluting) as midwives (Minturn and Hitchcock, 1963).

One could speculate that the frequency of Au in a community would be distributed according to jati affiliation, since affiliation is identified with pollution.

Transmission of Au

Maintenance of Au and its associated infectious agent in populations throughout the world depends upon its continual transmission form person to person, generation to generation. Known sources of infection are blood and feces. Routes of entry into the body are oral (ingestion) or parenteral (injection). Any action resulting in transmission of Au involves (a) a source of infected material, (b) a receptive and susceptible organism, and (c) an opportunity for contact.

The agent associated with Au remains infectious under extreme conditions. Blood, or other material containing the hepatitis agent, can apparently remain infective long after removal from a host. It is very difficult to destroy the agent by means other than severe ones (e.g., autoclaving). In addition, the disease can be transmitted by a very small amount of inoculum. Barker *et al.* (1970), in studies with human volunteers, showed that an inoculum that has been diluted 10^6 times and then administered intravenously could still transmit hepatitis. There are many cases where an individual has developed hepatitis following inoculation by the prick of a contaminated needle.

In the following section we consider some aspects of human life, and associated culturally variable patterns of behavior, that may permit or inhibit the transmission of Au. The broad areas to be considered are: women and maternity; ritual, cosmetic, and therapeutic surgical techniques; insect vectors; and animal contacts.

Women and maternity

The female's reproductive physiology, i.e., menstruation and child-bearing, and her social role as mother, provides opportunities for transmittal of such infectious agents as Au through the blood.

Mazzur (1973) has suggested that menstrual blood could be a source of Au transmission in some populations, depending on how the menstrual emission is dealt with. In most cultures, there is prescribed behavior concerning the menstruating women and/or menstrual blood. Beliefs in some power emanating from the person of the menstruating women and in the toxic and/or magical qualities of menstrual blood are commonly found. Practices often involve seclusion of the menstruating woman or avoidance of contact; taboos on food sharing or preparation; and taboos on sexual intercourse, with ritual purification following the menses. Less frequent are rules prescribing contact with the woman or with the menstrual blood. The following ethnographic excerpts illustrate such behavioral rules; some behaviors could conceivably expose one or more persons, or a class of people to the menstrual emission, whereas others would make such an event very unlikely.

Beidelman (1971) reports that the Kaguru of East Africa circumscribe the activities of a menstruating woman. She should not walk amongst garden crops, brew beer, prepare food, or come near people engaged in important tasks. Thought to be capable of polluting her husband, she could not share his bed, and was injuncted to bathe in the river downstream from the men. Similarly, the Kawai Papuaus of New Guinea were reported (Landtman, 1927) to consider "blood belong woman" as dangerous. All men and women were instructed to avoid contact with a menstruating or parturient woman, whereas the women must avoid food handling and must change their skirts and bed mats following menstruation or parturition.

Culturally formalized rules about menstruation are exemplified by Talmudic laws that seclude and limit the menstruating women for 2 weeks following the commencement of menses. Coitus and resumption of normal activities required first ablution and total immersion of the women following the menses. The menstruating female was considered "unclean." Islam also considers the woman unclean and forbids coitus during and after menstruation, until the woman has gone through a ritual purification.

In contrast to these stringent proscriptions against menstruating women are cases like that of the Kenya Gusii. There is no fear of menstrual blood, and, in fact, belief that conception occurs during menstruation means that sexual intercourse during menstruation is favored (LeVine and LeVine, 1963).

Beliefs attributing a kind of curative power to menstrual blood led to its use as a medicament by some people.

"Pliny reports that applications of menstrual blood were considered curative of gout, goitre, sore throat, boils, puerperal fever, the bites of mad dogs, epilepsy and even mere headaches," whereas St. Hildegare (fl. 1150) recommended ample baths of menstrual blood as an infallible preventive of leprosy (Ploss *et al.*, 1935).

Spencer and Gillen (1955) provide a colorful description of the Australian aborigine's use of genital blood for medicinal purposes. The Arunta of Australia "believe that [menstrual blood, or any blood from the genitals] will restore endangered life. While menstrual blood is supposed to restore power to the man, blood from the subincised penis is believed to have a similar effect on a woman. When menstrual blood is not available and a man is seriously ill, blood is drawn from the labia minora and one of the women takes a witchetty grub, dips it into the blood and gives it to the man to eat. Afterward his body is rubbed over with the blood. When an aboriginal woman is very sick, one of the sons of her younger sisters draws blood from the subincision wound; she drinks part of it and he rubs the remainder over her body."

Even in cases where menstrual blood is feared, and women are isolated from others, blood may remain in the environment, depending on how the emission is removed, and allow the possibility for transmission to occur, particularly to children, either in their play, or because of close physical contact with the mother. Where sexual contact is not forbidden during menstruation, conjugal transmission may occur. The increased incidence of hepatitis in conjugal pairs is suggestive (Hersh *et al.*, 1971) here.

The processes leading up to and surrounding birth obviously allow direct contact between a woman and her child, and may involve additional people as well. Maternal effects are of paramount importance in considering the transmission of some infectious agents. The data on maternal effect have been discussed above. These data are compatible with the explanation that the mother can affect the child any time from before birth until later in life.

Australia antigen is found in children only very rarely at the time of birth. If the mother has hepatitis and Au or, in some areas, if the mother is a carrier, it occurs in a large percentage of children within weeks or months of delivery. Although this does not rule out transplacental transmission (the antigen could be present in cord blood, but not detectable) (Matsuda *et al.*, 1972), it does favor the explanation that the infection occurs at birth, followed by an incubation period of several weeks or months. Australia antigen may be found in amniotic fluid (Matsuda *et al.*, 1972) and could be a source of infection of the child *in utero*.

The possibility for infection, primarily of the child, but also of others, is inherent in the birth process, which will be described here.

The first stage of labor is uterine contraction and dilation of the cervix. With dilation, there is a bloody "show" due to rupturing of capillaries in the cervix. The first stage lasts 7 to 12 hours. During the second stage of labor, with long and shortly spaced contractions, there is spontaneous rupture of the membranes, which is accompanied by a gush of amniotic fluid. Toward the end of the second stage, the increasing pressure of the emerging head may cause expulsion of fecal material. In the majority of nullipara, the perineum is unable to withstand the strain and tears unless an episiotomy has been performed. After the head has emerged, it first falls posteriorly (woman in supine position), bringing the face almost in contact with the anus, but, within a few moments, it assumes a transverse position. Continuing contractions expell the child completely. Immediately after extrusion, there is a gush of amniotic fluid, often tinged with blood. This stage may last 50 minutes in nullipara; 20 minutes in multipara.

In the third stage of labor, immediately following birth, there is a slight flow of blood, and usually within 8 minutes, the placenta separates from the uterus and is expelled. The volume of maternal blood shed during and very soon after the third stage of labor, with apparently uncomplicated vaginal delivery, commonly amounts to 500 ml or somewhat more (Hellman and Pritchard, 1971).

Delivery procedures can vary considerably, depending on (a) position of the mother; (b) use of appliances applied externally to the mother or child; (c) such manual manipulations as external massage or internal positioning of the child; (d) treatment of the umbilicus; (e) method of expelling the placenta; (f) the surface onto which the child is delivered and the treatment of the child after delivery; and (g) location of the delivery.

The possibilities for infecting other people reside in (a) the manner in which other people are involved in the birth process; (b) the disposal of birth "products"—the placenta, umbilical cord, blood, and fluid; and

(c) the place and accoutrements of birth and their treatment following delivery.

The concept that blood is unclean, contaminating, or polluting amongst the high status Rajputs of Khalapur, India, results in midwivery being the profession of untouchable women. Not only does the untouchable woman deliver the child, dispose of the placenta, and clean up following the birth, she is in charge of caring for the mother during a confinement in a separate room, of 10-14 days, during which time the mother and her utensils are considered to be unclean. Other persons avoid contact with the mother and the child. Following confinement, her room and utensils are purified, and the midwife is banished (Minturn and Hitchcock, 1963).

For the Dusun of North Borneo, childbirth is

> attended only by a midwife, . . . a female ritual specialist, the woman's mother, or her husband's mother. A location is selected near the upper wall of the house and an ordinary sleeping mat is spread out for the mother to kneel upon while she holds onto a strap of bark-cloth line suspended from a roof beam. The midwife kneels before the mother and massages her back and abdomen in the final stages of labor and takes the child at birth. The baby is given to the father's mother or wife's mother to be bathed in warm water and wrapped in a special cloth. With a specially made bamboo knife the cord is severed and with the afterbirth it is placed in a bamboo container that is sealed and hung under the porch eaves as a sign of a birth in the household.
>
> The personal effects of the wife and household equipment used in delivery are taken to the river and washed by the father. Contact with these materials is felt especially dangerous to unmarried girls and to other pregnant women due to danger of disease or malformations at birth. (Williams, 1965.)

Further description of the tremendous variety possible in the birth process can be found in Volume II of Ploss and Bartel, *Woman* (1935).

Whereas complete disposal of the placenta, by burial or burning, is most common, the practice of using or consuming all, or a portion of it (for a variety of reasons) has been reported from various parts of the world. A portion of the placenta or the blood is dried and pulverized and fed to women in Java, to increase their fertility; in Italy, to aid the flow of a mother's milk; and amongst the Chinese, to give energy prior to confinement. The whole placenta is reported to be eaten by some Brazilian Indians; it was eaten as a cure for epilepsy in Saxon Britain (Ploss *et al.*, 1935); and, in the Kuru region of New Guinea, both placenta and umbilical cord were sometimes consumed by the mother's kinswomen (Glasse, 1967).

In some areas it was thought necessary to dispose of the placenta in water—usually into running water of a river or the sea.

The possibilities for transmission of infectious agents resulting from the female reproductive physiology and role requires consideration of practices of menstruation and childbirth, of relationships between women and others, most especially, children, and those domestic functions (e.g., foodhandling) that may indirectly transmit such agents.

Cannibalism

Cannibalism, a practice once fairly widespread in some parts of the world (Hambly, 1925), may also have transmitted infectious agents. That such transmission might occur has been discussed by Glasse (1967) with regard to the transmission of kuru amongst the Fore of New Guinea. He states that "total consumption of the body, including brain, viscera and genitalia, often with little cooking, offer(s) a reasonably good chance for the transmission of micro-organisms from Kuru victim to the consumer. . . ."

Ritual, cosmetic, and therapeutic surgical practices

Practices likely to result in transmission of blood-borne diseases, both in modern and "primitive" populations, in the past and present, include any type of surgical procedure performed routinely with non-sterile instruments. Tattooing, cicatrization (scarring), circumcision (genital mutilation), inoculation, etc., are illustrative. Tattooing and scarification are practices of great antiquity and of world-wide occurrence and are known to affect the transmission of hepatitis (Fig. 10-1). Anecdotal information indicates, in Great Britain, a higher incidence of jaundice following tattooing in young people (Anon., 1967). In addition, Gostling (1971) reported on eight men who became jaundiced following tattooing in the same shop; five had Au in their blood.

Hambly (1925) documents the ubiquity of bodymarking. The earliest recorded tattoos are dated as early as 2000 b.c. in Egypt, and artifactual evidence suggests that tattooing could have been practiced by Cro-Magnon man (Seligman and Seligman, 1932). A map of the regions of the world, where incised body marking has been practiced, shows that it occurred everywhere, with the exception of northern Europe and inland China (Hambly, 1925).

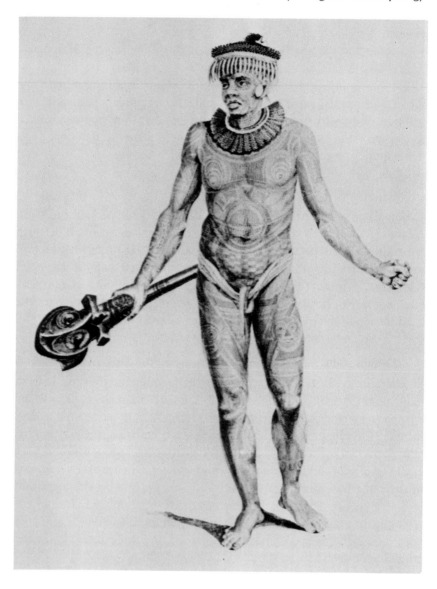

Fig. 10-1. Tattooed Marquesas man. Drawing from Cook Expedition of 1774. (Photograph courtesy, Pitt Rivers Museum, Oxford. B 1641 Q.)

Thomas (1968) reported on tattooing as practiced by the Kayan women of Borneo. Girls are tattooed extensively, beginning at the age of 6 to 13, with a major portion of tattooing occurring at puberty. The tattooing may be completed in a matter of weeks, or may take up to 4 years, with the tattooing taking place for a month each year. The tattooing is done by a female artist, who passes her skills and her equipment on to her daughter. The tattooing is done with a hammer-like instrument having two or three small metallic needles, ⅛ inch long. This hammer is a permanent tool, and there is no indication that it is cleaned between uses (Fig. 10-2).

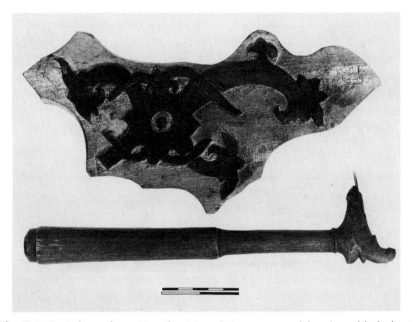

Fig. 10-2. Curved wooden pattern for tattoo design on arm of female and hafted set of tattooing needles in mallet from Sarawak-Borneo, 1920. (Photograph courtesy Pitt Rivers Museum, Oxford. Ref. #73.R611 IV.8 + VI.196.)

Firth (1936) describes the process of tattooing as it was practiced on Tikopia in the Pacific. Both men and women were tattooed after puberty. Tattooing was done by one of a few recognized experts who owned a kit. The primary instrument in the kit was "a small adze-like tool with a tiny blade made by cutting diagonally a piece of birdbone . . . and sharpening the edge into 5 or 6 teeth. The piece of bone . . . is lashed like an adze-blade to a small stick . . ." This is used to puncture the skin; pigment is rubbed into the puncture wounds. The same instrument is used for a number of people.

Hambly notes that, whereas both men and women are tattooed in many areas, the most remarkable and constant feature of the practice was the tattooing of women at puberty. A hypothesis about tattooing as a specific route of transmission in some populations could be tested.

Similarly, practices of cicatrization (Figs. 10-3 and 10-4), a well-known practice in African populations, has been implicated in two recent studies. Williams *et al.* (1972), in their investigation of Au carriers in a Nigerian population, suggest that widespread scarification practices amongst the indigenes may contribute to the much higher incidence of Au observed among them than among resident Europeans. Likewise, Swanepold and Cruikshank (1972) in a study of Au incidence among Europeans and Africans in Rhodesia, suggest that the much higher incidence (10%) in Africans may in part be due to the common African practices of scarring, tattooing, and ritual circumcision, as well as other minor surgical procedures.

Like tattooing and scarification, circumcisions (male and female) are

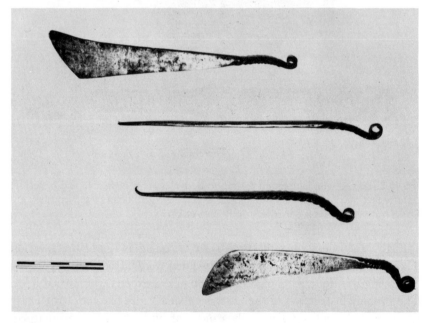

Fig. 10-3. Iron cicatricizing knives and hooks for making decorative keloids. Portuguese E. Africa (Mozambique) 1930. (Photograph courtesy Pitt Rivers Museum, Oxford. Ref. #68-L.6 VIII 448.)

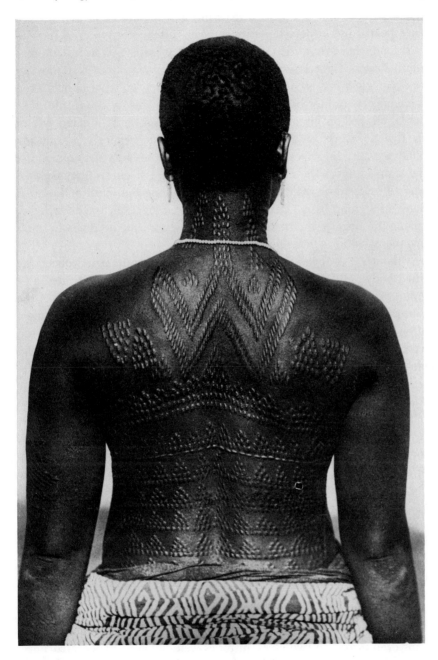

Fig. 10-4. African cicatrization from an unknown area. (Photograph courtesy Pitt Rivers Museum, Oxford. B 1476 Q.)

a common feature of puberty rituals in many societies and also involve the repeated use of non-sterile instruments, often on a group of individuals. Laubscher (1937) describes the process as it was performed amongst South Eastern Cape Bantu on a group of 18-year-old boys. "The [boy] to be circumcised first is chosen by the fathers. The isutu's ['head man'] son is second. He cannot be circumcised first as the rust on the [blade] may not be cleaned on him. [The operator] starts from the right-hand side of the row and works towards the left. He takes the prepuce . . . and amputates . . . [He] wipes the assigai [blade] on the boy's [clothing] . . . the isutu's son is . . . next and soon until the last one is circumcised." The clitoridectomy for the girls' initiation among the Gusii of Kenya is done on a group basis (LeVine and LeVine, 1963). On the other hand, among the Kaguru, the ritual labiadectomy is done at the time of a girl's first menstruation (Beidelman, 1971).

Although it is obviously difficult to make broad statements concerning ritual body mutilation, it appears that males are more often treated as a group, and females individually (as a consequence of the variability of the time of the first menses). It is also perhaps safe to suggest that males more often underwent a "surgical" initiation (e.g., circumcision) than did women—perhaps as a consequence of not having a clear-cut natural physiological sign, i.e., menstruation, indicating maturation.

Amongst the Nuba, of former British Central Africa, the girls are scarred individually at the time of the first menses, from sternum to umbilicus. At the first pregnancy, the whole face, body, arms, and legs are covered with scars (Seligman and Seligman, 1932). Amongst the Nuer, forehead scarring is part of the male initiation. This is done on a group of boys, age 13 to 16, by a single operator. They all are cut on the same day, with six parallel cuts being made across the forehead (Seligman and Seligman, 1932).

Some kinds of medical practice, notably those involving inoculations or injections, can readily transmit infectious agents, and may be responsible for numbers of cases observed in areas influenced or dominated by Western medical practices. Transfusion as a mechanism has already been discussed.

Amongst Rhodesian Africans, common factors in urban groups with high frequencies include sharing of eating and washing facilities and perhaps even razors. In two cases, histories were obtained of repeated injections performed by unqualified persons (Swanepold and Cruikshank, 1972). The illegal or indiscriminate use of hypodermic administration of drugs by unqualified persons is not uncommon in many parts of the world having contact and access to some Western medical practices (Fig. 10-5). Such practice is reportedly frequent among some peasants in South America.

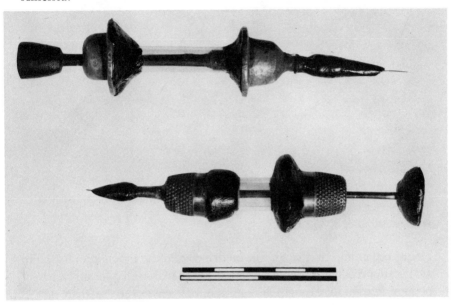

Fig. 10-5. Native-made syringes, China, 1908. (Photograph courtesy Pitt Rivers Museum, Oxford. 73 R. 6.5 IV 67; 18th C.)

"Inoculation hepatitis" outbreaks were frequently reported following mass vaccination or inoculation programs. There are accounts of epidemics in Germany in the 1880's after cowpox vaccinations with a lymph of human origin. Inoculation lancets, often of the type originally used by Jenner (Fig. 10-6), were non-disposable and repeatedly used. Non-disposable vaccinating equipment is still used in many parts of the world. The first definite hospital epidemics attributed to injection practices were described in 1926. During World War II, inoculation hepatitis was widespread all over the world. Twenty-seven thousand American World War II servicemen vaccinated against yellow fever with a contaminated serum developed hepatitis (Henschen, 1966).

Insect vectors

There is now evidence that the mosquito is a vector for transmitting Au. It has been shown experimentally that, in some mosquito species fed on

Fig. 10-6. Lancets used by Edward Jenner. (Photograph from the original lancets in the Wellcome Museum of the History of Medicine, London, by courtesy of the Trustees. Mus. Nos. R 73-76/1949.)

blood containing Au, the Au can be detected in the mosquitoes for up to 2 days after feeding. In some studies, it has been detected for much longer periods. Mosquitoes caught in communities where the Au frequency is likely to be high have been found to harbor Au. It has not yet been shown (to our knowledge) that Au can actually be transmitted by these mosquitoes, nor has growth of Au in the insect been demonstrated. If mechanical transfer alone could result in infection (and this would appear to be the case), mosquitoes (and other bloodsucking and biting insects) could be implicated in the maintenance of Au at relatively high frequencies in a number of populations, particularly in the tropics (Blumberg *et al.*, 1970).

It is also possible that insect vectors are responsible for transmitting Au between human and non-human primates. Though there is not yet evidence that primates in the wild are carriers of Au, it is known that primates can be infected and can transmit hepatitis to humans (Fiennes, 1967). They could act as reservoirs of the disease in regions where humans and other primates share a habitat or are close enough for winged vectors to transfer blood from one species to another.

Serving as an animal reservoir population for indirect transfer of infection is not the only way in which primates may contribute to the disease process. Rhesus monkeys freely share the urban habitat with humans in many cities in India. Regarded as sacred animals by some, these primates abound in the cities and survive, in large part, by foraging, which means raiding food shops, kitchens, and occasionally snatching food from people. They live in housetops, abandoned buildings, wherever a niche may be found. In short, their contact with humans is continuous and, in some sense, intimate (Singh, 1969).

More direct contact may occur when primates are kept as pets, in zoos, or for research. Old and new world monkeys imported into the United States include chimpanzees, gorillas, macaques, mangabeys and marmosets, squirrels, and capuchin, woolley, and spider monkeys. Held (1964) reported that seventy-eight cases of hepatitis in a research institution were associated with contacts with primates. Chimps were a source in sixty-one, gorillas in four, wooley monkeys in nine, and Celebes apes in four. Hillis (1961) reported on hepatitis associated with the handling of chimpanzees at Holloman Air Force Base, New Mexico. Fifty-two per cent of the handlers of newly arrived animals developed hepatitis, compared with a 0.4% incidence in all base personnel exclusive of handlers.

Spread of hepatitis and Au by fecal contaminators

Hepatitis and Au can in many cases be spread by the ingestion of feces from infected persons. Occasionally this may reach epidemic proportions. Many of the practices related to general public health will determine the spread of this form of feces-borne disease. Since many illustrations of this kind of spread are known and are discussed elsewhere, they will not be included here.

CONCLUSION

We selected a single disease (hepatitis) and infectious agent (Au) to illustrate the effects of anthropological practices on infectious disease. We hope that this has increased the clarity of the presentation and the discussion of specific hypotheses. The tests for Au are relatively simple, and, consequently, the carrier and disease states can be readily recognized. Because of its medical importance, tens of millions of people all over the world have been tested for Au. An enormous amount of data is already available, and more is being collected. The overt clinical symptoms of hepatitis are dramatic and can be readily recognized. The disease can be spread directly by blood and by other means (fecal-oral, insects); the conclusions drawn from the study of this disease may be generalized to other diseases that are similarly spread.

The complex distribution pattern of the carriers and disease and their interaction with genetic and environmental forces have been discussed. This includes a discussion of Au as a genetic polymorphism; sex and age effects, maternal effects; transmission by transfusion, tattooing and other kinds of blood-letting, and insects. These discussions have followed the general methods of medical anthropology in which an attempt is made to explain the observed distributions of disease in terms of social behavior, the environment, and genetics. Certain social and cultural practices that could influence the spread of the agent have been described. From these, and similar examples, specific prospective hypotheses can be advanced on the distribution of the agent. Consideration of these aspects of an infectious disease has led to some general concepts.

There are three categories of information available in the consideration of infectious disease and anthropology:

1. Information on the disease itself (microbiological). This includes identification of the infectious agent (the tubercle bacillus, cholera vibrio, Australia antigen, etc.); its life requirements; its mode of transmission (contaminated water or food, droplets in air, instruments used to pierce the skin, etc.); intermediary hosts (mosquitoes for malaria, yellow fever, elephantiasis, etc.); its symptoms; and the consequences of infection.

2. Information on the distribution of the disease (epidemiology). This includes geographic, age, and sex distribution, mortality, morbidity, and other parameters; its distribution in particular populations and its particular distribution within these populations. To use a now classic example, kuru was restricted to the Fore people of New Guinea and, in this population, to young people and women.

3. Information on the behavioral, genetic, and environmental characteristics of the "diseased" populations (anthropology).

Attention is usually called to a problem because of the presence of disease in a community (category 2). Then, armed with knowledge of the disease and its etiological agent (category 1) the social, environmental, and genetic characteristics of the population (category 3) are investigated in order to tell a story that can explain the disease distribution. A measure of the appropriateness of the story is the ability to use it to design public health strategies either to prevent the disease or to ameliorate its effects.

For example, as noted above, kuru was found to be common among the Fore. Investigation of this population resulted in the identification of an infectious agent, which appears to cause the disease. Information was also obtained on the social, environmental, and genetic characteristics of the population. A "story" was developed, linking the disease with cannibalism. The recent decrease in this practice appears to be associated with a concomitant decrease in the incidence of the disease.

Hence, in this approach, the initial stimulus for an investigation is through disease; and anthropological information is used to produce an explanation sufficiently good to lead to the prevention of the disease—an excellent test of reality.

In this chapter we have suggested an additional approach. It involves the same "categories" of information, but it arrives at them and utilizes them in a different sequence and for different reasons.

Information is available on the microbiological and epidemiological characteristics of an infectious agent (categories 1 and 2). Social, behavioral, environmental, and other characteristics of a variety of populations are known (category 3). Characteristics, in populations, that might interact with the disease and its agent are postulated in general. Hypotheses can be advanced on the distribution of the agent in a particular population, on the basis of the postulates. (In the case of Au, this refers primarily to the carrier state.) Testing of such hypotheses may provide a test of the reality of some kinds of social practices or social relationships.

For example, it might be possible, using Au as a tool, to test the effectiveness of a caste system in isolating classes of people from one another. How effective is the jati system in isolating classes? Is it effective enough to result in different frequencies of Au in the different groups, and, in particular, are the frequencies ranked in the order of the pollution meant to be inherent in caste classes? Are there differences in the strains (i.e., specificities) of Au in the different classes?

The use of tattooing or cicatrix marking may represent a bond between members of a community. Is the bond sufficiently strong that members of a common tattoo or cicatrix group all have the same infectious agents? In most societies, mothers are more intimate with their children than are other members of the family. Are they close enough so that mother and child are more likely to be infected with the same agents? If so, for how many years does this persist? How intimate are the relations with other family members? The study of the distribution of infectious agents could (perhaps) help answer such questions.

Hence, in this second approach, the initial entry into a problem is through observations on or questions about social behavior and the environmental, cultural, and/or genetic characteristics of the population; the disease, and its etiological agent, is used as a tool for the investigation. Obviously, the results of this approach may also be of medical importance; it gives a more detailed understanding of the dynamics of the disease and allows the planning of strategies to prevent illness. This may have a secondary value in that the investigation of social behavior in populations can be justified not only for its own sake, but also for its possible value in medical care.

REFERENCES

Anonymous. 1967. Tattooing of young people. *Brit. Med. J.* 1:376.

Barker, L. F., R. Shulman, R. Murray, R. J. Hirschman, F. Ratner, W. C. L. Diefenbach, and H. M. Geller. 1970. Transmission of serum hepatitis. *J.A.M.A.* 211.

Beidelman, T. O. 1971. *The Kaguru. A Matrilineal People of East Africa.* New York: Holt, Rinehart and Winston.

Blumberg, B. S. 1972. Australia antigen: The history of its discovery with comments on genetic and family aspects. In *Viral Hepatitis and Blood Transfusion,* eds. G. N. Vyas, H. A. Perkins, and R. Schmid. New York: Grune & Stratton, pp. 63-83.

Blumberg, B. S., H. J. Alter, and S. Visnich. 1965. A "new" antigen in leukemia sera. *J.A.M.A.* 191:541-546.

Blumberg, B. S., I. Millman, A. I. Sutnick, and W. T. London. 1971. The nature of Australia antigen and its relation to antigen-antibody complex formation. *J. Expl. Med.* 134:320-329.

Blumberg, B. S., A. I. Sutnick, W. T. London, and I. Millman. 1970. Current concepts. Australia antigen and hepatitis. *New Engl. J. Med.* 283:349-54.

Cazal, P., M. Robinet-Levy, and J.-M. Lemaire. 1972. Australia antigen, antibodies and hepatitis in families with chronic antigen. *Rev. Franc. Transfus.* 15:477-480.

Cepellini, R. 1970. *Considerazeoni sulla distribuzione dell' antigene Australia nells popolazione italiana.* Proceedings of the International Symposium on Australia Antigen and Viral Hepatitis. Milan.

Fiennes, R. 1967. *Zoonoses of Primates. The Epidemiology and Ecology of Simian Diseases in Relation to Man.* Ithaca, N.Y.: Cornell University Press, pp. 130-43.

Firth, R. 1936. Tattooing in Tikopia. *Man* 36:173-77.

Glasse, R. 1967. Cannibalism in the Kuru region of New Guinea. *Trans. N.Y. Acad. Sci.* 29:748-54.

Gostling, J. V. T. 1971. Long-incubation hepatitis and tattooing. *Lancet* 2: 1033.

Hambly, W. D. 1925. *The History of Tattooing or its Significance, with Some Account of Other Forms of Corporal Marking.* London: Witherby.

Hanevald, G. T. 1970. On the early history of tattooing. *Janus* 57:150-55.

Held, J. 1962. Hepatitis in humans associated with chimpanzees: U.S. Public Health Service, CDC Vet. Publ. #8 *Lab. Primate Newsletter*, Jan., 1964.

Hellman, L. M. and Pritchard, J. A. 1971. *Williams' Obstetrics*, 14th ed. London: Butterworths.

Henschen, F. 1966. *The History of Diseases*. London: Longmans.

Hersh, T., J. L. Melnick, R. K. Goyal, F. B. Hollinger. 1971. Non-parenteral transmission of viral hepatitis type B (Australia antigen-associated serum hepatitis). *N. Engl. J. Med.* 285:1363.

Hesser, J. E., I. Economidou, and B. S. Blumberg. Australia antigen in parents and sex ratio of offspring in a Greek population. (In preparation.)

Hillis, W. D. 1961. Human hepatitis with suspected sub-human primate source. *Amer. J. Hyg.* 73:316-32.

Kukowski, K., W. T. London, A. I. Sutnick, M. Kahn, and B. S. Blumberg. 1972. Comparison of progeny of mothers with and without Australia antigen. *Human Biol.* 44:489-500.

Landtman, G. 1927. *The Kiwai Papuans of British New Guinea*. London: Macmillan.

Laubscher, B. F. 1937. *Sex, Custom and Psychopathology*. London: George Routledge & Sons.

LeVine, R. and B. LeVine. 1963. Nyansongo: A Gusii Community in Kenya. In *Six Cultures. Studies of Child Rearing*, ed. B. B. Whiting. New York: Wiley.

London, W. T. 1970. Transmission of Australia antigen to man and non-human primates. *Proc. Nat. Acad. Sci.* (U.S.A.) 66:235.

London, W. T., Marion DiFiglia, A. I. Sutnick, and B. S. Blumberg. 1969. An epidemic of hepatitis in a chronic hemodialysis unit. Australia antigen and difference in host response. *N. Engl. J. Med.* 281:571-78.

London, W. T., H. J. Alter, J. Lander, and R. H. Purcell. 1972a. Serial transmission in Rhesus monkeys of an agent related to hepatitis-associated antigen. *J. Infect. Dis.* 125:382-89.

London, W. T., A. I. Sutnick, and B. S. Blumberg. 1972b. Current status of Australia antigen. In *Pathobiology Annual, 1972*, ed. Harry Ioachim. New York: Appleton-Century-Crofts, pp. 207-34.

MacArthur, W. P. 1957. Epidemic diseases and jaundice in history. *Brit. Med. Bull.* 13:146-49.

Matsuda, S., K. Tada, R. Shirachi, and N. Ishida. 1972. Australia antigen in amniotic fluid. *Lancet* 1:1117.

Mazzur, S. 1973. Menstrual blood as a vehicle of Australia antigen transmission. *Lancet* I:749.

Mazzur, S. and B. S. Blumberg. 1974. Silent maternal transmission of Australia antigen. *Nature* 247:41-43.

Meynard, J. E., K. R. Berquest, D. H. Krushok, and R. H. Purcell. 1972. Experimental infection of chimpanzees with the virus of hepatitis B. *Nature* 237:514-15.

Millman, I., S. N. Huang, V. Coyne, A. O'Connell, A. Aronoff, H. Gault, and B. S. Blumberg. 1972. Immunofluorescence and immunoelectron microscopy. In *Viral Hepatitis and Blood Transfusion*, ed. G. N. Vyas, H. A. Perkins, and R. Schmid. New York: Grune & Stratton, pp. 63-83.

Millman, I., H. Huhtanen, F. Merino, M. E. Bayer, and B. S. Blumberg. 1971. Australia antigen: Physical and chemical properties. *Res. Comm. Chem. Path. Pharm.* 2:667-86.

Minturn, L. and J. T. Hitchcock. 1963. The Rajputs of Khalapur, India. In *Six Cultures. Studies of Child Rearing*, ed. B. B. Whiting. New York: Wiley.

Nishioka, K., T. Hirayama, T. Sekine, K. Okochi, M. Mayumi, Sung Juei-Low, Lin Chen-Hui, and Lin Tong-Min. 1973. Australia antigen and hepatocellular carcinoma. In *Alpha-Fetoprotein and Hepatoma*, eds. H. Hirai and T. Miyaji. Tokyo: University of Tokyo Press, p. 167.

Okochi, K., M. Mayumi, and K. Nishioka. 1972. *The Natural History of Australia Antigen and Hepatocellular Carcinoma. Proceedings 3rd International Symposium*. Princess Takamatsu Cancer Research Fund. Tokyo, Nov., 1972.

Ploss, H. H., M. Bartels, and P. Bartels. 1935. *Woman*, ed. E. J. Dingwall. London: William Heineman.

Seligman, C. G. and B. L. Seligman. 1932. Pagan tribes of the Nilotic Sudan. London: George Routledge & Sons.

Singh, S. D. 1969. Urban monkeys. *Sci. Amer.* 221:108.

Spencer, B. and F. J. Gillen. 1955. The native tribes of Central Australia. MacMillan, London, 1899, cited in *Symbolic Wounds: Puberty Rites and the Envious Male*, ed. B. Bettelheim. Glencoe, Ill.: Macmillan.

Sukeno, N., R. Shirachi, H. Shiraishi, and N. Ishida. 1972. Conformational studies of Australia antigen by optical rotatory dispersion and circular dichroism. *J. Virol.* 10:157-58.

Sutnick, A. I., I. Millman, W. T. London, and B. S. Blumberg. 1972. The role of Australia antigen in viral hepatitis and other diseases. *Ann. Rev. Med.* 23:161-76.

Swanepold, R. and J. G. Cruikshank. 1972. Australia antigen in Rhodesia. *Lancet* 1:446.

Thomas, S. 1968. Women's tattoos of the upper Rajang. *Sarawak Museum J.* 16:209-34.

Williams, T. R. 1965. *The Dusun. A North Borneo Society*. New York: Holt Rinehart and Winston.

Williams, A. O. and A. I. O. Williams. 1972. Carrier stage prevalence of hepatitis associated antigen (Au/Sh) in Nigeria. *Amer. J. Epidem.* 96: 227-30.

11. Behavioral Response and Adaptation to Environmental Stimulation

JOACHIM F. WOHLWILL*

The view that the environment directly influences the individual's health, and is, thus, implicated in stress and disease, is an ancient one. It can be traced back at least as far as Hippocrates, as shown in the following excerpt from Dubos's (1965) summary of the Hippocratic Corpus:

> The well-being of man is under the influence of the environment, including in particular air, water, places, and the various regimens. The understanding of the effect of the environment on man is the fundamental basis of the physician's art.
>
> Health is the expression of a harmonious balance between the various components of man's nature . . . and the environment and ways of life. [p. 322.]

A long and distinguished line of leaders in the fields of biology and medicine—Claude Bernard, Lawrence Henderson, Ivan Setchenov, and, most recently, René Dubos—have extended and filled in this picture of the responsivity of the organism to features of the environment and the view of disease as an adaptation to conditions threatening a disturbance in the equilibrium between external and internal processes.

Although Hippocrates explicitly repudiated the value of a distinction between mental and physical health, the treatment of environmental stress and its effects on the individual has followed rather disparate lines.

* Division of Man-Environment Relations, Pennsylvania State University, University Park, Pennsylvania. A revised and shortened version of this paper has been published as "Human adaptation to levels of environmental stimulation" in *Human Ecology*, 1974, 2: 127-47.

Workers in biology and medicine have concerned themselves primarily with the effects of physical conditions of climate, nutrition, air-pollutants, etc., on body health and disease, following a homeostatic model; workers in psychology and psychiatry, in contrast, have focused more on environmental stressors emanating from interpersonal relations, occupational demands and responsibilities, and the like, with a predominant conception of stress as a product of conditions of frustration and interpersonal conflict and of defects in our social and cultural institutions.

Yet, without wishing in the least to minimize the major role of psychological stresses of the kind just mentioned in our everyday lives, we note with interest that continuous monitoring of pulse rate of a newspaper editor over the course of several days revealed that "his most stressful activity, judged by peaks in his pulse rate, was driving to and from work on a commuting San Francisco freeway" (U. Calif., n. d., p. 2).

The present paper is predicated on the assumption that there are attributes of our physical environment that may act as potential psychological stressors in their effects on behavior and psychological health. It is intended to provide a framework for studying such stressors and to consider the modes of adaptation and adjustment the individual has at his disposal in coping with them. Since the intent is to focus on generalized aspects or dimensions of environmental stimulation, as opposed to such specific stressors as noise and crowding, which are covered in other chapters of this volume, it will be necessary to present an analysis of the stimulus environment in terms of these generalized attributes in some detail before we can meaningfully consider the problem of adaptation as it applies in this realm.

LEVELS OF STIMULATION AND STRESS

Let us start with the assumption that the individual functions optimally within a certain range of environmental conditions, and, more particularly, of values on variables of stimulation contained within the environment. These include not only such properties exerting a direct effect on such physiological processes as temperature, air pressure, acidity, etc., but also the dimensions of the stimulus environment to which the individual responds primarily through the excitation of sensory receptor mechanisms, transmitting information to the higher centers of the central nervous system. We will presently consider the major stimulus dimensions that are relevant. For the moment, let us dwell on two important consequences of the assumption just stated.

The first consequence is that it is possible to look at environmental stressors at the behavioral level as acting in a manner similar to physiological stressors, i.e., as a deviation of some particular stimulus variable beyond the limits of tolerance built up within the individual for that variable. The second consequence is that, just as physiological equilibria may be disturbed by deviations in either direction (e.g., extreme hot or extreme cold), so psychological stressors may similarly involve departures from some modal level of stimulation in a bi-directional sense, i.e., in the direction of either over- or understimulation. This is an important point, since, in the past, psychologists have been prone to view the role of stimulation in the development and maintenance of behavior primarily from a "the-more-the-merrier" perspective. Both the animal research on the role of early sensory experience on subsequent development and the voluminous literature on the effects of human short-term sensory deprivation have given dramatic evidence of the deleterious effects on behavior of a marked reduction in the amount of stimulation present in an individual's environment. Very little attention, on the other hand, has been given to the effects of hyperstimulating conditions on behavior, and the possibility that such conditions may also have adverse effects on behavior has not been seriously examined, except for such intensive variables of stimulation as noise level or electric shock.

This is puzzling, since behavior theorists have increasingly invoked the concept of an *optimal level of stimulation* as essential to the maintenance of arousal and, thus, to maximally effective performance or to maximization of positive affect. Yet the limited evidence that we have in support of such an optimization principle is based entirely on research on preference responses, ratings of liking, and similar measures; extensions to possible impairment of performance or to deleterious effects on mental health have occasionally been suggested but rarely if ever put to an empirical test.

The case of the theoretical system proposed by Fiske and Maddi (1961) to deal with the role of variables in the stimulus environment in the activation of behavior and in the maintenance of arousal and hedonic tone is particularly illuminating, since these authors go to some length to bring out the relationship between high levels of activation (produced by high levels or intensities of stimulation) and negative affect, e.g.,

> Through experience, the organism learns to avoid markedly high or low levels of activation under most circumstances, because they are accompanied by unpleasantness. An extremely high level of activation is typically unpleasant because it is associated with such states as inability

to concentrate, anxiety, rapid heart beat, or a sinking feeling in the stomach. [p. 46.]

Yet the same authors, in their introductory chapter preceding the one just referrred to, state the following

> Since understimulation characterizes much of the material in this book, the reader may wonder why there is no chapter on overstimulation, *or stress*. Very strange and quite unexpected stimuli can be highly stressful, and a history of such stimulation, especially early in life, has important consequences for later behavior. . . . Yet stress is primarily a function of the intensity or meaning of stimulation. After the onset of the stressful conditions the contribution of temporal variation is minimal. Therefore the study of stress seems to add little to the understanding of varied experience. [p. 9, italics mine.]

The point of this quote, juxtaposed to the previous one, is that Fiske and Maddi appear to equate overstimulation to stress, to the exclusion of understimulation, and, in apparent contradiction to their proposition concerning the negative effect of extremely high levels of activation, they dismiss overstimulation as irrelevant to the effects of stimulus-variation on behavior, which is the focus of their volume. Both of these views are highly arguable, as we will try to show in this chapter. For one thing, if overstimulation may be viewed as stressful, so may understimulation, as the sensory-deprivation literature has made abundantly clear (e.g., Zubek, 1969). Furthermore, there appears to be no reason to dismiss out of hand the possibility that an excess of variation may be stressful in and of itself.

The proposition that stress can be viewed as a resultant of either hyper- or hypostimulating conditions, which is central to this chapter, is consonant with the *sensoristasis* concept advanced by Schultz (1965), i.e., "a state of cortical arousal which impels the organism (in a waking state) to strive to maintain an optimal level of sensory variation" (p. 30). In explicating his concept, Schultz draws the analogy to Cannon's homeostasis concept and explicitly considers increases of stimulation beyond the optimal level as disturbing the internal balance and disrupting behavior; he refers, furthermore, to Lindsley's (1961) analysis of the role of the reticular formation, postulating similar effects of sensory restriction and sensory overload. Yet Schultz, as did Fiske and Maddi before him, confines himself to the sensory-deprivation literature—possibly because of the paucity of evidence of the actual effects of overload.

Although the reference to Lindsley's reticular-formation model reinforces the plausibility of conceiving of hyper- and hypostimulation effects in comparable terms, i.e., as involving a disturbance in sensoristasis in either direction, it does not, of course, preclude the possibility—indeed, the strong likelihood—that the overt behavioral manifestations may be quite different in the two cases, just as body reactions to extreme heat and extreme cold take very different forms. It will, therefore, be necessary to maintain the distinction between hyper- and hypostimulation, while at the same time searching for possible similarities in the individual's general mode of response and adaptation to them.

Main varieties of hypo- and hyperstimulation

Let us examine, then, the main varieties of conditions of hypo- and hyperstimulation. At the hypostimulation end, we may usefully distinguish three different kinds: deprivation of sensory stimulation, deprivation of social interaction, and deprivation of movement.

1. *Deprivation of sensory stimulation.* This is the condition on which most of the experimental research has concentrated, inspired, in large measure, by the emphasis Hebb (1949) placed on a constant influx of stimulation as essential to the maintenance of behavior and the dramatic effects of sensory deprivation that the pioneering work originating in Hebb's laboratories at McGill University demonstrated (cf. Vernon, 1963). It typically involves the elimination of all potential sources of stimulus input, across some or all sensory modalities, usually by placing the individual in a dark, sound-proof room and preventing him from engaging in any self-stimulating movements or actions by encasing his hands and arms in cardboard tubes; at times even vocalization is denied the subject. Different experimenters have, inevitably, utilized varying degrees of such deprivation; a particularly significant variant on the absolute elimination of incoming visual stimulation is the use of translucent hemispheres (e.g., ping-pong ball halves) fitted over the subject's eyes.

It is obviously impossible to review the voluminous evidence on the behavioral effects of sensory deprivation here (cf. Zubek, 1969), nor is it essential to do so for the particular purpose of this chapter. It is sufficient to note the relevance of the sensory-deprivation work to an understanding of individual's responses to such environmental circumstances as those faced by individuals during extended stays in the Antarctic (e.g., Gunderson, 1968; Nelson, 1965) or by astronauts on prolonged space flights.

2. *Deprivation of social interaction (isolation).* The stimulation pro-

vided by interaction and communication with other human beings is clearly of a special sort and should be treated as separate from sensory deprivation. Most probably, the distinctive feature of social stimuli is the fact that they provide feedback to the individual's responses, and, perhaps as a consequence, arouse affect of a sort that the world of inanimate stimuli would be incapable of providing. (The world of animals is presumably intermediate between these two categories.)

Social isolation may, of course, be found in combination with sensory deprivation, as in the case of the prison inmate in solitary confinement. But it is not difficult to isolate its role independent of sensory deprivation in the laboratory, and research devoted to this question is indeed available (e.g., Zuckerman *et al.*, 1966). On the other hand, its role in a relatively pure state is brought out in accounts of adventures and explorers and scientists who have had occasion to spend extended periods away from their fellowmen (e.g., Lawick-Goodall, 1967).

3. *Deprivation or restriction of movement (confinement)*. Confinement represents still a different form of hypostimulation; most likely it owes its distinctiveness to the role of stimulation from the proprioceptors in maintaining posture and arousal. It, too, is typically found in conjunction with either sensory or social deprivation—or both, as in the case of the prison inmate in solitary confinement. Indeed, some of the experimental literature on the effects of impoverishment of stimulation during early experience on behavioral development is open to criticism on this ground: it is difficult to raise an organism under conditions of severe deprivation of sensory stimulation (e.g., by raising it in the dark) without at the same time substantially reducing the amount of movement the animal is likely to engage in. At the same time, it is not difficult to find at least one by no means rare example of a condition involving confinement to the point of immobilization, without either social isolation or sensory deprivation: the situation confronting a patient confined for an extended period to a hospital bed.

Turning now to the opposite end of the scale, that of hyperstimulation, we again find it useful to distinguish between an excess of stimulation and an excess of social interaction or contact. For reasons to be explained, there is no clear counterpart, at this end, of the confinement condition cited above, that is, we are not dealing here with a bi-polar dimension.

4. *Sensory Overload*. In sharp contrast to the topic of sensory deprivation, the effects of a hyperstimulating environment, that is, of very high levels of stimulation on the individual, have received virtually no atten-

tion on the part of psychologists, except within the very restricted realm of the effects of noise, which can hardly be considered to represent the counterpart at the hyperstimulation pole of the sensory deprivation condition. Precisely what "overstimulation" may mean will be more fully discussed below; we should recognize, in the meantime, that the use of the prefixes "hyper" and "over" may be begging the question, if anything more than a condition characterized by a relatively large amount of stimulus input is intended. Whether extreme amounts of stimulation will necessarily have negative effects on behavior remains to be determined, of course. But the relevance of the problem for an understanding of the conditions of human existence in some of our urban environments, for instance, should be apparent.

One particular determinant of this question must be noted here, since it relates to an important semantic distinction—that between *sensory* and *information overload*. This distinction concerns the question whether the stimuli impinging on the individual do so merely in the sense of passive exposure or whether they contain information requiring him to respond in a certain way. For obvious reasons, this distinction does not have a counterpart at the deprivation end, which is devoid of information, by definition; on the other hand, there is reason to believe, as we shall have occasion to point out, that sheer exposure to stimulation has much less marked effects on behavior or, at the very least, rather different effects than information overload. For this reason it appears advisable henceforth to designate the upper end as "sensory overstimulation," with the understanding that the prefix "over" is intended merely in a descriptive sense, and to reserve the term "over*load*" to situations where the individual must process information carried by the stimuli impinging on him.

5. *Crowding.* Again the presence, in large number, of other social objects can be treated as a special case of the preceding category, but it is most appropriately considered under a separate rubric. Effects of crowding have, most recently, become the subject of active research, both at the animal and the human levels, and this work has extended our grasp of this problem considerably beyond that reflected in the pioneering work of Calhoun (1962); it also calls into question some of the generalizations to the human condition that that work had inspired (e.g., Zlutnick and Altman, 1972). Yet it is undeniable that crowding does represent a commonly encountered aspect of urban existence, representing a potential form of psychological stress. Most probably, however, this stress potential of conditions of crowding derives less from the quality of stimulation

represented by people en masse than from the likelihood that crowding results in goal-blocking and, thus, in a state of frustration for the individual. (Exposure to crowds at parades or sporting events is not usually experienced as stressful.)

6. *"Hyperdynamic" conditions.* If restriction of movement did have an opposite pole, it would have to be a condition marked by an inordinate amount of physical movement. Although there are assuredly specific situations (e.g., sports) that may be characterized by high levels of activity, and possibly of movement per se, it is difficult to envisage an environment that would enforce such high amounts of movement. Conceivably, it might be rigged experimentally, as through the use of a treadmill, although that would only elicit a very restricted form of movement. More to the point, environmental circumstances corresponding to this condition do not readily come to mind.

MAJOR DIMENSIONS OF SENSORY DEPRIVATION AND OVERSTIMULATION

Whereas it is easy to define sensory deprivation in absolute terms as a condition of complete absence of stimulation, as soon as one attempts to operationalize the concept through the design of a study to investigate its effects, one is confronted with problem of identifying the relevant components of this condition. For instance, does it mean an absolute zero of stimulation (complete darkness, a sound-proof room), or simply an unvarying, homogeneous background of stimulation (as in the diffuse, unpatterned light transmitted through translucent hemispheres mentioned above or, in the auditory domain, a background of white noise)? Similarly, is restriction of movement, so as to eliminate proprioceptive stimulation, an essential component of the condition, and, if so, to what lengths should its implementation be carried? (For instance, should movements of the head or the mouth be eliminated?)

The problem becomes even more acute at the overstimulation end; we may take it for granted that it is impossible to incorporate every type and mode of stimulation that might be invented for this purpose into our experiment. But just what dimensions of stimulation shall we include in creating such a condition?

It is thus incumbent upon us to examine the various components into which the sensory-deprivation–overstimulation continuum may be analyzed. We distinguish five aspects: level, diversity, patterning, instability, and meaningfulness.

1. *Level*. This aspect is the only one that has been varied over a sufficiently large range of the continuum to bring out the bi-polar nature of the under- to overstimulation dimension, and it brings us closest to the physiological work on stress reactions to disturbance in the body's state of equilibrium. This is shown most clearly with respect to temperature, where we find similar types of reactions at the behavioral as at the physiological level, serving to restore the original equilibrium, ranging all the way from shivering or rubbing one's hands to putting on heavy clothing or lighting a fire, and from sweating and seeking out the shade to taking off clothing or turning on the air conditioner.

Is it legitimate to take the temperature dimension as a prototype in illustrating the effects of level of stimulation? It could be argued that the apparent bi-polarity of the effects have nothing to do with *under-* or *over-* stimulation, but is rather to be construed in a qualitative sense, equivalent, perhaps, to response to auditory *frequency* (very low- and very high-pitched tones are experienced as unpleasant). On the other hand, if we take such intensive dimensions as loudness and brightness, the symmetrical character of the effects of extreme levels at the low ends versus the high ends of the continuum is much more questionable, if only because physiological effects of pain and actual tissue damage enter at the high end and inevitably alter the picture.

2. *Diversity*. The role of *variation* in stimulation, both in a simultaneous and a successive sense, in eliciting and maintaining behavioral arousal and interest has been receiving increasing emphasis in recent experimental psychological literature. It is reflected in studies of effects of stimulus complexity, such as Berlyne's (e.g., 1960), in which heterogeneity of the elements of a stimulus represents one among several ways in which complexity is operationalized (Fig. 11-1). More fundamentally, it enters into the conceptualization of the role of stimulation in the arousal and maintenance of behavior offered by Fiske and Maddi (1961), among others, who postulate a need for stimulus variation as a basic property of living organisms and invoke the concept of "variation-seeking" in explaining particular forms of exploratory activity found to be a function of diversity of stimulation. As noted above with respect to Fiske and Maddi, the emphasis has been almost exclusively on the role of diversity, complexity, or variation in *raising* affect, arousal, or exploratory behavior. Yet our physical environment may at times produce stress, or mental fatigue, through a surfeit of diversity, akin perhaps to the tedium produced by the lack of it—as witness the phenomenon of "visual pollution," i.e., the wearisome hodgepodge of highly diverse sights, represented by the succes-

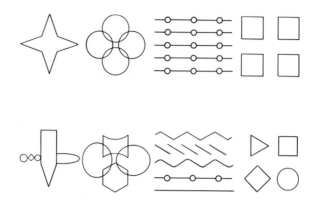

Fig. 11-1. Illustrative stimuli used by Berlyne in studies on the relationship between heterogeneity of elements of a stimulus field and interest, i.e., amount of voluntary exploration. (From Berlyne, 1960; reproduced by permission of McGraw-Hill Book Co.)

sion of gaudy signs, gas stations, and hamburger stands greeting the motorist at the outskirts of so many American cities.[1]

There is, in any event, considerable evidence to indicate that diversity conforms to the optimization principle, i.e., that the perceived attractiveness of a stimulus configuration is maximal for intermediate values of this variable. Thus, laboratory research on the relationship between stimulus complexity and preference has quite consistently shown that stimuli falling somewhere in between the two extremes of this continuum are most strongly preferred. This is true whether diversity is operationalized simply in terms of number of elements of random nonsense shapes (Day, 1967; Vitz, 1960; Thomas, 1966—data for high school subjects), of amount of variation contained in random sequences of tones (Vitz, 1966a), of number of *different* items (e.g., postage stamps) present in a constant-size matrix of such items (Wohlwill, 1975), or of pictures of the physical environment or non-representational modern art scaled in terms of the amount of variation they contain, along certain specified stimulus dimensions (Wohlwill, 1968, 1975). Particularly convincing evidence on this point comes from the latter of the two studies of the writers just men-

1 It might be argued that the effect of this type of scene is not so much a matter of too much variation, but simply one of ugliness. But that may be begging the question. The fact is that psychologists have done little so far to clarify the nature of ugliness; but it is a plausible hunch that it is the very diversity, i.e., lack of unity of a stimulus configuration that is responsible for the response "ugly" that it evokes in us.

tioned, in which children of different ages made preference judgments between pairs of slides of scenes from the physical environment that had been independently rated to vary along a seven-point scale of diversity, i.e., complexity. The results are shown in Fig. 11-2.

3. *Patterning.* We noted earlier, in reference to the sensory deprivation research, that deprivation of visual stimulation was frequently achieved by allowing the subject to be stimulated by a homogeneous field of diffuse light, i.e., one completely lacking in *patterned* information. At the same time, a diversified stimulus field completely devoid of structure

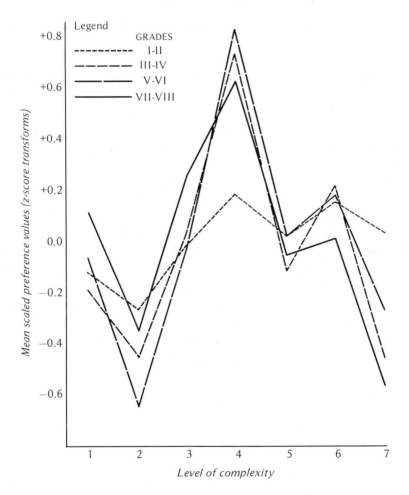

Fig. 11-2. Relationship between stimulus complexity level and preference, for scenes of the physical environment (Wohlwill, 1975).

or information would seem to represent a condition of overstimulation, i.e., one potentially overtaxing the individual's capacity to encode and transmit information. Here we have, then, a dimension with a virtually built-in optimization feature: some modal combination of structure and uncertainty is probably maximally conducive to the maintenance of attention and interest—a principle, incidentally, recognized in the field of aesthetics (cf. Meyer, 1956). Unfortunately, there is little evidence on this point available from laboratory research in which degree of patterning in a stimulus configuration has been subjected to systematic variation. We may refer, however, to the results of a study by Simon and Wohlwill (1968) in which ratings of degree of liking were obtained for short pieces of music, in their original versions and when altered so as to introduce progressively greater degrees of regularity of harmony and rhythm. For two of the four sets of musical passages thus obtained, the variant of the original that was intermediate in terms of regularity was preferred, on the average, over both the original version and the most regular transform. Significantly, this held true only for untrained listeners; subjects with formal training in music invariably preferred the most complex version, i.e., the original.

This demonstration of the role that experience may play in altering the nature of the individual's preference-for-complexity function—confirmed, incidentally, in Vitz's (1966a) research with random tone patterns—brings up a much more general question. It seems likely that experience changes the degree to which the individual is able to structure the stimulus input, i.e., to extract the information with respect to patterning contained in it. The difference between the two groups would thus relate, not so much to the preference function per se, but rather to the degree of patterning or information required for a given degree of *perceived* complexity. In other words, it is possible that, in the case of this variable, at least, the operation of the optimization principle is a consequence of the units of analysis in terms of which the individual perceives a stimulus pattern, rather than of preference for particular levels of stimulation. A stimulus configuration that is altogether devoid of patterning may, in fact, appear effectively as simple, and, thus, lacking in interest, only because the individual is no longer able to analyze it into its component units.

The problem has received all too little attention in the psychological laboratory, but it has been clearly recognized by such writers as Heckhausen (1964) and Rapoport and Hawkes (1970), who have been impressed with the inadequacy of a priori definitions of objective—as opposed to phenomenally perceived—stimulus complexity. It would not be difficult to find illustrations from the realm of art, as well as the physical environment, to remind us of the important role of the units of perceptual analysis into which the perceiver analyzes a complex stimulus field. One example may suffice: the view of an urban scene from the air may change from one of visual order and pattern to one of approaching chaos, as the plane descends from cruising altitude to a landing.

This point is of more than academic interest, since it may well be that one possible source of stress in our environment results from the difficulty an individual experiences in trying to impose a structure or pattern on the seemingly chaotic or random constellation of stimuli or events confronting him. Thus, as Lynch (1960) has argued on the basis of his work on urban imagery, where the urban environment contains clearly defined elements, landmarks, boundaries, etc., that aid the individual in structuring it, the satisfaction he is apt to derive from it is visibly enhanced.

4. *Stability/instability.* Quite possibly, the most critical attribute of a stimulus field, in terms of its potential for stress engendered through information overload, is the degree and type of *movement* it contains. The perception of movement in complex stimulus fields has been little investigated, but two reasons may be suggested for the projected role that movement will play in arousal and environmental stress. First, unlike stationary stimulus objects, a moving stimulus is difficult to ignore. It tends to impose itself on the individual's attention, and to demand a response to it at some level, ranging from simple tracking by eye to precise behavioral adjustments (as in driving a car). Second, once a dynamic element is introduced into a stimulus configuration, an entirely new dimension is added to the demands placed on the individual's information-processing capacity, owing to the need to identify and interpret stimuli without benefit of extensive examination and to maintain the sense of a structured field when the elements of that field are in a possibly continual state of flux. (One situation that brings out clearly the strain engendered by a problem of this kind is that confronting the air-traffic controller, whose job is well known for the manifestations of acute stress it engenders.)

Here, again, we undoubtedly confront a bi-polar dimension, in terms of its effects on the individual. A completely static world, frozen in time and space, as it were, is of course incompatible with a condition of life, but even when we encounter something approaching it, in a desert landscape, or in walking through downtown Manhattan on Labor Day, there may be a feeling of strangeness, amounting at times to actual discomfort in the stillness and quietude. At the opposite extreme, the hustle and bustle of places marked by a constant stream of randomly moving objects (e.g., Grand Central Station) may prove stressful, especially for the individual who is forced to live or work in such surroundings. Concrete evidence on this point is lacking, however.

5. *Meaningfulness*. It is hardly more than a truism to suggest that the extent to which a given stimulus field taxes the individual's information-processing capacity is a direct function of its meaningfulness to him—his familiarity with it, its degree of structure or organization, etc. There is some debate, however, as to the direction in which meaningfulness operates. Fiske and Maddi (1961), for instance, although they recognize meaning as a basic dimension modulating the role of stimulus variation in arousal, regard a stimulus lacking in meaning as low in its impact or arousal value; meaningfulness is thought of in an informational sense and, thus, positively related to arousal. There is, in fact, evidence (Munsinger and Kessen, 1964) that for the type of nonsense shapes considered above meaningfulness is a positive function of complexity. Yet this analysis of the matter ignores the opposite role of meaning, in the sense of familiarity, of reducing or inhibiting attention and interest. A good illustration of this point comes from studies comparing the attention-value of familiar, thus, meaningful pictures with similar stimuli that are novel or incongruous, and, thus, lacking in meaning (e.g., Smock and Holt, 1962; Berlyne, 1960). Familiarity, in other words, may not breed contempt, but neither does it enhance interest or arousal.

It seems, then, that meaningfulness is related to the deprivation-overload dimension in a bi-directional way. Perhaps this amounts to a problem of the definition of meaningfulness. Where "meaning" is intended as an attribute of each of the component perceptual units of a stimulus configuration, the effect of exposure to such units as an aggregate may well be in the direction of increasing arousal, possibly to the point of overstimulation. Such would be the case, perhaps, for reaction to a museum room that contained a surfeit of pictures, objects, or exhibits. On the other hand, where meaningfulness is taken as an attribute of the stimulus field as a whole, it certainly reduces the load on the information-processing capacity of the individual (where that is relevant to his situation) and may even result in a condition akin to sensory deprivation (e.g., being exposed *ad nauseam* to a too-familiar popular ditty).

THE PROBLEM OF ADAPTATION

One of the prime difficulties with any generalization concerning the effects of a given level or type of stimulation present in the environment on an individual living in that environment derives from the ubiquitous fact of adaptation. This is as true of the behavioral as it is of the physiological level. We do, in fact, seem to be able to become adapted to a vast range of circumstances, involving sometimes fairly extreme forms of deprivation and restriction, on the one hand, and overstimulation, on the other. In some cases, such as extended stays in the Antarctic, certain deleterious effects of the experience are observable (Gunderson, 1968; cf. also Zubek, 1969, p. 386). In others, such effects may be surmised, in the absence of good evidence pro or con. This question of the price we may pay for adapting to particular environments is a critical one, and we will return to it below. At this point, however, the fact of adaptation is what concerns us, since it inevitably affects the impact of a particular level or type of stimulation on the individual.

The concept of behavioral adaptation

Since the adaptation concept has been used in many different ways, both across disciplines (anthropology, biology, psychology) and within the discipline of psychology proper, it is important to define it in fairly rigorous terms for the purposes of this chapter. In this initial discussion of adaptation, at least, we will restrict ourselves to phenomena referring directly to dimensions, qualities, or attributes of the stimulus environment, where adaptation is defined as a quantitative shift in the distribution of judgmental or affective responses along a stimulus continuum, as a function of continued exposure to a stimulus.

This definition is presented with specific reference to Helson's (1964) adaptation-level theory, not only because this theory represents the most systematic and comprehensive attempt to encompass adaptation phenomena over a wide range of behavior, within a consistent framework, but also because it appears useful in conceptualizing the effects of prolonged exposure to a given stimulus environment on behavior.[2] Two points, in particular, warrant comment, in regard to this definition.

2 An excellent picture of the scope of this theory, as well as of recent developments and applications of it, is continued in a symposium edited by Appley (1971).

First, by defining adaptation as a shift in the distribution of responses, it may be seen that we are leaving out of our account adaptation phenomena involving a simple neutralization process, i.e., a reduction of the power of a given stimulus to evoke a response—as in the case of adaptation to an odor or a noise, for instance. Yet, in most, if not all, such cases, it is generally possible to reformulate the phenomenon in terms of shifts in distribution, by considering variations in response as a function of *intensity* of stimulation. In this connection, we may note that Helson conceives of sensory adaptation as relating to continua rather than fixed values, emphasizing sensitization and neutralization as frequently complementary aspects of adaptation, occurring over portions of a continuum (cf. Helson, 1964, pp. 46-50). Thus, one way of formulating the problem of adaptation in the case of smell, for instance, is in terms of a change in the intensity of the stimulus required for it to be detected or affectively reacted to—a view that is close to that implied in such aspects of biological adaptation as immunization (compare the change in the response of an animal to differential dosages of such a toxic substance as an insecticide).

The point may be illustrated by translating the function obtained by Holm (1903, in Osgood, 1953, p. 81), depicting the temporal course of adaptation to cold, into two curves: one to describe the hypothetical distribution of responses along an assumed continuum of perceived coldness at the beginning of adaptation; the other following 3.5 minutes of exposure of the skin to a stimulus at 10° C. The original and transformed functions are shown in Fig. 11-3.

The second point relating to our definition is that, by the criterion adopted, adaptation must be differentiated from *adjustment*, which, following Sonnenfeld (1966) may be viewed as a change in behavior that has the effect of modifying the stimulus or stimulus conditions to which the individual is exposed. The distinction is nicely illustrated with respect to temperature: the American on a visit to Great Britain in the winter is apt to feel uncomfortably cold at the prevailing indoor temperatures, and so may put on an extra sweater or leave on his overcoat. This would represent an adjustive response. After a prolonged stay in England, however, he may no longer experience a 65° temperature as uncomfortable: he has become adapted to it, or more precisely, his level of adaptation has shifted downward.

This distinction, as Sonnenfeld has shown, is an important one in evaluating long-range behavioral effects of environmental conditions on the individual, and we shall return to it below. Meanwhile, let us illustrate the

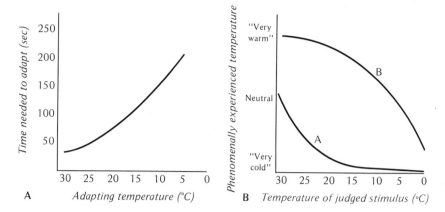

Fig. 11-3. (A) Time taken to adapt to cold, as a function of adapting temperature (Data from Holm, 1903; reproduced in Osgood, 1953.) (B) Hypothetical curves based on function, left, indicating the shift in relationship between phenomenally experienced temperatures and objective temperature, from that at start of the adaptation period (curve A, skin temperature assumed at 30° C) to that after 3.5 minutes of adaptation to cold (curve B, skin exposed at 5° C).

concept of adaptation in the sense we have defined it, and of adaptation level, more particularly. We will restrict ourselves to responses involving affect, preferential or evaluative judgment, or the like, as opposed to sensory sensitivity or perceptual judgment, even though the theory itself has been developed most extensively with respect to the latter aspect of behavior. This restriction is motivated both by considerations of length and by the more direct relevance of affective and evaluative functions to our treatment of behavioral effects of environmental stimulation.

Changes in preference as a function of adaptation to stimuli

Let us start out with a simple experiment, showing adaptation processes at work in reactions to temperature. This is a study by Haber (1958), who had his subjects immerse one hand in water of a given temperature and then determined their preference for waters at other temperatures, both warmer and colder than the original temperature. These preferences turned out to be a joint function of two factors: the deviation of the temperature of the sample from the one to which the subject had been pre-exposed and the absolute level of the temperature. Thus, for exposure temperatures in an intermediate range (e.g., 33° C) preference rose to a peak on either side of the adaptation level established by the exposure temperature, falling off beyond that point, according to a function originally postulated by McClelland *et al.* (1953) in their theory of affect (cf. Fig. 11-4). But, where more extreme exposure temperatures were used, Haber obtained preference functions decreasing monotonically for values beyond the adaptation temperature: thus, not surprisingly, after immersing his hand in water at 40° C, no subject consistently preferred water that was warmer than that temperature.

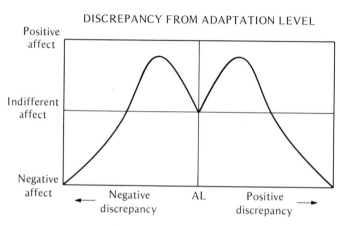

Fig. 11-4. Changes in affective response to stimuli as a function of extent of deviation from adaptation level. (After Haber, 1958; reproduced by permission of the American Psychological Association.)

Haber, following McClelland *et al.*, considers these data as evidence that discrepancy from adaptation level (AL) is a primary determinant of affective judgment, according to the function described in Fig. 11-4. It should be noted, however, that the study does not allow one to differentiate between the role of deviation from AL as opposed to that of absolute values along the continuum in question. In other words, it is conceivable that the falling off of the curves toward the two extremes owes as much to the approach to the limits of tolerance of the human body to water temperatures—presumably determined at a physiological level—as to the discrepancy of the values from the AL.

Adaptation of affect for diverse stimulus dimensions

Little evidence is available that would indicate how widely the function postulated by McClelland *et al.* can be generalized to other stimulus dimensions. Helson (1964, Ch. 6) reviews results from a variety of studies dealing with affective and aesthetic judgments, largely in support of his frame-of-reference theory, which postulates that any given stimulus will be evaluated in terms relative to the adaptation level established through previous experience with similar stimuli varying along some dimension. Thus, a given picture will be judged as relatively more beautiful if it follows exposure to a set of pictures independently rated near the "ugly" end of the continuum than when it is presented following exposure to a set rated near the "beautiful" end. But the double-bow shaped curve illustrated in Fig. 11-4, suggesting that an intermediate degree of deviation from the adaptation-level is maximally preferred, has seldom been verified elsewhere.

Two partial exceptions to this last statement may be cited, namely the studies of Terwilliger (1963) and Unikel (1971); they are of particular interest in dealing with adaptation along the variable of stimulus complexity. In Terwilliger's study, subjects were first shown a set of stimuli independently scaled for complexity and asked to give color associations for them; this was assumed to result in the establishment of a level of adaptation with respect to a complexity equivalent to the mean complexity value of all stimuli exposed. The subjects then saw the entire set again and rated them for pleasantness. Only one of two separate replications of this study yielded clear-cut evidence of a double-bow shaped function relating judged pleasantness to deviation from the adaptation level. There was, furthermore, no control over the role the exposure stimuli actually played in establishing an adaptation level—it is conceivable that the same results might have been obtained without any pre-exposure phase, based simply on the absolute complexity values of the stimuli and independent of the establishment of adaptation levels during that phase.

Unikel's study provides much more incisive evidence on this question. He pre-exposed his subjects for 30-minute periods to random patterns of lights at one of nine levels of complexity (defined in terms of the number of different lights included in the pattern, with lights varying in hue and spatial location). Subsequently, they were given a choice between the pattern to which they had become adapted and a new pattern of a level of complexity differing from the original by either one, five, or seven steps. The results, presented in Fig. 11-5, showed both a very marked bidirectional effect of discrepancy per se (the new patterns were preferred to an extent proportional to the number of steps by which they differed from the complexity level of the adaptation pattern, regardless of whether

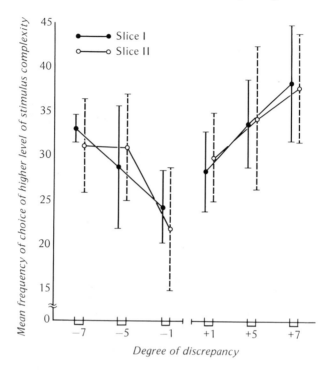

Fig. 11-5. Preference judgments as a function of deviation from adaptation level for stimuli varying on the dimension of complexity. (From Unikel, 1970; reproduced by permission of the American Psychological Association.)

they were *more* or *less* complex than the latter) and a smaller uni-directional effect of preference for higher complexity. Unfortunately, the study seems to lack a control for the effects of novelty: it is not clear to what extent the preference for the new pattern was based on satiation to the particular lights of the adaptation pattern rather than adaptation to a complexity level per se. This point would be particularly critical for those Ss whose adaptation patterns consisted of only one or two lights: since these subjects, given choice stimuli five or seven steps higher in complexity than the adaptation patterns, were responsible for the apparent absolute preference for higher complexity, the latter phenomenon may indeed by attributable to this novelty effect. Nevertheless, the study does show clearly the role of discrepancy from adaptation level as a determinant of a preferential response, and, by inference, the reality of adaptation levels formed with respect to such stimulus attributes as diversity.

The more general principle, that extended exposure to stimuli in a given range of a stimulus dimension will cause a shift in preference for stimuli varying along that scale, has similarly been applied to the dimension of stimulus complexity in research by Tennison (1968), who found that subjects exhibited a much higher degree of interest in a set of pictures rated at a medium complexity level if it had been preceded by a low-complexity series than when it had been preceded by a high-complexity set. An unpublished study by this writer, on the other hand, failed to reveal any shift in the preference function for a series of slides of non-representational modern art, scaled in complexity, following experience in viewing and making judgments of an interpolated set of slides of either high or low complexity.

The negative result just mentioned is plausibly attributable to the role of pre-existing levels of adaptation with respect to stimuli of this kind, against which the very limited experience with the set of adaptation stimuli presented in the laboratory was apparently ineffectual. As Helson (1964) has proposed, adaptation level represents a composite weighted average of all of an individual's prior experience with a given stimulus dimension; thus, although temporally more recent experience may exert a proportionally stronger effect than that which is more remote in time, one should nevertheless expect strongly established adaptation levels to be relatively resistant to alteration through short-term experience in the laboratory.

We know relatively little, finally, of either the formation or modification of adaptation levels with respect to such stimulus attributes as patterning, movement, or meaning, undoubtedly, in part, because of the difficulty of obtaining the kind of precise, reliable scaling of stimuli that would be needed to demonstrate shifts in adaptation level in terms of preference functions or to verify the double-bow shaped curve postulated by McClelland *et al.*

Adaptation as the basis for the optimization function

The preceding brief consideration of adaptation-level phenomena suggests an interesting hypothesis, i.e., that the optimization function stressed at the outset of this chapter as characteristic of preference and arousal measures as related to diverse dimensions of stimulation may, in fact, reflect the influence of adaptation levels established with respect to such dimensions through prior experience. In other words, rather than any particular intermediate value on such a dimension as loudness or complexity being intrinsically most conducive to eliciting arousal or positive affect, the typical inverted-U shaped functions actually observed with respect to these dimensions probably are attributable to the establishment of adaptation levels on the part of the individual. Since adaptation levels are the resultant of the averaging of all relevant prior experience along the given dimension, they would be expected to fall at some modal intermediate value. This interpretation of the basis for the optimization principle is not only of much theoretical consequence, e.g., in relation to such views of arousal as Berlyne's (1967) and Fiske and Maddi's (1961) but, as will be seen presently, of considerable relevance for dealing with differential responses to the conditions of stimulation characterizing particular physical environments. Let us briefly examine, therefore, what evidence may be adduced in its support.

Perhaps the most compelling evidence that could be cited in this regard comes from studies in which preference functions have been analyzed on a per-individual, rather than a per-group basis. This was done, for instance, in Vitz's (1965) study of preference for "random walks" of different lengths and in Dorfman and McKenna's (1966) study of preference for black and white patterns varying in fineness of grain, i.e., informational content. In both of these studies, the group data showed a moderately inverted-U shaped function for the group curves (cf. Fig. 11-6, a and b); when broken up into subsets of individuals grouped according to the most-preferred level of complexity, however, a whole series of differently shaped functions emerged, representing in the aggregate a distribution of optimal preference levels varying all along the continuum and, thus, resulting in progressively more nearly monotonic curves as the extremes are approached (cf. Fig. 11-7, a and b).

The independent isolation of these families of functions by Vitz and Dorfman and McKenna—curiously, at virtually the same time, but utilizing different kinds of stimuli—strongly suggests that differences in individual adaptation levels with respect to the dimension in question are operating here. Admittedly, we know little concerning the origin of these differences; separation of the subjects into art majors and non-art majors proved of only limited relevance in both of these studies. The possibility must even be recognized that factors other than sheer exposure to stimuli in the individual's past experience contribute to the establishment of individual adaptation levels. But this does not detract from the importance to be ascribed to these individual differences in throwing the meaning of the generalized inverted-U function into a new light—nor, it might be

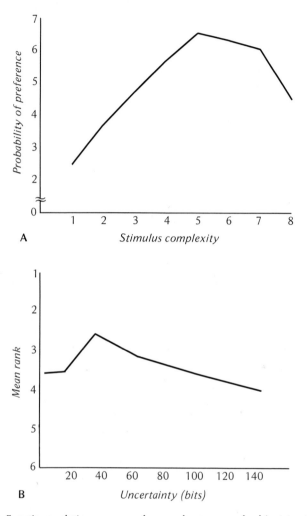

Fig. 11-6. Functions relating mean preference for groups of subject to stimulus complexity or uncertainty. (**A**) Data of Vitz (1966b), based on line-patterns ("random walks") varying in length. (**B**) Data of Dorfman and McKenna (1966) based on matrices of black and white cells varying in density of texture grain. (Reproduced by permission of *Behavioral Science* and the *Canadian Journal of Psychology*.)

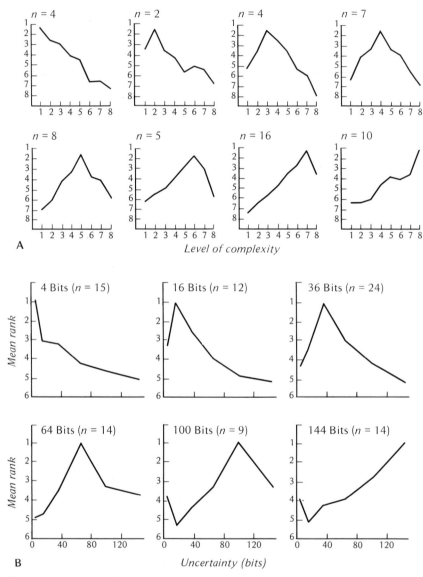

Fig. 11-7. Functions relating preference ranks to stimulus complexity or uncertainty, for subjects grouped according to most preferred level of complexity. (**A**) Data of Vitz (1966b); (**B**) data of Dorfman and McKenna (1966). (Reproduced by permission of *Behavioral Science and the Canadian Journal of Psychology*.)

noted, from the rather embarrassing methodological implications of these findings, since they cast doubt on the validity of functions based on group data in this type of situation.

One objection could be raised here, at least as long as we accept the hypothesis of McClelland *et al.*, embodied in Fig. 11-4, which stipulates that stimuli deviating by a certain amount from the adaptation level should be maximally preferred. The double-bow shaped function of McClelland *et al.* does not appear in any of the individual functions reported by Vitz and Dorfman and McKenna. It is possible, of course, that this function does not apply to a dimension such as stimulus complexity; in fact, for this attribute, Dember and Earl (1957) and Walker (1964) postulate rather a unidirectional effect, such that the most preferred or most actively explored level of stimulus complexity is one that is somewhat *above* the individual's own level, which, for our purposes may be identified with his adaptation level. Any of the functions shown in Fig. 11-7 would be compatible with this view, excepting those peaking at the lowest end of the complexity scale (even these could be explained in conformance with Dember and Earl's view, if we assume that the stimulus series did not span the total effective range of complexity levels that may characterize different individuals).

At the same time (as noted earlier), it must be recognized that verification of the McClelland *et al.* hypothesis requires the presentation of stimuli that are scaled at values spaced closely enough to ensure that peaks at points deviating perhaps only slightly from the subject's own position reveal themselves in the data. This represents a rather severe limitation, given the difficulty of obtaining finely graded series of stimuli (once we move away from such simple dimensions of intensity as temperature, amplitude, brightness, etc.) and of presenting a very large number of such stimuli to a single individual for evaluation.

BEHAVIORAL ADAPTATION TO THE ENVIRONMENT

The experimental evidence from the laboratory on the operation of the optimal-level-of-stimulation principle and its relationship to adaptation-level processes, as reviewed above, has several important implications for the individual's response to stimulation in his physical environment. Let us note two implications that appear to be particularly relevant and then conclude with a few further observations on processes and mechanisms of adaptation of a more qualitative kind.

The determinacy of previous experience

It is apparent from the adaptation-level research that individuals should be expected to respond to a given environment in terms of adaptation levels established in their prior experience with different environments. Some preliminary evidence on this point comes from a pilot investigation carried out by this writer, in collaboration with Imre Kohn (Wohwill and Kohn, 1973), which demonstrates the applicability of adaptation-level principles to complex dimensions of the urban environment, studied under naturalistic conditions. The study compared two groups of migrants with contrasting environments of origin, one from metropolitan areas, the other from small towns or rural areas, with respect to their assessment of various aspects of the community to which they had moved, which represented an urban environment of intermediate size, i.e., that of Harrisburg, Pennsylvania. Roughly one-half of the sample were adults, the other one-half high-school-age adolescents. A set of rating scales was employed to obtain evaluations of that environment with respect to such general-environmental conditions as pollution, noise and crowding, recreational opportunities, shopping facilities, and social conditions. On several of these dimensions, notably those of levels of noise, pollution, and incidence of vandalism and crime, significant differences were obtained in a direction conforming to that predicted by adaptation-level theory—e.g., rural migrants perceived noise and pollution levels as higher than metropolitan migrants. The study is subject to several severe limitations: the samples were very small, and made up disproportionately of Blacks and, in the case of the adults, of females; further, it was not possible to equate the two groups on several characteristics, notably that of age, although the results obtained are not readily attributable to that variable. It is also noteworthy that, in most cases where significant differences were obtained, they were accounted for in large part by the adults in the sample, rather than the adolescents. This result might be interpreted either as due to more firmly established adaptation levels in the older respondents or as due to an actual difference in the *effective* stimulus environments to which the rural adults and the adolescents had become adapted (e.g., high-school children's adaptation to noise might be relatively high, even in rural areas, through exposure to rock music, etc.).

Environmental preference responses should also be subject to the influence of adaptation levels formed in the individual's past experience. More particularly, extrapolating from the hypothesis of McClelland *et al.*

(1953), discussed above, one would predict that individuals will prefer levels of stimulation in their environment falling within close range of levels that predominated in their past and current experience. This seemingly innocuous conclusion—i.e., that we like best what we are most used to—is, in fact, partially borne out by data reported by Sonnenfeld (1967) on landscape preferences among Eskimo natives compared to white non-natives inhabiting different settlements in the Arctic, as well as to college-age whites living in Delaware. What makes this study significant for us is that, as a geographer, Sonnenfeld dealt with such dimensions of the natural terrain as amount of relief, vegetation, and water, as well as warm versus cold climate. These dimensions are, of course, not easily scalable so that Sonnenfeld had to limit himself to dichotomized representation of these dimensions, i.e., a flat terrain paired against a mountainous one, an arid scene paired against one in which water was prominent, etc. His subjects were simply asked to pick the scene from each pair that they preferred as a place to live. For the most part, subjects' preferences were in the direction of the geographic features characterizing their own habitat or, in the case of comparisons between natives and non-natives residing in the same area, their own home location.

Given the dichotomization of the stimulus attributes into high versus low in Sonnenfeld's study, this outcome is in accordance with a very weak form of adaptation-level theory. It is quite possible, in fact, that the considerable number of comparisons for which no significant differences in preferences could be demonstrated reflect cases where the adaptation levels for the two comparison groups on the dimension represented in the pair of slides were not sufficiently different to result in a clear pattern of differential choices. In order to verify this conjecture, one would, of course, need independent measures of the adaptation levels of the individuals in each sample with respect to each of the dimensions, as well as a quantitative scale that would allow one to place the pairs of slides on these same dimensions, so as to enable one to make specific predictions for any given case.

One seeming paradox in the above principle, that we prefer that which we are most used to, derives from the well-established contrary principle, that individuals seek out *change* or variation in their stimulus environment, and, in particular, are attracted to the unfamiliar or novel as opposed to the familiar (cf. Maddi, 1961). One way to resolve this apparent contradiction is to suggest that for purposes of short-term exploratory activity (i.e., vacationing or recreation), we may be biased toward novel stimuli and, thus, to conditions differing from the condition to which we have become adapted; in contrast, it is plausible that choices of permanent residence would prove more strongly dependent on adaptation levels established through extended prior experience. This interpretation is supported by evidence on a closely related distinction, between *interest* (as measured through ratings of "interestingness" or by the amount of time the individual spends voluntarily exploring a stimulus) and *liking* (indexed by ratings of "pleasingness" or degree of liking or comparative preference judgments). Thus, whereas the former typically increase monotonically with stimulus complexity, the latter are much more apt to reveal the type of inverted-U shaped function to which we have pointed repeatedly in this paper (cf. Day, 1967; Wohlwill, 1968). In this connection, is it not reasonable to see in the old saw concerning New York: "A nice place to visit, but I wouldn't want to live there" a recognition of this same differentation?

The range of inter-individual variation in adaptation level

A corollary of the preceding point, linking an individual's preferred level of stimulation to that to which his previous experience has exposed him, is that we can expect individuals to vary over a very wide range in the adaptation levels they will have established with reference to any particular stimulus dimension and, consequently, in their patterns of preference for levels of stimulation, simply on the basis of the tremendous variation in physical conditions that characterize different human habitats. This applies not only to such dimensions as temperature and climate, but to a variety of other attributes, such as the features of the terrain studied by Sonnenfeld. Yet more extreme instances of adaptation are represented by inhabitants of the desert (cf. Zubek, 1969, pp. 326ff). Of particular interest in this connection are two studies of sensory deprivation. The first by Gendreau *et al.* (1968) was carried out with prison inmates as subjects. Not only did these individuals appear to be able to tolerate a 7-day period of solitary confinement, under conditions of sharply reduced background illumination and auditory stimulation, without difficulty (i.e., without the typical incidence of subjects in this type of experiment who demand early release), but the experience served to reduce still further their adaptation level with respect to brightness stimulation as shown in the marked drop in their preferred level of background illumination from a base-level measure to one taken upon termination of the exposure period.

The second study by Haggard, Ås, and Borgen (1970) demonstrated more directly the influence of previously established adaptation levels on the individual's response to conditions of sensory deprivation. These investigators brought a group of young men from the northern regions of Norway, who had been living in virtual isolation as hermits, to their laboratory in Oslo to be subjects in a standard sensory deprivation experiment and compared their responses to a group of control subjects from Oslo. On a variety of responses, mostly measures of personality, the hermit group showed significantly less severe reactions than the control group.

We should not, of course, assume that adaptation to such (to us) extreme stimulus conditions is ever complete and uninfluenced by absolute levels. It is unlikely that temperatures of $-40°$ C are experienced as pleasurable even to the native Alaskan, or that the commuter comes to relish the conditions of congestion, of crawling traffic, etc., in the city at rush hour. The evidence, and the postulates derived from adaptation-level theory do indicate, however, that there is at least a neutralization of the negative affect that is evoked by these conditions in those who have been exposed to them, as well as a shift in the preference function, such that the optimal preferred level of stimulation remains displaced away from the norm and toward the extreme represented in the exposure conditions.

The process of adaptation

Up to this point we have treated behavioral adaptation to the environment as an essentially passive process, consequent upon mere exposure to a given stimulus condition. But this is, undoubtedly, an oversimplified view of the matter, even with respect to variables of physical stimulation (as opposed to inter-personal or social conditions), and even for adaptation proper, as opposed to responses of adjustment, i.e., behaviors available to the individual that effect an actual change in the stimulus conditions impinging on him. What, then, are some of the mechanisms the individual has at his disposal to facilitate his adaptation to a potentially unpleasant or noxious stimulus environment?

We have little direct evidence on this question, but Miller (1960) has suggested a number of such mechanisms in his systems-theoretical treatment of the problem of *information* overload, i.e., of the overtaxing of a system's power to process information required for a particular purpose. One of Miller's mechanisms, that of *filtering*, is of obvious relevance to the individual's adaptation to environmental stimulus conditions. This term refers to a person's tendency to process only a portion of the stimulus input impinging on him and to reject, i.e., shut out from awareness, the remainder. This mechanism cannot readily be applied to such primary stimulus dimensions as temperature, loudness, and the like, but it does apply to such higher-order variables of stimulation as complexity (e.g., in the sense of diversity), density of people, or to any other aspect of the stimulus environment that can be described in terms of quantities of discrete elements, creating an opportunity for selection or tuning-out to occur.

This mechanism of filtering is undoubtedly of great importance in adaptation to conditions of sensory overload, such as may be presumed to exist in our major urban centers. It demands a definite price, however, since it impairs the individual's ability to respond to information that may, in fact, be of relevance for him. Thus, it has been suggested that a possible contributing factor to the retardation in language development commonly found among "culturally deprived" children may be attributable to the overdose of visual and auditory stimuli, both verbal and nonverbal, with which they are bombarded at all hours of the day—from the TV screen, the ever-present horde of brothers and sisters, the neighbors brawling at close range, the human and vehicular traffic on the street below.

Milgram (1970) has presented a persuasive analysis of a particular aspect of this problem, i.e., of adaptation to overload in our urban environment, which results from the concentration of people. He cites a variety of mechanisms individuals may resort to in adapting to this condition, all of which have the effect of warding off some of the information originating in social stimuli or reducing their impact on the person. These mechanisms take such forms as a deliberate tuning-out of signals emanating from certain classes of people perceived as "strangers," of restricting communication with those known to the individual (e.g., by using an unlisted telephone number), and of reducing contacts with other individuals to a minimum level of personal involvement. This analysis is applied to such phenomena of urban life, confirmed by empirical data, as the reluctance to give assistance or information to strangers and similar manifestations of a weakened sense of social responsibility (e.g., the value placed on anonymity). In this case, it is apparent that this form of adaptation is, in part, at the expense of those individuals with whom the individual comes into contact and, in a larger sense, of his society. Yet there is a price to the individual, as well, in the form not only of a restricted range of social experiences, but of behavioral consequences such as the residue of tension or irritability that may result from repeated avoidance responses to other persons.

It should be noted that sheer numbers of people—i.e., intensity of potential overload deriving from the presence of people in large numbers in our big cities—is not the only determining factor in this type of adaptation syndrome; the perception of the possibility of danger or harm to the person undoubtedly contributes to the suspicion and distrust toward strangers, and there are other related cultural factors involved.[3] Milgram has recognized this point in the comparisons he makes between diverse American and European cities, utilizing both impressionistic evidence and data from empirical studies. Nevertheless, the suggestion that overload in the form of an excess of social stimulation forces the individual to disregard, tune-out, or avoid information from other persons, in order to keep from being overwhelmed by the concentrated dosages of it that he would otherwise be exposed to, does appear to be pertinent in considering the psychological stressors associated with urban life.

The cost of adaptation

The concept of the *cost* to the individual of adapting to particular environmental circumstances has been stressed by biologists, notably René Dubos, as basic to the understanding of disease. It has received less systematic attention on the part of psychologists, except perhaps those involved in work on psychosomatic illness. There is at least one set of studies, however, that deserves to be cited on this point, since it not only provides convincing experimental evidence, under carefully controlled laboratory conditions, of the reality of adaptation to a noxious stimulus, but also raises, in an interesting fashion, the question of the "psychic cost of adaptation"—an expression taken from the title of the report of this research. This is the work of Glass and his associates (Glass, Singer, and Friedman, 1969; Glass and Singer, 1972) of individuals' adaptation to noise.

Since this work is presented more fully in the chapter by Glass in this volume, we will limit ourselves to a brief reference to it. Glass *et al.* found

3 Evidence relevant to this point may be found in Milgram's own study, in the not too surprising finding that in both urban and small-town residences, people were much more ready to admit the female experimenters into their home for the alleged purpose of using the telephone than the male experimenters.

evidence, both at the physiological and the behavioral level, for adaptation to a situation in which subjects had to work at an arithmetic task while exposed to bursts of intermittent noise. Yet, on two post-test measures of resistance to frustration, as well as on a proofreading task, there was clear evidence that for the group originally exposed to unpredictable noise this exposure had left a residual effect, manifested in lower task performance and reduced frustration-tolerance. As Glass points out in his chapter, this evidence leaves in abeyance the question whether this residual effect does indeed represent the "price" of the adaptation that had occurred, i.e., whether it took place *because of* or *despite* the adaptation during the original exposure period. Glass cites subsequent evidence that appears to point rather to the latter alternative, but, at this point, the possibility of adaptation itself exacting a toll from the individual, as Dubos argues is the case in the realm of physiological processes, cannot be lightly dismissed, particularly for long-term adaptation.

There is a closely related source of ambiguity in the research of Glass, Singer *et al.* (1969). We do not know to what extent either the GSR data or the post-adaptation measures are to be attributed to the effort exerted by the subject to cope with the disruption by the noise of his performance on the arithmetic task, as opposed to the mere exposure to the aversive noise. In other words, if the subjects had had no task to perform, would they have adapted (i.e., at the physiological level) to the noise? And would there have been any residual effect?

This question is of some importance in research on the effects of the physical environment, since it is quite conceivable that the effects, not only of such aversive stimuli as noise in our environment, but of overstimulation may depend on the extent to which the stimulus conditions interfere with or disrupt some ongoing activity by the subject. Thus, a visitor to a busy factory, airport, or other environment replete with intense, diverse, and unpatterned stimulation may fail to respond aversively to it, and may even find fascination in watching it, whereas the person who is performing a job demanding concentration under these conditions may experience a much greater degree of stress. This point may underlie the predominantly negative results found by such investigators as Zuckerman *et al.* (1970), in investigating the effects of overstimulation. Thus, in the study being referred to, an 8-hour period of exposure to a remarkable conglomeration of visual and auditory stimulation of all kinds failed to exert any very marked effects on a variety of behavioral measures; indeed, the subjects rated their experience in predominantly favorable terms. A variety of physiological effects of exposure to overstimulation were, however, found; interestingly enough, these effects were, in several instances, comparable to those encountered as a result of sensory *deprivation* for an equivalent period of time. Perhaps we see here a manifestation of the aptness of the bi-polar sensoristasis model for looking at hyper- and hypostimulation to which we referred at the beginning of this chapter.

At the same time, we find at least one piece of evidence of the individual's ability to withstand even fairly drastic conditions of interfering visual and auditory stimulation while maintaining an almost unimpaired performance at a mental task. This comes from a study of Hovey (1928), which is noteworthy for having brought together what is undoubtedly the most bizarre collection of sounds and sights ever assembled for a psychological experiment, including bells, buzzers, a 5500-W spotlight, a 90,000-V rotary spark gap, a phonograph playing "Mary Lou" and "Petrushka," two organ pipes, three metal whistles, a 55-lb circular saw, several students performing stunts, and a photographer taking pictures of the proceedings! One might have thought that amid the din and chaos prevailing under the conditions of this experiment, the individual's ability to take an intelligence test, such as the Army Alpha, could not fail to be severely impaired, yet Hovey's results indicate that the effect was rather slight; indeed, the experimental group's mean score was actually higher under this condition than under a preceding base-line control condition. Although this improvement is in part attributable to the effects of practice, as revealed by a control group who took both tests under no-interference conditions, it still provides testimony to the remarkable capacity of the individual to tune-out interfering stimuli when the task demands it. There was only a slight suggestion that a certain toll may have been exacted from the subject in the process, in Hovey's incidental report that two of his 171 subjects—both of them female—broke down *after* the experiment into violent crying fits; possibly on a post-test measure such as Glass's, rather more pervasive aftereffects of this experience would have been found.

Conceivably, then, it is only when we are dealing with information rather than sensory overload—to revive the distinction offered in an earlier section—i.e., where the individual has to respond differentially to overlapping or competing channels of stimulation, that a major breakdown in performance will be registered. Miller's (1960) study of this phenomenon, referred to above in connection with the concept of filtering, is illustrative of the all too limited evidence we have on this point and the mechanisms utilized by the individual to cope with this kind of overload.

CONCLUSION

To conclude this overview of behavioral adaptation to environmental stimulation, it is appropriate that we try to place the problem of adaptation in a somewhat broader perspective, by considering it from a functional point of view and relating it to alternative mechanisms available to the individual to cope with potential or actual environmental stressors. More specifically, we will address ourselves to two interrelated questions: First, How adaptive is adaptation? And second, What are the pros and cons of adaptation, as compared to adjustment, as mechanisms for dealing with unpleasant or harmful environmental conditions? Although these questions are, at present, more in the realm of speculation and individual opinion than empirical fact, they are of sufficient importance from both a theoretical and a practical standpoint to warrant being raised, however briefly; we hope that presenting them in sharpened form will provide the impetus for a more systematic empirical attack on them.

As regards the first question, the adaptive value of adaptation to our stimulus environment, in the sense that we have discussed it, while far from being a matter of tautology, still might hardly seem subject to doubt. The individual cannot afford to respond continually to stimuli or aspects of his milieu of stimulation that are a constant feature of his environment (or nearly so) with the intensity or magnitude of affective arousal he exhibits on his initial confrontation with that environment. It is essential, in other words, that neutralization of affect occur, at least with respect to negatively experienced aspects of the stimulus environment over which the individual cannot exert any control.

At the same time it is apparent that such a neutralization or habituation process can be considered adaptive in a functional sense only as long as no undue price is exacted from the individual for resorting to it. We have already discussed the subject of the price of adaptation, but the problem in the functional sense is basically one of long-term effects of adaptation to environmental stressors confronting an individual over an extended period of time; on this point our knowledge is very limited as yet, particularly at the behavioral level, although we do have more evidence on prolonged adaptation of bodily functions to such extreme environmental conditions as life at high altitudes (Baker, 1969), as well as environmental insults of various sorts (e.g., Dubos, 1965).

From an evolutionary perspective, this problem is of relatively recent origin. We may take it for granted that until the advent of technology, with its pervasive and far-reaching alteration of the human environment, human beings, and human societies of the more recent historical past, were fairly well fitted to their habitats, and there were relatively few sources of chronic environmental stress that placed heavy demands on the individual's adaptation processes. Presumably where extremes of temperature, altitude, etc., did impose an undue burden on the adaptive capacities of the individual, human life would either have eventually vanished from those areas or selection would have produced a type of individual better able to withstand those conditions.

Technology has brought about two kinds of changes, which, curiously, operate in opposite directions. On the one hand, it has brought about a vast array of new types and sources of environmental stressors placing an increasingly heavy burden on the individual's capacity for psychological and biological adaptation—to conditions of noise, crowding, congestion, pollution, and other forms of environmental degradation and insult; to externally imposed alterations of the diurnal cycle, to life under highly artificial conditions and in such highly unusual environments as those of Sealab and the space capsule. At the same time, technology has provided us with an alternative to adaptation, which is being resorted to increasingly to reduce the extent or severity of the individual's exposure to environmental stressors—through central heating, air conditioning, and soundproofing in our homes and places of work, through the private automobile, which has reduced our exposure to the elements while in transit, and in various other ways, some of which are being devised to deal specifically with some of the newly created noxious stimuli in our environment. Furthermore, technology, as well as affluence, has increased our ability to avoid or escape from such environmental conditions, as evidenced in the flight to the suburbs and the boom in the summer-home business.

We are, in short, constantly confronted with the choice between adapting to environmental circumstances or resorting to a response of adjustment, whether by altering the environmental stimuli directly or avoiding or escaping from them. In introducing the topic of adaptation, we referred to this distinction of Sonnenfeld's (1966) between adaptation and adjustment, which is not only of great conceptual and theoretical importance but has far-reaching practical implications.

Sonnenfeld himself has argued provocatively that we have given insufficient recognition to adaptation as a mechanism for dealing with stimulation from the environment that deviates in some way from an individual's ideal and that, to this extent, the need for changing the environment to eliminate such stimuli and to create an aesthetically more satisfying one may have been overstressed. In contrast, Dubos (1965) among others, although less concerned with meeting individual preferences in regard to environmental aesthetics, and more with providing a satisfying milieu for all human beings, in conformance with the humanistic values he has so eloquently stressed (Dubos, 1968), has argued just as forcefully that we may be relying unduly on our capacity to adapt:

> Millions upon millions of human beings are so well adjusted to the urban and industrial environment that they no longer mind the stench of automobile exhausts, or the ugliness generated by the urban sprawl; they regard it as normal to be trapped in automobile traffic, to spend much of a sunny afternoon on concrete highways among the dreariness of anonymous and amorphous streams of motor cars. Life in the modern city has become a symbol of the fact that man can become adapted to starless skies, treeless avenues, shapeless buildings, tasteless bread, joyless celebrations, spiritless pleasures—to a life without reverence for the past, love for the present, or hope for the future.[pp. 278ff.]

It is impossible within the context of this chapter to do justice to this intricate problem, however great its importance and interest and however deserving of searching examination on the part of all who are concerned over the human condition. It is not only an issue of extreme complexity, from a cost-benefit point of view, but ultimately one that raises difficult questions of value, both personal and societal, which must be answered if one is to arrive at a rational decision as to the relative emphasis to be given to these alternative mechanisms. Within the framework of the present analysis, however, it is appropriate to raise two questions a complete account of the nature, purpose, and limitations of behavioral adaptation must face up to.

The first is whether the human's vaunted capacity for adaptation is itself subject to the role of experience, in this sense: Will an individual who has had no or only limited exposure to circumstances requiring adaptation be able to adapt as readily when confronted with a situation demanding it as someone who has had extensive exposure to a broad range of stimuli varying along some dimension? If we conceive of adaptation as an active process, and if we consider further that every change in level of stimulation calls this process into play to some degree, it is not altogether implausible to suggest that this process might conform to some "law of disuse" such that its effectiveness might be impaired following an extensive period during which the individual has minimized his exposure to any change in level of stimulation.

There is a somewhat different way of looking at this problem. If we try to analyze it in adaptation-level terms, we might look at the question as a matter of the *variability* of stimuli and its role in determining the slope of the adaptation-level function. More particularly, one might hypothesize that variability would be a parameter influencing the range of stimuli over which the change from neutral to positive to negative suggested by the McClelland *et al.* curve (Fig. 11-4) occurs—i.e., an individual whose AL has been established on the basis of a rather narrow range of stimuli would tolerate smaller discrepancies from his AL than someone who had been exposed to a greater diversity of stimuli. There appears, however, to be little empirical evidence available on this question.

The second question is a more basic one. It is suggested by Glass's findings that adaptation appears to take place differentially at different behavioral levels. In his own research there was clear evidence of adaptation at the physiological as well as task-performance level, but, at the same time, the post-test measures revealed marked residual effects of the original stressor stimuli on measures of persistence of behavior, as well as attentional efficiency. The relevance of this question in the present context is that an individual's decision as to whether to adapt or to effect an overt adjustment in his environment is apt to be based on considerations of his own subjective experience of satisfaction or comfort, as well as, of course, on the opportunities available to him for resorting to adjustment, in terms of cost, feasibility, etc. The consequence may be that where the individual is able to neutralize negative aspects of a stimulus environment in terms of his own subjective experience or awareness, he will see little necessity for adjusting his environment even though, at other levels, adaptation may be far from complete or bought at a high price. Conversely, a situation experienced as uncomfortable may create demands for adjustive mechanisms, whether through technology or avoidance behavior, even though in terms of efficiency of behavioral functioning or physiological health the situation is not particularly stressful. There is, thus, the possibility that we may be too readily tempted to resort to adjustment when it is relatively unnecessary and when it may place a heavy burden on our technological resources or our societal institutions, whereas, at the same time, we are content to adapt to situations that are, in fact, harmful. Thus, we demand air conditioning, where a few decades ago we were content to swelter in discomfort; at the same time we "put up with" the stresses of daily commuting to work through heavy traffic, even though, as the case of the San Francisco newspaper man cited at the start of this chapter indicates, there may be little if any adaptation occurring to these stresses at the physiological level—nor should we expect it to occur, since it is obviously dysfunctional to adapt to potentially dangerous situations.

The discussion of these questions just given, without providing any answers, should serve to bring out the complexity of adaptation as a multilevel problem, and the importance of considering a combination of criteria, both physiological and behavioral, in assessing the effects of environmental stress on the individual and his capacities to adapt to them. It is possible that our behavioral conception of adaptation, particularly under the influence of adaptation-level theory, has remained too exclusively focused on perceptual and affective judgment, leading up perhaps to a too facile relativism in our conception of the effects of environmental stimulation on personal satisfaction and well-being. Only by extending both the range of behavioral and physiological variables employed in our study of adaptation and the time scale over which the problem is investigated can we hope to arrive at a more adequate functional understanding of the virtues, as well as the limitations, of adaptation and of the role to be accorded it in our efforts to arrive at a healthier environment for human activity.

REFERENCES

Appley, M. (ed.). 1971. *Adaptation-Level Theory: A Symposium*. New York: Academic Press.
— Baker, P. T. 1969. Human adaptation to high altitude. *Science* 163:1149-56.
Berlyne, D. E. 1960. *Conflict, Arousal and Curiosity*. New York: McGraw-Hill.
Berlyne, D. E. 1967. Arousal and reinforcement. *Nebraska Symp. Motivation* 12:1-110.
Calhoun, J. B. 1962. Population density and social pathology. *Sci. Amer.* 206: 139-48.
Day, H. 1967. Evaluation of subjective complexity, pleasingness and interestingness for a series of random polygons varying in complexity. *Percept. & Psychophys.* 2:281-86.
Dember, W. N. and R. W. Earl. 1957. Analysis of exploratory, manipulatory, and curiosity behavior. *Psychol. Rev.* 64:91-96.
Dorfman, D. D. and H. McKenna. 1966. Pattern preference as a function of pattern uncertainty. *Can. J. Psychol.* 20:143-53.
Dubos, R. 1965. *Man Adapting*. New Haven: Yale University Press.
Dubos, R. 1968. *So Human an Animal*. New York: Scribners.

Fiske, D. W. and S. R. Maddi. 1961. A conceptual framework. In *Functions of Varied Experience*, eds. D. W. Fiske and S. R. Maddi. Homewood, Ill.: Dorsey Press, pp. 11-56.

Gendreau, P. E., N. Freedman, G. J. S. Wilde, and G. D. Scott. 1968. Stimulation seeking after seven days of perceptual deprivation. *Percept. and Mot. Skills* 26:547-50.

Glass, D. C. and J. E. Singer. 1972. *Urban Stress: Experiments on Noise and Social Stressors*. New York: Academic Press.

Glass, D. C., J. E. Singer, and L. N. Friedman. 1969. Psychic cost of adaptation to an environment stressor. *J. Person. Soc. Psychol.* 12:200-10.

Gunderson, E. K. 1968. Mental health problems in Antarctica. *Arch. Environ. Hlth.* 17:558-64.

Haber, R. N. 1958. Discrepancy from adaptation level as a source of affect. *J. Exptl. Psychol.* 56:370-75.

Haggard, E. A., A. Ås, and C. M. Borgen. 1970. Social isolates and urbanites in perceptual isolation. *J. Abnorm. Psychol.* 76:1-9.

Hebb, D. O. 1949. *The Organization of Behavior*. New York: Wiley.

Heckhausen, H. 1964. Complexity in perception: Phenomenal criteria and information theoretic calculus—A note on D. E. Berlyne's "complexity effects." *Can. J. Psychol.* 18:168-73.

Helson, H. 1964. *Adaptation-Level Theory*. New York: Harper & Row.

Holm, K. G. 1903. Dauer Temperaturempfindungen. *Skand. Arch. f. Physiol.* 14:242.

Hovey, H. B. 1928. Effects of general distraction on the higher thought processes. *Amer. J. Psychol.* 40:585-91.

Lee, D. H. K. 1966. The role of attitude in response to environmental stress. *J. Soc. Issues* 22:83-91.

Lindsley, D. B. 1961. Common factors in sensory deprivation, sensory distortion, and sensory overload. In *Sensory Deprivation*, eds. P. Solomon *et al.*, Cambridge: Harvard University Press, pp. 174-194.

Lynch, K. 1960. *The Image of the City*. Cambridge: MIT Press.

Maddi, S. R. 1961. Exploratory behavior and variation-seeking in man. In *Functions of Varied Experience*, eds. D. W. Fiske and S. R. Maddi. Homewood, Ill.: Dorsey Press, pp. 253-77.

Meyer, L. B. 1956. *Emotion and Meaning in Music*. Chicago: University of Chicago Press.

Lawick-Goodall, J. V. 1967. *My Friends the Wild Chimpanzees*. Washington, D.C.: National Geographic Society.

McClelland, D. C., J. W. Atkinson, R. A. Clark, and E. L. Lowell. 1953. *The Achievement Motive*. New York: Appleton-Century.

Milgram, S. 1970. The experience of living in cities. *Science* 167:1461-68.

Miller, J. G. 1960. Information input overload and psychopathology. *Amer. J. Psychiat.* 116:695-704.

Munsinger, H. and W. Kessen. 1964. Uncertainty, structure and preference. *Psychol. Monogr.* 78:#9 (Whole #586).

Nelson, P. D. 1965. Psychological aspects of Antarctic living. *Military Med.* 130:485-89.

Osgood, C. E. 1953. *Method and Theory in Experimental Psychology*. Urbana, Ill.: University of Illinois Press.

Rapoport, A. and R. Hawkes. 1970. The perception of urban complexity. *J. Amer. Inst. Planners* 36:106-11.

Schultz, D. P. 1965. *Sensory Restriction: Effects on Behavior.* New York: Academic Press.

Simon, C. and J. F. Wohlwill. 1968. An experimental study of the role of expectation and variation in music. *J. Res. Mus. Educ.* 16:227-38.

Smock, C. D. and B. G. Holt. 1962. Children's reactions to novelty: An experimental study of "curiosity motivation." *Child Devel.* 33:631-42.

Sonnenfeld, J. 1966. Variable values in space landscape: An inquiry into the nature of environmental necessity. *J. Soc. Issues* 22:71-82.

Sonnenfeld, J. 1967. Environmental perception and adaptation level in the Arctic. In *Environmental Perception and Behavior,* ed. D. Lowenthal. (Dept. of Geography, *Research Paper* #109). Chicago: University of Chicago Press, pp. 42-59.

Tennison, J. C. 1968. Duration of visual attention as a function of an adaptation to stimulus complexity. Unpublished Ph.D. Thesis. Ohio University.

Terwilliger, R. F. 1963. Pattern complexity and affective arousal. *Percept. & Mot. Skills* 17:387-95.

Thomas, H. 1966. Preferences for random shapes: Ages six through nineteen years. *Child Develop.* 37:343-59.

Unikel, I. P. 1971. Effects of changes in stimulation upon preference for stimulus complexity. *J. Exper. Psychol.* 88:246-50.

University of California. n. d. *Man under Stress: California and the Challenge of Growth* (Conference VII). San Francisco: n. p.

Vernon, J. 1963. *Inside the Black Room.* New York: Potter.

Vitz, P. C. 1966a. Affect as a function of stimulus variation. *J. Exptl. Psychol.* 71:74-79.

Vitz, P. C. 1966b. Preference for different amounts of visual complexity. *Behav. Sci.* 11:105-14.

Walker, E. L. 1964. Psychological complexity as a theory of motivation and choice. *Nebraska Symp. Motivation* 12:47-95.

Wohlwill, J. F. 1968. Amount of stimulus exploration and preference as differential functions of stimulus complexity. *Percept. & Psychophys.* 4:307-12.

Wohlwill, J. F. 1975. Children's response to meaningful pictures varying in diversity: Exploration time vs. preference. *J. Exp. Child Psychol.* (in press).

Wohlwill, J. F. and I. Kohn. 1973. The environment as perceived by the migrant: An adaptation-level view. *Repres. Res. in Soc. Psychol.* 4:135-64.

Zlutnick, S. and I. Altman. 1972. Crowding and human behavior. In *Environment and the Social Sciences: Perspectives and Applications,* eds. J. F. Wohlwill and D. H. Carson. Washington, D.C.: American Psychological Association, pp. 44-58.

Zubek, J. P. (ed.). 1969. *Sensory Deprivation: Fifteen Years of Research.* New York: Appleton-Century-Crofts.

Zuckerman, M., H. Persky, T. R. Hopkins, T. Murtaugh, G. K. Basu, and M. Schilling. 1966. Comparison of stress effects of perceptual and social isolation. *Arch. gen. Psychiat.* 14:356-65.

Zuckerman, M., H. Persky, L. Miller, and B. Levin. 1970. Sensory deprivation versus sensory variation. *J. abnorm. Psychol.* 76:76-82.

12. Effects of Noise on Human Performance

DAVID C. GLASS*

JEROME E. SINGER**

Several years ago, we happened to read the following account in a *Fortune* magazine article:

> In the Bronx borough of New York City one evening last spring, four boys were at play, shouting and racing in and out of an apartment building. Suddenly, from a second-floor window, came the crack of a pistol. One of the boys sprawled dead on the pavement. . . . The killer . . . confessed to police that he was a night worker who had lost control of himself because the noise from the boys prevented him from sleeping (Mecklin, 1969)

This incident may be an extreme example of the impact of noise on man, but it does highlight potential consequences of the increasing deterioration of our "sound environment." The research we reported in this chapter[1] does not attempt to document such dramatic effects; rather, it is confined to an examination of the influence of noise and related stressors on more mundane behavioral and psychophysiological processes. And even these effects are difficult to demonstrate, for, in time, people simply

* Department of Psychology, The University of Texas, Austin, Texas.
** Department of Sociology, The State University of New York, Stony Brook, New York.

1 The research discussed in this paper was supported by the National Science Foundation (GS-2405 and GS-2412) and the Russell Sage Foundation. Modified versions of the paper appeared in the *American Scientist*, July-August, 1972, and *Representative Research in Social Psychology*, 1973, 4, 165-183.

learn to ignore noise. The proposition that man is adaptable, however, has an important corollary; namely, man pays a price for adaptation that is observable in behavior (Selye, 1956; Dubos, 1965; Wohlwill, 1970).

Our research was initially undertaken as a test of the hypothesis that adaptation is costly to the organism. But, as we shall see later, the results suggest a somewhat different interpretation. The original idea was to allow subjects to adapt to repeatedly presented high-intensity sound and then to determine whether the process of adaptation or habituation left subjects less able to cope with subsequent environmental demands. [We use the terms habituation and adaptation interchangeably throughout this paper; the convention is adopted with full knowledge that not all forms of adaptation necessarily involve the same basic processes (cf. Thompson and Spencer, 1966; Lazarus, 1968).]

The basic notion was that mental effort entailed in the adaptive process affects subsequent behavior adversely. Following Lazarus (e.g., 1968), we assumed that adaptation is a cognitive process, involving re-evaluation of the noise stressor as benign or the use of more direct action strategies for coping with noise—e.g., "filtering" noise out of awareness by becoming engrossed in some task. We did not attempt to measure various adaptive strategies; instead, we assumed that subjects would use one or another strategy, resulting in a decrement of autonomic response to noise. This decrement was, in effect, our principal index of adaptation.

NOISE AND TASK PERFORMANCE

Before describing behavioral aftereffects of noise adaptation, we will first consider noise effects occurring during the process of acoustic stimulation. Noise may be defined as any sound that is physiologically arousing and stressful, subjectively annoying, or disruptive of performance (Anastasi, 1964). But do we have any evidence that noise is, in fact, a stressor with measurable consequences resulting from its repeated application? There are dozens of newspaper accounts and magazine stories that suggest an affirmative answer. Psychoacousticians, however, are not at all convinced that noise has deleterious effects on man. Comprehensive reviews of systematic research on noise (e.g., Broadbent, 1957; Kryter, 1970) conclude that there is no compelling evidence of adverse effects of high-intensity noise per se on human task performance. Laboratory-produced noise does not affect a subject's ability to do mental and psychomotor tasks ranging from the boringly simple to the interesting and challenging. Other than as a damaging agent to the ear, or as a source of interference with tasks requiring communication, or an indirect effect from interference with sleep and, thus, lowered task efficiency, noise does not seem to impair human performance.

Data from our own research provide support for this conclusion. On relatively simple mental tasks—arithmetic addition, number comparison, verbal skills—there appears to be little evidence of task impairment during noise stimulation, even when sound approaches levels of 110 dbA. (The abbreviation dbA refers to the decibel measurement made on the A-scale of a sound-level meter, where higher frequencies are weighted more heavily because they are more annoying to the human ear. A sound of 110 dbA is about what one would hear if one were operating a riveting machine.) We have tested well over 200 subjects in our laboratories, and a typical set of results is presented in Table 12-1. The test—number comparison—required

Table 12-1   *Average number of errors on Part 1 and average decrements in errors from Part 1 to Part 2 of the number comparison test*

	Experimental Condition		
	Loud noise (108 dbA) (n = 18)	Soft noise (56 dbA) (n = 20)	No noise (control) (n = 10)
Part 1 errors	3.28	3.30	2.80
Decrement in errors from Part 1 to Part 2	−1.85	−1.48	−0.20

the subject to indicate whether successive sets of multiple digits were the same or different (French *et al.*, 1963). There are obviously no differences in average number of errors between noise conditions during the first part of the testing session (about 12 minutes), but the errors that do appear tend to decline during the second 12-minute period. We interpret these decrements in number of errors as behavioral evidence of noise adaptation. As we shall see later, physiological indicators of adaptation were also obtained in these studies.

Our research has customarily used broad-band noise consisting of a specially prepared tape recording of the following sounds superimposed upon one another: (a) two people speaking Spanish; (b) one person speaking Armenian; (c) a mimeograph machine; (d) a desk calculator; (e) a typewriter. We selected this particular concatenation of sounds as an analogue of the spectrum of complex noise often present in the urban environment. A sound-spectrographic analysis of the noise recording showed that energy did indeed range broadly from 500 Hz to 7000 Hz, with the mode at about 700 Hz. Free field stimulation was used throughout most of the research, with the noise delivered over a speaker mounted on the wall directly behind the seated subject.

We have suggested that noise per se has minimal effects on task performance. There are, however, several exceptions to this generalization. In particular, performance is impaired when (a) long-term vigilance demands are placed on the subject; (b) the task is otherwise complex; (c) noise is intermittent. Evidence for vigilance-task impairments has been extensively documented elsewhere (e.g., Broadbent, 1971) and does not need to be repeated at this time. Evidence of intermittency effects has also been reported by other investigators (Broadbent, 1957), but a word or two is needed here. Briefly, this research has shown that intermittent noise is experienced as more aversive than continuous noise, and, if the intermittency is aperiodic (i.e., unpredictable), felt aversiveness is still greater. Other studies have reported corresponding effects for task efficiency; for example, aperiodic noise degrades performance more than does continuous or periodic noise (e.g., Sanders, 1961). The tasks used in most of this research were relatively simple verbal and numerical tests.

We have not been able to replicate the aperiodicity effect in our own laboratories. Our results for periodic and aperiodic noise, on tasks like number comparison and addition, are presented in Table 12-2. It is clear

Table 12-2   *Average number of errors on Part 1 and average decrements in errors from Part 1 to Part 2 of the addition test*

	Experimental Condition		
	Aperiodic noise ($n = 18$)	Periodic noise ($n = 20$)	No noise (control) ($n = 10$)
Part 1 errors	5.28	5.76	2.20
Decrement in errors from Part 1 to Part 2	−0.54	−1.78	⊢0.08

from even casual examination of the table that aperiodic noise does not produce more task deficits than periodic noise, even when both are at 108 dbA levels of intensity. It should also be noted that unsignaled noise does not result in greater performance errors than signaled noise. Signaling and periodicity are each a form of predictability, and we have studied the influence of both variables in our research.

Although unpredictable noise does not degrade *simple* task performance, it does exert a greater impact on *complex* task performance than predictable noise. In two of our experiments, deterioration of performance was observed if excessive demands were placed on the subject's information-processing capacities—as when he was working on two tasks simultaneously or maintaining continual vigilance on a tracking task (Finkleman and Glass, 1970; Glass and Singer, 1972). It would appear that unpredictable noise directly affects performance only when the subject is working at maximum capacity.

There is one general consistency in these exceptions to the earlier conclusion that noise itself does not have adverse effects on performance. All three exceptions appear to reflect the operation, not of noise alone, but of noise mediated by cognitive processes. Two are presumably situations in which the organism becomes overloaded; that is, task inputs are so numerous that they inhibit adequate information processing, and noise becomes still another input for the organism to monitor. The noise continually overloads the subject and, in such situations, produces performance deficits that do not wane with repeated exposure. The deleterious effects of aperiodic noise probably reflect the fact that unpredictable stressors have a more aversive impact on behavior than predictable stressors (e.g., Berlyne, 1960). These observations underscore the importance of cognitive factors in mediating the effects of noise on behavior. For unpredictability is an extra-stimulus variable, and task complexity and vigilance may be viewed as instances of cognitive overload.

AFTEREFFECTS OF UNPREDICTABLE NOISE

At the outset, we stated that the principal rationale for our research was the notion that adaptation to noise results in adverse behavioral aftereffects. Our implicit assumption has been that the individual expends "psychic energy" in the course of the adaptive process, and this leaves him less able to cope with subsequent environmental demands and frustrations (cf. Selye, 1956). Since there is some evidence to suggest that unpredictable noise is more aversive than predictable noise, we anticipated that adaptation to the former type of stimulation would be more costly to the individual. Specifically, we hypothesized that unpredictable noise, in contrast to predictable noise, would lead to greater reductions in tolerance for post-noise frustration and greater impairments of performance on a task requiring care and attention.

The prototypic procedure used to test this hypothesis is as follows. Upon entering the laboratory, the subject was told that the purpose of the study was to investigate "the effects of noise levels on task performance and physiological processes." The use of skin electrodes was then explained, and leads were attached to the subject's fingers and arm. After a brief resting period, the experimenter outlined the tasks the subject would be working on during noise exposure—usually verbal and numerical tests.

Following the task instructions, the noise session proper began. Sound was delivered intermittently—at either random or fixed intervals—throughout a 23-, 24-, or 25-minute period, depending on the particular experiment being conducted. In fixed or predictable conditions, the noise was presented at the end of every minute for about 9 seconds. In random, or unpredictable, conditions, delivery of noise was randomized with respect to both length of the bursts and intervals between them. In some studies, the intensity of each type of noise was varied so that one-half the subjects in the unpredictable and predictable conditions heard 108 dbA sound, whereas the other one-half heard 56 dbA sound. The total time of exposure was identical in all conditions—about 3.5 to 5 minutes, depending on the particular study. Following termination of the noise, the experimenter re-entered the chamber and administered the tasks designed to measure aftereffects of adaptation. Subjects assigned to no-noise control conditions were treated identically to experimental subjects, except for the absence of the noise stimuli.

Let us now consider illustrative results from the first of these noise experiments (Glass *et al.*, 1969, Experiment 1). We begin with evidence pertaining to noise adaptation. Phasic skin conductance (GSR) was monitored throughout the noise session, and, as noted earlier, the decrement in reactivity on this measure was taken as an index of adaptation. Figure 12-1 shows these adaptation data as mean log conductance change scores within each of four successive blocks of noise bursts (Montagu and Coles, 1966). There is a clear decline in GSR response on successive blocks of trials in each noise condition. Since initial reactions to loud noise (108 dbA) were greater than to soft noise (56 dbA), the magnitude of GSR decline is understandably greater in the former condition. The mag-

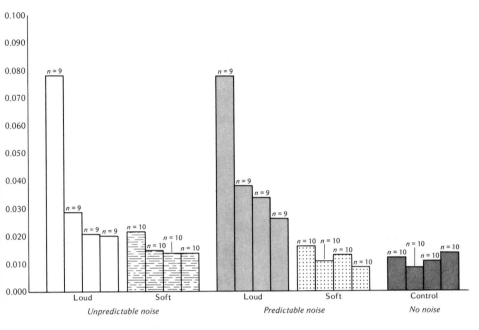

Fig. 12-1. Mean log conductance change scores for four successive blocks of noise bursts.

nitude and rate of adaptation, however, is virtually identical in predictable and unpredictable conditions within each noise-intensity treatment: that is, subjects were equally reactive at the beginning of the noise session and equally unreactive at the end.

It would appear that phasic skin conductance responses to noise occur during initial exposure and wane with repeated stimulation. Assuming that physiological stress reactions interfere with performance efficiency, we may also expect initial task errors to decline over the course of noise exposure. Recall that the task results presented earlier generally conformed to such expectations (see Tables 12-1 and 12-2). This phenomenon of adaptation is indeed pervasive; it characterized almost every subject in each of our experiments, and it appeared on several different autonomic channels—GSR, vasoconstriction of peripheral blood vessels, muscle action potentials. We may thus conclude that there is a generalized stress response to noise, which habituates with repeated stimulation.

Our major hypothesis stated that noise adaptation would lead to deleterious behavioral aftereffects, and this expectation was, in fact, con-

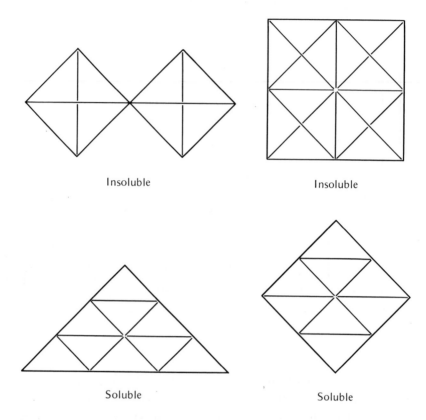

Fig. 12-2. Insoluble and soluble puzzles.

firmed. Exposure to unpredictable noise, in contrast to predictable noise, was followed by impaired task performance and lowered tolerance for post-noise frustrations. Even though noise adaptation took place to an equivalent degree under both predictable and unpredictable conditions, the magnitude of adverse aftereffects was greater under unpredictable conditions. Before presenting results in support of this general conclusion, we must first explain how frustration tolerance was measured.

Following noise termination, four line diagrams (Fig. 12-2) printed on 5 × 7 inch cards were arranged in four piles in front of the subject (Feather, 1961; Glass and Singer, 1972). Each pile consisted of cards with the same diagram on them. The subject's task was to trace over all the lines of a given diagram, or puzzle, without tracing any line twice and without lifting his pencil from the figure. He was told that he could take as many trials at a given puzzle as he wished but that there was a time limit on how long he could work on a particular trial, and the experimenter would inform him when his time was up. At the end of that time, he had to decide whether to take another card from the same pile and try that puzzle again or move on to the puzzle in the next pile. If he decided to move on, he could not go back to the previous puzzle.

Two of the line diagrams were, in fact, insoluble, but very few subjects were able to see this. The insoluble puzzles were presumed to lead to failure and frustration. Indeed, we repeatedly observed outward signs of exasperation as subjects attempted over and over again to solve the insoluble. While this was going on in the experimental chamber, the experimenter was in the control room observing and recording the number of trials taken by a subject on each puzzle. These data provided us with a measure of his persistence on the insoluble puzzles: namely, the fewer the number of trials, the less the persistence, and, by interpretation, the lower the subject's tolerance for an inherently frustrating task.

Typical results on this task are shown in Fig. 12-3. As can be seen, subjects took significantly fewer trials following exposure to loud unpredictable noise than to loud and soft predictable noise, and this effect was true for both of the insoluble puzzles. Almost all subjects solved the soluble puzzles within four or five trials. It would appear, then, that lowered tolerance for frustration is an adverse consequence of exposure to the presumably more aversive unpredictable noise. There is also an unexpected tendency for this effect to appear even when the unpredictable noise is not particularly loud. Soft unpredictable noise was associated with a lower tolerance of frustration than loud predictable noise. Unpredictability is indeed a potent factor in the production of noise aftereffects.

It should be noted, however, that our measures of frustration tolerance could be regarded as an index of adaptive lack of persistence on an insoluble task. Put somewhat differently, it may be that taking fewer trials on the insoluble puzzles was an adaptive rather than a maladaptive response. Such an interpretation is theoretically possible, but we find it difficult to understand why unpredictable noise would lead to more adaptive responses to insoluble problems than predictable noise. Unpredictable stressors have been shown by others to exert a more aversive impact on behavior than predictable stressors (e.g., Berlyne, 1960), and, thus, we might expect maladaptive responses after exposure to the former type of stimulation. The alternative interpretation of our frustration-tolerance measure is also difficult to maintain in the face of results obtained on an-

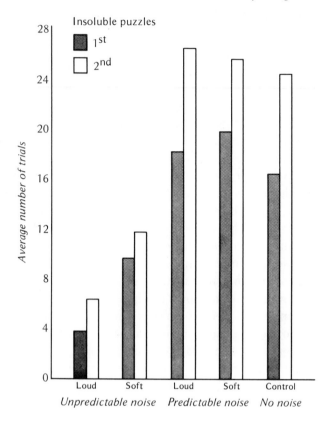

Fig. 12-3. Average number of trials on the first and second insoluble puzzles.

other post-noise task. It was expected that unpredictable noise, in contrast to predictable noise, would impair quality of performance on a task requiring care and attention. Subjects were therefore given a proofreading test immediately following completion of the insoluble puzzle test. They were asked to correct errors, such as transpositions and misspellings, that had been deliberately introduced into a seven-page passage. Each subject was given 15 minutes on this task, and quality of performance was measured as the percentage of "errors not found" of the total number of errors that could have been found at the point the subject was told to stop work.

There were no significant differences between noise conditions in the total amount read by subjects. Figure 12-4, however, shows the predicted differences in average percentage of errors missed in the completed part of the proofreading task. Loud unpredictable noise is associated with a greater percentage of proofreading errors than either loud or soft predictable noise. Although soft unpredictable noise leads to greater impairment of proofreading accuracy than loud predictable noise, the difference is not statistically significant, as in the case of the frustration-tolerance measure.

Taken together, our findings suggest that people adapt to noise but show behavioral deficits after noise termination. We cannot say that these deficits are the direct result of noise adaptation; it is just as likely that they occur in spite of adaptation. Later, we refer to data that, in fact, support the second interpretation. For the moment, however, we have simply shown that exposure to unpredictable noise leads to more adverse aftereffects than exposure to predictable noise. A psychological factor, unpre-

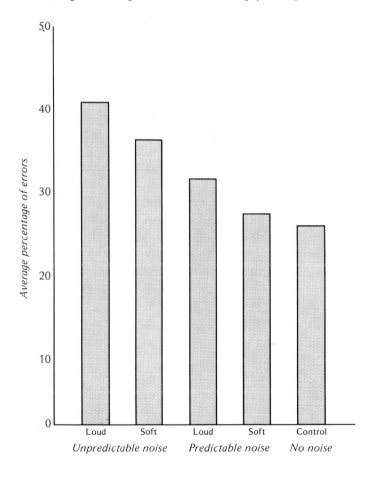

Fig. 12-4. Average percentage of errors missed in the proofreading task.

dictability, appears to be more important than physical parameters of noise (e.g., intensity) in producing post-noise deficits. The case for the existence of this phenomenon is strengthened by the range of conditions over which it has been found in various replications (see Glass and Singer, 1972). These include: (a) different ways of manipulating unpredictability, (b) different levels of physical noise intensity, (c) different male and female subject populations, and (d) different laboratory locations.

PERCEIVED CONTROL OVER NOISE

The research described thus far does not provide precise theoretical understanding of the relationship between unpredictable noise and adverse aftereffects. It is not enough to assume that unpredictable noise is more aversive than predictable noise; we still need to specify why it is more aversive and, indeed, why negative effects appear primarily after noise termination. A possible answer to the first question is based on the notion that exposure to an unpredictable stressor induces feelings in the individual that he cannot control his environment—or at least certain stressful aspects of it. He cannot determine onset and offset of the stressor, and he is even unable to anticipate its occurrence (see, e.g., Haggard, 1946; Pervin, 1963; Corah and Boffa, 1970; Geer *et al.*, 1970). Under these conditions, we might well expect lowered frustration tolerance and impaired proofreading accuracy following stress arousal. The individual has experienced not only the aversiveness of the noise but also the "anxiety" of being incapable of doing anything about it. On the other hand, providing him with information about when to expect the noise affords a measure of cognitive control over the situation, which reduces the adverse effects of unpredictability. The validity of this line of reasoning was tested in a series of eight experiments, but we will present only one illustrative study here. Additional data can be found in a monograph summarizing our research (Glass and Singer, 1972).

The prototypic experiment involved two groups of subjects who listened to the unpredictable noise tape played at 108 dbA. One group (perceived control) was given control over the noise, whereas the other (no perceived control) did not receive this option. At the beginning of the experiment, subjects in the perceived-control condition were shown a microswitch attached to the side of their chair and told that they could at any time terminate the noise for the remainder of the session by pressing the switch. They were further informed that the experimenter preferred that they not press the switch, but the choice was entirely up to them. The latter instruction was given particular emphasis in order to induce forces against pressing the switch, while giving subjects a feeling that they could press it if they so desired. In fact, few subjects used the switch throughout noise exposure. All other details of procedure and measurement in this experiment were virtually identical to those used in the unpredictability experiments.

In order to determine whether or not the manipulations were success-

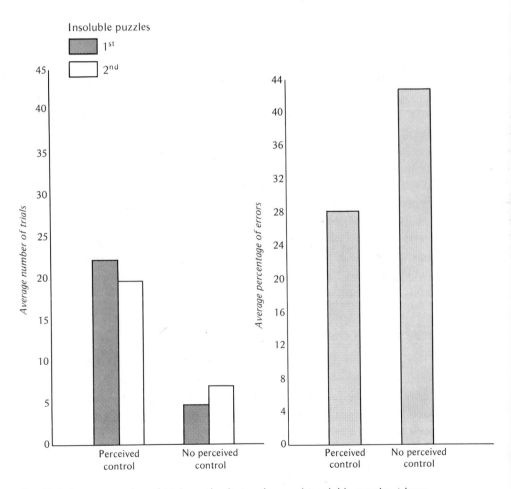

Fig. 12-5. Average number of trials on the first and second insoluble puzzles (above, left).
Fig. 12-6. Average percentage of errors missed in the proofreading task (above, right).

ful in inducing the perception of control, all subjects were asked in a post-experimental questionnaire: "To what extent did you feel that you really could have had the noise stopped during today's session?" The rating scale on the questionnaire was from 1, "No control at all" to 9, "Complete control." The mean for the nine subjects in the perceived-control condition was 7.4 and for the nine subjects in the no-perceived-control condition, 3.0. The difference was statistically significant at better than the 0.01 level.

Subjects in both conditions adapted to the noise as measured by phasic skin conductance decrements and decline in task errors. The aftereffect results present a somewhat different picture, however. Figures 12-5 and 12-6 show these data. It is immediately obvious that perception of control over noise termination had a dramatic impact on the aftereffect measures. Tolerance for post-noise frustration was appreciably increased, and proofreading errors substantially declined.

These ameliorative effects have been obtained with a number of experimental variations of perceived control, including the induction of a perceived contingency between instrumental responding and avoidance of noise (see Glass and Singer, 1972). Other data from these studies indicate a tendency toward reduced physiological reactions to initial noise bursts when subjects believed they could escape or avoid the noise. The results of our research thus suggest that perception of control reduces the aversive impact of unpredictable noise, and hence, deleterious aftereffects of exposure to such stimulation. To reiterate our earlier conclusion, psychological (i.e., cognitive) factors, not simply physical parameters of noise, are the important elements in the production of noise aftereffects.

PERCEIVED CONTROL AND HELPLESSNESS

The perception of control appears to reduce negative aftereffects of unpredictable noise—but why? What specific stress-reducing mechanisms are aroused by the manipulation of controllability? In answering this question, we reasoned that inescapable and unpredictable noise confronts the individual with a situation in which he is at the mercy of his environment. As we noted earlier, he is powerless to affect the occurrence of the stressor, and he certainly cannot anticipate its onset. We may describe his psychological state under these circumstances as one of helplessness.

The notion that uncontrollable stress results in a sense of helplessness has been developed in several previous studies (e.g., Grinker and Spiegel, 1945; Janis, 1962; Mandler and Watson, 1966; Lazarus, 1966), and even in animal research there have been a number of treatments of helplessness and the closely related theme of hopelessness (Mowrer, 1960; Richter, 1957). More recently, Seligman and his colleagues (e.g., Seligman *et al.*, 1971) have proposed a theory of "learned helplessness," the basic premises of which are as follows: (a) when aversive stimuli are uncontrollable, the organism learns that his responses do not influence the outcome; (b) the realization of this relationship interferes with the learning of a subsequent relationship in which the organism's responses would in fact control and thereby ameliorate the aversive stimulus. In other words, it is not the stressful event itself that causes interference but the individual's lack of control over the event. This lack of control induces a state of helplessness in which there is no incentive for initiating actions aimed at avoiding or escaping from the aversive stimulus. If, on the other hand, the individual has learned that he can control the stimulus, escape and avoidance behaviors will be facilitated in subsequent exposures to the same and similar stressors.

Seligman explicitly states that his definition of control is in terms of the experimenter's arrangement of experimental events, not in terms of the individual's perception of them. Our primary concern, by contrast, has been with perceived control—that is, the belief that control over aversive stimulation is possible even though the individual does not actually exert control. This difference in definition does not necessarily imply an inconsistency, and, for our purposes, we may consider Seligman's theory as one version of a more general helplessness hypothesis, which deals with a wide gamut of consequences resulting from uncontrollable stressful events.

The helplessness hypothesis provides a nice explanation of the relationship between unpredictable and uncontrollable noise and deleterious aftereffects. If the impact of a repeatedly presented aversive event is greatest where feelings of helplessness are maximal, it follows that adverse aftereffects will also be maximal. Our working thesis is, then, that exposure to uncontrollable noise produces feelings of helplessness, which interfere with later functioning. Perceived-control subjects learn to label their situation as one in which they are not helpless. By contrast, no-perceived-control subjects do not develop such expectations.

Subsequent performance after noise stimulation is affected in a way that is consistent with prior experience, when control was or was not perceived as available. Presumably, the helpless group experience not only the aversiveness of unpredictable noise but also the "anxiety" connected with their felt inability to do anything about it. Perceived-control subjects, on the other hand, are exposed only to the stress of the noise itself; they do not experience additional anxiety produced by feelings of helplessness. We tentatively conclude, therefore, that unpredictable noise produces adverse aftereffects because it is more aversive than prdictable noise, its greater aversiveness being a function of the sense of helplessness induced in an individual who is unable to control and/or predict its onset and offset.

OTHER COGNITIVE FACTORS

The importance of unpredictability and uncontrollability in determining noise aftereffects led us to examine other cognitive factors that might be expected, on a priori grounds, to interact with noise (cf. Zimbardo, 1969). These additional studies illustrate the extension of our cognitive approach, while delimiting the scope of our effects; it is as important to know which cognitive variables do not affect noise as to know which do. In the first of these experiments, we considered the extent to which "relative deprivation" would, under certain circumstances, modify the consequences of a noise stressor (cf. Pettigrew, 1967).

An individual exposed to noise will experience a certain amount of discomfort and incur a certain measure of negative aftereffects. If that same individual is exposed to the noise under identical physical conditions, but with the knowledge that someone else is being exposed to less intense noise, his resulting feelings of relative deprivation should increase the aversiveness of the noise and its consequent negative aftereffects. This prediction assumes that frustration stemming from relative deprivation generalizes to the stressful event itself and makes for a more generally aversive experience. In those instances where a subject finds himself better off relative to a comparison person, there should be an arousal of relative satisfaction rather than relative deprivation. This satisfaction will lower the total aversiveness of the noise situation by a similar process of generalization and, therefore, reduce adverse post-noise consequences.

An experiment designed to test these propositions was conducted by two of our students, Brett Silverstein and Ilene Staff. The results were unequivocal. When the subjects were relatively deprived with respect to noise—when they thought another person (i.e., a confederate of the experimenter) was undergoing less noise—they showed greater impairment on a somewhat modified version of the proofreading task and on the Stroop Color Word Test (aftereffect measures used in this study). Conversely, when they believed that the confederate was undergoing more severe noise, the subjects showed few aftereffect deficits. [The Stroop test, widely used in psychology (Jensen and Rohwer, 1966), consists of a series of color names, each of which is printed in incongruent colors. The subject's task, in this version of the test, is to write the letter of the appropriate color under each color name. For example, if the word "red" is printed in blue, the subject should write "b" for "blue" under the word. This moderately stressful test requires that a subject be alert in order to resolve competition between opposing response tendencies.]

The results of the Stroop and proofreading tests, based on ten cases in each condition, are shown in Figs. 12-7 and 12-8. The no-relative-deprivation subjects (those who were ostensibly exposed to the same noise as the confederate) provide a bench mark for comparison purposes. They were told they would receive moderately intense noise, and they behaved as though this is what they did hear, although the sound was actually an intense 108 dbA. The high-relative-deprivation subjects underwent the same promised level of noise, but they were informed that the confederate would receive a less intense set of stimuli. They did significantly less well on the aftertasks than the no-relative-deprivation subjects. As expected, the low-relative-deprivation subjects behaved like the no-deprivation controls. It should be noted that questionnaire data confirmed the success of the deprivation manipulation. Subjects in the high-relative deprivation category felt they had received more intense noise than the confederates; subjects in the low-relative-deprivation group felt they had received less noise; and the no-relative-deprivation subjects perceived no difference.

This experiment underscores the importance of still another cognitive factor in reactivity to noise. It is both fascinating and ironic to note that stress aftereffects decline when others are perceived to be in more stressful circumstances and increase when others are ostensibly experiencing less stress. There are at least two ways in which these effects can be explained. First, exposure to the relative deprivation condition amounts to victimization by an arbitrary and unfair experimenter, which should evoke anger in addition to stress. The experience of anger could directly impair task performance or lower the subject's motivation to do well as a means

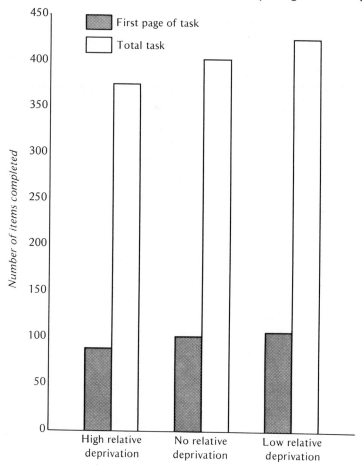

Fig. 12-7. Number of items completed on the Stroop test.

of expressing anger against the experimenter. In either case, we would expect performance on the proofreading and Stroop tests to be impaired among the relative-deprivation group as compared to the no-deprivation controls. Subjects in the low-relative-deprivation condition should show superior performance compared to the controls. Knowing that they had received favored treatment from the experimenter may have evoked positive feelings, which directly counteracted the effects of the noise stress or motivated them to do well on the tasks as a way of thanking the experimenter. The results shown in Figs. 12-7 and 12-8 are, of course, consistent with these explanations.

Alternatively, we might interpret the effects of the relative deprivation manipulation in a manner similar to that which was used to explain the effects of perceived control. Although this approach is somewhat less compelling than the explanation given above, it does have the advantage of being coordinate with our previous theorizing about controllability and its impact on stress aftereffects. Thus, we assume that the noxiousness of a stress depends, in part, on the person's evaluation of the stress in relation to his ability to cope with it. The more overwhelming it seems, and the fewer his adaptive resources, the more likely he is to label the situation as one in which he is helpless. Perceived control would reduce the stressor's effects primarily by increasing the person's evaluation of his coping resources, thereby leading him to label the situation as one in which he is not helpless.

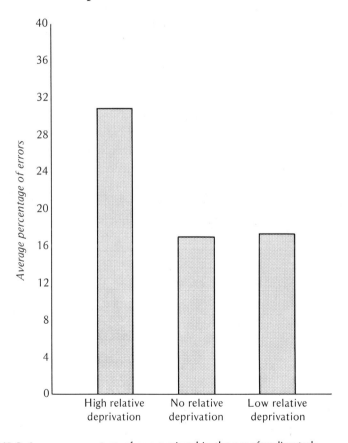

Fig. 12-8. Average percentage of errors missed in the proofreading task.

In analogous fashion, relative deprivation may exert its effects by providing the individual with additional information about his helplessness. If others are less deprived with respect to a stressor, and if there seems to be little opportunity to change this state of affairs, the individual may well conclude that he is relatively powerless to cope with the resultant stress. This labeling process may cause him to reassess the stressor's magnitude, and, hence, to increase negative aftereffects. By contrast, the person in a state of low relative deprivation realizes that there are others who are in even worse circumstances. This will enable him to revise his assessment of his coping resources and reduce perceived aversiveness of the stressor and, therefore, the severity of the aftereffects.

The relative deprivation experiment was one of a series aimed at exploring the impact of various cognitive factors (other than controllability and predictability) upon noise effects and aftereffects. Thus, a choice of whether or not to experience noise was also found to influence the severity of aftereffects. When people were required to work under noisy conditions, they suffered aftereffects of a given level of severity; if, however, people worked under noisy circumstances as a consequence of a free and informed decision on their part, the aftereffects of noise were mitigated. The necessity of the noise, whether defined as an unavoidable concomitant of an important activity or as gratuitous, was also investigated in our research. It is presently equivocal whether this factor affects noise-produced aftereffect performance; there are indications, however that an adequate test has yet to be made of the effects of the necessity variable. We intend to examine this and related cognitive factors in future stress research in our laboratories.

PROLONGED EXPOSURE TO NOISE

All of the studies described up to this point were carried out in the laboratory. The aftereffects of prolonged noise exposure cannot easily be investigated within this type of research context. This limitation, however, was at least partly overcome in one of our field studies conducted in New York City (Cohen et al., 1972). Expressway traffic was the principal source of intermittent noise. It was assumed that the subjects, 54 elementary school boys and girls, had minimal control over this noise source. Initial decibel measurements in a high-rise housing development built over an expressway permitted the use of floor level as an index of noise intensity in the children's apartments.

The study showed inverse relationships between the children's verbal skills and the noisiness of their apartments. Children living on lower floors of the 32-story buildings showed greater impairment of auditory discrimination and reading ability than those living in higher-floor apartments, where noise level was, in fact, lower. Auditory discrimination mediated the association between noise and reading deficits, and length of residence in the building increased the magnitude of the correlation between noise and auditory discrimination. Additional analyses ruled out explanations of the result in terms of social class variables and physiological damage. It would appear that there are indeed negative aftereffects of prolonged exposure to noise.

NON-NOISE STRESSORS

Although noise was the stressor used in the studies described up to this point, we do not believe our findings and interpretations hinge upon the unique characteristics of noise as a stressor. The pattern of results obtained with noise—almost universal adaptation followed by adverse aftereffects as a function of cognitive factors surrounding noise exposure—has been obtained with other stressors (Glass and Singer, 1972). For example, data from experiments using electric shock demonstrate that adverse behavioral consequences are reduced if this form of stimulation is both predictable and controllable. Still other research in our laboratories has indicated that these two cognitive variables produce similar effects with social stressors, such as bureaucratic frustration and arbitrary discrimination.

The bureaucracy experiment is a good illustration. Subjects who were exposed to a contrived experience with bureaucratic red tape showed adverse aftereffects, both general and specific. The general aftereffect was a drop in efficiency of cognitive functioning as measured by proofreading. The specific effects were that subjects who attributed their bureaucratic troubles to an immutable system over which they felt little control became docile and compliant; subjects who attributed their bureaucratic troubles to the people involved (presumably over whom control was more likely) became reactive and negative. Although subjects who were exposed to the stress of bureaucratic harassment showed adverse aftereffects, they demonstrated them in different ways, as a function of what they learned about the controllability of their environment. Subjects who were harassed by a bureaucratic official learned of their potential control of the system, had this control rendered ineffectual, and then attempted to reduce their sense of helplessness by exercising control over those with whom they subsequently interacted. Subjects who were harassed by bureaucratic regulations, rather than by the bureaucrat, learned that they were in a system in which they could not exercise control—there was no point of leverage—and, in subsequent exchanges, they quickly acceded to the other's control rather than expend useless effort in a chimerical attempt to establish their own control.

The electric shock experiments allowed us to generalize the effects of unpredictability and perceived uncontrollability. We realize that a somewhat liberal interpretation is required to assume that the bureaucracy experiment manipulated perceived control, and it is certainly not reasonable to argue that it varied the predictability of stressful stimulation. Broadness of application, however, is perhaps more important in new areas of research than point-by-point comparability between two or more similar types of variables. The strategy of testing for aftereffects over a number of physical and social stressors was part of the general rationale underlying our program of research. A strong case can now be made that exposure to a variety of aversive events leads to negative aftereffects.

PSYCHIC COSTS OF STRESS

Analogues of urban stress, whether physical or social, have few direct effects; people adapt to stress. But, stressors do have disruptive aftereffects, and they are more a function of the cognitive circumstances in which stimulation takes place than of the sheer magnitude or intensity of stimulation. These conclusions do not mean that aftereffect phenomena are the "psychic price" paid by an individual for adaptation to noxious stimulation. Such a hypothesis was indeed the original basis for our research, but the results presented thus far do not provide confirmation. It is entirely possible that aftereffects are as much post-stressor phenomena as post-adaptation phenomena. The designs and findings of our research do not indicate whether aftereffects occurred in spite of adaptation or because of the effort entailed in the adaptive process. Further analysis and experimentation with the noise stressor enabled us to reach a partial adjudication of this rather nice theoretical issue.

As we noted earlier, adaptation is a cognitive process involving one or another mechanism designed to filter out of awareness certain aspects of the aversive agent or, in some other way, reappraise it as benign. We assumed that physiological adaptation is one index of this process and that the effort entailed in achieving adaptation is reflected in the magnitude of decline of physiological response to the stressor. Given these assumptions, we were able to conclude that greater amounts of adaptation are not systematically related to greater post-noise deficits. We inferred this lack of association from two analyses (see Glass and Singer, 1972).

First, there was a very low correlation (—0.20) between aftereffect scores (i.e., proofreading) and indices of adaptation magnitude for subjects in various unpredictable and uncontrollable noise conditions. Second, we conducted still another noise experiment in which we failed to find differences in adverse aftereffects in two unpredictable conditions— one in which the usual autonomic adaptation took place and one in which GSR decrements were inhibited by using long intervals between noise bursts. On the basis of these and related data, we tentatively suggest that aftereffect phenomena represent behavioral consequences of cumulative exposure to noxious stimulation. It is not the adaptive process itself that causes deleterious aftereffects but mere exposure in spite of adaptation.

Stress aftereffects, whether caused by noise or by some other aversive event, may be viewed as an instance of the "delayed reaction" effect observed in a number of field studies of psychological stress (e.g., Grinker and Spiegel, 1945; Basowitz *et al.*, 1955). They may be observed relatively soon after termination of the aversive event, as in the case of increased anxiety among army personnel in the period immediately following graduation from airborne training school. On the other hand, they may not become evident for several months, as in the case of soldiers who are relatively calm during combat but manifest severe attacks of anxiety months after and miles removed from the battle. The fact that adaptation takes place during the stress period suggests that reactivity is being minimized and that the individual is learning to work in spite of stress.

Continued exposure to the stressor, however, may produce cumulative effects that appear only after stimulation is terminated. It is as if the person does not experience maximal stress until he is no longer required to cope with the stressor; only then do the behavioral consequences of the event become evident. Korchin (1965) has nicely summarized the dynamics of delayed reaction in the following terms: "This [the delayed reaction] might represent a release phenomenon from the control of feelings and associated stress behaviors which had been necessary for adaptive behavior [during stress exposure]." In other words, aftereffects of the kind observed in our research may well represent residues of cumulative stress that occur only after maintenance of effective functioning is no longer required. The adaptive process may not be directly implicated in the production of stress aftereffects, but it would still seem important to question the validity of the simplistic idea that man's adaptability is of unqualified benefit to his subsequent functioning.

REFERENCES

Anastasi, A. 1964. *Fields of Applied Psychology*. New York: McGraw-Hill.
Basowitz, H., H. Persky, S. J. Korchin, and R. R. Grinker. 1955. *Anxiety and Stress*. New York: McGraw-Hill.
Berlyne, D. E. 1960. *Conflict, Arousal, and Curiosity*. New York: McGraw-Hill.
Broadbent, D. E. 1957. Effects of noise on behavior. In *Handbook of Noise Control*, ed. C. M. Harris. New York: McGraw-Hill.
Broadbent, D. E. 1971. *Decision and Stress*. New York: Academic Press.
Cohen, S., D. C. Glass, and S. E. Singer. 1973. Apartment noise, auditory discrimination, and reading ability in children. *J. of Exptl. Soc. Psychol.* 9: 407-22.
Corah, N. L. and J. Boffa. 1970. Perceived control, self-observation, and response to aversive stimulation. *J. Pers. Soc. Psychol.* 16:1-14.
Dubos, R. 1965. *Man Adapting*. New Haven: Yale University Press.
Feather, N. T. 1961. The relationship of persistence at a task to expectation of success and achievement related motives. *J. Abnorm. Soc. Psychol.* 63: 552-61.
Finkelman, J. M. and D. C. Glass. 1970. Reappraisal of the relationship between noise and human performance by means of a subsidiary task measure. *J. Appl. Psychol.* 54:211-13.
French, J. W., R. B. Ekstrom, and L. A. Price. 1963. *Manual for Kit of Reference Tests for Cognitive Factors*. Princeton, N.J.: Educational Testing Service.
Geer, J. H., G. C. Davison, and R. I. Gatchel. 1970. Reduction of stress in humans through nonveridical perceived control of aversive stimulation. *J. Pers. Soc. Psychol.* 16:731-38.
Glass, D. C., J. E. Singer, and Lucy N. Friedman. 1969. Psychic cost of adaptation to an environmental stressor. *J. Pers. Soc. Psychol.* 12:200-10.
Glass, D. C. and J. E. Singer. 1972. *Urban Stress: Experiments in Noise and Social Stressors*. New York: Academic Press.
Grinker, R. R. and J. P. Spiegel. 1945. *Men under Stress*. New York: McGraw-Hill.
Haggard, E. A. 1975. Some conditions determining adjustment during and readjustment following experimentally induced stress. In *Contemporary Psychopathology*, ed. S. S. Tomkins. Cambridge, Mass.: Harvard University Press.
Janis, I. L. 1962. Psychological effects of warnings. In *Man and Society in Disaster*, eds. G. W. Baker and D. W. Chapman. New York: Basic Books.

Jensen, A. R. and W. D. Rohwer, Jr. 1966. The Stroop color-word test: A review. *Acta Psychologica* 25:36-93.

Korchin, S. J. 1965. Some psychological determinants of stress behavior. In *The Quest for Self-Control*, ed. S. Z. Klausner. New York: Free Press, p. 260.

Kryter, K. 1970. *The Effects of Noise on Man*. New York: Academic Press.

Lazarus, R. S. 1966. *Psychological Stress and the Coping Process*. New York: McGraw-Hill.

Lazarus, R. S. 1968. Emotions and adaptation: Conceptual and empirical relations. In *Nebraska Symposium on Motivation*, ed. W. J. Arnold. Lincoln: University of Nebraska Press.

Mandler, G. and D. L. Watson. 1966. Anxiety and the interruption of behavior. In *Anxiety and Behavior*, ed. C. D. Spielberger. New York: Academic Press.

Mecklin, J. M. 1969. It's time to turn down all that noise. *Fortune*. October 1969, p. 130.

Montagu, J. D. and E. M. Coles. 1966. Mechanism and measurement of the galvanic skin response. *Psychol. Bull.* 65:261-79.

Mowrer, O. H. 1960. *Learning Theory and Behavior*. New York: Wiley.

Pervin, L. A. 1963. The need to predict and control under conditions of threat. *J. Pers.* 31:570-87.

Pettigrew, T. F. 1967. Social evaluation theory: Convergences and applications. In *Nebraska Symposium on Motivation*, ed. D. Levine. Lincoln: University of Nebraska Press.

Richter, C. P. 1957. On the phenomenon of sudden death in animals and man. *Psychosom. Med.* 19:191-98.

Sanders, A. F. 1961. The influence of noise on two discrimination tasks. *Ergonomics* 4:253-58.

Seligman, M. E. P., S. F. Maier, and R. L. Solomon. 1971. Unpredictable and uncontrollable aversive events. In *Aversive Conditioning and Learning*, ed. F. R. Brush. New York: Academic Press.

Selye, H. 1956. *The Stress of Life*. New York: McGraw-Hill.

Thompson, R. F. and W. A. Spencer. 1966. Habituation: A model phenomenon for the study of neural substrates of behavior. *Psycholog. Rev.* 73: 16-43.

Wohlwill, J. F. 1970. The emerging discipline of environmental psychology. *Amer. Psychol.* 25:303-12.

Zimbardo, P. G. 1969. *The Cognitive Control of Motivation*. Glenview, Ill.: Scott, Foresman.

13. Biological Anthropology as an Applied Science

ALBERT DAMON*

We need a new science of man. For the moment, let us call it human biology and ecology, the study of man's ability to live in his ecosystem, which is physical, biological, and cultural. This need has not yet been acknowledged by most anthropologists, and I suspect that this is because anthropology, like other academically oriented fields, is discipline- rather than problem-, mission-, or action-oriented. Faced with one of mankind's most urgent crises, uncontrolled urbanization, the response of the American Anthropological Association and, particularly, of the biological anthropologists, was to organize a symposium on biological adaptations in the city for their 1968 meetings. Despite the promising title, most of the participants deplored the absence of data, called for more research, or presented irrelevant material that happened to concern city dwellers but might just as well have concerned non-city dwellers. One participant studied Apaches on reservations in Arizona. These anthropologists, on the whole, pursued their own interests, whether in evolution, genetics, or disease, but with city dwellers as the new object of study. They asked not what they could do for man in the city, but what man in the city could do for them. Most of them seemed unaware that there was a problem or that they, as scientists, could help solve the problem.

These remarks are not meant personally. Some of the participants acknowledged the problem but thought that biological anthropology had little to offer at the moment. This was, indeed, the case, and it was not their fault alone. The whole profession had been caught unprepared. Social an-

* Late Professor of Anthropology, Harvard University, Cambridge, Massachusetts.

thropologists define problems in the same way as biological anthropologists. A problem is something you would like to study because it fits into your theoretical disciplinary interest, not something you can or should help with or do something about.

It is by no means too late to change this attitude. Biological anthropologists can make a vital and desperately needed contribution to human welfare, here and now. Some of the necessary technical methods and the norms, such as anthropometric and radiological standards of growth and maturation and nutrition, are available now. Data are beginning to accumulate in other areas, including, for example, man's short-range responses and long-range adaptations to various environmental extremes—heat, cold, altitude, aridity. What we need, particularly, is information on the less extreme, less exotic, perhaps less acute, but subtler and longer-acting stresses of modern life. Some of these stresses are physical, some are biological, and some are psychosocial. They include crowding, noise, artificial lighting, arousal, conflict, insecurity, mobility, accelerating change, and the tensions related to the necessity of being constantly alert. One concept that summarizes many of the features of modern life is "information input overload" ("just too bloody much"), which is demonstrably harmful to many forms of life and even machines. Our biological environment includes chemical and physical mutagens and carcinogens, many microbiological hazards, and pollutants; many aspects of the environment disrupt important biological rhythms. Many of us eat too much or too little or unwisely; most of us don't exercise enough. My thesis is that biological anthropologists should provide some of the information on how these phenomena affect man and that biological anthropologists should certainly integrate and apply this kind of information. Let me pursue this theme further.

First of all, consider the need for an applied science of human biology and ecology, that is, applied biological anthropology. In an article in *Science*, John Platt (1969) offers a brilliant analysis of mankind's most critical concern, namely, how to survive the next 20 years. By that time, he argues, we will either have solved, or be on the road to solving, a few major problems, or we may be literally dead or dying. If we can solve these major problems, all of which contribute to a single "crisis of transformation," mankind faces a glorious future. Platt advocates an all-out crash program to solve these problems, dropping or postponing "research as usual." We may agree or disagree, but we should examine Platt's program. He ranks mankind's problems into eight grades based on the magnitude of their effects and the number of people affected by them: In grade 1 is the possibility of total annihilation by nuclear or chemical or biological warfare. Grade 2 includes the problem of participatory democracy (that is, the crisis of authority), ecological unbalance, the population explosion, and maladaptive patterns of living. And so on, down to grades 7 and 8, which include problems that have been exaggerated or even overstudied. Here Platt lists mind control, heart transplants, sperm banks, eugenics, man in space, and, at the very bottom, much so-called basic research. These problems are overstudied in the sense that they can wait. The major problems cannot wait.

In Platt's list of major problems, the biological anthropologist can help solve the problems of population, ecological balance, and living patterns, including urban blight. The biological anthropologist has not been very active so far, but I hope this book will help show him what he might be doing and how he might be gathering the information we so badly need.

Leaving Platt's apocalpytic vision, let us listen to René Dubos, an outstanding microbiologist, and, more recently, a social philosopher. His book, *Man Adapting,* is a plea for just such a new science of human biology and ecology, a science Dubos believes will prove as revolutionary for the well-being of mankind as the biochemical revolution 50 years ago and the discovery of antibiotics 30 years ago. Epidemiologists have known for some time that, in this century, there has been a remarkable shift in the leading causes of illness and death in the developed countries. The infectious diseases have given way to such non-infectious, chronic diseases as heart disease, cancer, stroke, cirrhosis of the liver, diabetes, and even peptic ulcer. These are the diseases of civilization, in that some are seen because the individual lives long enough to develop them and some are the result of maladaptive practices of the individual or the technologist. Now, everyone must die at some time of some cause, but I think we all would rather take our chances with a heart attack at age 60 than with acute gastroenteritis at age 5.

Dubos points out that these gains have come about chiefly as a result of a higher standard of living and the application of science to the prevention of nutritional and infectious diseases and not solely through new therapies for old diseases. Our health problems, he says, arise largely in the man-environment relationship. The environment affects the development of human characteristics directly, in health as well as in disease. Our current environment is dangerous on two counts: it contains frankly harmful elements, and it changes so rapidly that man cannot adapt fast enough to maintain his health.

Now man, in one sense, is remarkably adaptable. For 200 years the inhabitants of northern Europe have been exposed to high concentrations of many types of air pollutants produced by incomplete burning of coal and pollutants released by factories, which, recently, have been augmented by automobile fumes; the whole is compounded by miserable weather for much of the year. Yet northern Europeans seem cheerfully adapted, on the whole—they raise families, produce goods, engage in scientific and artistic activities, and so on.

Populations all over the world are growing—the usual biological indication of successful adaptation. So, on the surface, man seems to be adapting. But here Dubos points out that the general biological concept of adaptation and the suitability of the environment, if it facilitates such adaptation, does not apply to man. In his words, "an environment allowing man to produce a family and to be economically effective during his adult years should be regarded as unacceptable if it generates disease late in life." "Human ecology," he goes on to say, "differs from orthodox biomedical sciences in the much greater emphasis it should place on indirect, delayed effects of environmental forces." In particular, forces working on the child, as in nutritional or psychosocial deprivation or overfeeding and overstimulation, may have long-lasting effects.

After pointing out our lack of systematic knowledge about man in his environment, Dubos concludes by saying that "the social need for human ecology is acute."

Another plea for the new science comes from Dr. Lawrence Hinkle of Cornell Medical College. In an unpublished memorandum on the study of human biology, Hinkle defines human biology as that branch of science that seeks to understand the biological characteristics of man. Such a science will, in the first place, be based on an understanding of the place of man in the natural world, and it will be pursued in the context of general biology. In this context, it might well begin with the study of human evolution. Since cultural adaptation has been such an outstanding feature of human evolution, the new human biology will include the study of the origin, development, and important features of human culture, as well as the physical evolution of man. It will include human genetics, human development, human physiology, and human reproduction. It will include human behavior, its evolution, with a special concern for the biological basis of human behavior and its relation to animal behavior. Since man is pre-eminently a social animal, it will include the study of social groups, the interactions between groups, and the effect of groups on individual behavior; it will also include the study of the evolutionary origin of social groups and their relation to social grouping in animals. Finally, it will include human ecology—the study of how men interrelate with the world in which they live and with the people around them and how this interrelationship affects their health and behavior.

Many of the man-created features of the human environment have important biological effects. For example, the nature, location, and arrangement of our space for living; our methods of transportation and communication; our methods of energy production and a host of technological processes; our methods of utilizing or disposing of waste products; and our methods of growing, preparing, and preserving food, and, especially, the emphasis on and advertisements for refined and convenience foods. A knowledge of human biology has, thus, become increasingly important for those who would enter such diverse fields as urban planning, architecture, engineering, agriculture, food science, environmental toxicology, industrial hygiene, business administration, and political science and certain areas of government; but, currently, there is no provision for a fundamental education in human biology for people entering these fields.

Men are rapidly changing the characteristics of their environment, to the detriment of all forms of life, themselves included; yet, it is evident that our present level of civilization and well-being has been attained largely through manipulation of our environment and that any change in the way we handle our physical surroundings may have social and economic implications for people everywhere. Despite the pressing nature of the biological and social problems that face us, we are not teaching scientists the basics of human biology so that they can begin to develop a scientific approach to a study of the ecosystems that include man.

Hinkle concludes that, in the great forum of the scientific and academic communities, there have been few, if any biologists who represent biological man as he exists in the modern world. There have been botanists and zoologists who represent plant and animal biology; anthropologists who represent primitive or ancient man; sociologists and psychologists who represent social and behavioral man; and physicians who represent ill or disabled man. There have not been the human biologists who bridge the "two cultures" of science and the humanities and who speak for man as we now understand him as a biological and social being, nor have there been the graduate schools to provide a home for those who would so study man.

I can add further testimony to the desperate need for human biological knowledge on the part of those who design environments. Decisions about the environment must be made and are being made all the time, often on a large scale, and often irrevocably, without any solid, biologically based input as to human needs. We human biologists have finally convinced the urban and regional planners, architects, and civil engineers, and even some developers, that certain types of physical environments can damage people. They now ask the biological and social scientists, "What should we do? How much can people tolerate? What is optimal?" It is our turn now to hem and haw. The simple fact is, we don't know. Only recently, a group of government planners, physicians, architects, engineers, and social scientists met, under Hinkle's direction, to plan research to find out what to do.

Here again, biological anthropologists are not the only ones caught unprepared. Psychologists are in the same position, as Dr. Wohlwill points out in an earlier chapter. Other social scientists are in an even more difficult position. The public and the politicians, disillusioned with natural science and technology as harbingers of the good life, have discovered the social sciences and look to them for the solutions to our social problems—war, violence, and poverty. What they find, when they turn to social anthropology, is a very different set of concerns—kinships, linguistics, and the social structure of remote tribes. We have preferred to observe man, not serve man.

I think we can agree that the new science is needed. Some of us may have thought that this is what physical or biological anthropology is all about—or what it should be about. Let us take a look. A biological anthropologist is trained to analyze the biological variations of man, both the genetic variations and the variations that involve responses to the environment. His particular competence is the description of the human organism and his orientation is primarily toward the group or population, although he may also be concerned with individuals. Since man is a social as well as a biological being, the biological anthropologist must concern himself with both psychology and physiology.

As a science, biological anthropology has two aspects, theoretical, or basic, and applied. Human variation is studied by the theoretical biological anthropologist as dependent upon climate, habitat, migration, inbreeding, or other environmental and genetic factors. The applied biological anthropologist, on the other hand, studies the biological manifestations of human variation and tries to turn them to practical ends. These ends could be identifying and preventing diseases, designing healthful habitats, or setting standards for normal dietary variation within subcultures. This book attempts to broaden the horizons of both theoretical and applied biological anthropology to include more physiology, and, hence, medicine and ecology.

Theoretical biological anthropology is the study of human evolution and differentiation, of biological variation in primates, fossil man, and living man; here, we attempt to explain such processes and products of evolution as anatomy, serology, and behavior in terms of natural selection, including genetics and environmental and cultural adaptation, and to reconstruct past events and project current trends.

Applied biological anthropology is less familiar. The biological anthropologist applies his knowledge in two main areas; medicine and bioengineering. For example, anthropologists have played a leading role in the current International Biology Program. In this book, the authors have extended the horizons of human biology in the broad sense of human ecosystems.

The applications of biological anthropology, medically, lie in anatomy, in medical education, for the most part; in physiology, in the study of environmental adaptation; in legal medicine, in the identification of remains, the determination of paternity, and the analysis of criminal behavior (the writer served on a team of scientists appointed by the attorney general of the State of Massachusetts to act on an advisory board in the apprehension of the Boston Strangler); in preventive medicine, in the identification of high-risk groups or persons (persons with sickle-cell anemia, carriers of hepatitis); and in biomedical engineering, in the design of safety and other clothing and equipment and work space (the astronautical clothing and work spaces were built to anthropometric specifications). Measurements, norms, and standards derived from a host of anthropological studies are used in such areas as general and pediatric medicine and dentistry and in surveys of nutritional levels and etiology of disease in diverse populations as well as within a population. The list for applied biological anthropology is almost endless.

The reader might well ask whether all is not going well. What more should biological anthropologists be doing that they are not already doing? The answer is that there are too few of them, and they are not working in the areas of greatest social need, i.e., applied anthropology. Moreover, departments of anthropology offer too few courses to meet these so-cial needs. Applied biological anthropology can fairly be termed a shortage area in the biomedical sciences, at a time when students, research-funding agencies, politicians, and, ultimately, the public, are increasingly seeking "relevance" in science. This shortage must be met if an ecological night-mare is to be avoided. Man is increasingly beset by man-made environ-mental problems and "diseases of civilization," and at least some of the solutions can come from us.